THE MYSTICAL
CITY OF GOD

VOLUME II

"THE INCARNATION"

THE DIVINE HISTORY AND
LIFE OF THE VIRGIN
MOTHER OF GOD

VENERABLE MARY OF AGREDA

TRANSLATED FROM THE SPANISH BY
REVEREND GEORGE J. BLATTER

CATHOLIC WAY
PUBLISHING

Copyright © 1914, So. Chicago, Ill., The Theopolitan;
Hammond, Ind., W.B. Conkey Co., US.
Re-typeset and re-published in 2013 by Catholic Way Publishing.
Cover design by Catholic Way Publishing.

IMPRIMATUR:
+H.J. Alerding
Bishop of Fort Wayne

Mystical City of God, the miracle of his omnipotence and the abyss of his grace
the divine history and life of the Virgin Mother of God our Queen and our Lady,
most holy Mary expiatrix of the fault of eve and mediatrix of grace. The history
and life of the Virgin Mother of God our Queen and our Mother and Mediatrix
of Grace, manifested to Sister Mary of Jesus, Prioress of the convent of the
Immaculate Conception in Agreda, Spain. For new enlightenment of the world,
for rejoicing of the Catholic Church, and encouragement of men. Completed in
1665.

Translation from the Original Authorized Spanish Edition by Fiscar Marison
(George J. Blatter). Begun on the Feast of the Assumption 1902, completed
1912.

The Mystical City of God consists of four volumes; The Conception, The
Incarnation, The Transfixion and The Coronation. These four Volumes and
Popular Abridgement are available from the Publisher in E-Book and Paperback.

This work is published for the greater glory of Jesus Christ through His
most holy mother Mary and for the sanctification of the Church militant.

ISBN-13: 978-1-78379-283-2

11 10 9 8 7 6 5 4 3 2

Available in E-Book.

www.catholicwaypublishing.com
London, England, UK
2013

CONTENTS

CITY OF GOD PART II
THE INCARNATION
BOOK IV

THE MYSTICAL CITY OF GOD

VOLUME II

THE INCARNATION

CITY OF GOD

INTRODUCTION TO PART II

1. When I was ready to present before the throne of God the insignificant results of my labors in writing the first part of the most holy life of Mary, the Mother of God, I wished to subject it to the scrutiny and correction of the divine light, by which I had been guided in my shortcomings. I was very anxious to be, consoled by the renewed assurance, and benign approval of the Most High, and to know, whether He wished me to continue or to abandon this work, which is so far above my lowliness. The Lord responded saying: "Thou hast written well, and according to our pleasure; but We desire thee to understand, that in order to manifest the mysteries and most high sacraments of the rest of the life of our only and chosen Spouse, Mother of our Onlybegotten, thou hast need of a new and more exalted preparation. It is our wish that thou die to all that is imperfect and visible, and that thou live according to the spirit; that thou renounce all the occupations and habits of an earthly creature and assume instead those of an angel, striving to attain in them a still greater purity and an entire conformity with what thou art to understand and write."

2. In this answer of the Most High I understood, that such a high perfection of life and habits and such an unwont-

ed exercise of virtues was proposed and required of me, that, full of diffidence, I became disturbed and fearful of undertaking a work so arduous and difficult for an earthly creature. I felt within myself great repugnance rising up in the flesh against the spirit. The spirit called me with interior force, urging me to strive after the disposition, which was required of me, and advancing as argument the pleasure of the Lord and the benefits accruing to myself. On the other hand the law of sin (Rom. 7, 23), which I felt in my members, opposed the divine promptings and discouraged me by the fear of my own inconstancy. I felt a great distaste, which deterred me and a great pusillanimity which filled me with fear. In this excitement I began to believe, that I was not capable of treating about such high things, especially as they were so foreign to the condition and estate of a woman.

3. Overcome by fears and difficulties, I resolved not to continue this work, and to use all possible means to adhere to this determination. The common enemy knew my fear and cowardice, and, as his utmost cruelty is more aroused against the weak and disheartened, he made use of this very disposition to attack me with incredible fury. It seemed to him, that I was left without help in his hands. In order to conceal his malice, he sought to transform himself into an angel of light, pretending to be very solicitous for my soul and for my welfare. Under this false pretext he perfidiously deluged me with his suggestions and doubts; he represented to me the danger of damnation and frightened me with punishments similar to those of the chief of the angels (Is. 14, 12), since I had sought in my pride to comprehend, what was above my powers and in opposition to God himself.

4. He pointed out to me many souls, who, professing virtue, were deceived by some secret presumption and by yielding to the insinuations of the devil; and he made me believe, that in so far as I sought to scrutinize the secrets of the divine

Majesty (Prov. 25, 27), I could not but be guilty of pride and presumption, thus being already judged. He urged very strongly, that the present times were ill suited for such matters and sought to confirm his assertion by what happened to some well known persons, who were found to labor under deceit and error. He reminded me of the dread of the spiritual life in others; how great would be the discredit, which would arise by any mistake of mine and what evil effect it would have on those of little piety; all this I would know by experience and to my regret, if I persisted in writing about this matter. And as it is true evidently, that all the opposition to the spiritual life and the small esteem in which the mystic virtues are held, is caused by that mortal enemy, so, for the purpose of doing away with Christian devotion and piety in many souls, he succeeds in deceiving some and in sowing the cockle among the good seed of the Lord (Matth. 13,25). Thus he causes confusion and obscures the true sentiment concerning it, making it more difficult to distinguish the darkness from the light. I am not surprised to see him succeed therein, as the true discernment is the special work of God and of those, who participate in his true wisdom, and do not govern themselves only by earthly insight.

5. It is not easy during this mortal life to discern true prudence from the false; for often also the good intention and zeal warp the human judgment, when counsel and light from on high are wanting. I had occasion to learn this in the execution of that which I am about to undertake: for some persons, well known as devout, not only those who loved me on account of their piety and desired my welfare, but also those who were less loving and considerate: all alike at one time wished to deter me from this undertaking, and also from the path, which I was going, as if I was proceeding upon it by my own choice. Their fear of drawing discredit or confusion upon those who were striving after piety with me,

or upon religion or my neighbors, and especially upon the convent in which I lived, caused them anxiety and to me, affliction. I was much enamoured by the security, which the ordinary paths of the other nuns seemed to offer; I acknowledge, that this suited more my own insight and my inclination and desires, and was urged upon me still more by my timidity and my great fears.

6. Cast about upon these impetuous waves, my heart sought to reach the port of obedience in order to reassure me in the bitter sea of my confusion. To add to my tribulation, it began to be rumored about in our order, that my spiritual father and superior, who had for many years directed my soul and who well understood my interior trials, who moreover had commanded me to write the preceding part of this history, who would most likely encourage, quiet, and console me, was suggested for removal to a higher office. The suggestion was not acted upon, but it occasioned his absence for many days, and the dragon took advantage of all this in order to pour out against me the furious river of his wrath (Apoc. 13, 15). Thus, though in vain, he exerted all his malice, on this occasion and others, to entice me from obedience and deprive me of the guidance of my superior and master.

7. In addition to all the contradictions and temptations already mentioned, and many others not possible to describe, the demon sought to deprive me of my health, causing many aches, indispositions and disorders of the whole body. He harassed me with insurmountable sadness and conflicting thoughts; he seemed to confuse my understanding, hinder correct thinking, weaken my will power, and sift me in body and soul. And it happened that in the midst of this confusion I committed some faults, which were serious enough in me, although they were committed not so much in malice as from human frailty. Nevertheless the serpent sought to use them for my destruction more than any other means; for

thus having interrupted the flow of good works, his fury was let loose to cause still greater faults in this embarrassment by inveigling me to exaggerate my guilt. To this he drove me by impious and most insidious suggestions, seeking to persuade me, that all that I had experienced in the path which I had trodden, was false and erroneous.

8. As these insinuations, on account of the faults committed and on account of my continual consternation and fears, began to appear plausible, I resisted them less than others; and it was only through the special mercies of the Lord, that I did not fall entirely from all belief and hope in a remedy. But I found myself so entangled in difficulties and surrounded by darkness, that I may say, the groanings of death encompassed me and the sorrows of hell engulfed me (Ps. 17, 5) inspiring me with dread of extreme peril. I resolved to burn the manuscripts of the first part of this divine history and to desist from writing the second. The angel of satan, who inspired me with this resolution, induced me also to withdraw myself from the whole undertaking: to put an end to the pursuit of the spiritual life, to neglect my interior life, and not to communicate about it with anyone. Thus would I be able to do penance for my sins, appease the Lord, propitiate Him, and retain his friendship. In order to make sure of the effects of his concealed malice he proposed, that I make a vow not to write any more on account of the danger of being deceived and of deceiving; but that instead, I amend my life, retrench my imperfections and embrace penance.

9. With this masque of seeming virtue the dragon pretended to establish his damnable counsels and cover himself with the skin of a sheep, while in reality he acted as a bloodthirsty and devouring wolf. He persevered for some time in this attack and all alone I remained for fifteen days in a night of darkness, without relief or consolation either human or divine: without the former, because I was without the help

and the counsel of obedience, and without the latter, because the Lord had interrupted the flow of his favors, his enlightenments and continual inspiration. Above all was I distressed by despair of salvation and in it, the persuasion, that death and the danger of my eternal damnation was approaching; all this was instigated and fostered in me by the enemy.

10. But as the aftertastes of his temptations are so bitter and end but in despair, the very disturbance, by which he upset the whole republic of my powers and acquired habits, made me more wary of fulfilling anything which he urged on me and proposed to me. He availed himself of the continual fear, which tormented me with the dread of offending God and of losing his friendship and when, in my doubts, I applied myself to works of piety, he sought to draw me away. This very fear however made me hesitate at what the astute dragon had tried to convince me of and in this uncertainty I deferred giving assent to it My high regard for obedience also, by which I had been ordered to write, and the contrariness of that which I felt in my interior, helped me to resist and to recoil at his suggestions. Above all the assistance of the Most High defended me and permitted not the beasts to snatch my soul, which amid sighs and groans confessed Him. I cannot describe in words the temptations, combats, troubles, dismays and afflictions, which I suffered in this battle: for I saw myself placed in such a state, that in my judgment there was really no greater difference between my condition and that of the damned, except that in hell there is no redemption, while in mine it was still possible.

11. One day, in order to get some respite, I cried out from the bottom of my heart saying: "0 woe is me, that I have come to such a state! and woe to my soul, which finds itself therein! Whither shall I turn, since all the portals of my salvation are closed?" Immediately a strong and sweet voice gave answer within myself:

"Whither dost thou wish to go outside of God himself?" By this answer I perceived that my cure was at hand in the Lord, and at the breaking of this dawn I began to raise myself from the depth of the confusion, into which I was cast, and I felt a powerful increase in the fervor of my desires and in the acts of faith, hope and charity. I debased myself in the presence of the Most High and, in firm confidence in his goodness, I wept over my faults with bitter sorrow. I confessed them many times and sighing from the depth of heart, I began to seek again the former light and truth. And as the divine Wisdom comes forth to meet those by whom it is invoked (Wis. 6, 17), it advanced toward me in delight and cleared away the night of my confusion and tormenting afflictions.

12. Presently that bright day broke, which I had desired so much; the quiet possession of peace returned; I enjoyed the sweet love and vision of my Lord and Master, and with it I again perceived, why I should believe, accept and esteem the benefits and favors, which his mighty arm wrought in me. I gave Him thanks as far as was in my power; and I saw, who I was and who God is; that a creature by itself can do nothing, that it is nothing, because sin is nothing. I saw also what man can do when raised up and assisted up by the divine right hand, being much more than can be imagined by our earthly faculites. Humbled in the perception of these truths and in the presence of the inaccessible light, (which is vast and strong, without deceit or falsehood), my heart flowed over in sweet affections of love, praise and thanksgiving. For now I understood, that He had guarded and defended me, so that in the confused night of temptations my lamp might not be extinguished (Prov. 31, 18); and in the depth of my gratitude I annihilated myself to the dust and humiliated myself as a worm of the earth.

13. To make this benefit more certain, I immediately heard an interior exhortation, without knowing clearly from whence it proceeded; while it severely reprehended me for my disloyalty and my wrongful ways, it at the same time admonished and enlightened, instructed and corrected me. It furnished me with a deep understanding of good and evil, of virtue and vice, of what was secure, useful and beneficial, as well as their contraries; it laid open to me the way of eternity, gave me a knowledge of the means and of the end, of the value of life everlasting, and of the miserable unhappiness and the so little considered ruin of endless perdition.

14. In the profound knowledge of these two extremes, I confess that I was dumbfounded and cast about between the fear of my dreadful infirmity and the desire of reaching the happiness, of which I was unworthy on account of my demerits. I was full of the thought of the kindness and mercy of the Most High; and the fear of losing Him: I beheld the two different ends awaiting the creatures: eternal glory and eternal misery; and it seemed a small matter to me to suffer all the pains and torments of the world, of purgatory and hell itself, in order to attain to the one and to avoid the other. And although I perceived, that the divine help is assured to those who seek to make use of it, yet as I also saw by this light, that life and death are in our hands (Eccli. 15, 18), and that our weakness or malice may prevent the proper use of grace, and that the tree will lie for all eternity as it once has fallen (Eccles. 11, 3), on this account I was overcome by the deepest sorrow, which penetrated my heart.

15. This sorrow was increased by a most severe answer or inquiry, which came from the Lord. For while I found myself thus annihilated in the consciousness of my weakness and danger and by the thought of having offended his justice, so that I dared not raise my eyes toward Him, He met my

speechless sorrow by the advances of his mercy, saying to me in answer to them:

"Which dost thou wish, my soul? Which dost thou seek? Which of these ways wilt thou choose? What is thy resolve?" This question was an arrow to my heart: for although I knew for certain, that the Lord knew my desires better than I myself, the delay between the question and the answer was incredibly painful to me; I wished, if possible, that the Lord should anticipate my answer and should not show Himself ignorant of the response, which I would give. But, impelled by great emotion, I made response in words coming from the innermost of soul, and said; "Lord and omnipotent God! The path of virtue, the way of eternal life do I chose, this do I desire, and in this do Thou place me; and as I do not merit it in thy justice, I appeal to they mercy, and I offer for myself the infinite merits of thy most holy Son and my Redeemer, Jesus Christ."

16. I was made aware, that this highest Judge remembered the promise, which is given to the Church, that He would grant all that is asked in the name of his Onlybegotten (John 16, 23), that in Him and on his account my petition was granted and its fulfillment hastened according to my poor wishes. Certain conditions were made and proposed to me by an intellectual voice, saying to me interiorly: "Soul, created by the hand of the Almighty, if thou wishest, as one of the elect, to follow in the path of the true light and attain the position of a most chaste spouse of the Lord, who calls thee, it is befitting, that thou observe the laws and precepts of love. The first thing required of thee is, that thou reject entirely all earthly inclinations, renouncing all and every affection toward the transient things, so that thou have no love or affection toward any created being, no matter how useful, beautiful or agreeable it may appear to thee. Cherish no created image, harbor no earthly affection; let thy will rest

in no created object, except in so far as thy Lord and Spouse shall command thee for the well ordering of thy love, or in so far as thou canst be aided thereby to love Him alone."

17. "And when, after thus reaching this perfect abnegation and renunciation of thyself, thou shalt have freed and disentangled .thyself from all earthly things, seek the Lord, raising thyself with the swift wings of the dove toward the high habitation, in which He, in his condescension, wishes to place thy spirit; so that there thou mayest live in his presence and have a secure dwelling-place. This great Lord is a most jealous Spouse and his love and emulation are strong as death (Cant. 8, 6). He wishes to adorn thee and set thee in a secure place, in order that thou mayest not issue from it, or leave his presence for another, where thou findst Him not or enjoyest not his caresses. He, with whom thou art to converse without mistrust, wishes to sign thee with his own hand, and this is a most equitable law, which the spouses of the great King must observe; for even those in the world observe it, in order to show their faithfulness. It is due to the nobility of thy Spouse, that thou observe a behavior corresponding to the dignity and position conferred by Him, without descending to anything not befitting this estate or making thee unworthy of the adornment lavished upon thee for entrance into his bridal chamber."

18. "Next I require of thee, that thou despoil thyself with diligence of the vestments torn by thy faults and imperfections, soiled by the effects of sin, and made odious by the inclinations of nature. His Majesty wishes to wash off the stains, to purify and renew thee with his beauty, but under condition, that thou never lose sight of the poor and despicable vestments of which thou .hast been divested, so that in the memory and knowledge of this benefit, thou mayest spread the odor of sweetness for this great King by the nard of thy humility (Cant. 1, 11), and so that thou mayest never

forget the return, which thou owest to the Author of thy salvation. Thus will He, by the precious balsam of his blood, purify thee, heal thy wounds and enlighten thee copiously."

19. "In addition to all this" (this voice continued to say) "in order that thus forgetting all earthly things thou mayest be coveted by the highest King, seek to adorn thyself with the jewels, which He in his pleasure has prepared for thee. The vestments, which shall cover thee, are to be whiter than the snow, more brilliant than the diamond, more resplendent than the sun and yet they will be at the same time so delicate, that they wilt easily be spoiled by any negligence, making thee abominable in the sight of thy Spouse. But if thou preserve them in the purity which He desires, thy steps will be beautiful as the Prince's daughter (Cant. 7, 1), and his Majesty will be pleased with thy sentiments and thy words. As a cincture of thy vestment He will give thee the knowledge of his divine power and his holy fear, in order that, having bound thy inclinations, thou mayest direct thyself by his pleasure. The jewels of thy necklace, which adorn thy neck, signifying thy humble submission, shall be the costly stones of faith, hope and charity. As a clasp for thy hair (which are the high and exalted thoughts and thy heavenly intelligences), thou wilt have from Him the infused science and wisdom, and the embroideries of thy vestments shall be all the beauty and richness of the virtues. Thy diligence in performing what is most perfect shall serve thee as sandals. and thy laces shall be the avoidance and restraints, that thou wilt use in order to keep from evil. The rings, which will beautify thy fingers, shall be the seven gifts of the Holy Ghost; and the beauty of thy face shall be the participation of the Divinity, which on account of his holy love, shall shine there from. Thereto thou shalt add the coloring of confusion for having offended Him, in order that it may make thee ashamed of offending Him in the future, compar-

ing at the same time the coarse and sordid habits of the past with those that now adorn thee."

20. "And because thy own merits would make but a poor and miserable return for such a high espousal, the Most High wishes to ratify this contract by singling out, as if for thee alone, the infinite merits of thy Spouse Jesus Christ, and He makes thee a partaker of all his possessions and treasures in the heavens and upon earth. For all belongs to this supreme Lord (Esther 13, 11), and of all this thou shalt be mistress as his spouse for thy own use and for the greater love of Him. But remember, soul, that in order to obtain such a gift, thou must hide all this within thyself, without ever losing thy secret; for I warn thee of the danger of soiling thy beauty with the least imperfection; but if at any time thou committest such an imperfection out of weakness, rise from it at once, like a strong one, and acknowledging it, weep over the small fault as if it had been the most grievous."

21. "And in order that thou mayest have a dwelling place and habitation befitting such a great estate, thy Spouse does not wish to set thee any limit, but it is his pleasure, that thou dwell in the infinite regions of his Divinity and that thou roam about and disport thyself through the illimitable fields of his attributes and perfections, where the view of the intellect is without restraint, where the will is delighted without shadow of misgiving, and where the inclinations are satiated without bitterness. This is the paradise always delightful, where the most beloved brides of Christ find their recreation, where they gather the fragrant flowers and myrrh, and where the infinite is found for those that have renounced the imperfect nothing. There will thy habitation be secure; and in order that thy intercourse and companionship may be in correspondence with it, I desire that thou converse with the angels, holding them as friends and companions, and copy-

ing from them, during their frequent conversations and intercourse with thee, their virtues by faithful imitation."

22. "Take notice" (continued the voice) "0 soul, of the greatness of this benefit; for the Mother of thy Spouse and the Queen of heaven adopts thee anew for her daughter, receives thee as her disciple, and assumes the place of a Mother and of a Teacher toward thee. Through her intercession dost thou receive those special favors and they are all granted to thee that thou mayest write her most holy life. On this account thou hast been pardoned without thy merit, and that, which otherwise thou wouldst not have reached, has been conceded to thee. What would become of thee, O soul, if it were not for the Mother of mercy? Thou wouldst already have perished, if her intercession had failed thee; poor and useless would have been thy works, if, by divine condescension, thou hadst not been selected to write this history, but the eternal Father chose thee for his daughter, in view of this work, and for a spouse of his Onlybegotten Son; and the Son received thee to his close embraces, and the Holy Spirit selected thee for his enlightenments. The document of this contract and espousal is written and imprinted on the white parchment of the purity of most holy Mary: there the finger and the power of the Most High have written it; the ink is the blood of the Lamb; the executor is the eternal Father; the tie which binds thee to Christ is the Holy Spirit; the bondsmen are the merits of the same Jesus Christ and of his Mother; for thou art but a vile worm, having nothing to offer and being expected to give merely thy free consent."

23. So far the admonishing voice, which I heard. Although I judged it to be that of an angel, yet whether such it was, I could not ascertain clearly, for I did not perceive it in the same way as at other times. Such manifestations and disclosures accommodate themselves to the dispositions of the soul at the time of their reception, as for instance it

happened to the disciples at Emmaus (Luke 24, 16). Many other experiences I had in order to overcome the opposition of the serpent against the writing of this history, but it would draw out this introduction too much to mention them now. I continued my prayers for some days, asking the Lord to govern and direct me in order not to make a mistake, and representing to Him my incapacity and timidity. His Majesty persisted in exhorting me to ordain my life toward all purity and the greatest perfection, and in urging me to continue in it after having begun. And especially the Queen of the angels intimated to me her will many times, and with great sweetness and tenderness commanded me to obey Her as her daughter and write her most holy life, which I had commenced.

24. To all this I wished to add the security of obedience. Without saying anything of that, which I had heard from the Lord and from his most holy Mother, I asked my confessor and superior what he would direct me to do in this matter. He answered by commanding me under obedience to continue and to write the second part of this history. Finding myself thus compelled both by the Lord and by obedience, I returned again to the presence of the Most High, where I found myself one day in prayer, and, renouncing my whole self and recognizing my insignificance and liability to err, I prostrated myself before his Majesty and said: "My Lord, my Lord, what wishest Thou to do with me?" Whereupon I received the following intelligence.

25. It seemed to me, that the divine light of the blessed Trinity showed me my own self full of poverty and defects, and severely reprehending me for them, furnished me at the same time with the highest doctrine and salutary directions for a perfect life, and for this purpose God purified and enlightened me anew. I became aware that the Mother of grace, most holy Mary, standing before the throne of the

Divinity, was interceding and pleading for me. With such assistance my confidence took new life and profiting by the clemency of such a Mother, I addressed myself to Her and spoke to Her only these words: "My Lady and my Refuge, consider, as a true Mother, the poverty of thy slave." It seemed to me as if She heard my prayer and speaking with the Most High, She said: "My Lord, I wish to receive this useless and poor creature anew as a daughter and adopt her as my own." (Truly this was the act of a most liberal and mighty Queen!) But the Most High answered:

"My Spouse, for such a great favor as this, what does this soul bring in return? She does not deserve it, being a useless and destitute worm, and thankless for our gifts."

26. O wonderful power of the divine word! How shall I describe the effects produced in me by this answer of the Allpowerful? I humbled myself to the depth of my nothingness and I was filled with the knowledge of the misery of creatures and of my own ingratitude toward God. My heart sank within me in sorrow for my sins and in the desire of obtaining the unmerited happiness of being the child of that Sovereign. I raised my eyes full of dread to the throne of the Most High and my visage was transported in fear and hope; I turned toward my Advocate, and desiring to be admitted as her slave, since I did not merit the title of daughter, I spoke from the bottom of my heart without forming any words; and I heard the great Lady say to the Lord:

27. "Divine Lord and my God, it is true, this poor creature has nothing to offer to thy justice, but I offer for her the merits and the blood, which my most holy Son poured out for her and with it I present also the dignity of Mother of thy Onlybegotten Son, which I received from thy ineffable kindness, all the works, which I performed in thy service in having borne Him in my womb, and nourished Him with the milk of my breast, and above all I offer Thee thy own

bounty and Divinity; I earnestly entreat Thee to consider this creature as my adopted daughter and disciple for whom I will stand security. Under my guidance She will amend her faults and perform her works according to thy pleasure."

28. The Most High, (may He be eternally praised for hearing the petition of the great Queen interceding for the least of his creatures), yielded to these prayers, and immediately in the joy of my soul I felt immense effects, such as are impossible to describe; with my whole heart I turned toward all the creatures of heaven and earth, and, not being able to contain my exultation, I invited them to exalt for me and with me the Author of grace. It seemed to me that I addressed them in the following words: "0 ye inhabitants and courtiers of heaven and all ye living creatures, formed by the hand of the Most High, behold this marvel of his liberality and mercy and bless and exalt Him for all eternity, since He has raised from the dust the most vile of the universe and has enriched the most destitute; He has honored the most unworthy, though He is the highest God and the powerful King. And since you, sons of Adam, here see the poorest orphan succored, the greatest sinner pardoned; issue forth from your ignorance, raise yourself from your listlessness and renew your hope; for if his powerful arm has assisted me, if He has called and forgiven me, all of you can hope for your salvation; and if you wish to assure yourselves of it, seek, seek the protection of the most holy Mary, ask Her for her intercession, and you will find Her to be the Mother of ineffable mercy and clemency."

29. I turned also to this most exalted Queen and said to Her: "Aye, O my Lady, now I do not call myself an orphan, since I have a Mother, and a Mother, who is the Queen of all creation; I shall not any more be ignorant, since I have as Teacher the Mistress of divine wisdom, not poor, since I have as Lord Him, who is Master of all the treasures of

heaven and earth; I have a Mother, who protects me; an Instructress, who teaches and corrects me; a Mistress, who commands and governs me. Blessed art Thou amongst all women, wonderful among all creatures, admirable in heaven and on earth, and let all confess thy greatness with eternal praises. Since it is not easy or possible for the least among creatures, the lowest worm of the earth to give Thee any return: receive it then from the divine right hand and in the divine vision, where Thou standest in the presence of God enjoying Thyself through all eternity: I shall remain thy acknowledged and bounden slave, praising the Almighty as long as my life shall last, since his liberal mercy has so favored me, as to give me my Queen as my Mother and Teacher. Let my loving muteness praise Thee, since my tongue has not words or terms adequate for doing it; for all of them are strained and limited."

30. It is not possible to describe what the soul feels during such mysterious favors. They were the source of great good to my soul, for immediately I was made aware of a perfection of life, and of works for which I fail to find terms. But all this, the Most High told me, was given to me on account of the most holy Mary and in order to write her life. It was intimated to me, that by ratifying this blessing, the eternal Father chose me to manifest the sacraments of his Daughter; that the Holy Spirit poured out his light and inspirations that I might declare the hidden gifts of his Spouse; and that the most holy Son appointed me to manifest the mysteries of his most pure Mother Mary. And in order that I might become capable of this work, the Holy Trinity enlightened and bathed my soul in a special light of the Divinity and the divine power touched up my faculties as with a pencil, furnishing them with new habits for the perfect execution of this work.

31. The Most High also commanded me to strive to imitate with all my heart, according to my weak powers, all that I should understand and write about the heroic virtues and the most holy operations of the heavenly Queen, guiding my life according to her example. Knowing how unfit I am for the fulfillment of this obligation, the same most kind Queen offered to me anew her favor, help and instruction for all that the Lord commanded and pointed out to me. Then I asked for the blessing of the most holy Trinity in order to begin the second part of this heavenly history. I felt that all three persons of the Godhead conferred their blessing upon me. Issuing from the trance, I sought to wash my soul in the Sacraments and, full of contrition for my sins, in the name of the Lord and of obedience, I set myself about this work for the glory of the Most High and for his most holy Mother, the ever immaculate Virgin Mary.

32. This second part comprises the life of the Queen of the angels from the mystery of the Incarnation to the Ascension of Christ our Lord into heaven, which is the principal and the most important part of this history, for it includes the whole life and mysteries of the Lord himself with his Passion and most holy Death. I wish only to remark here, that the graces and blessings conceded to most holy Mary in preparation for the Incarnation, began to flow from the moment of her Immaculate Conception; already at that time, in the intention and the decree of God, She was the Mother of the Word. But in the measure as the realization of the Incarnation drew nigh, the favors and gifts of grace continued to increase. Although they seemed to be all of the same kind and nature from the beginning, yet they continued to augment and increase; and there are not terms new and varied enough to equal in their significance these increases and advances in the blessings conferred. Thus it becomes necessary in this narrative to measure all by the infinite

power of the Lord, who, giving much, retains enough to give infinitely more, while the capacity of each soul, and especially the soul of the Queen of heaven, is in its way infinite, being able to receive ever more and more. And this happened with the soul of holy Mary, until She arrived at a summit of holiness and participation of the Divinity, to which no other creature has attained nor will ever attain in all eternity. May the Lord himself enlighten me, that I may follow up this work according to his divine pleasure. Amen

CITY OF GOD PART II

THE INCARNATION

BOOK III

Containing the most Exquisite Preparations of the Almighty for the Incarnation of the Word In Mary most Holy; the Circumstances Accompanying this Mystery; the Exalted State, In which the Blessed Mother was placed; her Visit to Saint Elisabeth and the Sanctification of the Baptist: Her Rapture to Nazareth and a Memorable Battle of the Virgin with Lucifer.

Chapter I

THE MOST HIGH BEGINS TO PREPARE IN MOST HOLY MARY
THE MYSTERY OF THE INCARNATION; THE EVENTS OF THE
NINE DAYS PRECEDING THIS MYSTERY, ESPECIALLY THE
HAPPENINGS OF THE FIRST DAY.

1. In order that most faultless life might be to all an example
of the highest holiness, the Most High had placed upon our
Queen and Mistress the duties of a spouse of saint Joseph
which was a position requiring more intercourse with neighbors. The heavenly Mistress, finding self in this new estate,
was filled with such exalted thoughts and sentiments in the
fulfillment of duties, and ordered all the activities of life with
such wisdom, that She was an object of admirable emulation
to the angelic spirits and an unparalleled example for men.
Few knew and still fewer had spoken with Her; but these
happy ones were so filled with that celestial influence of
Mary, that with a wonderful joy and with unwonted flights
of spirit they sought to express and manifest the light, which
illumined their hearts and which they knew came from . The
most prudent Queen was not unaware of these operations of
the Most High; but neither was it yet time, nor would most
profound humility as yet consent to their becoming known
to the world. She continually besought the Lord to hide
them from men, to make all the favors of his right hand
redound solely to his praise, and to permit to be ignored and

despised by all the mortals, in as far as his infinite goodness would not be offended thereby.

2. These prayers were accepted by her divine Spouse with great benignity and his providence arranged all things in such a manner, that the very light, which incited men to proclaim her greatness, at the same time caused them to be mute. Moved by divine power, they refrained from expressing their thoughts, inwardly praising the Lord for the light, which they felt within themselves. Filled with marvel they suspended their judgment, and leaving behind the creatures, they sought their Creator. Many turned from sin at the mere sight of; others amended their lives; all were affected at seeing and experienced heavenly influences in their souls. But immediately they forgot the source of these influences; for if they could have remained in her presence, or could have retained the memory of her image, and if God had not prevented it by a mystery, nothing would have been able to divert their attention from and all would have sought without wavering.

3. In such fruitful occupations and in augmenting the gifts and graces from which all this good proceeded, our Queen, the Spouse of Joseph, busied Herself during the six months and seventeen days, which intervened between her espousal and the Incarnation of the Word. I cannot pretend to refer even briefly to her great heroic acts of all the virtues, interior and exterior, to all her deeds of charity, humility, religion, and all her works of mercy, the alms and benefactions; for this exceeds the power of the pen. The best I can do is to sum up and say: that the Most High found in most holy Mary the fulfillment of all his pleasure and of his wishes, as far as is possible in the correspondence of a creature with its Creator. By her sanctity and merits God felt Himself as it were obliged, and, (according to our way of speaking), compelled, to hasten his steps and extend the arms of his Omnipotence to bring about the greatest of wonders conceivable

in the world before or after: namely the Incarnation of the Onlybegotten of the Father in the virginal womb of this Lady.

4. In order to proceed with a dignity befitting Himself, God prepared most holy Mary in a singular manner during the nine days immediately preceding this mystery, and allowed the river of his Divinity to rush impetuously forth (Psalm 45, 5) to inundate this City of God with its floods. He communicated such great graces and gifts and favors, that I am struck dumb by the perception of what has been made known to me concerning this miracle, and my lowliness is filled with dread at even the mention of what I understood. For the tongue, the pen, and all the faculties of a creature fall far below any possibility of revealing such incomprehensible sacraments. Therefore I wish it to be understood, that all I say here is only an insignificant shadow of the smallest part of these wonders and ineffable prodigies, which are not at all to be encompassed by our limited words, but only by the power divine, which I do not possess.

5. On the first day of this most blessed novena the heavenly Princess Mary, after a slight rest, according to the example of her father David and according to the diurnal order and arrangement laid out for Her by the Lord, left her couch at midnight (Psalm 118, 62), and, prostrate in the presence of the Most High, commenced her accustomed prayer and holy exercises. The angels, who attended upon Her, spoke to Her and said: "Spouse of our King and Lord, arise, for his Majesty calls Thee." She raised Herself with fervent affection and answered:

"The Lord commands the dust to raise itself from the dust." And turning toward the countenance of the Lord, who called Her, She added: "Most high and powerful Master, what wishest Thou to do with me?" At these words her most holy soul was raised in spirit to a new and higher habitation, closer to the same Lord and more remote from all earthly and passing things.

6. She felt at once, that She was being prepared by those illuminations and purifications, which at other times She had experienced in some of the most exalted visions of the Divinity. I do not dwell on them, since I have described them in the first part (Part I, 620–629). The Divinity manifested Itself not by an intuitive, but by an abstractive vision; however so clearly, that by it She understood more of this incomprehensible Object, than what the blessed see and enjoy by intuition. For this vision was more exalted and more profound than the others of that kind; since this heavenly Lady made Herself more capable day by day and, because She made such perfect use of graces, She disposed Herself for ever greater ones. Moreover, the repeated enlightenments and visions of the Divinity continually enabled Her to respond more and more befittingly to its infinite operations.

7. In this vision our Princess Mary learned most high secrets of the Divinity and of its perfections, and especially of God's communications ad extra in the work of creation. She saw that it originated in the goodness and liberality of God, that creatures were not necessary for supplementing his Divine existence, nor for his infinite glory, since without them He was glorious through the interminable eternities before the creation of the world. Many sacraments and secrets were manifested to our Queen, which neither can nor should be made known to all; for She alone was the only One (Cant. 6, 8; 7, 6), the chosen One, selected by the highest King and Lord of creation for these delights. But as her Highness in this vision perceived this impulse and inclination of the Divinity to communicate Itself ad extra with a force greater than that which makes all the elements tend toward their center, and as She was drawn within the sphere of this divine love, She besought the eternal Father with heart

aflame, that He send his Onlybegotten into the world and give salvation to men, since in this manner He should satisfy, and, (speaking humanly), execute the promptings of his Divinity and its perfections.

8. These petitions of his Spouse were very sweet to the Lord, they were the scarlet lace, with which She bound and secured his love. And in order to put his desires into execution He sought first to prepare the tabernacle or temple, whither He was to descend from the bosom of the eternal Father. He resolved to furnish his beloved and chosen Mother with a clear knowledge of all his works ad extra, just as his Omnipotence had made them. On the first day therefore, and in this same vision, He manifested to Her all that He had made on the first day of the creation of the world, as it is recorded in Genesis, and She perceived all with greater clearness and comprehension, than if She had been an eyewitness; for She knew them first as they are in God, and then as they are in themselves.

9. She perceived and understood, how the Lord in the beginning (Gen. 1; 1, 5), created heaven and earth; in how far and in what way it was void, and how the darkness was over the face of the abyss; how the spirit of the Lord hovered over the waters and how, at the divine command, light was made, and what was its nature; how, after the darkness was divided, it was called night and the light day, and how thus the first day was made. She knew the size of the earth, its longitude, latitude and depth, its caverns, hell, limbo and purgatory with their inhabitants; the countries, climes, the meridians and divisions of the world, and all its inhabitants and occupants. With the same clearness She knew the inferior orbs and the empyrean heaven; how the angels were made on the first day; She was informed of their nature, conditions, diversity, hierarchies, offices, grades and virtues. The rebellion of the bad angels was revealed to Her, their fall and the

occasion and the cause of that fall, though the Lord always concealed from Her that which concerned Herself. She understood the punishment and the effects of sin in the demons, beholding them as they are in themselves; and at the conclusion of the first day, the Lord showed to Her, how She too was formed of this lowly earthly material and endowed with the same nature as all those, who return to the dust; He did not however say, that She would again return to it; yet He gave Her such a profound knowledge of the earthly existence, that the great Queen humiliated Herself to the abyss of nothingness; being without fault, She debased Herself more than all the children of Adam with all their miseries.

10. This whole vision and all its effects the Most High arranged in such a way as to open up in the heart of Mary the deep trenches that were required for the foundations of the edifice, which He wished to erect in Her: namely so high a one, that it would reach up to the substantial and hypostatic union of the human and divine nature. And as the dignity of Mother of God was without limits and to a certain extent infinite, it was becoming that She should be grounded in a proportionate humility, such as would be without limits though still within the bounds of reason itself. Attaining the summit of virtue, this blessed One among women humiliated Herself to such an extent, that the most holy Trinity was, as it were, fully paid and satisfied, and (according to our mode of understanding) constrained to raise Her to the highest position and dignity possible among creatures and nearest to the Divinity itself. In this highest benevolence his Majesty spoke and said to Her:

11. "My Spouse and Dove, great is my desire of redeeming man from sin and my immense kindness is as it were strained in waiting for the time, in which I shall descend in order to repair the world; ask Me continually during these

days and with great affection for the fulfillment of this desire. Prostrate in my royal presence let not thy petitions and clamors cease, asking Me that the Onlybegotten of the Father descend in reality to unite Himself with the human nature." Whereupon the heavenly Princess responded and said: "Lord and God eternal, whose is all the power and wisdom, whose wish none can resist (Esther 13, 9), who shall hinder thy Omnipotence? Who shall detain the impetuous current of thy Divinity, so that thy pleasure in conferring this benefit upon the whole human race remain unfulfilled? If perhaps, O my Beloved, I am a hindrance to such an immeasurable benefit, let me perish before I impede thy pleasure; this blessing cannot depend upon the merits of any creature; therefore, my Lord and Master, do not wait, as we might later on merit it so much the less. The sins of men increase and the offenses against Thee are multiplied; how shall we merit the very blessing, of which we become daily more unworthy? In Thee thyself, my Lord, exists the last cause and motive of our salvation; thy infinite bounty, thy numberless mercies incite Thee, the groans of thy Prophets and of the Fathers of thy people solicit Thee, the saints sigh after Thee, the sinners look for Thee and all of them together call out to Thee; and if I, insignificant wormlet, on account of my ingratitude, am not unworthy of thy merciful condescension, I venture to beseech Thee, from the bottom of my heart, to speed thy coming and to hasten thy Redemption for thy greater glory."

12. When the Princess of heaven had finished this prayer, She returned to her ordinary and more natural state; but anxious to fulfill the mandate of the Lord, She continued during that whole day her petitions for the Incarnation of the Word and with the deepest humility She repeated the exercises of prostrating Herself to the ground and praying in the form of a cross. For the Holy Ghost, who governed Her, had

taught Her this posture, by which She so highly pleased the most blessed Trinity. God saw, in the body of the future Mother of the Word, as it were the crucified person of Christ and therefore He received this morning sacrifice of the most pure Virgin as an advance offering of that of his most holy Son.

Words of the Queen

THE VIRGIN MARY SPEAKS TO SISTER MARY OF AGREDA

13. My daughter, the mortals are not capable of understanding the ineffable operations of the arm of the Omnipotent in preparing me for the Incarnation of the eternal Word, Especially during the nine days, which preceded this exalted sacrament was my spirit elevated and united with the immutable being of the Divinity. I was submerged in the ocean of his infinite perfections, participating in all those eminent and divine effect, which are beyond all presentiment of the human hearts. The knowledge of creatures communicated to me penetrated into their very essence, so that it was more profound and piercing than that of all the angelic spirits, though their knowledge of creation, on account of the beatific vision, is altogether admirable. Moreover the images of them all were impressed upon my mind to be used by me according as I desired.

14. What I wish of thee today is to take notice how I used this knowledge and to imitate me according to thy power with the help of the infused light, which thou hast received for this purpose. Profit by the knowledge of creatures by making of them a ladder to ascend unto God thy Creator; so that thou mayest seek in all of them their first beginning and their last end. Let them serve thee as a mirror from which the Godhead is reflected, reminding thee of his Omnipotence and inciting thee to the love, which He seeks in thee. Be

thou filled with wonder and praise at the greatness and magnificence of the Creator and in his presence humiliate thyself to the dust. Shun no difficulty or suffering in order to become meek and humble of heart. Take notice, my dearest, that this virtue of humility was the firm foundation of all the wonders, which the Most High wrought in me; and in order that thou mayest esteem this virtue so much the more, remember that of all others, it is at the same time the most precious, the most delicate and perishable; for if thou lose it in any respect, and if thou be not humble in all things without exception, thou wilt not be humble in anything. Remember thy earthly and corruptible nature, and be not ignorant of the fact, that the Most High has providentially formed man in such a way that his own existence and formation intimate and rehearse the important lesson of humility never allowing him to be without this salutary teaching. On this account He has not formed him of the most excellent material, and has concealed the noblest part of his being in the sanctuary of his interior (Exod, 30, 24), teaching him to weigh as in a balance on the one side, the infinite and eternal existence of the Lord, and on the other, his own ignoble material existence. Thus he is to give unto God what belongs to Him, and to himself what belongs to his own self (Matth. 22, 21).

15. Most zealously I attended to this adjustment, becoming an example and guide therein to all the mortals. I wish that thou also do it in imitation of me, and that thou zealously study to acquire the humility, which pleases the Most High and myself, who desire thy true advancement. I wish that thy perfection be built up in the deep trenches of thy own self-knowledge; in order that the deeper its foundations are laid, to so much the higher and more exalted perfection may rise the edifice of thy virtue. Thus thy will shall find a most intimate conformity with that of the Lord, who looks

down from the eminence of his throne upon the humble of
the earth.

Chapter II

THE LORD ON THE SECOND DAY CONTINUES HIS FAVORS
IN PREPARATION FOR THE INCARNATION OF THE WORD IN
THE MOST HOLY MARY.

16. In the first part of this history (Part I, 219), I mentioned,
that the most pure body of Mary was conceived and perfectly
formed within the space of seven days. The Most High
wished to work this miracle, in order that this most holy soul
might not have to wait so long as the souls of ordinary
mortals. He wished it to be created and infused before the
usual time, (as it also really happened), in order that this
beginning of the reparation of the world might have some
similarity to the beginning of its creation. This correspondence again took place at the coming of the Redeemer so that,
having formed the new Adam, Christ, God might rest as one
who had strained all the powers of his Omnipotence in the
greatest of his works; and that He might enjoy the most
delicious Sabbath of all his delights. And as these wonders
necessitated the intervention of the Mother of the divine
Word, who was to give Him a visible form, and as She was to
unite the two extremes, man and God, it was proper that She
should bear relation to both. Her dignity was inferior only to
that of God and superior to all that was not God; to this
dignity belonged also a proportionate knowledge and under-

standing, as well of the highest essence of the Divinity, as also of all the inferior creatures.

17. Following up his intention, the supreme Lord continued the favors, by which He wished to dispose most holy Mary for the Incarnation during nine days, as I have begun to explain. On the second day, at the same hour of midnight, the Virgin Mary was visited in the same way as described in the last chapter. The divine power raised Her up by the same elevations and illuminings to prepare Her for the visions of the Divinity. He manifested Himself again in an abstractive manner as on the first day, and She was shown the works performed on the second day of the creation. She learnt how and when God divided the waters (Gen. 1, 6), some above and others below, establishing the firmament, and above it the crystal, known also as the watery heaven. Her insight penetrated into the greatness, order, conditions, movements and all the other qualities and conditions of the heavens.

18. And in the most prudent Virgin this knowledge did not lay idle, nor remain sterile; for immediately the most clear light of the Divinity overflowed in Her, and inflamed and emblazoned Her with admiration, praise and love of the goodness and power of God. Being transformed as it were with a godlike excellence, She produced heroic acts of all the virtues, entirely pleasing to his divine Majesty. And as in the preceding first day God had made Her a participant of his wisdom, so on this second day, He made Her in corresponding measure a participant in the divine Omnipotence, and gave Her power over the influences of the heavens, of the planets and elements, commanding them all to obey Her. Thus was this great Queen raised to Sovereignty over the sea, the earth, the elements and the celestial orbs, with all the creatures, which are contained therein.

19. This sovereignty and supreme power belonged to the dignity of most holy Mary on account of the reason men-

tioned above; and besides for two other special ones; the first: because this Lady was the privileged Queen, exempt from the common law of sin and its consequences: therefore She was not to be put in the same general class with the insensate sons of Adam, against whom the Omnipotent armed the creatures (Wisd. 5, 18) for vengeance of his injuries and for the punishment of their frenzy. For if they had not in their disobedience turned against their Creator, neither would the elements nor their dependencies have been disobedient toward them, nor would they have molested them, nor turned against them the rigor and inclemency of their activity. And if this rebellion of the creatures is a punishment of sin, it could not justly extend itself to the most holy Mary, who was immaculate and without fault. Nor was it just, that She should be less privileged than the angels, who were not subject to these consequences of sin, or deprived of the dominion over the elementary powers. Although most holy Mary was of corporeal and terrestrial substance, yet She raised Herself above all corporeal and spiritual creatures, and made Herself Queen and Mistress of all creation. In this, therefore, She deserved so much the higher credit, as it was the rarer and the more precious. More must be conceded to the Queen than to her vassals, more to the Mistress than to the servants.

20. The second reason is, because her most holy Son was Himself to obey this heavenly Queen and his Mother. Since He was the Creator of the elements and of all things, it follows naturally that they should obey Her, to whom the Creator subjected Himself, and that they should be commanded by Her. Was not the person of Christ himself, in so far as his human nature was concerned, to be governed by his Mother according to the constitution and law of nature? This privilege of sovereignty tended also greatly to enhance the virtues and merits of most holy Mary, for thereby that which in ourselves is usually done under constraint and against our

will, was performed by Her freely and meritoriously. This most prudent Queen did not use her sovereignty over the elements and the creatures indiscriminately and for her own alleviation and comfort; but She commanded the creatures not to suspend their activities and influences in as far as they would naturally be painful and inconvenient to Her. For in these things She was to be like her most holy Son and suffer conjointly with Him. Her love and humility did not permit Her to withhold and suspend the inclemencies of the creatures in her regard, since She knew how valuable suffering is and how estimable in the eyes of the Lord.

21. Only on some occasions, when She knew that it was not for her benefit but necessary for her Son and Creator, the sweet Mother restrained the force of the elements and their influences, as we shall see farther on during her journey to Egypt and on other occasions, where She most prudently judged it proper, that the creatures recognize their Creator and reverence Him, or protect and serve Him in some necessity (Infr. 543, 590, 633). What mortal will not marvel at the knowledge of such a new miracle? To see a mere earthly creature, yet One clothed with the sovereignty and dominion of the whole creation, esteem Herself in her own eyes as the most unworthy and insignificant of the creatures, and, in these humble sentiments, command the wrath of the winds and all the rigors of the natural elements to turn against Her and under obedience fulfill her command! In obeying Her, however, these elements. full of reverence and courtesy toward such a Mistress, yielded to her wishes, not in vengeance of the wrongs of their Creator, as they do in regard to the rest of the children of Adam, but in order to respect her commands.

22. In the presence of this humility of our invincible Queen, we mortals cannot deny our most arrogant vanity and presumption, or rather our audacity, since, seeing that

on account of our insane outrages we merit the furious rebellion of the elements and of all the harmful forces of the universe against us, we complain of their rigor, as if their molestations were an injury. We deprecate the rigor of the cold, we complain of the exhaustion of heat; all painful things we abhor, and we condemn with all energy these ministers of divine justice and seek our own comforts and delights, as if they were to last forever and as if it were not certain that we are only drawing therefrom a heavier punishment of our faults.

23. But returning to the consideration of the knowledge and power given to the Princess of heaven and the other gifts preparing Her worthily for the position of Mother of God, we can understand their excellence, for we see in them a certain infinity or boundlessness, participating of the Divinity, and similar to that which was afterwards possessed by the most holy soul of Christ. For She not only knew all creatures in God, but comprehended them in such a way as to master them and at the same time reserve capacity for knowing many others, if there had existed more to be known. I call this knowledge an infinity, because it seems to partake of the qualities of infinite knowledge and because, in one and the same action of her mind and without successive advertence, She saw and perceived the number of the heavens, their latitude and profundity, their order, motions, qualities, their matter and form; the elements with all their changes and accidents: all of these She knew at the same time. The only thing the most wise Virgin did not know was the immediate end of this knowledge until the moment of her consent and the fulfillment of the ineffable mercy of the Most High. She continued during these days her most fervent prayers for the coming of the Messias, according to the command of the Lord. And He had given Her to understand that He would not tarry, as the time destined for his arrival was at hand.

Words of the Queen

THE VIRGIN MARY SPEAKS TO SISTER MARY OF AGREDA

24. My daughter, from what thou art going to learn of the favors and blessings conferred upon me in preparation for the dignity of Mother of God, I wish thee to perceive the admirable order of his wisdom in the creation of man. Take notice, therefore, that his Creator made him out of nothing, not in order to be a slave, but in order to be the king and the master of all creation (Gen. 1, 26), and in order that he make use of creatures in sovereignty, command and mastery; yet at the same time man was to recognize himself as the image of his Maker and the work of his hand, remaining more devoted to God and more submissive to his will than the creatures to man; for all this was demanded by justice and reason. And in order that man might not be without information and knowledge of the Creator and of the means of perceiving and executing his will, He added to his natural light a greater one, more penetrating, more limpid, more certain, more free and extensive, namely the light of divine faith, by which man might know the existence of God and of his perfections, and conjointly with these, his works. Furnished with this knowledge and dominion man was established in good standing, honored and enriched, having no excuse for not devoting himself entirely to the fulfillment of the divine will.

25. But the foolishness of man disturbs this order and destroys this harmony, when, being created as the lord and king of creatures, he enslaves himself, subjecting himself to them, and degrading his dignity in using visible things not as a prudent master, but as an unworthy vassal. For he debases himself beneath the lowest of creatures, by losing sight of the fact that he is their superior. All this perversity arises from the use of creatures not for the service of the Creator through well ordered faith, but for the indulgence of the passions and

the delights of the senses. Hence also arises man's great abhorrence of those things which are not pleasing to the senses.

26. Thou, my dearest, look faithfully toward thy Creator and Lord and in thy soul seek to copy the image of his divine perfections: lose not the mastery and dominion over creatures, let none of them infringe upon thy liberty; but seek to triumph over all of them, allowing nothing to interpose itself between thee and thy Creator. Subject thyself gladly, not to the pleasurable in creatures, since that will obscure thy understanding and weaken thy will, but to the adverse and the painful resulting from their activity. Suffer this with joyous willingness, for I have done the same in imitation of my Son, although I had the power to neutralize their molestations and had no sins to atone for.

Chapter III

WHAT FAVORS THE MOST HIGH CONFERRED ON MOST
HOLY MARY ON THE THIRD DAY OF THE NOVENA BEFORE
THE INCARNATION.

27. The right arm of the Most High, which threw open the
doors of the Divinity to most holy Mary, continued to enrich
and adorn at the expense of his infinite attributes this most
pure spirit and virginal body which He had chosen as his
tabernacle, as his temple, and as the holy city of his habitation. And the heavenly Lady, engulfed in this vastness of the
Divinity, winged her flight day by day farther away from
earthly things, and transformed Herself more and more into
a heavenly being, discovering ever new sacraments in the
Most High. For as He is the infinite Object of desire, although the appetite is satiated with that which is received,
always more remains to be desired and understood. Not all
the hierarchies of the angels, nor all men together, have
attained such preferment in blessings, mysteries and sacraments as this Princess attained, especially as regards those due
to Her as Mother of the Creator.

28. On the third day of preparation at which I have now
arrived, having again been prepared as on the first day, the
Divinity manifested Itself anew in abstractive vision. Too
slow and inadequate are our powers for understanding the
increase of the gifts and graces, which the Most High then

lavished on heavenly Mary; and at this juncture I am at a loss for words to explain even the least portion of what I perceived. I can only express myself by saying, that the divine wisdom and power proceeded in a manner worthy of Her, who was to be the Mother of the Word, so as to ensure, as far as is possible for a creature, that likeness and proportion, which was due to the divine Persons. Whoever has even a faint understanding of the distance which lies between the two extremes, the infinite God and the limited human creature, can comprehend so much the better, what is necessary to bring them together and establish a proportion.

29. More and more the Queen of heaven reflected his infinite attributes and virtues; more and more brilliantly shone forth her beauty under the touch of the pencil of the divine Wisdom and under the colors and lights added to it from on high. On this day She was informed of the works of creation as they happened on the third day. She learned when and how the waters, which were beneath the firmament, flowed together in one place (Gen. 1, 9), disclosing the dry land, which the Lord called earth, while He called the waters the sea. She learned in what way the earth brought forth the fresh herbs, and all plants and fructiferous trees with their seeds, each one according to its kind. She was taught and She comprehended the greatness of the sea, its depth and its divisions, its correspondence with the streams and the fountains, that take their rise from it and flow back into it; the different plants and herbs, the flowers, trees, roots, fruits and seeds; She perceived how all and each one of them serve for the use of man. All this our Queen understood and penetrated with the keenest insight more clearly, distinctly and comprehensibly than Adam or Solomon. In comparison with Her all those skilled in medicine in the world would appear but ignorant even after the most thorough studies and largest experience. The most holy Mary knew all that was hidden

from sight, as Wisdom says (Wis. 7, 21); and just as She learned it without any fiction, She also communicates it without envy. Whatever Solomon says there in the book of Wisdom was realized in Her with incomparable and eminent perfection.

30. On some occasions our Queen made use of this science in order to exercise her charity toward the poor and needy, as will be related in the sequence of this history (No. 668, 867, 868, 1048; III. 159,423). She had it under perfect control, and it was as familiar to Her as the well-trained musician is with his instrument. The same was true of all the rest of the sciences, whenever She found it desirable or necessary to make use of them in the service of the Most High. For She was Mistress of all of them more perfectly than any of the mortals who ever did excel in any art or science. She was versed in the virtuous qualities and activities of the stones, herbs and plants, and in Her was true what Christ our Lord promised to the Apostles and first Christians, that poisonous draughts would not hurt them. This privilege belonged to the Queen as a sovereign, so that neither poison or any other thing could ever injure Her or cause Her any harm except with her permission.

31. These privileges and favors the most prudent Princess and Lady always kept concealed, and She made no use of them for Herself, as I have said, desiring not to be deprived of a share in the suffering, which had been chosen by her most holy Son. Before conceiving Him and becoming his Mother, She was inspired with divine knowledge and science concerning the passibility of the Word made flesh. And when She became Mother She saw and experienced this truth in her Son and Lord himself and therefore She gave a greater license, or rather a more strict command, to creatures to afflict Her, since She saw the results of this activity in their own Creator. Hence, as the Most High did not wish his only

and chosen Spouse to be continually molested by the creatures, even though She herself desired it, He often restrained them and neutralized their operations, so that the heavenly Princess, unhindered by them, might occasionally enjoy the delights of the most high King.

32. There is another special favor, which the most holy Mary received for the benefit of the mortals on the third day and in that vision of the Divinity; for during this vision God manifested to Her in a special way the desire of his divine love to come to the aid of men and to raise them up from all their miseries. In accordance with the knowledge of his infinite mercy and the object for which it was conceded, the Most High gave to Mary a certain kind of participation of his own attributes, in order that afterwards, as the Mother and Advocate of sinners, She might intercede for them. This participation of the most holy Mary in the love of God and in his inclination to help Her, was so heavenly and powerful that if from that time on the strength of the Lord had not come to her aid, She would not have been able to bear the impetuosity of her desire to assist and save mankind. Filled with this love and charity, She would, if necessary or feasible, have delivered Herself an infinite number of times to the flames, to the sword and to the most exquisite torments of death for their salvation. All the torments, sorrows, tribulations, pains, infirmities She would have accepted and suffered; and She would have considered them a great delight for the salvation of sinners. Whatever all men have suffered from the beginning of the world till this hour, and whatever they will suffer till the end, would have been a small matter for the love of this most merciful Mother. Let therefore mortals and sinners understand what they owe to most holy Mary.

33. From that day on, we can say, the heavenly Lady continued to be the Mother of kindness and great mercy, and for

two reasons: first, because from that moment She sought with an especial and anxious desire to communicate without envy the treasures of grace, which She had comprehended and received; and therefore such an admirable sweetness grew up in her heart, that She was ready to communicate it to all men and to shelter them in her heart in order to make them participants of the divine love, which there was enkindled. Secondly, because this love of most holy Mary for the salvation of men was one of the principal dispositions required for conceiving the eternal Word in her virginal womb. It was eminently befitting that She should be all mercy, kindness, piety and clemency, who was Herself to conceive and give birth to the Word made man, since He in his mercy, clemency and love desired to humiliate Himself to the lowliness of our nature, and wished to be born of Her in order to suffer for men. It is said: like begets like: just as the water partakes of the qualities of the minerals through which it flows; and although the birth of Christ originated in the Divinity, yet it also partook of the conditions of the Mother as far as was possible. She therefore would not have been suitable' for concurrence with the Holy Ghost in this conception, in which only the activity of the man was wanting, if She had not been endowed with perfections corresponding to those of the humanity of Christ.

34. The most holy Mary issued from this vision with ever increasing fervor, and during all the rest of the day She occupied Herself in the prayers and petitions commanded Her by the Lord. The heart of her Spouse was wounded with love, so that (according to our mode of thinking) He already longed for the day and the hour when He should rest in the arms and recline at the breast of his Beloved.

Words of the Queen

THE VIRGIN MARY SPEAKS TO SISTER MARY OF AGREDA

35. My dearest daughter, great were the favors which the hand of the Most High showered upon me in the visions of the Divinity, vouchsafed me during the nine days before his conception in my womb. And although He did not manifest Himself intuitively and altogether unveiled, yet He did it in an exalted manner and with such effects as are reserved to his wisdom. In the remembrance of what I perceived in this vision, I rose to the true perception of the position which God held in comparison to men and men in comparison to God; my heart was inflamed with love and was torn with sorrow; for I realized the immensity of his love towards mortals, and their most ungrateful oblivion of his incomprehensible goodness. Many times would I have died at the thought of these extremes, if God himself had not comforted and preserved me. This sacrifice of his servant was most pleasing to his Majesty and He accepted it with greater complacency than all the holocausts of the old Law; for He beheld my humility and delighted in it very much. Whenever I performed these exercises, He showed great mercy to me and to my people.

36. These sacraments, my dearest, I manifest to thee in order to encourage thee to imitate me, as far as is possible with thy weak forces aided by grace. Look upon the works, which thou hast learnt of, as a pattern and example to be closely followed. Meditate much, and weigh over and over again as well in the light of grace as in that of reason, how exactly mortals ought to correspond to this immense kindness of God and to his eagerness to assist them. Compare at the same time the heartless obduracy of the children of Adam. I wish that thy heart be softened in affectionate thankfulness toward the Lord and melted in sorrow at these

unhappy proceedings of men. I assure thee, my. daughter, that on the day of the general adjustment, the cause of the greatest wrath of the just Judge shall be man's most ungrateful forgetfulness of this truth; and the confusion of men on account of this wrath shall be such, that on that day they would of their own accord cast themselves into the abyss of pain, if there were no ministers of divine justice to visit this retribution upon them.

37. In order to avoid such an abominable fault and in order to forestall such a horrible chastisement, renew in thyself the memory of the blessings, which thou hast received at the hands of his love and infinite clemency; and remember that God has distinguished thee in preference to the souls of many generations. Do not make the mistake of considering these great favors and special gifts as conferred on thee for thyself alone: they were conferred also for the sake of thy brethren: for the divine mercy is extended to all men. Therefore the return, which thou owest to the Lord, must be made first for thyself and then for thy brethren. And because thou art poor, offer up the life and merits of my most holy Son, and with them, all that I have suffered by the forces of my love. Thus wilt thou make thyself pleasing to God and tender some recompense for the ingratitude of mortals. In all these things exercise thyself repeatedly many times, remembering in the meanwhile what I thought and felt in similar acts and exercises.

Chapter IV

THE MOST HIGH CONTINUES HIS FAVORS TO MOST HOLY
MARY ON THE FOURTH DAY.

38. Still the favors and most exalted mysteries of the Most
High toward our Queen and Lady in preparing Her for
approaching dignity of Motherhood continued. The fourth
day of this preparation had arrived and at the same hour She
was again raised to the abstractive vision of the Divinity. But
this vision was accompanied by new effects of exalted enlightenments in this most pure Soul. The divine power and
wisdom has no bounds or limits; to his operations only our
will, or the limitation of our created nature, offers resistance.
But in the will of most holy Mary the divine power found no
hindrance, for all her works were executed with plenitude of
holiness and entirely according to the pleasure of the Lord,
drawing Him on, as He himself said, and wounding his heart
with love (Cant. 4, 9). Only in so far as most holy Mary was
a mere creature was the power of the divine arm limited; but
within these limits it could act without bound or restriction,
and without measure, offering Her the waters of wisdom
from the purest and most crystalline founts of the Divinity.

39. The Most High manifested to Her in this vision, by
most special enlightenments, the new Law of grace which the
Redeemer of the world was to establish, the Sacraments

contained in it, the end for which He would leave them in his new Church of the Gospel, the gifts and blessings prepared for men, and his desire, that all should be saved and that all should reap the fruit of the Redemption. And so great was the wisdom, which the most holy Mary drew from these visions, wherein She was taught by the highest Teacher and the Corrector of the wise (Wis. 7, 15), that, if by any means man or angel could describe it, more books would have to be written of this science of our Lady than all those which have been composed in this world concerning all the arts and sciences, and all the inventions of men. And no wonder her science was greater than that of all other men: for into the heart and mind of our Princess was emptied and exhausted the ocean of the Divinity, which the sins and the evil disposition of the creatures had confined, repressed and circumscribed. It was concealed within its own source until the proper time, which was no other than the hour in which She was chosen as Mother of the Onlybegotten of the Father.

40. Joined with the sweetness of this divine science, our Queen felt a loving, yet piercing sorrow, which this very science continued to renew. She perceived in the Most High the ineffable treasures of grace and blessings, which He had prepared for mortals and She saw the weight of the Divinity as it were inclined toward the desire of seeing all men enjoy them eternally. At the same time She saw and considered the wicked disposition of the world, and how blindly mortals impeded the flow of these treasures and deprived themselves of participation of the Divinity. From this resulted a new kind of martyrdom full of grief for the perdition of men and of the desire of remedying such lamentable loss. This caused Her to offer up the most exalted prayers, petitions, sacrifices, humiliations and heroic acts of love of God and of men, in order that no one, if possible, should henceforth damn himself, and that all should recognize their Creator, and

Redeemer, confess Him, adore and love Him. All this took place in this very vision; but as these petitions were of the same kind as those already described, I do not expatiate on them here.

41. In conjunction therewith the Lord showed Her also the works of creation performed on the fourth day (Gen. I, 14–17). The heavenly Princess Mary learned how and when the luminaries of heaven were formed in the firmament for dividing day and night and for indicating the seasons, the days and the years; how for this purpose was created the great light of heaven, the sun, presiding as the lord of the day, and joined with it, the moon, the lesser light, which reigns over the darkness of the night. In like manner were formed the stars of the eighth heaven, in order that they might gladden the night with their brilliance and preside with their various influences over both the day and the night. She understood what was the material substance of these luminous orbs, their form, their size, their properties, their various movements and the uniformity as well as the inequality of the planets. She knew the number of the stars, and all their influences exerted upon the earth, both in regard to the living and the lifeless creatures; the effects and changes, which they cause in them by these influences.

42. This is not in conflict with what the Prophet says, (Psalm 146, 4), that God knows the number of the stars and has called them by their names; for David does not thereby deny to his Majesty the liberty of conceding to a creature that as a privilege which He possesses by nature. It is plain, that since this knowledge is communicable and since it would contribute to Mary's excellence, it should not be denied to Her. Has He not conferred upon Her greater favors, and has He not made Her the Queen of the stars and of all other creatures? And this knowledge was as it were only a sequel of her dominion and sovereignty over the powers, influences

and movements of all the celestial orbs, since they were commanded to obey Her as their Queen and Lady.

43. In consequence of this command, which the Lord gave to the celestial orbs and in accordance with the dominion which most holy Mary obtained over them, She possessed such power, that if She commanded the stars to leave their positions in heaven, they would obey Her instantly and would hasten to the regions which She chose to designate. The same is true of the sun and the planets: all would pause in their course and suspend their operations to execute the command of Mary. I have already said above (No. 21) that sometimes her Highness made use of this sovereignty; for, as we shall see farther on, it happened a few times in Egypt, where the rays of the sun are exceedingly strong, that She commanded the sun to moderate its heat and not to molest or fatigue the infant God, its Master. And the sun obeyed Her therein, causing inconvenience and suffering to Her, because She wished it, and yet respecting the tender years of the Sun of justice, whom She held in her arms. The same happened also with other stars, and on a few occasions She detained the sun in its course, as I will mention later.

44. Many other hidden sacraments the Most High manifested to our great Queen in this vision, and what I have said and will say of all these mysteries, leaves me dissatisfied and with a heart as it were torn asunder: for I see, that I can say little of that which I understand and, in proportion, I understand still less of what really did happen to the heavenly Lady. Many of the mysteries concerning Her are reserved for the last day, when her most holy Son shall proclaim them, since now we are not capable of receiving their revelation. The most holy Mary issued from this vision still more inflamed and filled with the Divinity, entirely transformed by the knowledge of God's attributes and perfections; and her advance in virtues kept pace with her progress in divine

favors. She multiplied her requests, her fervent sighs, and her meritorious works, in order to hasten the Incarnation of the Word and our salvation.

Words of the Queen

THE VIRGIN MARY SPEAKS TO SISTER MARY OF AGREDA

45. My dearest daughter, I wish that thou busy thyself much in meditating and pondering upon that which thou hast understood of my doings and sufferings at the time, when the Most High gave me such a deep insight into his goodness, which drew Him as with an infinite force to enrich men, and when He showed me the want of correspondence and the dark ingratitude of the mortals. When I turned from the consideration of this most liberal condescension of the Most High, to the perception and understanding of the foolish hard-heartedness of the sinners, my soul was pierced with an arrow of mortal anguish, which remained for life. And I wish to tell thee of another mystery: many times the Most High in order to heal the affliction and consternation of my heart in this sorrow, sought to console me by saying: "Accept Thou, my Spouse, the gifts, which the blind and ignorant world in its unworthiness despises and is incapable of receiving and understanding." With these words the Most High was accustomed to set free the currents of his divine bounty, which rejoiced my soul more than human powers can comprehend, or tongue explain.

46. I desire, therefore, that thou, my friend, be now my companion in the sorrow which I suffered and which is so little noticed by the living. In order to imitate me therein and in the effects of this most just grief, thou must deny thyself, forget thyself entirely, and crown thy heart with the thorns of sorrow at the behavior of mortals. Weep thou in seeing them laugh at their eternal damnation, for such weeping is the

most legitimate occupation of the true spouses of my most holy Son. Let them seek their delight only in the tears, which they pour out on account of their sins and those of the ignorant world. Thus prepare thy heart in order that the Lord may make thee a participant of his treasures; not in order to become rich, but in order that his Majesty may fulfill his most generous love toward thee and in order that souls may find justification. Imitate me in all that I teach thee, since thou knowest that this is my desire in favoring thee.

Chapter V

HIS MAJESTY MANIFESTS NEW MYSTERIES AND SACRAMENTS
TOGETHER WITH THE WORKS OF THE FIFTH DAY OF THE
CREATION TO MOST HOLY MARY, AND HER HIGHNESS
CONTINUES TO PRAY FOR THE INCARNATION OF THE
WORD.

47. The fifth day of the novena, which the most blessed
Trinity celebrated in the temple of most holy Mary, in order
that the eternal Word might assume human shape in Her,
had arrived. Just as in the preceding days She was elevated to
an abstractive vision of the Divinity, and, as the veil fell more
and more from the secrets of the infinite wisdom, She discovered new mysteries also during this day. For the preparations and enlightenments emitted ever stronger rays of light
and divine graces, which flashed into her most holy soul and
emptied the treasures of infinity into her faculties, assimilating and transforming the heavenly Lady more and more to a
likeness of her God in order to make Her worthy of being his
Mother.

48. In this vision, showing Himself to Her with ineffable
signs of affection, the Most High spoke to the heavenly
Queen and manifested to Her additional secrets, saying: "My
Spouse and my Dove, in the secret of my bosom thou hast
perceived the immense bounty, to which my love for the
human race inclines Me, and the treasures, which are secretly

prepared for their happiness: so powerful is this love in Me, that I wish to give them my Onlybegotten for their instruction and salvation. Thou hast also seen something of the small returns, of their most listless ingratitude and contempt, in which men hold my clemency and love. Yet, although I have shown thee part of their malice, I wish, my friend, that thou shouldst once more know in Me, how small is the number of those who are to know and love me as my chosen ones; and how great and extended is the number of the ungrateful and the reprobate. The innumerable sins and abominations of these impure and defiled men, whom I have foreseen in my infinite knowledge, retard my bounteous mercy and have locked up the treasurehouse of my Divinity, making the world entirely unworthy of receiving my gifts."

49. The Princess Mary, through these words of the Most High, was instructed in the great mysteries regarding the number of the predestined and the reprobate; and also regarding the hindrances and impediments by which sinful men delayed the coming of the eternal Word as man into the world. Having present before Herself the vision both of the infinite bounty and equity of the Creator and of the measureless iniquity and malice of men, the most prudent Mistress, inflamed by the fire of divine love, spoke to his Majesty and said:

50. "My Lord and infinite God of wisdom and incomprehensible sanctity, what mystery is this, which Thou hast manifested to me? Without measure are the misdeeds of men, so that only thy wisdom can comprehend them. But can all these and many more, perhaps, extinguish thy bounty and love, or vie with them? No, my Lord and Master, it must not be so; the malice of men must not detain thy mercy. I am the most useless of all the human race; yet on its behalf I remind Thee of thy fidelity. Infallibly true it is, that heaven and earth will come to naught, before thy word can fail (Is.

51, 6), and it is also true, that Thou hast many times given thy word through the holy Prophets; and Thou hast promised them by word of mouth, a Redeemer and our salvation. How then, my God, can these promises fail of fulfillment without conflicting with thy infinite wisdom; or how can man be deceived without conflicting with thy goodness? In order to induce Thee to fulfill thy promise and to secure them eternal felicity through thy incarnate Word, I have nothing to offer on the part of mortals nor can any creature oblige Thee; and if this blessing could be merited, then thy infinite and bounteous clemency would not thereby be glorified. Only through thy own Self can this obligation be imposed upon Thee, for only in God can a sufficient reason be found for his becoming man: in Thee alone was the reason and the motive for our creation, and therefore in Thee alone also the reason for our reparation after our fall. Do not seek, my God and most high King, for merits, nor for a greater motive, than thy own mercy and the exaltation of thy holy name."

51. "It is true, my Spouse," answered the Most High, "that on account of my goodness I bound Myself to the promise of vesting Myself in human nature and of dwelling among them, and that no one could merit in my sight such a promise; but the ungrateful behavior of men, so abominable in my sight and in my justice, does not merit the execution of this promise. For though I seek only their eternal happiness as a return of my love, I perceive and find only obduracy, by which they are certain to waste and despise the treasures of my grace and blessing. They will yield thorns instead of fruit, great insults for benefits, and base ingratitude for my unbounded and generous mercy; and the end of all these evils will be for them the privation of my vision in eternal torments. Take notice of these truths recorded in the secrets of my wisdom, my Friend, and weigh these great sacraments;

for to thee my heart is laid open, so that thou canst see the justice of my proceeding."

52. It is impossible to describe the hidden secrets, which most holy Mary then saw in the Lord; for She perceived in Him all the creatures of the past, present and the future, and the position of each one in creation, the good and bad actions and the final ending of each one. If She had not been strengthened, She could not have preserved her life under the effects and feelings caused by the knowledge and insight into these hidden sacraments and mysteries. But as his Majesty, in these new miracles and blessings had such high ends in view, He was not sparing but most liberal with the beloved One, whom He had chosen as his Mother. And as our Queen derived this science from the bosom of God itself, She participated also in the fire of his eternal Charity, which inflamed Her with the love of God and the neighbor. Therefore, continuing her intercession, She said:

53. "Lord and eternal God, invisible and immortal, I confess thy justice, I magnify thy works, I adore thy infinite Essence and hold in reverence thy judgments. My heart melts within me with tenderest affection, when I perceive thy unlimited bounty toward men and their dark ingratitude and grossness toward Thee. For all of them, O my God, Thou seekest eternal life; but there are few who are thankful for this inestimable benefit, and many who will perish by their malice. If on this account, O my eternal Good, Thou relinquishest thy undertaking, we mortals are lost; but while Thou, in thy divine fore-knowledge, perceivest the sins and the malice of men who offend Thee so much, Thou also foreseest thy Onlybegotten made man and his works of infinite price and value in thy sight; and these will counterbalance and exceed the malice of sin beyond all comparison. Through this Godman let thy equity be conquered and on his account give us Him now! And, in order to urge my

petitions upon Thee once more in the name of the human race, I unite myself with the spirit of this Word, already made man in thy mind, and pray for his coming in fact and for the eternal life of men through his hands."

54. At this prayer of most pure Mary, the eternal Father (in our way of speaking) represented to Himself his Onlybegotten as borne in the virginal womb of this great Queen; and He was moved by her humble and loving petitions. His apparent hesitation was merely a device of his tender love in order to enjoy so much the longer the voice of his Beloved, causing her sweet lips to distil most sweet honey (Cant. 4, 11) and her emissions to be like those of paradise (Cant. 4, 13). And to draw out still more this loving contention, the Lord answered Her: "My sweetest Spouse and chosen Dove, great is that which thou askest of Me and little is that which obliges Me on the part of men; how then shall such a singular blessing be conferred on those unworthy ones? Leave Me, my friend, to treat them according to their evil deserts." Our powerful and kind Advocate responded: "No, my Master, I will not desist from my importunity; if much I ask, I ask it of Thee, who are rich in mercies, powerful in action, true in thy words. My father David said of Thee and of the eternal Word: "The Lord hath sworn, and He will not repent: Thou art a priest forever according to the order of Melchisedech" (Ps. 109, 4). Let then that Priest come, who is at the same time to be the sacrifice for our rescue; let Him come, since Thou canst not repent of thy promise; for Thou dost not promise in ignorance. Let me be clothed, O my sweet love, with the strength of this Man God, which will not allow me to put a stop to my importunity, until Thou give me thy blessing as to my father Jacob" (Gen. 32,26).

55. In this contest (just as it once happened to Jacob) our Lady and Queen was asked, what was her name; and She said: "I am a daughter of Adam, formed by thy hands from

the insignificant dust." And the Most High answered: "Henceforth Thou shalt be called: Chosen for the Mother of the Onlybegotten." But the latter part of this name was heard only by the courtiers of heaven, while to Her it was as yet hidden until the proper time. She therefore heard only the word "Chosen." Having thus protracted this amorous contention according to the disposition of his divine wisdom and as far as served to inflame the heart of this elected One, the whole blessed Trinity gave to Mary, our most pure Queen, the explicit promise, that They would now send into the world the eternal Word made man. Filled with incomparable joy and exultation by this fiat, She asked and received the benediction of the Most High. Thus this strong Woman issued forth from the contest with God more victorious than Jacob; for She came out rich, strong and laden with spoils, and the One that was wounded and weakened (to speak in our way) was God himself; for He was drawn by the love of this Lady to clothe Himself in that sacred bridal chamber of her womb with the weakness of our passible nature. He disguised and enveloped the strength of his Divinity, so as to conquer in allowing Himself to be conquered, and in order to give us life by his death. Let the mortals see and acknowledge, how most holy Mary, next to her most blessed Son, is the cause of their salvation.

56. During this vision were also revealed to this great Queen the works of the fifth day of the creation in the manner in which they happened; She saw how, by the force of the divine command, were engendered and produced in the waters beneath the firmament, the imperfect reptiles, which creep upon the earth, the winged animals that course through the air, and the finny tribes that glide through the watery regions. Of all these creatures She knew the beginnings, the substance, the form and figure according to their kinds; She knew all the species of the animals that inhabit the

fields and woods, their conditions, peculiarities, their uses
and connections; She knew the birds of heaven (for so we call
the atmosphere), with the varied forms of each kind, their
ornaments, feathers, their lightness; the innumerable fishes of
the seas and the rivers, the differences between the whales,
their forms, composition and qualities, their caverns and the
foods furnished them by the sea, the ends which they serve,
the use to which they can be put in the world. And his
Majesty especially commanded all these hosts of creatures to
recognize and obey most holy Mary, giving Her the power to
command all of them, as it happened on many occasions to
be mentioned later on (No. 185, 431, 636). Therewith She
issued from the trance of this day and She occupied Herself
during the rest of it in the exercises and petitions, which the
Most High had pointed out to Her.

Words of the Queen

THE VIRGIN MARY SPEAKS TO SISTER MARY OF AGREDA

57. My daughter, the more complete knowledge of the
wonderful operations of the arm of the Almighty in raising
me during the abstractive visions of the Divinity to the
dignity of Mother, is reserved for the predestined when they
shall come to know them in the heavenly Jerusalem. There
they shall understand and see them in the Lord Himself and
with that special delight and astonishment, which the angels
experienced, when the Most High revealed these things to
them for his exaltation and praise. And since his Majesty has
shown Himself so lovingly generous toward thee, giving thee
in preference to all the generations of men, such great
knowledge and light concerning these so hidden sacraments,
I desire, my friend, that thou signalize thyself above all
creatures in praising and magnifying his holy name for the
works of his powerful arm in my regard.

58. At the same time thou must strive, with all thy power, to imitate me in the works, which I performed by the aid of these great and wonderful blessings. Pray and sigh for the eternal salvation of thy brethren, and that the name of my Son may be extolled by all and known to the whole world. Thou must establish the habit of this kind of prayer, by a constant resolve, founded upon firm faith and unshaken confidence, and by never losing sight of thy misery in profound humility and self-abasement. Thus prepared, thou must battle with the divine love for the good of thy people, firmly convinced, that the most glorious triumphs of divine love may especially be looked for in its dealings with the humble, who love God in uprightness. Raise thyself above thyself and give Him thanks for the special blessings conferred upon thee and for those conferred upon the human race. Transformed by this divine love, thou wilt merit other gifts, both for thyself and for thy brethren; and whenever thou findest thyself in his divine presence, do thou ask for his benediction.

Chapter VI

THE MOST HIGH MANIFESTS TO MARY, OUR MISTRESS, ADDITIONAL MYSTERIES AND SHOWS HER THE WORKS OF THE SIXTH DAY OF CREATION.

59. While the Most High continued the proximate preparation of our heavenly Princess for the reception of the eternal Word in her virginal womb, She, on her part, persevered without intermission in her fervent sighs and prayers to hasten his coming into the world. When the night of the sixth of these days, which I have begun to describe, had arrived, and when She had previously been elevated by still more profound illuminations, She was again called and invited in spirit to the abstractive vision of the Divinity. Although this happened in the same manner as at other times, yet it was accompanied by more heavenly effects and by a more profound insight into the attributes of the Most High. She remained nine hours in this trance and issued from it at the third hour. Yet, although the high vision of the essence of God ceased at that hour, the most holy Mary continued to enjoy another kind of vision and prayer. This was indeed inferior to the first, but in itself was most exalted and more excellent than that experienced by any of the saints or the just. The gifts and favors so far described partook more and more of the divine during the last days preceding the Incarnation, without at the same time being a hindrance

to the active occupations of her married state, for here Martha had no right to complain, that Mary forsook her in her ministrations (Luc. 10, 40).

60. Having seen God in this vision She was immediately shown the works on the sixth day of the creation of the world. She witnessed, as if She Herself had been present, how at the command of the Lord the earth brought forth the living beings according to their kinds, as Moses says (Gen. 1, 24). Holy Scripture here refers to the terrestrial animals, which being more perfect than the fishes and birds in life and activity, are called by a name signifying the more important part of their nature. She saw and understood all the kinds and species of animals, which were created on this sixth day, and by what name they were called: some, beasts of burden, because they serve and assist man, others, wild beasts, as being more fierce and untamed; others, reptiles, because they do not raise themselves or very little from the earth. She knew and comprehended the qualities of all of them: their fury, their strength, the useful purposes which they serve, and all their distinctions and singularities. Over all these She was invested with dominion and they were commanded to obey Her. She could without opposition on their part have trodden upon asps and basilisks, for all would have meekly borne her heel. Many times did some of these animals show their subjection to her commands, as when, at the birth of her most Holy Son, the ox and the ass prostrated themselves and by their breaths warmed the infant God at the command of his blessed Mother.

61. In this plenitude of knowledge and science our heavenly Queen understood perfectly the secret ways of God in making all creation serve for the benefit of man, and how much man owes to his Creator on this account. And it was most proper that She should possess this knowledge and understanding, so that with it She might be able to give

fitting thanks for these blessings. Neither men nor angels have done so, failing to correspond and falling short of their duty in this regard. All these voids were filled by the Queen of all, and She satisfied for the debt of gratitude, which we could not or would not pay. Through Her, divine equity was duly satisfied, considering Her as a medium between itself and the creatures. By her innocence and gratitude She became more pleasing to his Majesty than all the rest of the creatures. The mysterious advent of God into the world was thus being prepared: for the last hindrance was removed by the sanctification of Her, who was to be his Mother.

62. After seeing the creation of all the irrational creatures, She became aware, how the most blessed Trinity, in order to complete and perfect the world, said: "Let us make man to our image and likeness" (Gen. 1, 26), and how by virtue of this divine decree the first man was formed of the earth as the first parent of all the rest. She had a profound insight into the harmonious composition of the human body and soul and of their faculties, of the creation and infusion of the soul into the body and of its intimate union with the body. Of the structure of the human body and all its parts, She obtained a deep knowledge: She was informed of the number of the bones, veins, arteries, nerves and ligatures; of the concourse of humors to compose the befitting temperaments, the faculties of nutrition, growth and locomotion; She learned in what manner the disturbances or changes in this harmony caused the sicknesses, and how these can be cured. All this the most prudent Virgin understood and comprehended without the least error, better than all the wise men of the world and better than even the angels.

63. The Lord manifested to Her also the happy state of original justice, in which He placed the first parents Adam and Eve; She understood their condition, beauty and perfection of innocence and grace, and for how short a time they

persevered in it. She perceived how they were tempted and overcome by the astuteness of the serpent (Gen. 2, 51), and what were the consequences of their sin; and how great were the fury and hate of the demon against the human race. At the vision of all these things our Queen made great and heroic acts of virtue, highly pleasing to God. She understood, that She was a daughter of these first parents and that She descended from a nature so thankless to its Creator. In the remembrance of this She humiliated Herself in his divine presence, thereby wounding the heart of God and obliging Him to raise Her above all that is created. She took it upon Herself to weep for the first sin and for all the rest, that followed from it, as if She Herself had been guilty of them all. Hence, even at that time, that first sin might have been called a fortunate fault, which caused tears so precious in the eyes of the Lord, and which earned us such sureties and pledges of our Redemption.

64. Rendering worthy thanks to the Creator for the magnificent work of the creation of man, She reflected deeply on his disobedience, the seduction and deception of Eve, and She inwardly resolved to yield that perpetual obedience, which these first parents had refused to their Creator. So acceptable in his eyes was this subjection, that his Majesty in the presence of the heavenly courtiers decreed the immediate fulfillment and execution of that, which was prefigured in the history of the king Assuerus, by whom the queen Vashti was repudiated and deprived of royal dignity on account of disobedience, while the humble and gracious Esther was raised to her place (Esther 7, 2).

65. There was an admirable similarity between that event and these mysteries; for the exalted and true King, in order to show the greatness of his powers and the treasures of his Divinity, had prepared the great banquet of his creation, and having spread the liberal repast for all the creatures, invited

the guests, that is the human race, by the creation of its first parents. Vashti, our mother Eve, disobeyed, failing to submit herself to the divine command, and now amid the wonderful acclamation and jubilee of the angels, the true Assuerus ordered the most humble Esther to be on that day elevated to Sovereignty over all creation, this Esther being none other than the most holy Mary, full of grace and beauty, chosen among all the daughters of men as their Restoratrix and the Mother of his Christ.

66. In the plenitude of this mystery the Most High infused into the heart of our Queen a new abhorrence of the demon, such as filled Esther toward Aman (Esther 7, 10); and thus it happened, that She thrust him from his position of superiority and command over the world. She crushed the head of his pride, hanging him on the gallows of the Cross, where he had hoped to destroy and conquer the Godman, but was himself chastised and overcome by it. Toward all this the most holy Mary was instrumental, as we shall relate in its place (Vol. III, 653). Just as the envy of the dragon against the Woman, that is this heavenly Lady, commenced in heaven, when he saw Her clothed with the sun (Apoc. 12, 4, Part I, 95) ; so this strife continued until he was deprived of his tyrannous dominion. Just as the most faithful Mardocheus was given the position of the proud Aman (Esther 6, 10); so also was honored the most chaste and faithful Joseph, who continually urged Her to pray for the liberty of her people. This was the constant subject of conversation between Joseph and his most pure Spouse; for this very purpose was he raised to the summit of sanctity, and to the exalted dignity of holding the sealing ring of the highest King (Esther 8, 2), whereby he received authority to command the Godman himself, as is related in the Gospel. Having experienced all these mysteries, our Queen issued from her vision.

Words of the Queen

THE VIRGIN MARY SPEAKS TO SISTER MARY OF AGREDA

67. Wonderful, my daughter, was the gift of humility, which the Most High conferred upon me in the event described by thee. And since his Majesty does not reject the prayers of those, that dispose themselves to receive it, I desire that thou imitate me and be my companion in the exercise of this virtue. I had no part in the sin of Adam, for I was exempted from his disobedience; but because I partook of his nature and by it was his daughter, I humiliated myself in my estimation to nothingness. In the light of this example then, how far must those humiliate themselves, who not only have had a part in the first sin, but also have committed other sins without number? The aim and motive of this humiliation moreover, should not be to remove the punishments of those sins, but to make restoration and recompense for the diminution and loss of honor, which was thereby occasioned to the Creator and Lord.

68. If a brother of thine should grievously offend thy natural father, thou wouldst not be a loving and loyal daughter of thy father, nor a true sister to thy brother, if thou wouldst not grieve for the offense and weep not over his ruin as over thy own; for to the father is due reverence and to thy brother thou owest love as to thyself. Consider then, dearest, and examine in the proper light, how much difference there is between thy Father who is in heaven and thy natural father, and how all of you are his children, bound together by the strictest obligation of brethren and of servants of one true Master. Just as thou wouldst shed tears of humiliation and confusion at some ignominious fault of thy natural brother; so I wish that thou do it for the sins, which the mortals commit against God, sorrowing for them in confusion as if thou wert responsible for them thyself. That is what I did at

the thought of the disobedience of Adam and Eve and of all the evils, which ensued therefrom to the human race. And the Most High was pleased with my charitable interest; for most agreeable in his sight are the tears shed for the sins, which are forgotten by those, that have committed them.

69. At the same time see thou bear ever in mind, that, no matter how great and rare are the favors received from the Most High, thou do not despise the danger of sin nor contemn the solicitous and humble performance of the ordinary duties of precept and charity. For these do not oblige thee to leave the presence of God: faith teaches thee, and inspiration should govern thee, to bear Him with thee in all occupations and places, quitting thyself and thy inclinations, but fulfilling in all things the will of thy Lord and Spouse. Do not allow thyself to be led in these sentiments by the trend of thy own inclinations, nor by that which seems to agree with thy own interior liking and taste; for many times the greatest danger is hidden beneath this cloak. In such doubts and hesitations let holy obedience be thy umpire and master; through it thou canst decide securely, and thou wilt need no other criterion for thy actions. Great victories and advances in merit are connected with the true submission of self and subjection of our own judgments to those of others. Thou shouldst never wish to retain for thyself the power to will or not to will: then thou shalt sing of victories and overcome thy enemies.

Chapter VII

THE MOST HIGH CELEBRATES A NEW ESPOUSAL WITH THE PRINCESS OF HEAVEN IN ORDER TO INAUGURATE THE NUPTIALS OF THE INCARNATION. HE ADORNS HER FOR IT.

70. Great are the works of the Most High, for all of them were and are executed with the plenitude of knowledge and goodness, ordained in equity and number (Wis. 11, 21). None of them is faulty, useless or ineffectual, superfluous or vain; all are exquisite and magnificent, finished and executed according to the full measure of his holy will. Such He desired them to be, in order that He might be known and magnified in them. But in comparison to the mystery of the Incarnation, all the works of God ad extra, although they are in themselves great, stupendous and marvelous, more to be admired than comprehended, are only a small spark, issuing from the unfathomable abyss of the Divinity. This great sacrament of vesting Himself in a passible and mortal nature is pre-eminently the great work of his infinite power and wisdom and the one which immeasurably excels all the other works and wonders of his powerful arm. For in this mystery, not merely a spark of the Divinity, but that whole vast volcano of the infinite Godhead, broke forth and communicated itself to men, uniting Itself by an indissoluble and eternal union to our terrestrial human nature.

71. If this wonderful sacrament of the King is to be measured only by his own vastness, it follows that the Woman, in whose womb He was to become man, deserved to be so perfectly adorned with the plenitude of his treasures, that no gift or grace within the range of possibility be omitted, and all these gifts be so consummate, that nothing is wanting to them. As all this was reasonable and altogether befitting the greatness of the Omnipotent, He certainly fulfilled it in the most holy Mary, much better than king Assuerus did with the gracious Esther (Esther 2, 9), when he raised her to his magnificent throne. The Most High visited our Queen Mary with such great favors, privileges and gifts, that the like was never even conceived in the mind of creatures, and, when She issued forth in the presence of the courtiers of this great King of the eternal ages (I Tim. I, 17), they recognized and exalted in Her the power of God, at the same time understanding, that He, who chose to select a woman for his Mother, knew also how to make her worthy of assuming that position.

72. The seventh day of this mysterious preparation for the approaching sacrament arrived, and in the same hour as already mentioned, the heavenly Lady was called and elevated in spirit, but with this difference, that She was bodily raised by her holy angels to the empyrean heaven, while in her stead one of them remained to represent Her in corporeal appearance. Placed into this highest heaven, She saw the Divinity by abstract vision as in other days; but always with new and more penetrating light, piercing to new and more profound mysteries, which God according to his free will can conceal or reveal. Presently She heard a voice proceeding from the royal throne, which said: "Our Spouse and chosen Dove, our gracious Friend, who hast been found pleasing in our eyes and hast been chosen among thousands: We wish to accept

thee anew as our Bride, and therefore We wish to adorn and beautify thee in a manner worthy of our design."

73. On hearing these words the most Humble among the humble abased and annihilated Herself in the presence of the Most High more than can be comprehended by human power. Entirely submissive to the divine pleasure and with entrancing modesty, She responded: "At thy feet, O Lord, lies the dust and abject worm, ready is thy poor slave for the fulfillment of all thy pleasure in her. Make use, O eternal Good, of this thy insignificant instrument according to thy desire, and dispose of it with thy right hand." Presently the Most High commanded two seraphim, of those nearest to his throne and highest in dignity to attend on this heavenly Virgin. Accompanied by others, they presented themselves in visible form before the throne, and there surrounded the most holy Mary, who was more inflamed with divine love than they.

74. It was a spectacle worthy of new wonder and jubilee for all the angelic spirits to see in this heavenly place, never touched by other feet, a humble Maiden consecrated as their Queen and raised to the closest proximity to God of all the created beings; to see that Woman, whom the world ignored and held in oblivious contempt, so highly esteemed and appreciated (Prov. 31, 10) ; to see our human nature in its first fruits receiving the pledge of superiority over the celestial choirs and already assuming its place among them. O what a holy and just envy must such a strange wonder have caused in the ancient courtiers of that heavenly Jerusalem! What thoughts rose up within them in praise of its Author! What sentiments of humility did it awaken in them, subjecting all their high understandings to the decrees of the divine Will! They saw that He was holy and just, who exalted the humble, who favored human lowliness and raised it above the angelic choirs.

75. While the inhabitants of heaven were lost in their praiseworthy admiration, the most blessed Trinity, (according to our imperfect mode of understanding and speaking), conferred within Itself, how pleasing in its sight was the Princess Mary, how perfectly and completely She had corresponded with the blessings and gifts confided to Her, how adequately She had augmented the glory of the Lord; and how free She was of any fault, defect or hindrance, that might compromise the dignity of her predestined Motherhood of the Word. Accordingly the three Persons of the Trinity resolved to raise this Creature to the highest position of grace and friendship of God, such as no creature had ever or would ever attain; and then and there They gave to Her more than to all the rest of creatures together. The most blessed Trinity was pleased and rejoiced in seeing that the supreme holiness of Mary was such as had been conceived and determined for Her in the divine intellect.

76. In correspondence with this holiness, and as a completion of it, and as a testimony of the benevolence with which the Lord wished to communicate to Her ever new influences of his Divinity, He ordained and commanded, that most holy Mary be visibly clothed and adorned with mysterious vestments and jewels, which should symbolize the interior graces and privileges of a Queen and of a heavenly Spouse. Although such bridal adornment had already been conferred upon Her before that time, when She was presented in the temple (Part I, 436); yet now this was done under new and wonderful conditions; for it was to serve as the immediate preparation for the miracle of the Incarnation.

77. Presently therefore, upon the command of the Lord the two seraphim clothed most holy Mary with a tunic or ample robe, which, as a symbol of her purity and grace, was so exquisitely white and resplendent, that if one single ray of the light so profusely emitted by it would flash into the

world, it would by itself give more refulgence than all the stars combined, even if they were all suns; and in comparison with it, all the light, which is known to us, would appear as darkness. While the seraphim vested Her, the Most High gave Her a profound understanding of the obligation entailed thereby: namely, that She must make a befitting return to his Majesty, by proportioning her faithful love and the exalted perfection of her actions to that, which She had now learnt. Nevertheless, the purpose, for which the Lord intended these blessings, that is his Incarnation through Her, continued to be hidden to her mind. All the rest of the mysteries our Lady understood and for all of them She humiliated Herself with ineffable prudence, and She asked the divine assistance for corresponding to these favors and blessings.

78. Over this robe the same seraphim placed a girdle, as a symbol of the holy fear, which was infused into Her. It was very rich, with jewels of extreme refulgence and beauty. At the same time the fountain of light bursting forth from the Divinity enlightened and illumined the heavenly Princess, so that She understood the exalted reasons, why God should be feared by all the creatures. With this gift of fear of the Lord She was appropriately girded, as befitted a Creature, who was to treat and converse so familiarly with her Creator as his Mother.

79. Presently She perceived, that the seraphim adorned Her with most beautiful and abundant hair, held together by a rich clasp, more brilliant than pure and polished gold. She understood, that in this embellishment was conceded to Her the privilege of spending her whole life in exalted and divine thoughts, inflamed by the subtlest charity as signified by the gold. In connection with this privilege She was established anew in the habits of unclouded wisdom and science, exquisitely binding up the hair of exalted thoughts by an ineffable

participation in the wisdom and science of God himself. Sandals or shoes were also given to Her, to indicate, that all her steps and movements would be most beauteous (Cant. 7, 1), tending always to the high and holy aim of the greater glory of the Most High. And these shoes were laced with the especial grace of anxious diligence in doing good both before God and man (Luke 1, 39), as it happened when She hastened to visit saint Elisabeth and saint John; and thus this Daughter of the Prince issued most beautiful in her footsteps (Cant. 7, 1).

80. Her arms were adorned with bracelets, filling Her with magnanimity for undertaking great works in participation of the divine magnificence; and thus She always extended them toward courageous deeds (Prov, 31, 19). Her fingers were embellished by rings, in order that in smaller or more inferior matters She might act in a superior manner, exalted in aim and purpose and in all respect making her doings grand and admirable. To this they added a necklace, set with inestimable and brilliant jewels and containing symbols of the three most excellent virtues of faith, hope and charity in correspondence with the three divine Persons. Conjointly with this gift they renewed in Her the habits of these most noble virtues, which She would especially need in the mysteries of the Incarnation and Redemption.

81. In her ears they hung earrings of gold, filigreed with silver (Cant. 1, 10), thus preparing her ears for the message, which She was shortly to hear from the archangel Gabriel, and at the same time they furnished Her with knowledge in order that She might listen attentively and give discreet and acceptable answers to the divine proposals. Thus would the pure silver of her innocence resound in the ears of the Lord and re-echo, in the bosom of the Divinity, those charming and sacred words: "Fiat mihi secundum verbum tuum." "Be it done to me according to thy word" (Luke 1, 38).

82. Then they spread over her garment inscriptions, which at the same time served as embroidery or borders of the finest colors mixed with gold. Some of them bore the legend: "Mary, Mother of God;" others: "Mary, Virgin and Mother." But these inscriptions were not intelligible to Her, nor were they explained to Her, but their meaning was known to the holy angels. The different colors symbolized the habits of all the virtues in the most excellent degree and their active exercise, surpassing all that was ever practiced by the rest of the intellectual creatures. And as a complement of all this beauty, they furnished Her as if with lotions for her face, by illuminating Her with the light drawn from the proximity and participation of the inexhaustible Being and perfection of God himself. For as She was destined actually and truly to shelter within Her virginal womb the infinite perfection of God, it was befitting, that She should have received it beforehand by grace in the highest measure possible to a mere creature.

83. In this adornment and beauty our Princess Mary stood before the Lord so beautiful and charming, that even the supreme King could desire Her as Spouse (Ps. 44, 12). I do not detain myself here in repeating what I have already said, what I will yet say in this history about her virtues; I only say that this adornment was accompanied by new features and effects altogether divine. All this was proper to the infinite power and to its immense perfection and sanctity, which offer to our comprehension ever new fields of speculation. And when there is question of this ocean of perfection in most holy Mary, we certainly can hope only to skirt its shores. My understanding of that which I perceive, is always pregnant with vast fields of thought, on which I cannot expatiate.

Words of the Queen

THE VIRGIN MARY SPEAKS TO SISTER MARY OF AGREDA

84. My daughter, the work-shops and treasure-rooms of the Most High are those of a divine Lord and omnipotent King, and therefore without number or limit are the riches and treasures which they contain for the endowment of his chosen brides. He can enrich innumerable others just as He has enriched my soul, and yet infinitely more will remain. Although He will give to no creature as much as He has conferred upon me, it is not because He is not able or does not wish, but because no one will dispose himself for his grace as I did. But the Almighty is most liberal with some souls and enriches them so munificently, because they impede his gifts less, and dispose themselves better than others.

85. I desire, my most beloved, that thou place no obstacle to the love of thy Lord; but I wish, that thou dispose thyself for the jewels and gifts, intended for thee in order to make thee worthy of his bridal chamber. Remember that all the just souls receive this adornment from his hands, though each one according to the degree of the friendship and grace, which makes them capable of receiving them. If thou wishest to attain the highest purity of that perfection and become worthy of standing in the presence of thy Lord and Spouse, strive to be robust and strong in love; and thou knowest, that this is augmented in the same degree, as mortification and self-abnegation are practiced. Thou must deny thyself and forget all earthly things; thou must expel all thy meanings toward thyself and toward visible things, in the divine love solely thou must increase and advance. Wash and purify thyself in the blood of thy Redeemer, Christ, and apply this cleansing many times by renewing thy loving sorrow for thy sins. Thereby wilt thou find grace in his eyes and thy beauty

will be desired by Him, and all thy adornments will be full of the greatest perfection and purity.

86. And as thou hast been so highly favored and distinguished by the blessings of the Lord, it is just that thou, more than many generations of men, give thanks and with incessant praises magnify Him for what, He has condescended to do for thee. If this vice of ingratitude is so vile and reprehensible in the creatures, who owe Him little and in their earthliness and coarseness, forget the benefits of the Lord; greater will thy guilt be in falling short of thy obligations. And do not deceive thyself with the pretext of being humble; for there is a great difference between thankful humility and humble thanklessness. Remember that the Lord very often shows great favors to the unworthy, in order to manifest his goodness and munificence. On the contrary let no one become inflated, but let everyone acknowledge so much the more his unworthiness, using it as a medicine and treacle against the poison of presumption. But gratitude will agree with this humble opinion of self, since we must acknowledge, that every good gift comes from the Father of lights and cannot ever be merited by creatures (James 1, 17). All have their source only in his goodness, binding us and obliging us to grateful recognition.

Chapter VIII

OUR GREAT QUEEN, IN THE PRESENCE OF THE LORD, PLEADS FOR THE HASTENING OF THE INCARNATION AND OF THE REDEMPTION OF MAN, AND HIS MAJESTY YIELDS TO HIS PRAYER.

87. The heavenly Princess, most holy Mary, had now attained such fullness of grace and beauty and the heart of God was so wounded by her tender affections and desires (Cant. 4, 9), that He was so to say irresistibly drawn to begin his flight from the bosom of the eternal Father to the bridal-chamber of her virginal womb and end the long delay of more than five thousand years. Nevertheless, since this new wonder was to be executed in the plenitude of his wisdom and equity, the Lord arranged this event in such a way, that the Princess of the heavens Herself, being the worthy Mother of the incarnate Word, should at the same time be also the most powerful Mediatrix of his coming and the Redeemer of his people much more than Esther was of Israel (Esther ch. 7 and 8). In the heart of most holy Mary burned the flame, which God himself had enkindled, and without intermission She prayed for the salvation of the human race. However, as yet the most humble Lady restrained Herself in modesty, knowing that on account of the sin of Adam, the sentence of death and of eternal privation from the vision of God had been promulgated (Gen. 3, 19).

88. A heavenly strife thus arose in the most pure heart of Mary between her love and her humility, and, lost in these sentiments, She repeated many times: "Oh who shall be able to secure the salvation of my brethren! Oh who shall be able to draw from the bosom of the eternal Father his Onlybegotten and make Him a partaker of our mortality! Oh who shall oblige Him to give to our human nature the kiss of his mouth, for which the bride asks Him! (Cant. 1, 1). But how can we, the children and descendants of the malefactor, who committed the crime, ask for this favor? How can we draw Him toward us, whom our fathers repelled? Oh my Love, if I could but see Thee at the breasts of thy Mother, the human nature! (Cant 8, 1). Oh Light of lights, God of the true God, would that Thou descend, bending down thy heavens (Ps. 143, 5) and shedding thy light upon those that live sitting in darkness! (Is. 9,2). Would that Thou pacify thy Father, and, by thy right hand that is by his Onlybegotten, hurl the proud Aman, thy enemy, the devil, from his height! Who shall be the Mediatrix, who shall draw from the celestial altar, as with tongs of gold (Is. 6, 6), that ember of the Divinity, for the purification of the world, as once did the seraphim, according to the word of the prophet Isaias !"

89. This prayer most holy Mary repeated during the eighth day of her preparation, and at midnight, being wrapped and entranced in the Lord, She heard his Majesty responding to Her: "My Spouse and my Dove, come, my Chosen one, for the common law does not apply to thee (Esther 15, 13). Thou art exempt from sin and thou art free from its effects since the moment of thy Conception. When I gave being to thee, I turned away from thee the sceptre of my justice and laid upon thy neck that of my great clemency, in order that the general edict of sin might not touch thee. Come to Me, and be not dismayed in the consciousness of thy human nature; I am He, that raises the humble, and fills

with riches those that are poor. Thou hast Me for thy Friend
and my liberal mercies shall be at thy disposal."

90. These words our Queen heard intellectually and, as in
the preceding night, She presently felt Herself raised by the
holy angels bodily to heaven, while in her stead remained one
of the angels of her guard. Again She ascended to the presence of the Most High, so enriched by the treasures of his
graces and gifts, so fortunate and beautiful, that She singularly excited the wonder of the supernal spirits. They broke out
in praise of the Almighty, saying: "Who is this, that ascends
from the desert, overflowing with delights? (Cant. 8, 5). Who
is She, that so attracts and compels her Beloved as to bear
Him with Her to the earthly habitation? Who is She, that
rises as the dawn, more beautiful than the moon, chosen as
the sun? (Cant. 6, 9). How refulgent doth She rise from the
darkness of the earth? How is She so courageous and strong,
being clothed in such fragile nature? How does She in her
strength overcome the Almighty? And how comes it that the
heavens, which are closed against the children of Adam, are
thus thrown open to this singular Woman, sprung from the
same race ?"

91. The Most High received his holy and chosen Bride,
most holy Mary, into his presence. Although this happened
not in an intuitive, but in an abstractive vision of the Divinity, it was accompanied with incomparable favors of light and
purification proceeding from the Lord himself, such as were
specially reserved for this day. For they were so divine, that,
in our way of speaking, God himself who wrought them, was
astonished and was charmed with the work of his hand. As if
entranced with love, He spoke to Her and said: "Revertere,
revertere, Sulamitis, ut intueamur te" (Return, return, O
Sulamitess, that We may behold thee). "My Spouse, my most
perfect and beloved Dove, pleasing in my sight, turn and
advance toward Us, that We may behold thee and be

charmed by thy beauty. I do not regret to have created man and I delight in his formation, since thou hast been born of him. Let my celestial spirits see how justly I have desired and do desire to choose thee as my Spouse and the Queen of all the creatures. Let them see what good reason I have to rejoice in this my bridal chamber, from whence my Onlybegotten, next to that of my own bosom, shall derive the greatest glory. Let all understand, that if I justly repudiated Eve, the first queen of the earth, on account of her disobedience, I now place thee and establish thee in the highest dignity, showing my magnificence and power in dealing with thy purest humility and self-abasement."

92. This day was for the angels a day of jubilation and rejoicing greater than any since their creation. And when the most blessed Trinity thus chose and appointed his Spouse and Mother of the Word for the Queen and Lady of the creatures, the holy angels and all the celestial court of Spirits acknowledged and received Her as their Mistress and Superior, and they sung sweet hymns of glory in her honor and in praise of her Author. During these hidden and admirable mysteries the heavenly Queen Mary was absorbed in the abyss of the Divinity and in the light of his infinite perfections: and thereby the Lord prevented Her from attending to all that happened. Thus the sacrament of her Mothership of the Onlybegotten still remained hidden to Her until the proper time. Never did the Lord deal in such a manner with any nation (Ps. 147, 20), nor did He ever show Himself so great and powerful in any creature, as on this day in most holy Mary.

93. The Most High added yet other favors, saying to Her with extreme condescension: "My chosen Spouse, since Thou hast found grace in my eyes, ask of Me without restraint, what thou desirest, and I assure thee, as the most faithful God and powerful King, that I shall not reject thy petitions

nor deny thee what thou askest." Our great Princess humiliated Herself profoundly and relying on the promise and royal
word of the Lord, and inspired with highest confidence, She
answered saying: "My Lord and highest God, if I have found
grace in thy eyes (Gen. 18, 3, 27), although I am dust and
ashes, I will speak in thy divine presence and pour out to
Thee my heart" (Ps. 61,9). Again his Majesty assured Her
and commanded Her to ask in the presence of all the heavenly court, for whatever She desired, even if it were a part of his
kingdom (Esther 5, 3). "I do not ask, O Lord, for a part of
thy kingdom in my own behalf," answered most holy Mary,
"but I ask for the whole of it for all the race of men, who are
my brothers. I beseech Thee, highest and powerful King, that
according to thy immense kindness Thou send us thy Only
begotten our Redeemer, in order that He may satisfy for the
sins of all the world, that thy people may gain the freedom so
much desired, and that, through the satisfaction thus rendered to thy justice, peace may be declared among men upon
(Ezech, 34, 25) earth, and that the portals of heaven, closed
by sin, may be thrown open for its inhabitants. Let all flesh
see thy salvation (Is. 52, 10); let peace and justice give each
other that close embrace and the kiss, which David asked for
(Ps. 84, 11) ; let us mortals possess a Teacher, a Guide and a
Savior (Is. 30, 20), a Chief, who shall live and dwell with us
(Baruch. 3, 38). Let the day of thy promises dawn upon us,
O my God, let thy words be fulfilled, and let the Messias,
expected for so many ages, arrive. These are my anxious
desires, and for this do I breathe forth my sighs, since Thou
showest to me the condescension of thy infinite clemency."

94. The highest Lord, who wished to bind Himself by her
prayer, disposed and incited the petitions of his beloved
Spouse; benignly He inclined toward Her and answered Her
with singular clemency: "Pleasing to my Will are thy requests, and acceptable are thy petitions: it shall be done as

thou askest. I desire, my Daughter and Spouse, what thou seekest; and as a pledge of this, I give thee my word and promise thee, that very shortly my Onlybegotten shall descend to the earth and shall vest Himself and unite Himself with the human nature. Thus thy acceptable wishes shall be executed and fulfilled."

95. With this assurance and divine promise our great Queen Princess felt new enlightenment and security in her spirit, convincing Her, that the end of that long protracted and prolix night of sin and of the ancient Law was approaching and that the brightness of human Redemption was about to dawn. And because the rays of the Sun of Justice, whose dawn was soon to arise from Her, so closely and so intensely enveloped Her about, She became Herself the most beautiful aurora, inflamed and refulgent as it were with the fiery clouds of the Divinity, which transformed all things within Her. All afire with love and gratitude for the approaching Redemption, She gave unceasing praise to the Lord both in her own name and in that of all the mortals. In this occupation She passed that day, after the angels had again restored Her to the earth. I must grieve at my ignorance and shortcomings in explaining these so exalted mysteries; and if learned men and great students cannot give an adequate explanation of these things, how shall it be given by a poor and lowly woman? May my ignorance be supplemented by the light of Christian charity and my presumption be atoned for by my obedience.

Words of the Queen

THE VIRGIN MARY SPEAKS TO SISTER MARY OF AGREDA

96. My dearest daughter, how far removed is worldly wisdom from the admirable operations of the divine power in these sacraments of the Incarnation of the divine Word in my womb! Flesh and blood cannot reach them, and not the

angels and seraphim, though they be of the highest; nor can they know mysteries so deeply hidden and so far above the ordinary course of grace. Praise thou, my beloved, the Lord for them with incessant love and thankfulness. Be thou not any longer slow in understanding the greatness of his divine love and his readiness to benefit his friends and dear ones, whom He desires to elevate from the dust and enrich in diverse manners. As soon as thou hast penetrated into this truth, it will oblige thee to thank Him and incite thee to undertake the great things, that become a most faithful daughter and spouse.

97. And in order that thou mayest dispose thyself and be inspired so much the more, I remind thee, that the Lord often says these same words to his chosen ones: "Revertere, revertere, ut intueamur te." For He derives just as great pleasure from their deeds, as when a father rejoices in his beloved and well-behaved son, whom he looks upon many times with great affection; or as an artist, when he beholds with pride the perfect works of his hands; or as a king, who inspects the rich city, which he has added to his dominions; or as one, who is pleased with his much beloved friend. There is only this difference: the Most High finds incomparably more delight than all these in the souls, which He has chosen for his blessings; and in proportion as they dispose themselves and advance in virtue, the Lord also multiplies his favors and benefits. If the mortals, that attain to the light of faith, would enter into this truth, they would, merely on account of this complacence of the Almighty in their good deeds, not only preserve themselves from sin, but they would zealously engage in great works until death and eagerly show their loving servitude to Him, who is so liberal in rewarding, and so generous in his favors.

98. When, on this eighth day which thou hast described, the Lord in heaven spoke to me these words: "Revertere,

revertere," asking me to turn toward Him and allow the celestial spirits to look upon me; I was made aware, that the pleasure, which his divine Majesty derived in beholding me, by itself exceeded all the delight and complacency, which He ever derived from all the most saintly souls in the height of their sanctity. In his gracious condescension He was more pleased in me than in all the Apostles, Martyrs, Confessors, Virgins and all the rest of the saints. And this pleasure and complacency of the Most High overflowed and enriched my spirit with such an influx of grace and participation of the Divinity, that thou canst neither understand nor explain it as long as thou art in the mortal flesh. But I tell thee of this hidden mystery, in order that thou mayest bless its Author, and that, while yet thy exile from the fatherland continues, thou dispose and exert thyself in my place and name to extend and reach out thy hands to great things (Prov, 31, 19). Give to the Lord the satisfaction expected of thee, and strive after it, thus earning his blessings and soliciting them for thyself and thy neighbor with perfect charity.

Chapter IX

THE MOST HIGH RENEWS ALL HIS FAVORS AND BENEFITS IN
THE MOST HOLY MARY AND, AS THE ULTIMATE PREPARA-
TION FOR THE INCARNATION, MAKES HER SOVEREIGN AND
QUEEN OF ALL THE UNIVERSE.

99. On the last day of the novena of immediate preparation
of the tabernacle (Ps. 45, 5), which He was to sanctify by his
coming, the Most High resolved to renew his wonders and
multiply his tokens of love, repeating the favors and benefits
which up to this day He had conferred upon the Princess
Mary. But the Almighty chose to work in such a way, that in
drawing forth from his infinite treasures his gifts of old, He
always added thereto such as were new. All of these different
kinds of wonders were appropriate to the end He had in
view: lowering his Divinity to the human nature and raising
a woman to the dignity of Mother of God. In descending to
the lowliness of man's estate, God neither could, nor needed
to change his essence: for, remaining immutable in Himself,
He could unite. his Person to our nature; but an earthly
woman, in ascending to such an excellence that God should
unite with Her and become man of her substance, apparently
must traverse an infinite space and be raised so far above
other creatures, as to approach God's infinite being itself.

100. The day had then arrived, in which most holy Mary
was to reach the last stage and be placed so close to God, as

to become his Mother. In that night, at the hour of greatest silence, She was again called by the same Lord as it had happened on the other days. The humble and prudent Queen responded: "My heart is prepared (Ps, 107,2), my Lord and exalted Sovereign: let thy divine pleasure be fulfilled in me." Immediately She was, as on the preceding day, borne body and soul by the hands of her angels to the empyrean and placed in the presence of the royal throne of the Most High; and his divine Majesty raised Her up and seated Her at his side, assigning to Her the position and throne, which She was to occupy forever in his presence. Next to the one reserved for the incarnate Word, it was the highest and the most proximate to God himself; for it excelled incomparably that of any of the other blessed, and that of all of them together.

101. From this position She saw the Divinity by an abstractive vision, as at other times, and his Majesty, hiding from Her the dignity of Mother of God, manifested to Her such unusual and such high sacraments, that on account of their sublimity and my insignificant capacities, I cannot describe them. Again She saw in the Divinity all things created and many other possible and future ones. The corporeal things God manifested and made known to Her by corporeal and sensible images, as if they had been presented to her ocular vision. The fabric of the universe, which before this She had known in parts, now appeared to Her in its entirety, distinctly pictured as upon canvas, with all the creatures contained therein. She saw the harmony, order, connection and dependence of each toward each, and of the divine will, which had created them, governs and preserves them, each in its place and mode of existence. Again She saw all the heavens and the stars, the elements, and those that lived in them, purgatory, limbo, hell and all the occupants of these caverns. Just as the position of the Queen of creation

was above all creatures and inferior only to that of God, so also the knowledge given to Her was superior to that of all created things being inferior only to that of the Lord.

102. While thus the heavenly Lady was lost in admiration of what the Almighty showed to Her, and was wrapped in praise and exaltation of the Lord, his Majesty spoke to Her and said: "My chosen Dove, all the visible creatures, which thou beholdest, I have created and preserved in all their variety and beauty by my Providence, solely for the love of men. And from all the souls, which I have until now created and which are predestined to be created unto the end, I shall choose and select the congregation of the faithful, who shall be set apart and washed in the blood of the Lamb in the Redemption of the world. They shall be the special fruit of his Redemption, and they shall enjoy its blessings through the new law of grace and the sacraments to be instituted by the Redeemer; and afterwards those that persevere shall partake of my eternal glory and friendship. For these chosen ones I have primarily created these wonderful works! And, if all of them would strive to serve Me, adore and acknowledge my holy name; as far as I am concerned, I would for each and every one of them create these great treasures and assign all over to them as their possession.

103. "And if I had created only one being capable of my grace and glory, I would have made it the lord and master of all creation; for this would be a much smaller favor than to make it partaker of my friendship and of eternal happiness. Thou, my Spouse, shalt be my chosen One and thou hast found grace in my sight; and therefore I make thee Mistress of all these goods and I give thee dominion and possession of them all, so that, if thou art a faithful spouse according to my wishes, thou mayest distribute and dispose of them according as thou desirest and according as thy intercession shall direct; for this is the purpose, for which they are given into thy

possession." Therewith the most blessed Trinity placed a crown on the head of our Princess Mary, consecrating Her as the sovereign Queen of all creation. Upon it was spread and enameled the inscription: Mother of God; but its meaning was not known to Her at this time. The heavenly spirits, however, knew it and they were filled with admiration at the magnificence of the Lord toward this Maiden, most fortunate and blessed among womankind. They revered and honored Her as their legitimate Queen and as Sovereign of all creation.

104. All these portents of love the right hand of the Most High wrought according to the order most befitting his infinite wisdom; for before coming down to assume flesh in the virginal womb of this Lady, it was proper that all his courtiers should acknowledge his Mother as their Queen and Mistress, and give Her due honor as such. It was certainly proper and just that God should first make Her Queen before making Her Mother of the Prince of eternities; for She that was to bear a Prince, must necessarily first be a Queen and be acknowledged as Queen by her vassals. That the angels should know Her as Mother, was not improper, nor was there any necessity of concealing it from them. But on the other hand it seemed due to the majesty of the Divinity, that the tabernacle chosen for his indwelling should appear before them prepared and adorned with all that was highest in dignity and perfection, in nobility and magnificence to the full extent, in which it was possible. Thus then, was She presented to the holy angels, and recognized by them, as their honored Queen and Lady.

105. In order to put the last touch to this prodigious work of preparing the most holy Mary, the Lord extended his powerful arm and expressly renewed the spirit and the faculties of the great Lady, giving Her new inclinations, habits and qualities, the greatness and excellence of which are

inexpressible in terrestrial terms. It was the finishing act and the final retouching of the living image of God, in order to form, in it and of it, the very shape, into which the eternal Word, the essential image of the eternal Father (II Cor. 4; 4) and the figure of his substance (Heb. 1,3), was to be cast. Thus the whole temple of most holy Mary, more so than that of Solomon, was covered with the purest gold of the Divinity inside and out, (III Kings, 6, 30), so that nowhere could be seen in Her any grossness of an earthly daughter of Adam. Her entire being was made to shine forth the Divinity; for since the divine Word was to issue from the bosom of the eternal Father to descend to that of Mary, He provided for the greatest possible similarity between the Mother and the Father.

106. No words at my disposal could ever suffice to describe as I would wish, the effects of these favors in the heart of our great Queen and Mistress. Human thought cannot conceive them, how then can human words express them? But what has caused the greatest wonder in me, when I considered these things in the light given to me, is the humility of this heavenly Woman and the mutual contest between her humility and the divine power. Rare and astonishing prodigy of humility, to see this Maiden, most holy Mary, though raised to the supremest dignity and holiness next to God, yet humiliating Herself and debasing Herself below the meanest of the creatures; so that, by the force of this humility, no thought of her being destined for the Mothership of the Messias could find entrance into her mind! And not only this: She did not even have a suspicion of anything great or admirable in Herself (Ps. 130, 1). Her eyes and heart were not elated; on the contrary the higher She ascended by the operation of the right hand of her God, so much the more lowly were her thoughts concerning Herself. It was therefore just, that the Almighty should look upon her humility (Luke

1,48), and that therefore all generations should call her fortunate and blessed.

THE VIRGIN MARY SPEAKS TO SISTER MARY OF AGREDA

107. My daughter, the soul that has only a selfish and servile love is not a worthy spouse of the Most High, for she must not love or fear like a slave, nor is she supposed to serve for her daily wages. Yet although her heart must be a filial and generous love on account of the excellence and immense goodness of her Spouse, she must nevertheless also feel herself much bounden to Him, when she considers how rich and liberal He is; how, on account of his love for souls, He has created such a variety of visible goods in order that they might serve those who serve Him; and especially, when she considers how many hidden treasures He has in readiness in the abundance of his sweetness (Ps. 30, 20) for those that fear Him as his true children. I wish that thou feel deeply obliged to thy Lord and Father, thy Spouse and Friend, at the thought of the riches given to those souls, who become his dearest children. For, as a powerful Father, He holds in readiness these great and manifold gifts for his children, and if necessary, all of his gifts for each one of them in particular. In the midst of such motives and incentives of love the disaffection of men is inexcusable, and at the sight of so many blessings, given without measure, their ingratitude is unpardonable.

108. Remember, also, my dearest, that thou wast no foreigner, or stranger in this house of the Lord, his holy Church (Ephes, 2, 19); but thou wast made a domestic and a spouse of Christ among the saints, favored by his gifts and by the dowry of a bride. Since all the treasures and riches of the bridegroom belong to the legitimate spouse, consider of how

great possessions He makes thee participant and mistress. Enjoy them all, then, as his domestic, and be zealous for his honor as a much-favored daughter and spouse; thank Him for all these works and benefits, as if they had all been prepared for thee alone by the Lord. Love and reverence Him for thyself and for all thy neighbors, to whom God has been so liberal. In all this imitate, with thy weak faculties, that which thou hast understood of what I have done. I assure thee also, daughter, that it will be very pleasing to me, if thou magnify and praise the Omnipotent with fervent affection, for the favors and riches which, beyond all human conception, the divine right hand showered upon me.

Chapter X

THE BLESSED TRINITY SENDS THE ARCHANGEL GABRIEL AS
A MESSENGER TO ANNOUNCE TO MOST HOLY MARY THAT
SHE IS CHOSEN AS THE MOTHER OF GOD.

109. For infinite ages had been appointed the convenient
hour and time, in which the great mystery of piety (I Tim. 3,
16), which was approved by the Spirit, prophesied to men,
foretold to the angels, and expected in the world, was to be
drawn from the hidden recesses of the divine wisdom in
order to be appropriately manifested in the flesh. The plenitude of time (Gal. 4, 4) had arrived, that time which until
then, although filled with prophecies and promises, was
nevertheless void and empty. For it wanted the fullness of the
most holy Mary, by whose will and consent all the ages were
to receive their complement, namely the eternal Word made
flesh, capable of suffering and redeeming man. Before all ages
this mystery was prearranged in such a way, that it should be
fulfilled through the mediation of this heavenly Maiden.
Since now She existed in the world the Redemption of man
and the coming of the Onlybegotten of the Father was not
longer to be delayed. For now He would not need to come
and live as if by sufferance merely in tents (II Kings 7, 6) or
in a strange house; but He could enjoy a free welcome as in
His temple and as in his own house, one that had been built
and enriched at his own preordained expense, more so than

the temple of Solomon at the expense of his father David (I Par. 22, 5).

110. In this predetermined time then the Most High resolved to send his Onlybegotten Son into the world. And comparing, (according to our way of understanding and speaking), the decrees of his eternity with the prophecies and testimonies made to man from the beginning of the world, and all this together with the position of sanctity to which He had raised most holy Mary, He judged that all the circumstances were favorable for the exaltation of his holy name, and that the execution of his eternal will and decree should be made manifest to the angels and be commenced by them. His Majesty spoke to the archangel Gabriel in such words or language as He was accustomed to use in intimating his will to the holy angels. Although God usually illumines the holy spirits by commencing with the higher angels, who in turn purify and illumine the others in their order down to the least among them, thus making known the revelations of the Divinity; yet on this occasion this usage was not maintained, for the holy archangel received his message immediately from the mouth of God.

111. At the bidding of the divine will the holy Gabriel presented himself at the foot of the throne intent upon the immutable essence of the Most High. His Majesty then expressly charged him with the message, which he was to bring to the most holy Mary and instructed him in the very words with which he was to salute and address Her. Thus the first Author of the message was God himself, who formed the exact words in his divine mind, and revealed them to the holy archangel for transmission to the most pure Mary. At the same time the Lord revealed to the holy prince Gabriel many hidden sacraments concerning the Incarnation. The blessed Trinity commanded him to betake himself to the heavenly Maiden and announce to Her, that the Lord had

chosen Her among women to be the Mother of the eternal Word, that She should conceive Him in her virginal womb through operation of the Holy Ghost without injury to her virginity. In this and in all the rest of the message, which he was to declare and manifest to this great Queen and Mistress, the archangel was instructed by the blessed Trinity itself.

112. Thereupon his Majesty announced to all the other angels that the time of the Redemption had come and that He had commanded it to be brought to the world without delay; for already, in their own presence, the most holy Mary had been prepared and adorned to be his Mother, and had been exalted to the supreme dignity. The heavenly spirits heard the voice of their Creator, and with incomparable joy and thanksgiving for the fulfillment of his eternal and perfect will, they intoned new canticles of praise, repeating therein that hymn of Sion: "Holy, holy, holy art thou, God and Lord Sabaoth (Is. 6, 3). Just and powerful art Thou, Lord our God, who livest in the highest (Ps. 112, 5) and lookest upon the lowly of the earth. Admirable are all thy works, most high and exalted in thy designs."

113. The supernal prince Gabriel, obeying with singular delight the divine command and accompanied by many thousands of most beautiful angels in visible forms, descended from the highest heaven. The appearance of the great prince and legate was that of a most handsome youth of rarest beauty; his face emitted resplendent rays of light, his bearing was grave and majestic, his advance measured, his motions composed, his words weighty and powerful, his whole presence displayed a pleasing, kindly gravity and more of godlike qualities than all the other angels until then seen in visible form by the heavenly Mistress. He wore a diadem of exquisite splendor and his vestments glowed in various colors full of refulgent beauty. Enchased on his breast, he bore a most beautiful cross, disclosing the mystery of the

Incarnation, which He had come to announce. All these circumstances were calculated to rivet the affectionate attention of the most prudent Queen.

114. The whole of this celestial army with their princely leader holy Gabriel directed their flight to Nazareth, a town of the province of Galilee, to the dwelling place of most holy Mary. This was an humble cottage and her chamber was a narrow room, bare of all those furnishings which are wont to be used by the world in order to hide its own meanness and want of all higher goods. The heavenly Mistress was at this time fourteen years, six months and seventeen days of age; for her birthday anniversary fell on the eighth of September and six months seventeen days had passed since that date, when this greatest of all mysteries ever performed by God in this world, was enacted in Her.

115. The bodily shape of the heavenly Queen was well proportioned and taller than is usual with other maidens of her age; yet extremely elegant and perfect in all its parts. Her face was rather more oblong than round, gracious and beautiful, without leanness or grossness; its complexion clear, yet of a slightly brownish hue; her forehead spacious yet symmetrical; her eyebrows perfectly arched; her eyes large and serious, of incredible and ineffable beauty and dovelike sweetness, dark in color with a mixture tending toward green; her nose straight and well shaped; her mouth small, with red-colored lips, neither too thin nor too thick. All the gifts of nature in Her were so symmetrical and beautiful, that no other human being ever had the like. To look upon Her caused feelings at the same time of joy and seriousness, love and reverential fear. She attracted the heart and yet restrained it in sweet reverence; her beauty impelled the tongue to sound her praise, and yet her grandeur and her overwhelming perfections and graces hushed it to silence. In all that approached Her, She caused divine effects not easily explained;

She filled the heart with heavenly influences and divine operations, tending toward the Divinity.

116. Her garments were humble and poor, yet clean, of a dark silvery hue, somewhat like the color of ashes. and they were arranged and worn without pretense, but with the greatest modesty and propriety. At the time when, without her noticing it, the embassy of heaven drew nigh unto Her, She was engaged in the highest contemplation concerning the mysteries which the Lord had renewed in Her by so many favors during the nine preceding days. And since, as we have said above, the Lord himself had assured Her that his Onlybegotten would soon descend to assume human form, this great Queen was full of fervent and joyful affection in the expectation of its execution and inflamed with humble love. She spoke in her heart: "Is it possible that the blessed time has arrived, in which the Word of the eternal Father is to be born and to converse with men? (Baruch 10, 38). That the world should possess Him? That men are to see Him in the flesh? (Is. 40. 5). That his inaccessible light is to shine forth to illumine those who sit in darkness? (Is. 9, 2). O, who shall be worthy to see and know Him ! O, who shall be allowed to kiss the earth touched by his feet !"

117. "Rejoice, ye heavens, and console thyself, O earth (Ps. 95, 11); let all things bless and extol Him, since already his eternal happiness is nigh! O children of Adam, afflicted with sin, and yet creatures of my Beloved, now shall you raise your heads and throw off the yoke of your ancient servitude! (Is. 14,25). O, ye ancient Forefathers and Prophets, and all ye just, that are detained in limbo and are waiting in the bosom of Abraham, now shall you be consoled and your much desired and long promised Redeemer shall tarry no longer! (Agg. 2, 8). Let us all magnify Him and sing to Him hymns of praise! O who shall be the slave of Her, whom Isaias points out as his Mother (Is. 7,4); O Emmanuel, true

God and Man! O key of David, who art to unlock heaven!
(Is. 22,22). O eternal Wisdom! O Lawgiver of the new
Church! Come, come to us, O Lord, and end the captivity of
thy people; let all flesh see thy salvation!" (Is. 40, 5).

118. In these petitions and aspirations, and in many more
too deep for my tongue to explain, the most holy Mary was
engaged at the hour, when the holy angel Gabriel arrived.
She was most pure in soul, most perfect in body, most noble
in her sentiments, most exalted in sanctity, full of grace and
so deified and pleasing in the sight of God, that She was fit
to be his Mother and an instrument adapted for drawing
Him from the bosom of the Father to her virginal womb.
She was the powerful means of our Redemption and to Her
we owe it on many accounts. And therefore it is just, that all
generations and nations shall bless and forever extol Her
(Luke 1, 48). What happened at the entrance of the heavenly
embassy, I will relate in the following chapter.

119. I wish only to state here a fact worthy of admiration,
that for the reception of the message of the archangel and for
the execution of the exalted mystery, which was to be
wrought in the heavenly Lady by her consent, his Majesty left
Her without any other aid than the resources of her common
human nature and those furnished Her by the faculties and
virtues of her ordinary condition, such as have been described
in the first part of this history (Part I, 674–714). The Most
High disposed it thus, because this mystery was to be enacted
as a sacrament of faith conjointly with hope and charity. And
therefore the Lord provided Her with no special aid, leaving
Her to her belief and hope in his divine promises. Thus
prepared She experienced what I shall try to relate in my
inadequate and limited terms. The greatness of these sacraments makes my ability to explain them appear so much the
more insufficient.

Words of the Queen

THE VIRGIN MARY SPEAKS TO SISTER MARY OF AGREDA

My daughter, with special affection I manifest to thee now my will and desire that thou make thyself worthy of the intimate and familiar converse with God, and that for this purpose thou dispose thyself with great zeal and solicitude, weeping over thy sins, and forgetting and rejecting all the visible things, so that thou have no thought henceforth for any other thing outside of God. Therefore thou must begin to practice all that I have taught thee until now, and whatever I will yet teach thee in the balance of this history. I will accompany thee and guide thee on the course with which thou must maintain in this familiar intercourse and in regard to the favors, which thou receivest through his condescension, entertaining Him in thy heart by means of the faith, light and grace given to thee. If thou dost not first conform to this my admonition, and prepare thyself accordingly, thou wilt not reach the fulfillment of thy desires, nor shall I reap the fruit of my instructions, which I give to thee as thy Teacher.

121. Since thou has found, without any merit of thine, the hidden treasure and the precious pearl of my teachings and instruction (Matth. 13, 44), despise all other things, in order to possess and secure for thyself this prize of inestimable value; for with it thou shalt receive all other goods and thou wilt make thyself worthy of the intimate friendship of the Lord and of his perpetual indwelling in your heart. In exchange for this great blessing, I desire that thou die to all earthly things and that thou offer the thankful love of an entirely purified will. In imitation of me be thou so humble, that as far as thou art concerned, thou be persuaded and convinced of thy entire worthlessness and incapability, not

meriting to be considered even as a slave of the servants of Christ.

122. Remember, I was far from imagining, that the Most High had designed me for the dignity of Mother of God; and this was my state of mind although He had already promised his speedy coming into the world and although He had commanded me to desire after Him with such great affection, that on the day before the execution of this mystery I thought I would die and my heart would burst with loving sighs, if the divine Providence had not comforted me. He dilated my spirit with the firm hope, that the Onlybegotten of the eternal Father would descend from heaven without delay; yet on the other hand, my humility inclined me to fear, lest my presence in the world might perhaps retard his coming. Contemplate then, my beloved, this secret of my breast, and what an example it is for thee and for all the mortals. And since it is difficult for thee to understand and describe such high wisdom, look upon me in the Lord, in order that by his divine light, thou mayest meditate and comprehend the perfection of my actions; follow me by imitating me, and walk in my footsteps.

Chapter XI

MARY LISTENS TO THE MESSAGE OF THE HOLY ANGEL: THE MYSTERY OF THE INCARNATION IS ENACTED BY THE CONCEPTION OF THE ETERNAL WORD IN HER WOMB.

123. I wish to confess before heaven and earth and its inhabitants, and in the presence of the Creator of the universe and the eternal God, that in setting myself to write of the profound mystery of the Incarnation, my feeble strength deserts me, my tongue is struck mute, my discourse is silenced, my faculties are benumbed, my understanding is eclipsed and overwhelmed by the divine light, which guides and instructs me. In it all is perceived without error and without any deviousness; I see my insignificance and I am made aware of the emptiness of words and the insufficiency of human terms for doing justice to my concepts of this sacrament, which comprehends at one and the same time God himself and the greatest and most wonderful work of his Omnipotence. I see in this mystery the divine and admirable harmony of his infinite providence and wisdom, with which from all eternity He has ordained and prearranged it, and by which He directed all creation toward its fulfillment. All his works and all his creatures were only well adjusted means of advancing toward this apex of his aims, the condescension of a God in assuming human nature.

124. I saw that the eternal Word had awaited and chosen, as the most opportune time and hour for his descent from the bosom of the Father, the midnight of mortal perversion (Wis. 18, 14), when the whole posterity of Adam was buried and absorbed in the sleep of forgetfulness and ignorance of their true God, and when there was no one to open his mouth in confessing and blessing Him, except some chosen souls among his people. All the rest of the world was lost in silent darkness, having passed a protracted night of five thousand and about two hundred years. Age had succeeded age, and generations followed upon generations, each one in the time predestined and decreed by the eternal Wisdom, each also having an opportunity to know and find Him, its Creator; for all had Him so nigh to them, that He gave them life, movement and existence within their own selves (Acts 17, 28). But as the clear day of his inaccessible. light had not arrived, though some of the mortals, like the blind, came nigh to Him and touched Him in his creatures, yet they did not attain to the Divinity (Rom. 1, 23) and in failing to recognize Him, they cast themselves upon the sensible and most vile things of the earth.

125. The day then had arrived in which the Most High, setting aside the long ages of this dark ignorance, resolved to manifest Himself to men and begin the Redemption of the human race by assuming their nature in the womb of most holy Mary, now prepared for this event. In order to be able to describe what was revealed concerning this event to me, it is necessary to make mention of some hidden sacraments connected with the descent of the Onlybegotten from the bosom of the Father. I assume as firmly established what the holy faith teaches in regard to the divine Persons, that although there is a real personal distinction between the three Persons, yet there is no inequality in wisdom, omnipotence or other attributes, just as little as there is in the divine

nature; and just as They are equal in dignity and infinite perfection, so They are also equal in these operations ad extra, which proceed from God himself for the production of some creature or temporal object. these operations are indivisibly wrought by three divine Persons; for not one Person alone produces them, but all Three in so far as They are one and the same God, possessing one and the same wisdom, one and the same understanding and will. Thus what the Son knows and wishes, that also the Father knows and wishes; and so also the Holy Ghost knows and wishes whatever is known and willed by the Father and the Son.

126. In this indivisibility of action the three Persons wrought and executed, by one and the same act, the mystery of the Incarnation, although only the person of the Son accepted for Himself the nature of man, uniting it to Himself hypostatically. Therefore we say that the Son was sent by the eternal Father, from whose intelligence He proceeds, and that the Father sent Him by the intervening operations of the Holy Ghost. As it was the Person of the Son which came to be made man, this same Person before descending from the heavens and the bosom of the Father, in the name of that same humanity to be received by Him, made a conditional request, that, on account of his foreseen merits, his salvation and satisfaction of the divine justice for sins be extended to the whole human race. He desired the fiat or ratification of the most blessed will of the Father, who sent Him, for the acceptance of this Redemption by means of his most holy works and his passion, and through the mysteries, which He was to enact in the new Church and in the law of grace.

127. The eternal Father accepted this petition and the foreseen merits of the Word; He conceded all that was proposed and asked for the mortals, and He himself confirmed the elect and predestined souls as the inheritance and possession of Christ forever. Hence, Christ himself, our

Lord, through saint John says that He has not lost nor has allowed to perish, those whom the Father had given him (John 18,9). In another place it is said: that no one shall snatch his sheep from his hands nor from those of his Father (John 17, 12). The same would hold good of all those that are born, if they would avail themselves of the Redemption, which, as it is sufficient, should also be efficacious for all and in all; since his divine mercy desired to exclude no one, if only all of them would make themselves capable of receiving its benefits through the Redeemer.

128. All this, according to our way of understanding, happened in heaven at the throne of the most blessed Trinity as a prelude to the fiat of the most holy Mary, of which I will presently speak. At the moment, in which the Onlybegotten of the Father descended to her virginal womb, all the heavens and the creatures were set in commotion. On account of the inseparable union of the divine Persons, the Three of Them descended with the Word, though the Word alone was to become incarnate. And with the Lord their God, all the hosts of the celestial army, issued from heaven, full of invincible strength and splendor. Although it was not necessary to prepare the way, since the Divinity fills the universe, is present in all places and cannot be impeded by anything; nevertheless all the eleven material heavens showed deference to their Creator, and, together with the inferior elements, opened up and parted as it were, for his passage; the stars shone with greater brilliancy, the moon and sun with the planets hastened their course in the service of their Maker, anxious to witness the greatest of his wonderful works.

129. Mortals did not perceive this commotion and renewal of all the creatures; both because it happened during the night, as well as because the Lord wished it to be known only to the angels. These with new wonder praised Him, knowing these profound and venerable mysteries to be

hidden from men. For they knew that men were far removed from understanding these wonderful benefits, so admirable even in the eyes of angelic spirits. To these angelic spirits alone was at that time assigned the duty of giving glory, praise and reverence for these benefits to their Maker. However, in the hearts of some of the just the Most High infused at that hour a new feeling and affection of extraordinary joy of which they became conscious. They conceived new and grand ideas concerning the Lord; some of them were inspired and began to confer within themselves, whether this new sensation, which they felt, was not the effect of the coming of the Messias in order to redeem the world; but all this remained concealed, for each one thought, that he alone had experienced this renewal of his interior.

130. In the other creatures there was a like renovation and change. The birds moved about with new songs and joyousness; the plants and trees gave forth more fruit and fragrance; and in like proportion all the rest of the creatures received and felt some kind of vivifying change. But among those that received the greatest share, were the Fathers and Saints in limbo, whither the archangel Michael was sent with the glad message, in order to console them and cause in them the fullness of jubilee and praise. Only for hell it was a cause of new consternation and grief; for at the descent of the eternal Word from on high, the demons felt an impetuous force of the divine power, which came upon them like the waves of the sea and buried all of them in the deepest caverns of their darkness without leaving them any strength of resistance or recovery. When by divine permission they were again able to rise, they poured forth upon the world and hastened about to discover what strange happening had thus undone them. However, although they held several conferences among themselves, they were unable to find the cause. The divine Power concealed from them the sacrament of the Incarnation

and the manner in which most holy Mary conceived the incarnate Word (No. 326). Not until the death of Christ on the cross did they arrive at the certainty, that He was God and true man, as we shalt there relate.

131. In order that the mystery of the Most High might be fulfilled, the holy archangel Gabriel, in the shape described in the preceding chapter and accompanied by innumerable angels in visible human forms and resplendent with incomparable beauty, entered into the chamber, where most holy Mary was praying. It was on a Thursday at six o'clock in the evening and at the approach of night. The great modesty and restraint of the Princess of heaven did not permit Her to look at him more than was necessary to recognize him as an angel of the Lord. Recognizing him as such, She, in her usual humility, wished to do him reverence; the holy prince would not allow it; on the contrary he himself bowed profoundly as before his Queen and Mistress, in whom he adored the heavenly mysteries of his Creator. At the same time he understood that from that day on the ancient times and the custom of old whereby men should worship angels, as Abraham had done (Gen. 28, 2), were changed. For as human nature was raised to the dignity of God himself in the person of the Word, men now held the position of adopted children, of companions and brethren of the angels, as the angel said to Evangelist Saint John, when he refused to be worshipped (Apoc, 19, 10).

132. The holy archangel saluted our and his Queen and said: "Ave gratia plena, Dominus tecum, benedicta tu in mulieribus" (Luke 1, 28). Hearing this new salutation of the angel, this most humble of all creatures was disturbed, but not confused in mind (Luke 1, 29). This disturbance arose from two causes: first, from her humility, for She thought Herself the lowest of the creatures and thus in her humility, was taken unawares at hearing Herself saluted and called the

"Blessed among women;" secondly, when She heard this salute and began to consider within Herself how She should receive it, She was interiorly made to understand by the Lord, that He chose Her for his Mother, and this caused a still greater perturbance, having such a humble opinion of Herself. On account of this perturbance the angel proceeded to explain to Her the decree of the Lord, saying: "Do not fear, Mary, for thou hast found grace before the Lord (Luke 1, 30); behold thou shalt conceive a Son in thy womb, and thou shalt give birth to Him, and thou shalt name Him Jesus; He shall be great, and He shall be called Son of the Most High," and the rest as recorded of the holy archangel.

133. Our most prudent and humble Queen alone, among all the creatures, was sufficiently intelligent and magnanimous to estimate at its true value such a new and unheard of sacrament; and in proportion as She realized its greatness, so She was also moved with admiration. But She raised her humble heart to the Lord, who could not refuse Her any petition, and in the secret of her spirit She asked new light and assistance by which to govern Herself in such an arduous transaction; for, as we have said in the preceding chapter, the Most High, in order to permit Her to act in this mystery solely in faith, hope and charity, left Her in the common state and suspended all other kinds of favors and interior elevations, which She so frequently or continually enjoyed. In this disposition She replied and said to holy Gabriel, what is written in saint Luke: "How shall this happen, that I conceive and bear; since I know not, nor can know, man?" At the same time She interiorly represented to the Lord the vow of chastity, which She had made and the espousal, which his Majesty had celebrated with Her.

134. The holy prince Gabriel replied (Luke 1, 24) : "Lady, it is easy for the divine power to make Thee a Mother without the co-operation of man; the Holy Spirit shall

remain with Thee by a new presence and the virtue of the Most High shall overshadow Thee, so that the Holy of holies can be born of Thee, who shall himself be called the Son of God. And behold, thy cousin Elisabeth has likewise conceived a son in her sterile years and this is the sixth month of her conception; for nothing is impossible with God. He that can make her conceive, who was sterile, can bring it about, that Thou, Lady, be his Mother, still preserving thy virginity and enhancing thy purity. To the Son whom Thou shalt bear, God will give the throne of his father David and his reign shall be everlasting in the house of Jacob. Thou art not ignorant, O Lady, of the prophecy of Isaias (Is. 7, 14), that a Virgin shall conceive and shall bear a son, whose name shall be Emmanuel, God with us. This prophecy is infallible and it shall be fulfilled in thy person. Thou knowest also of the great mystery of the bush, which Moses saw burning without its being consumed by the fire (Exod, 3, 2). This signified that the two natures, divine and human, are to be united in such a manner, that the latter is not consumed by the divine, and that the Mother of the Messias shall conceive and give birth without violation of her virginal purity. Remember also, Lady, the promise of the eternal God to the Patriarch Abraham, that, after the captivity of his posterity for four generations, they should return to this land; the mysterious signification of which was, that in this, the fourth generation, (In the autograph manuscript Mary of Agreda explains this fourth generation as follows: "The mystery of this fourth generation is that there are four generations: first that of Adam without a father or mother; second, that of Eve without a mother; third, of our own, from a father and mother; fourth, that of our Lord Jesus Christ, from a Mother without a father. The incarnate God is to rescue the whole race of Adam through thy cooperation from the oppression of the devil (Gen. 15, 16). And the ladder, which Jacob saw in his sleep (Gen. 28, 12), was an express figure of the royal way, which the eternal Word was to open up and by which the mortals are to ascend to heaven and the angels to descend to earth. To this earth the Onlybegotten of the Father shall lower Himself in order to converse with men and communicate to them the treasures of his Divinity, imparting to them his virtues and his immutable and eternal perfections."

135. With these and many other words the ambassador of heaven instructed the most holy Mary, in order that, by the remembrance of the ancient promises and prophecies of holy Writ, by the reliance and trust in them and in the infinite power of the Most High, She might overcome her hesitancy at the heavenly message. But as the Lady herself exceeded the angels in wisdom, prudence and in all sanctity, She withheld her answer, in order to be able to give it in accordance with the divine will and that it might be worthy of the greatest of all the mysteries and sacraments of the divine power. She reflected that upon her answer depended the pledge of the most blessed Trinity, the fulfillment of his promises and prophecies, the most pleasing and acceptable of all sacrifices, the opening of the gates of paradise, the victory and triumph over hell, the Redemption of all the human race, the satisfaction of the divine justice, the foundation of the new law of grace, the glorification of men, the rejoicing of the angels, and whatever was connected with the Incarnation of the Onlybegotten of the Father and his assuming the form of servant in her virginal womb (Philip 2, 7).

136. A great wonder, indeed, and worthy of our admiration, that all these mysteries and whatever others they included, should be intrusted by the Almighty to an humble Maiden and made dependent upon her fiat. But befittingly and securely He left them to the wise and strong decision of this courageous Woman (Prov. 31, 11), since She would consider them with such magnanimity and nobility, that perforce his

confidence in Her was not misplaced. The operations, which proceed within the divine Essence, depend not on the co-operation of creatures, for they have no part in them and God could not expect such co-operations for executing the works ad intra; but in the works ad extra and such as were contingent, among which that of becoming man was the most exalted, He could not proceed without the co-operation of most holy Mary and without her free consent. For He wished to reach this acme of all the works outside Himself in Her and through Her and He wished that we should owe this benefit to this Mother of wisdom and our Reparatrix.

137. Therefore this great Lady considered and inspected profoundly this spacious field of the dignity of Mother of God (Prov, 21, 11) in order to purchase it by her fiat; She clothed Herself in fortitude more than human, and She tasted and saw how profitable was this enterprise and commerce with the Divinity. She comprehended the ways of his hidden benevolence and adorned Herself with fortitude and beauty. And having conferred with Herself and with the heavenly messenger Gabriel about the grandeur of these high and divine sacraments, and finding Herself in excellent condition to receive the message sent to Her, her purest soul was absorbed and elevated in admiration, reverence and highest intensity of divine love. By the intensity of these movements and supernal affections, her most pure heart, as it were by natural consequence, was contracted and compressed with such force, that it distilled three drops of her most pure blood, and these, finding their way to the natural place for the act of conception, were formed by the power of the divine and holy Spirit, into the body of Christ our Lord. Thus the matter, from which the most holy humanity of the Word for our Redemption is composed, was furnished and administered by the most pure heart of Mary and through the sheer force of her true love. At the same moment, with a

humility never sufficiently to be extolled, inclining slightly her head and joining her hands, She pronounced these words, which were the beginning of our salvation: "Fiat mihi secundum verbum tuum" (Luke 1, 31).

138. At the pronouncing of this "fiat," so sweet to the hearing of God and so fortunate for us, in one instant, four things happened. First, the most holy body of Christ our Lord was formed from the three drops of blood furnished by the heart of most holy Mary. Secondly, the most holy soul of the same Lord was created, just as the other souls. Thirdly, the soul and the body united in order to compose his perfect humanity. Fourthly, the Divinity united Itself in the Person of the Word with the humanity, which together became one composite being in hypostatical union; and thus was formed Christ true God and Man, our Lord and Redeemer. This happened in springtime on the twenty-fifth of March, at break or dawning of the day, in the same hour, in which our first father Adam was made and in the year of the creation of the world 5199, which agrees also with the count of the Roman Church in her Martyrology under the guidance of the Holy Ghost. This reckoning is the true and certain one, as was told me, when I inquired at command of my superiors. Conformable to this the world was created in the month of March, which corresponds to the beginning of creation. And as the works of the Most High are perfect and complete (Deut. 32, 4), the plants and trees come forth from the hands of his Majesty bearing fruit, and they would have borne them continually without intermission, if sin had not changed the whole nature, as I will expressly relate in another treatise, if it is the will of the Lord; now however I will not detain myself therewith, since it does not pertain to our subject.

139. In the same instant, in which the Almighty celebrated the nuptials of the hypostatic union in the womb of most holy Mary, the heavenly Lady was elevated to the beatific

vision and the Divinity manifested Itself to Her clearly and intuitively. She saw most high sacraments, of which I will speak in the next chapter. The mysteries of the inscriptions, with which She was adorned and which the angels exhibited as related in the seventh chapter (No. 82, also Part I, 207, 363–4), were made clear to Her each in particular. The divine Child began to grow in the natural manner in the recess of the womb, being nourished by the substance and the blood of its most holy Mother, just as other men; yet it was more free and exempt from the imperfections, to which other children of Adam are subject in that place and period. For from some of these, namely those that are accidental and unnecessary to the substance of the act of generation, being merely effects of sin, the Empress of heaven was free. She was also free from the superfluities caused by sin, which in other women are common and happen naturally in the formation, sustenance and growth of their children. For the necessary matter, which is proper to the infected nature of the descendants of Eve and which was wanting in Her, was supplied and administered in Her by the exercise of heroic acts of virtue and especially by charity. By the fervor of her soul and her loving affections the blood and humors of her body were changed and thereby divine Providence provided for the sustenance of the divine Child. Thus in a natural manner the humanity of our Redeemer was nourished, while his Divinity was recreated and pleased with her heroic virtues. Most holy Mary furnished to the Holy Ghost, for the formation of this body, pure and limpid blood, free from sin and all its tendencies. And whatever impure and imperfect matter is supplied by other mothers for the growth of their children was administered by the Queen of heaven most pure and delicate in substance. For it was built up and supplied by the power of her loving affections and her other virtues. In a like manner was purified whatever served as food for the heavenly

Queen. For, as She knew that her nourishment was at the same time to sustain and nourish the Son of God, She partook of it with such heroic acts of virtue, that the angelic spirits wondered how such common human actions could be connected with such supernal heights of merit and perfection in the sight of God.

140. The heavenly Lady was thus established in such high privileges in her position as Mother of God, that those which I have already mentioned and which I shall yet mention, convey not even the smallest idea of her excellence, and my tongue cannot describe it. For, neither is it possible to conceive it by the understanding, nor can the most learned, nor the most wise of men find adequate terms to express it. The humble, who are proficient in the art of divine love, become aware of it by infused light and by the interior taste and feeling, by which such sacraments are perceived. Not only was most holy Mary become a heaven ,a temple and dwelling place of the most holy Trinity, transformed thereto, elevated and made godlike by the special and unheard of operation of the Divinity in her most pure womb; but her humble cottage and her poor little oratory was consecrated by the Divinity as a new sanctuary of God. The heavenly spirits, who as witnesses of this marvelous transformation were present to contemplate it, magnified the Almighty with ineffable praise and jubilee; in union with this most happy Mother, they blessed Him in his name and in the name of the human race, which was ignorant of this the greatest of his benefits and mercies.

Words of the Queen

THE VIRGIN MARY SPEAKS TO SISTER MARY OF AGREDA

141. My daughter, thou art filled with astonishment at seeing, by means of new light, the mystery of the humiliation

of the Divinity in uniting Himself with the human nature in
the womb of a poor maiden such as I was. I wish, however,
my dearest, that thou turn thy attention toward thyself and
consider, how God humiliated Himself, and came into my
womb, not only for myself alone, but for thee as well. The
Lord is infinite in his mercy and his love has no limit, and
thus He attends and esteems and assists every soul who
receives Him, and He rejoices in it, as if He had created it
alone, and as if He had been made man for it alone. Therefore with all the affection of thy soul thou must, as it were,
consider thyself as being thyself in person bound to render
the full measure of thanks of all the world for his coming;
and for his coming to redeem all. And if, with a lively faith
thou art convinced and confessest, that the same God who,
infinite in his attributes and eternal in his majesty, lowered
Himself to assume human flesh in my womb, seeks also thee,
calls thee, rejoices thee, caresses thee, and thinks of thee
alone, as if thou wert his only creature (Gal. 2, 20) ; think
well and reflect to what his admirable condescension obliges
thee. Convert this admiration into living acts of faith and
love; for, that He condescends to come to thee, thou owest
entirely to the goodness of the King and Savior, since thou
thyself couldst never find Him nor attain Him.

142. Considering merely that which this Lord can give
thee outside of Himself, it will appear to thee grand, even
when thou perceivest it only by a mere human intelligence
and affection. It is certainly true that any gift from such an
eminent and supreme King is worthy of all estimation. But
when thou beginst to consider and know by divine light, that
this gift is God Himself and that He makes Thee partaker of
his Divinity, when thou wilt understand, that without thy
God and without his coming, all creation would be as nothing and despicable in thy sight; thou wouldst want to enjoy
thyself and find rest only in the consciousness of possessing

such a God, so loving, so amiable, so powerful, sweet and affluent; who, being such a great and infinite God, humiliates Himself to thy lowliness in order to raise thee from the dust and enrich thy poverty, performing toward thee the duties of a Shepherd, of a Father, a Spouse and most faithful Friend.

143. Attend, therefore, my daughter, in the secret of thy heart to all the consequences of these truths. Ponder and confer within thyself about this sweetest love of the great King for thee; how faithful He is in his gifts and caresses, in his favors, in the works confided to thee, in the enlightenment of thy interior, instructing thee by divine science in the infinite greatness of his Being, in his admirable works and most hidden mysteries, in universal truth and in the nothingness of visible existence. This science is the first beginning and principle, the basis and foundation of the knowledge which I have given thee in order that thou mayest attain to the decorum and magnanimity, with which thou art to treat the favors and benefits of this thy Lord and God, thy true blessedness, thy treasure, thy light and thy Guide. Look upon Him as upon the infinite God, loving, yet terrible. Listen, my dearest, to my words, to my teachings and discipline, for therein are contained the peace and the enlightenment of thy soul.

Chapter XII

OF THE FIRST ACTS OF THE MOST HOLY SOUL OF CHRIST
OUR LORD IN THE FIRST INSTANT OF HIS CONCEPTION
AND OF THE CORRESPONDING ACTS OF HIS MOST PURE
MOTHER.

144. In order to understand what were the first acts of the
most holy Soul of Christ our Lord, we must refer to that
which has been said in the preceding chapter (No. 138),
namely, that all that substantially belonged to this divine
mystery, the formation of the body, the creation and the
infusion of the soul, and the union of the individual humanity with the person of the Word, happened and was completed in one act or instant; so that we cannot say that in any
moment of time Christ our highest Good was only man. For
from the first instant He was man and true God; as soon as
his humanity arrived at being man, He was also God; therefore He could not at any time be called a mere man, not for
one instant; but from the very beginning He was Godman or
Mangod. And as the active exercise of the faculties is co-
existent with operative essences, therefore the most holy soul
of Christ our Lord, in the same instant in which the Incarnation took place, was beatified by intuitive vision and love.
According to our way of speaking, the powers of his intellect
and will immediately united with the Divinity itself. For his
human essence joined the Divinity in one instant by hypo-

static union, and thus his human faculties in their most perfect activity were united with the essence of God himself, so that both in essence and in operation He was entirely deified.

145. The wonder about this sacrament is that so much glory, yea, the greatness of the immense Divinity, was enclosed within such a small compass, not larger than the body of a bee, or not greater than a small almond. For the dimension of the most holy body of Christ was not any greater than that at the instant when the conception and hypostatic union took place. Moreover in this small compass was included the highest glory as well as the capability for suffering; for the humanity was at the same time glorified and also passible, it was both a Comprehensor and a Viator, possessing heaven though yet on his pilgrimage to heaven. God, however, in his infinite power and wisdom, could thus contract Himself and enclose his infinite Deity within the sphere of a body thus minute by a new and admirable mode of existence, without in the least ceasing to be God. By the same Omnipotence He provided that this most holy soul of Christ, in its superior faculties and in its most noble operations, should be in the state of glory and enjoying beatitude; while all this immense glory was at the same time compressed, as it were, into the superior parts of his soul, suspending the effects and gifts of glory, that would otherwise naturally have communicated themselves to his body. On this account He could be at the same time a viator, subject to suffering, enabling Him to procure our salvation by means of his Cross, Passion and Death.

146. In order to be fully equipped for these and for whatever the most holy humanity was to perform, all the habits, natural to his faculties and necessary for their activity and operation both as Comprehensor and as Viator, were infused into it at the moment of his conception, Thus He was fur-

nished with the infused science of the blessed; with the
sanctifying grace and the gifts of the Holy Ghost, which
according to Isaias rested upon the Christ (Is. 11, 2). He
possessed all the virtues, except faith and hope; for these are
incompatible with the beatific vision and possession, and
were wanting in Him; likewise were wanting in the Holy of
the holy ones, all other virtues, which presuppose any imperfection; since He could not sin, nor was deceit found in his
mouth (I Pet. 2, 22). The dignity and excellence of his
science and grace, the virtues and perfections of Christ our
Lord need not be mentioned here, for that is taught by the
sacred doctors and masters of theology in a profuse manner.
For me it is sufficient to state that all this was as perfect as
was possible to the divine power and that it cannot be encompassed by human understanding. For the most holy soul
of Christ drank from the very fountain of the Divinity (Ps.
35, 10) and could do so without limit or retrenchment, as
David says (Ps, 109, 7). Therefore He must have been possessed of the plenitude of all virtues and perfections.

147. Thus adorned and deified by the Divinity and its
gifts, the most holy soul of Christ our Lord proceeded in its
operations in the following order: immediately it began to see
and know the Divinity intuitively as It is in Itself and as It is
united to his most holy humanity, loving It with the highest
beatific love and perceiving the inferiority of the human
nature in comparison with the essence of God. The soul of
Christ humiliated itself profoundly, and in this humility it
gave thanks to the immutable being of God for having
created it and for the benefit of the hypostatic union, by
which, though remaining human, it was raised to the essence
of God. It also recognized that his most holy humanity was
made capable of suffering, and was adapted for attaining the
end of the Redemption. In this knowledge it offered itself as
the Redeemer in sacrifice for the human race (Ps. 39, 8),

accepting the state of suffering and giving thanks in his own name and in the name of mankind to the eternal Father. He recognized the composition of his most holy humanity, the substance of which it was made, and how most holy Mary by the force of her charity and of her heroic virtues, furnished its substance. He took possession of this holy tabernacle and dwelling; rejoicing in its most exquisite beauty, and, well pleased, reserved as his own property the soul of this most perfect and most pure Creature for all eternity. He praised the eternal Father for having created Her and endowed Her with such vast graces and gifts; for having exempted Her and freed Her from the common law of sin, as his Daughter, while all the other descendants of Adam have incurred its guilt (Rom. S, 18). He prayed for the most pure Lady and for saint Joseph, asking eternal salvation for them. All these acts, and many others, were most exalted and proceeded from Him as true God and Man. Not taking into account those that pertain to the beatific vision and love, these acts and each one by itself, were of such merit that they alone would have sufficed to redeem infinite worlds, if such could exist.

148. Even the act of obedience alone, by which the most holy humanity of the Word subjected itself to suffering and prevented the glory of his soul from being communicated to his body, was abundantly sufficient for our salvation. But although this sufficed for our salvation, nothing would satisfy his immense love for men except the full limit of effective love (John 13, 1); for this was the purpose of his life, that He should consume it in demonstrations and tokens of such intense love, that neither the understanding of men nor of angels was able to comprehend it. And if in the first instant of his entrance into the world He enriched it so immeasurably, what treasures, what riches of merits must He have stored up for it, when He left it by his Passion and Death on the cross after thirty-three years of labor and activity all

divine! O immense love! O charity without limit! O mercy without measure! O most generous kindness! And, on the other hand, O ingratitude and base forgetfulness of mortals in the face of such unheard of and such vast benefaction! What would have become of us without Him? How much less could we do for this our Redeemer and Lord, even if He had conferred on us but small favors, while now we are scarcely moved and obliged by his doing for us all that He could? If we do not wish to treat as a Redeemer Him, who has given us eternal life and liberty, let us at least hear Him as our Teacher, let us follow Him as our Leader, as our guiding light, which shows us the way to our true happiness.

149. This Lord and Master did not work for Himself, nor did He preempt his soul, nor gain this augmentation of grace, for Himself, but entirely for us. He had no need of all this, nor could He receive an increase of grace or glory, since He was filled with them (John 1, 14), as saint John says; for He was the Onlybegotten of the Father at the same time that He was man. In this He had no equal, nor could He have an imitator. All the saints and mere creatures gained merits for themselves and labored for reward; the love of Christ alone was without self interest and altogether for us. And if He wished to enter and go through the school of bodily experience of this life (Luke 2, 52), it was in order to teach us and enrich us by his obedience (Heb. 5, 8), while He turned over to us his infinite merits and his example, in order that we might be wisely instructed in the art of loving. For this is not learned perfectly by affection and desire, unless it is truly and effectively practiced in deeds. I do not enlarge upon the mysteries of the most holy life of Christ our Lord, on account of my incapacity, and I refer to the Gospels, selecting only that which will seem necessary for the heavenly history of his Mother, our Lady. For the lives of this Son and his most holy Mother are so intimately connected and inter-

twined with each other, that I cannot avoid making references to the Gospels and besides add other facts, which are not mentioned by them concerning the Lord and which were not necessary in their narratives for the first ages of the Catholic Church.

150. These operations of Christ our Lord in the first instant of his conception were followed, in another essential instant, by the beatific vision of the Divinity, which we have mentioned in the preceding chapter (No. 139) ; for in one instant of time many instants of essence can take place. In this vision the heavenly Lady perceived with clearness and distinction the mystery of the hypostatic union of the divine and the human natures in the person of the eternal Word, and the most holy Trinity confirmed Her in the title and the rights of Mother of God. This in all rigor of truth She was, since She was the natural Mother of a Son, who was eternal God with the same certainty and truth as He was man. Although this great Lady did not directly cooperate in the union of the Divinity with the humanity, She did not on this account lose her right to be called the Mother of the true God; for She concurred by administering the material and by exerting her faculties, as far as it pertained to a true Mother; and to a greater extent than to ordinary mothers, since in Her the conception and the generation took place without the aid of a man. Just as in other generations the agents, which bring them about in the natural course, are called father and mother, each furnishing that which is necessary, without however concurring directly in the creation of the soul, nor in its infusion into the body of the child; so also, and with greater reason, most holy Mary must be called, and did call Herself, Mother of God; for She alone concurred in the generation of Christ, true God and Man, as a Mother, to the exclusion of any other natural cause; and only through

this concurrence of Mary in the generation, Christ, the Man-God, was born.

151. The Virgin Mother of Christ also understood in this vision the future mysteries of the life and death of her sweetest Son and of the Redemption of the human race, together with those of the new law of the Gospel, which was to be established in connection therewith. To Her were also manifested other great and profound secrets, which were made known to none other of the saints. The most prudent Queen, seeing Herself thus in the immediate presence of the Deity and furnished with the plenitude of divine gifts and science as became the Mother of the Word, lost in humility and love, adored the Lord in his infinite essence, and without delay also in its union with the most holy humanity. She gave Him thanks for having favored Her with the dignity of Mother of God and for the favors done to the whole human race. She gave thanks and glory also for all the mortals. She offered Herself as an acceptable sacrifice in his service, in the rearing up and nourishing of her sweetest Son, ready to assist and co-operate (as far as on her part it would be possible), in the work of the Redemption; and the holy Trinity accepted and appointed Her as the Coadjutrix in this sacrament. She asked for new graces and divine light for this purpose and for directing Herself in the worthy ministration of Her office as Mother of the incarnate Word, that She might treat Him with the veneration and magnanimity due to God himself. She offered to her holiest Son all the children of Adam yet to be born and the saints of limbo; and in the name of all and of Herself She performed many acts of heroic virtue and asked for great favors, which however I will not stop to mention, as I have already done in regard to others on different occasions. For from these it can easily be conjectured what petitions this heavenly Queen made on this occasion, which so far excelled all the other fortunate and happy days of her previous life.

152. But She was especially persistent and fervent in her prayer to obtain guidance of the Almighty for the worthy fulfillment of her office as Mother of the Onlybegotten of the Father. For this, before all other graces, Her humble heart urged Her to desire, and this was especially the subject of her solicitude, that She might be guided in all her actions as becomes the Mother of God. The Almighty answered Her: "My Dove, do not fear, for I will assist thee and guide thee, directing thee in all things necessary for the service of my Onlybegotten Son." With this promise She came to Herself and issued from her ecstasy, in which all that I have said had happened, and which was the most wonderful She ever had. Restored to her faculties, her first action was to prostrate Herself on the earth and adore her holiest Son, God and Man, conceived in her virginal womb; for this She had not yet done with her external and bodily senses and faculties. Nothing that She could do in the service of her Creator, did this most prudent Mother leave undone. From that time on She was conscious of feeling new and divine effects in her holiest soul and in her exterior and interior faculties. And although the whole tenor of her life had been most noble both as regards her body as her soul; yet on this day of the incarnation of the Word it rose to still greater nobility of spirit and was made more godlike by still higher reaches of grace and indescribable gifts.

153. But let no one think that the purest Mother was thus favored and so closely united with the humanity and Divinity of her holiest Son, only in order to continue to enjoy spiritual delights and pleasures, free from suffering and pain. Not so, for in closest possible imitation of her sweetest Son, this Lady lived to share both joy and sorrow with Him; the memory of what She had so vividly been taught concerning the labors and the death of her holiest Son, was like a sword piercing her heart. This sorrow was proportionate to

the knowledge and love, which such a Mother had of such a Son, and which his presence and intercourse so continually recalled to her mind. Although the whole life of Christ and of his most holy Mother was a continued martyrdom and suffering like that of the cross, and was filled with incessant pain and labors; yet in the most pure and loving heart of the heavenly Queen there was also this special feature of suffering, that to her inward sight as a most loving Mother, the passion, torments, ignominies and death of her Son were forever present. And by this continued sorrow of thirty-three years She took upon Herself the long vigil of our Redemption and during all this time this sacrament was concealed in her bosom without companionship or alleviation from any creatures.

154. With this loving sorrow, full of the sweetest anguish, She often looked upon her holiest Son both before and after his birth, and speaking to Him from her innermost heart, She would repeat these words: "Lord and God of my soul, most sweet Son of my womb, why hast Thou given me the position as Mother and yet connected with it the sorrowful thought of losing Thee, leaving me an orphan, bereft of thy desirable company? Scarcely art Thou put in possession of a body for thy earthly life, when Thou art notified of the sentence of a sorrowful death for the rescue of men. The first of thy actions is one of superabundant merit in satisfaction for his sins. O would that the justice of the eternal Father were thereby satisfied and thy sufferings and death fall upon me! From my body and blood Thou hast composed thine own, without which it would not be possible for Thee to suffer, since Thou art the immutable and immortal God. If therefore I have furnished Thee the instrument or the matter of thy sufferings, let me too suffer with Thee the same death. O inhuman sin, how, being so cruel and the cause of so much evil, couldst thou nevertheless be so fortunate, that thy

Repairer should be One, who on account of his infinite Goodness, can make thee a "happy fault!" O my sweetest Son and my love, who shall be thy guard, who shall defend Thee from thy enemies? O would that it were the will of the Father, that I guard Thee and save Thee from death, or die in thy company, and that Thou never leave mine! But that which happened to the patriarch Abraham, shall not now take place (Gen. 22, 11); for the predestined decree shall be executed. Let the will of the Lord be fulfilled." These loving sighs were many times repeated by our Queen, as I shall say farther on, and the eternal Father accepted them as an agreeable sacrifice, while they were the sweetest diversion of her most holy Son.

Words of the Queen

THE VIRGIN MARY SPEAKS TO SISTER MARY OF AGREDA

155. My daughter, since thou hast, by faith and divine light, arrived at a knowledge of the grandeur of God and of his ineffable condescension in coming down from heaven for thee and for all the mortals, let not this benefit be for thee idle and fruitless. Adore the essence of God with profound reverence, and praise Him for what thou knowest of his goodness. Receive not light and grace in vain (II Cor. 6, 1) ; and study the encouraging example given by my most holy Son and myself in imitation of Him, as thou hast come to be instructed in it; for as He was the true God, and I his Mother (for in so far as He was man his most holy humanity was created), let us humiliate ourselves in the remembrance of our lowly human nature and confess the greatness of the Divinity, greater than any creature can comprehend. Do this especially when thou receivest the same Lord in the holy Sacrament. In this admirable Sacrament my most holy Son with Divinity and humanity comes to thee and remains with

thee in a new and incomprehensible way. His great condescension is manifest, though it is little taken notice of and
respected by mortals, nor does it find the return due to such
love.

156. Let then thy acknowledgment be accompanied with
as much humility, reverence and worship as is possible to thy
combined powers and faculties; for though they be exerted to
the utmost limit, they will always fall short of what thou
owest to God and of what He deserves. And in order that
thou mayest as far as possible make up for thy deficiencies,
offer up that, which my most holy Son and I have done;
unite thy spirit and thy affections in union with the Church
triumphant and militant, offering at the same time thy life as
a sacrifice and praying that all nations may know, confess and
adore their true God who became man for all. Thank Him
for the benefits, which He has conferred and confers on all,
whether they know Him or not, whether they confess or
repudiate Him. Above all I ask of thee, my dearest, to do that
which is most acceptable to the Lord and most pleasing to
me; that thou grieve, and in sweet affection mourn over the
gross ignorance and dangerous tardiness of the sons of men;
over the ingratitude also of the children of the Church, who,
having received the light of the divine faith, yet live in such
interior forgetfulness of the works and benefits of the Incarnation, yea, of God himself, and so much so, that they seem
to differ from infidels only in some ceremonies and exterior
worship. They perform these without spirit or heartiness,
many times offending and provoking the divine justice which
they should placate.

157. Through this ignorance and torpidity it happens
that they are not prepared to receive and acquire the true
science of the Most High. They bring upon themselves the
loss of the divine light and they deserve to be left in the heavy
darkness, making themselves more unworthy than the infi-

dels themselves and entailing upon themselves an incomparably greater chastisement. Mourn over such great damage of thy neighbors and pray for help from the bottom of thy heart. And in order that thou mayest put away from thy own self such formidable dangers, do not undervalue the favors and benefits, which thou receivest, nor, even under pretense of humility, belittle or forget them. Remember and consider how distant was the journey, which the grace of the Most High has made in order to call thee (Ps. 18, 7). Ponder in thy mind, how it has waited upon thee and consoled thee, assured thee in thy doubts, quieted thee in thy fears, ignored and pardoned thy faults, multiplied favors, caresses and blessings. I assure thee, my daughter, that thou must confess in thy heart, that the Most High has not done such things with any other generation; thou of thyself canst do nothing; thou art poor and more useless than others. Let then thy thanks be greater than that of all the creatures.

Chapter XIII

AN EXPLANATION OF THE STATE IN WHICH MOST HOLY
MARY FOUND HERSELF AFTER THE INCARNATION OF THE
DIVINE WORD IN HER VIRGINAL WOMB.

158. The deeper I begin to understand the divine effects and
conditions which were caused by the conception of the
eternal Word in the Queen of heaven, the more am I involved in the difficulties of describing this event. For I find
myself immersed in exalted and complicated mysteries, while
my intellect and my power of expression are entirely insufficient for encompassing what is presented to me. Nevertheless
my soul experiences such great sweetness and such delight in
spite of this deficiency, that I cannot bring myself to repent
entirely of my undertaking; at the same time obedience
animates me and also compels me to overcome the hardships,
which in a weak and womanly mind would be insuperable, if
the assurance and encouragement coming from this source
would not assist me. This is true especially of this chapter, in
which I am to treat of the gifts of glory enjoyed by the
blessed in heaven. Taking their prerogatives as models I will
try to describe the state of the heavenly Empress Mary after
becoming the Mother of God.

159. For this purpose I will speak of the blessed from two
points of view: of their own perfection and of their relation
to God. As regards the latter, the Divinity is made clear and

manifest to them with all its perfections and attributes. This is called the object of their beatitude, their glory, the substantial joy, the ultimate end, wherein the whole creature finds its adequate end and rest. On the part of the saints there are the beatific operations of vision and love, and of others necessarily connected with that most happy state, which neither the eyes have seen, nor ears have heard, nor can enter into the thoughts of men (Is. 64, 4; I Cor. 2, 29). Among the gifts and prerogatives of this glory of the saints, some are called endowments freely given as to a spouse entering upon the spiritual matrimony, which is consummated in the joys of the eternal felicity. Just as the earthly spouse acquires possession and dominion of her endowments and enjoys in common with her husband the use of them, so also in glory these gifts are made to the saints as their own, while their use is common both to them, in as far as they themselves rejoice in them, and to God, in as far as He is glorified in them by the saints. And these ineffable gifts are more or less excellent according to the merits and the dignities of each. But they are not given to those, who are not of the same nature as the Spouse, namely Christ our Lord; hence only to men, not to angels. For the incarnate Word has not entered into any espousals with the angels, (Heb.2, 16) as He has done with men, by uniting Himself with them in that great sacrament mentioned by the Apostle, (Eph. 5, 32), in Christ and in the Church. Since, however, the Bridegroom Christ, as man, is composed of body and soul, just like the rest of men, therefore both body and soul are to be glorified in his presence and the gifts of glory are both for the body and the soul. Three of these gifts pertain to the soul and they are called vision, comprehension and fruition; and four pertain to the body: clearness, impassibility, subtility and agility, and these are properly the effects of intuitive vision overflowing from the glory of the soul.

160. In all these gifts our Queen Mary participated to a certain extent already in this life; especially after the Incarnation of the Word in her virginal womb. It is true that these gifts are given to the saints as comprehensors, being pledges and dowries of the eternal and imperishable felicity, and as it were securities for the unchangeableness of their state. On that account they are not conferred upon those still on the way to heaven. But upon holy Mary these gifts were conferred as a viator; hence not as on a comprehensor, not permanently, but from time to time and step by step, and with a certain difference, as we shall explain. In order that the appropriateness of this rare blessing in the sovereign Queen may be the better understood, let that, which I have said in the seventh and following chapters before the Incarnation, be remembered; for there the preparation and espousal with which the Most High favored his most blessed Mother in accordance with her dignity, are explained. On the day in which the divine Lord assumed human nature in her virginal womb, this spiritual marriage, as far as the heavenly Lady is concerned, was consummated by that most exalted and exquisite beatific vision, which, as we have said, was then vouchsafed to Her. But for the other faithful the Incarnation was as it were an espousal, which is to be consummated in their heavenly fatherland (Osea 2, 19).

161. Our great Queen possessed another prerequisite for these privileges: She was exempt from all stain of original and actual sin and was confirmed in grace by actual impeccability. Thus She was capable of celebrating this marriage in the name of the Church militant and to make promises in the name of all its members (Eph, 5, 32) ; for in this matter, as She was the Mother of the Savior, his foreseen merits found their application through Her. By her transient vision of the glory of the Divinity, She became the accepted surety for all the children of Adam, that this same reward will not be

denied to any of those, who shall use the grace of their Redeemer to merit it. The divine incarnate Word certainly was highly pleased to find, that his most burning love and his infinite merits should immediately bear fruit in Her, who at the same time was his Mother, his first Spouse and the bridal chamber of his Divinity; and that his rewards should fall upon One, in whom there was no hindrance. By conferring these privileges and favors upon his most holy Mother, Christ our Salvation, indulged and partly satiated his love for Her and in Her, for all the mortals; too long a delay did it seem to the divine love, to wait thirty-three years until He should manifest his Divinity to his own Mother. Although He had shown Her this favor at other times, as related in the first part (No. 382, 429), yet on this occasion of his Incarnation He did it in a more excellent manner; one which corresponded with the glory of his most holy soul. However, all this in Her was not permanent, but renewed from moment to moment with the flow of time, in as far as was compatible with the ordinary state of pilgrimage.

162. Conformably to this, God, on the day in which most holy Mary assumed the position of Mother of the eternal Word by conceiving Him in Her womb, invested us with a right to our Redemption, founded upon the espousal of the human nature with Himself. In the consummation of this spiritual marriage by the beatification of the most holy Mary and the conferring upon Her the gifts of glory, the same reward was also promised to us, if we should make ourselves worthy of it through the merits of his most holy Son, our Redeemer. But so far did the Lord raise his Mother above all the glory of the saints in the blessings of this day, that all the angels and men, even in their highest reaches of beatific vision and love, cannot attain to that which the heavenly Queen then attained; the same must also be said of the gifts of glory, which overflowed from the soul to her body; for all

of them corresponded with her innocence, holiness and merits, and these again correspond with that highest of all dignities possible to a creature: that of being the Mother of her Creator.

163. Coming now to these gifts in particular, the first gift to her soul was the clear and beatific vision, which corresponds to the obscure knowledge of faith in the viators, This vision was given to the most holy Mary at the times and in the manner already explained and to be explained later. Besides these intuitive visions, She had many other abstractive ones of the Divinity, of the kind mentioned above. Although all these were transient, yet they left in her mind most exquisite and various images furnishing Her with such a clear and exalted knowledge of the Divinity, that no words can be found to express it. In this our Lady was singularly privileged before all other creatures, and thus She possessed the permanent effects of the gifts of glory as far as compatible with her position as viator. When at times the Lord hid himself from Her, suspending the use of these images for certain high ends, She made use of infused faith, which in Her was superexcellent and most efficacious. In such manner, one way or the other, her soul never lost sight of that divine Object, nor wandered from It even for a moment. However, during the nine months in which She bore in her womb the incarnate Word, She enjoyed even greater visions and gifts of the Divinity.

164. The second of these gifts is comprehension, possession or apprehension. This consists in the attainment of the end, corresponding to the virtue of hope, whereby we seek after the final Object in order to possess It without danger of ever losing It. This possession and comprehension in most holy Mary corresponded to the visions mentioned; because seeing the Divinity, She possessed It. Whenever She depended on faith alone, hope was in Her more firm and secure

than in any other creature; and more than this; for, as the security of possession in the creature is founded to a great extent upon sanctity and impeccability, our heavenly Lady on this account was so privileged, that the firmness and security of her possession of God, although She was a pilgrim, equaled in certain respects the firmness and security of the blessed. For on account of her stainless and unimpeachable sanctity She was assured of never losing, God; although the cause of this security in Her as Viatrix was not the same as in the glorified saints. During the months of her pregnancy She enjoyed this possession of God in various ways by special and wonderful graces, through which the Most High manifested Himself and united Himself to her most pure Soul.

165. The third gift is fruition, which corresponds to charity, since charity does not cease but is perfected in glory (I Cor. 13, 8) ; for fruition consists in loving the highest Good possessed by us. This is the charity of heaven, that, just as God is known and possessed as He is in "Himself, so also He is loved for his own sake. True, even now, while we are yet viators, we love Him for his own sake; but there is a great difference. Now we love him in desire and we know Him not as He is in Himself, but as He is represented to us by incongruous images or by enigmas (I Cor. 13, 12; John 3, 2) ; therefore our love is not perfected, nor do we rest in it, or find the plenitude of delight therein, though there is much to incite us. But in the clear vision and possession we shall see Him as He is in Himself and we shall see Him through Himself, not through enigmas; thus we shall love Him as He should be loved and as far as we can love Him respectively; our love will be perfected and the fruition of Him will be satiated, without leaving anything to be desired.

166. Most holy Mary participated in this fruition more abundantly than in any other; for even though her most

ardent love might, in a certain respect, have been inferior to that of the blessed whenever She was without the clear vision of the Divinity, yet it was superior in many other points of excellence, even while remaining in the lower state. No one ever possessed the divine science in the same degree as this Lady, and by it She understood how God is to be loved for Himself. This science was perfected by the memory of what She had seen and enjoyed higher in degree than the angels. And as her love was nourished by this knowledge of God, it necessarily exceeded that of the blessed in all that did not pertain to immediate fruition and unchangeableness as to increase or augmentation. On account of her profound humility the Lord condescended to an arrangement, whereby She could act as a Viatrix remaining in a holy fear of displeasing her Beloved. This burning love was of the most perfect kind and tended entirely toward God himself; it caused in Her ineffable joy and delight, proportioned to the excellence of her love.

167. In regard to the gifts of the body, redounding from the gifts of glory, and other gifts of the soul constituting the accidental part of the glory of the blessed, I will say, that they serve for the perfection of the glorious bodies in the activity of their senses and motive powers. By them the bodies are assimilated to the soul and throw off the impediments of their earthly grossness, enabling them to obey the wishes of the souls, which in that most happy state cannot be imperfect or opposed to the will of God. The senses require two gifts: one to refine the reception of sensible images, and this is perfected by the gift of clearness; the other, to repel all activity or passivity hurtful and destructive of the body, and this is done by the gift of impassibility. Two other gifts are required in order to perfect the power of motion: one, in order to overcome the resistance or impediment of gravity, furnished by the gift of agility; the other, in order to overcome the

resistance of other bodies, furnished by the gift of subtlety. With these gifts the body becomes glorious, clear, incorruptible, agile and subtle.

168. In all these privileges our great Queen and Lady participated during her mortal life. The gift of clearness disposes the body to receive the light and at the same time to give it forth, doing away with earthly opaqueness and obscurity and making it more transparent than clearest crystal. Whenever most holy Mary enjoyed the clear and beatific vision, her virginal body participated in this privilege in a measure beyond all human calculation. The after-effects of this purity and clearness would have been most wonderful and astounding, if they could have been made perceptible to the senses. Sometimes they were noticeable in her most beautiful face, as I will say later on, especially in the third part; yet they were not known or perceived by all who conversed with Her, for the Lord interposed a curtain or veil, in order that they might not always or indiscriminately be manifested. But in many respects She herself enjoyed the advantages of this gift, though it was disguised, suspended or hidden to the gaze of others; She for instance was not inconvenienced by earthly opaqueness, as the rest of men.

169. Saint Elisabeth perceived something of this clearness, when at the sight of Mary she exclaimed: "And whence is this to me, that the Mother of my Lord should come to me?" (Luke 1, 43). The world was not capable of perceiving this sacrament of the King (Tob. 12, 7), nor was it opportune to manifest it at that time. Yet to a certain extent her face was always more bright and lustrous than that of other creatures. Also in other respects it exhibited qualities altogether above the natural order of other bodies, which produced in Her a most delicate and spiritualized complexion, like that of an animated crystal. This presented to the touch not the asperity natural to the flesh, but the softness as it were of the purest

and the finest silk, so that I cannot find any other comparison to make myself understood. Yet all this should not appear strange in the Mother of God; for She bore Him in her womb and She had seen Him often, even face to face. For the Israelites could not look upon Moses face to face, nor bear the splendor, which shone forth from him after his communication with the Lord upon the mountain (Exod. 34, 29), though it was much inferior to that vouchsafed to most holy Mary. There is no doubt, that if God had not by a special providence withheld and hidden the splendor in reality due to the countenance and the body of his most pure Mother, it would have brightened the world more than a thousand suns combined. None of the mortals could, by natural power, have sustained its brilliancy; since, even thus restrained and concealed, it was sufficient to cause in them the same effects, which saint Dionysius the Areopagite experienced in looking upon Her and which he describes in his letter to Paul.

170. Impassibility produces in the glorified body such a condition, that no agent, except God himself, can by any activity or influence, change or disturb it, no matter how powerful this activity may be. Our Queen participated in this gift in two ways: first, in regard to the temperament and humors of the body. She possessed these in such a delicate measure and proportion, that She could not contract or suffer any infirmities, nor was She subject to any other human hardships which arise from the inequality of the four humors, being in this regard as it were almost impassible. Secondly, in regard to the dominion and commanding power, which She had over all the creatures, as mentioned above, (No. 13, 18,43, 56,60) ; for none of them had power to act contrary to her will and consent. We can add still another participation of impassibility: the assistance of the divine power in proportion to her innocence. For, if it is said,

that the first parents in paradise could not suffer a violent death as long as they persevered in original justice, it must not be understood to mean that they enjoyed this privilege by intrinsic or inherent powers (for if a lance would have wounded them they could die), but they enjoyed it through the assistance of the Lord, who would always prevent them from being wounded. If then the first parents possessed this privilege and could transmit it to their descendants as their servants and vassals, it was due, by a much better title, to the innocence of the sovereign Mary; and so in truth was She endowed with it.

171. Our most humble Queen made no use of these privileges, for She renounced them in imitation of her most holy Son and in order to labor and gain merits for our benefit; in spite of them She, wished to suffer and She really suffered more than the martyrs. Human intellect cannot weigh correctly the greatness of these labors. We shall speak of them throughout this heavenly history, leaving much more untold, for common language and words cannot encompass them. But I must advert to two things: first, that the sufferings of our Queen bore no relation to any sins of her own, for She had none to atone for; and therefore She suffered none of the bitterness, which is mixed with pains endured in the memory and consciousness of our own guilt of sins committed. Secondly: that in her sufferings She was divinely sustained in accordance with the ardors of her love, for She could not naturally endure so much sufferings, as her love called for, or as much as, on account of this very love, the Lord allowed Her to endure.

172. Subtility is a gift, which takes away from the glorified body the density or grossness natural to quantitative matter and which enables it to penetrate other bodies and to occupy the same place with them. The subtilized bodies of the blessed therefore are endowed with qualities peculiar to

the spirit and can without difficulty penetrate the quantitative matter of other bodies. Without dividing or separating them it can occupy the same place. Thus our Lord's body, coming forth from the grave (Matth. 28, 2) and entering the closed doors (John 20, 19), penetrated the material enclosing these places. Most holy Mary participated in this gift not only while She enjoyed the beatific visions, but also otherwise according to her will and desire, as happened many times in her life in her bodily appearances to some persons, of which we shall yet relate; for in all these She made use of her gift of subtlety penetrating other bodies.

173. The last gift of the body enables the glorified body to move from place to place instantly and without the impediment of terrene gravity, in the manner of pure spirits, which move by their own volition. Mary most holy possessed a continual and wonderful participation in this agility, especially as a direct result of the divine visions. She did not feel in her body the force of weight and gravity; therefore She could walk without feeling the inconvenience usual to that kind of exercise; She could move about with instantaneous speed, without feeling any shock or fatigue as we would feel. All this belonged naturally to the quality and condition of her body, so spiritualized and well-formed. During the time of her pregnancy She felt even less the weight of her body; although, in order to bear her share of labors, She allowed hardships to produce their effect. She was so admirable and perfect in the possession and use of these privileges, that I find myself wanting in words to express all that has been made manifest to me concerning them; for it exceeds all that I have said or am able to say.

174. Queen of heaven and my Mistress, since Thou hast condescended to adopt me as thy daughter, thy word will remain a pledge, that Thou wilt be my Guide and Teacher. Relying on this promise I presume to propose a difficulty, in

which I find myself: How does it come, my Mother and Lady, that thy most blessed soul, after it had enjoyed the clear intuition of God according to the disposition of his Majesty, did not remain in the state of blessedness? And why can we not say, that Thou didst remain in this state of beatitude, since there was no sin nor any other obstacle to this state in Thee, according to the dignity and sanctity revealed to me by the supernatural light?

Words of the Queen

THE VIRGIN MARY SPEAKS TO SISTER MARY OF AGREDA

175. My dearest daughter, thou doubtest as one that loves me and askest as one not knowing. Consider then, that the perpetuity and durability of blessedness and felicity is destined for the saints, since their happiness is to be entirely perfect; if it would last only for some time, it would be wanting in the completeness and adequacy necessary for constituting it as the highest and most perfect happiness. At the same time it is incompatible with the common law and ordinary course, that the creature be glorified and at the same time be subject to sufferings, even though it be without sin. If this law did not hold good with my most holy Son (John 1, 18), it was because He was at the same time God and man and it was not befitting that his most holy soul, being hypostatic ally united with the Divinity, should be without the beatific vision; and as He was at the same time Redeemer of the human race, He could not suffer nor pay the debt of sin, that is pain, if He had not possessed a body capable of suffering. But I was a mere creature, and therefore I could have no claim to the vision, which' to Him was due as a God. Moreover I could not be said to have permanently enjoyed the state of blessedness, because it was conceded to me from one time to another. Under these conditions I was capable of

suffering at one time and enjoying blessedness at another; moreover it was more usual for me to suffer and to gain merits, than to be blessed, since I belonged to the viators and not to the comprehensors.

176. Justly the Most High has ordained, that the blessedness of eternal life should not be enjoyed in this mortal existence (Exod, 33, 20), and that immortality should be reached by passing through existence in a mortal body and by gaining merits in a state of suffering, such as is the present life of men (Rom. 6, 23). Although death in all the sons of Adam was the stipend and punishment of sin (Rom. 6, 23), and therefore death and all the other effects and chastisements had no rights in me, who had not sinned; yet the Most High ordained, that I also, in imitation of my most holy Son, should enter into felicity and eternal life by the death of the body (Luke 24, 26). There was nothing incongruous in this for me, but it afforded me many advantages, allowing me to follow the royal way of all men and gain many merits and great glory by suffering and dying. Another advantage resulted therefrom for men, for they saw that my most holy Son and I myself, who was his Mother, were truly human as they themselves, since we proved to them our mortality. Thereby the example, which we left them became much more efficacious and they would be induced to imitate the life, which we led and which redounded so much to the greater glory and exaltation of my Son and Lord, and of myself. All this would have come to nought, if the visions of the Divinity had been continuous in me. However, after I conceived the eternal Word, the benefits and favors were more frequent and greater, since I was then brought into close connection with Him. This is my answer to thy questions. No matter how much thou hast meditated and labored in manifesting the privileges and their effects enjoyed by me in mortal life, thou wilt never be able to comprehend all that the powerful

arm of the Omnipotent wrought in me. And much less canst thou describe in human words what thou hast understood.

177. Now attend to the instruction, which I will give thee regarding the preceding chapters. If I was the model to be imitated in the way I responded to the coming of God into the soul and into the world by showing due reverence, worship, humility, and thankful love, it follows, that if thou, (and in the same way the rest of the souls), art solicitous in imitating me, the Most High will come and produce the same effects in thee as in myself; though they may be not so great and efficacious. For if the creature, as soon as it obtains the use of reason, begins to advance toward the Lord as it should, directing its footsteps in the path of life and salvation, his Most High Majesty will issue forth to meet it, (Wis. 6, 15), being beforehand with his favors and communications; for to Him it seems a long time to wait for the end of the pilgrimage in order to manifest Himself to his friends.

178. Thus it happens, that by means of faith, hope and charity, and by the worthy reception of the Sacraments, many divine effects, wrought by his condescension, are communicated to the souls. Some are communicated according to the ordinary course of grace and others according to a more supernatural and wonderful order; and each one will be more or less conformable to the disposition of the soul and to the ends intended by the Lord, which are not known at present. And if the souls do not place any obstacle on their part, He will be just as liberal with them as with those who dispose themselves, giving them greater light and knowledge of his immutable being, and by a divine and exceedingly sweet infusion of grace, transforming them into a likeness of Himself and communicating to them many of the privileges of the beatified. For after He is found He allows Himself to be taken possession of and enjoyed by that hidden embrace, which the Spouse felt, when She said: "I will hold Him and

not dismiss Him" (Cant. 3, 4). Of this possession and of his presence the Lord himself will give many token and pledges, in order that the soul may possess Him in peace like the blessed, although always only for a limited time. So liberal as this will God, our Master and Lord, be in rewarding the objects of his love for the labors accepted by them for his sake and fearlessly undertaken to gain possession of Him.

179. In this sweet violence of love the creature begins to withdraw from and die to all earthly things; and that is why love is called strong as death. From this death arises a new spiritual life, which makes the soul capable of receiving new participations of the blessed and their gifts; for it enjoys more frequently the overshadowing of the Most High and the fruits of the highest Good, which it loves. These mysterious influences cause a sort of overflow into the interior and animal parts of the creature, producing a certain transparency and purifying it from the effects of the spiritual darknesses; it makes it courageous and as it were indifferent to suffering, ready to meet and endure all that is adverse to the inclinations of the flesh. With a certain subtle thirst it begins to seek after all the difficulty and violence incident to the attainment of the kingdom of heaven (Matth. 11, 12); it becomes alert and unhindered by earthly grossness, so that many times the body itself begins to feel this lightness in regard to its own self; the labors, which before seemed burdensome, become easy. Of all these effects thou hast knowledge and experience, my daughter, and I have described and rehearsed them for thee, in order that thou mayest dispose thyself and labor so much the more earnestly; so that the divine activity and power of the Most High, in working out his pleasure in thee, may find thee well disposed and free from resistance and hindrance.

Chapter XIV

OF THE ATTENTION AND CARE, WHICH THE MOST HOLY
MARY BESTOWS UPON THE FRUIT OF HER WOMB AND SOME
HAPPENINGS IN REGARD TO IT.

180. As soon as our Lady and Queen issued from the trance,
in which She had conceived the eternal incarnate Word, She
prostrated Herself upon the earth and adored Him in her
womb, as I have already said in the twelfth chapter (No.
152). This adoration She continued all her life, commencing
it at midnight every day and repeating these genuflexions
three hundred times, until the same hour of the following
night, and oftener, whenever She had opportunity; in this
She was even more diligent during the nine months of her
divine pregnancy. In order to comply entirely with the new
duties consequent upon the guarding of this Treasure of the
eternal Father in the virginal bridal chamber, She directed all
her attention toward frequent and fervent prayer. She was
solicitous in sending up many and reiterated petitions to be
able worthily to preserve the heavenly Treasure confided to
Her. Accordingly She dedicated anew to the Lord her soul
and all her faculties, practicing all virtues in a heroic and
supreme degree, so that She caused new astonishment in the
angels. She also consecrated and offered up all the motions of
her body to the worship and service of the infant Godman
within Her. Whether She ate, slept, labored or rested, She

did it all for the nourishment and conservation of her sweetest Son, and in all these actions She was inflamed more and more with divine love.

181. On the day following the Incarnation, the thousand guardian angels which attended upon most holy Mary, appeared in corporeal form and with profound humility adored their incarnate King in the womb of the Mother. Her also they acknowledged anew as their Queen and Mistress and rendered Her due homage and reverence, saying: "Now, O Lady, Thou art the true Ark of the testament (Deut. 10, 5), since Thou containest the Lawgiver himself and preservest the Manna of heaven (Heg. 9, 4), which is our true bread. Receive, O Queen, our congratulations on account of thy dignity and happiness, for which we also thank the Most High; since He has befittingly chosen Thee for his Mother and his tabernacle. We offer anew to Thee our homage and service, and wish to obey Thee as vassals and servants of the supreme and omnipotent King, whose Mother Thou art." These protestations and homages of the holy angels excited in the Mother of wisdom incomparable sentiments of humility, gratitude and love of God. For in this most prudent heart, where all things were weighed with the scales of the sanctuary according to their true value and weight, this reverence and acknowledgment of the angelic spirits proclaiming Her as their Queen, was held in high esteem. Although it was a greater thing to see Herself the Mother of the King and Lord of all creation, yet all her blessings and dignities were made more evident by these demonstrations and homages of the holy angels.

182. The angels rendered this homage as executors and ministers of the will of the Most High. When their Queen and our Lady was alone, all of them attended upon Her in corporeal form, and they assisted Her in her outward actions and occupations; and when She was engaged in manual

labor, they administered to Her what was needed. Whenever She happened to eat alone in the absence of saint Joseph, they waited upon Her at her poor table and at her humble meals. Everywhere they followed Her and formed an escort, and helped Her in the services rendered to saint Joseph. Amid all these favors and obsequious attendance the heavenly Lady did not forget to ask permission from the Master of masters for all her operations and undertakings and to implore his direction and assistance. So exact and so well governed were all her exercises according to the plenitude of perfection, that the Lord alone could comprehend and properly weigh them.

183. Besides the ordinary guidance during the time in which She carried in her most holy womb the incarnate Word, She felt his divine presence in diverse ways, all admirable and most sweet. Sometimes He showed Himself to Her by abstractive vision, as mentioned above. At other times She saw and beheld Him as He was now present in the virginal temple, united hypostatically with the human nature. At other times the most holy humanity was manifested to Her, as if in a crystalline monstrance, composed of her own maternal womb and purest body; this kind of vision afforded special consolation and delight to the great Queen. At other times She perceived how the glory of his most holy soul overflowed into the body of the divine Child, communicating to It some of the effects of its own blessedness and glory and how the clarity and light of the natural body of her Son passed over in a wonderfully sweet ineffable and divine manner into Herself as Mother. This favor transformed Her entirely into another kind of being, inflaming her heart and causing in Her such effects as no created capacity can explain. Let the intellect of the highest seraphim extend and dilate as much as it may, it would nevertheless find itself overwhelmed by this glory (Prov. 25, 27); for the entire being of the

heavenly Queen was an intellectual and animated heaven, and in Her was summarized the divine glory and greatness, in a measure that even the vast confines of the heavens themselves could not encompass.

184. These and other prerogatives alternated and succeeded each other in accordance with the exercises of the divine Mother, and such variety as suited the different kinds of work which She performed. All her doings, whether spiritual or manual or otherwise of the body, served her God or benefited her neighbors, being undertaken and accomplished by this prudent Maiden to produce a harmony admirable and most sweet before the Lord, and wonderful to the angelic spirits. And when, by the disposition of the Most High, the Mistress of the world returned to a more natural state, She suffered mortal agony, caused by the force and violence of her love; for to Her could in truth be applied what Solomon says in the name of the Spouse: "Stay me with flowers, compass me about with apples" (Cant. 2, 5) ; and thus it would happen, that by the piercing wounds of these sweet arrows of love She was brought near to the ending of her life. But in this necessity the powerful arm of the Most High was wont to strengthen Her in a supernatural manner.

185. Sometimes, in order to afford Her sensible relief, innumerable birds would come to visit Her by the command of the Lord. As if they were endowed with intellect, they would salute Her by their lively movements, and dividing into harmonious choirs, would furnish Her with sweetest music, and they would wait for her blessing before again dispersing. This happened in a special manner soon after She had conceived the divine Word, as if they wished to congratulate Her on her dignity in imitation of the angels. The Mistress of all creatures on that day spoke to the different kinds of birds and commanded them to remain and praise with Her the Creator, in thanksgiving for the creation, and for the exist-

ence and beauty given to them and to sing his praises for their conservation. Immediately they obeyed Her as their Mistress and anew they began to form choirs, singing in sweetest harmony and bowed low to the ground to worship their Creator and honor the Mother, who bore Him in her womb. They were accustomed to bring flowers to Her in their beaks and place them into her hands, waiting until She should command them to sing or to be silent according to her wishes. It also happened that in bad weather some birds would come and seek the protection of the heavenly Lady, and She took them in and nourished them, in her admirable innocence glorifying the Creator of all things.

186. And our weak ignorance must not be estranged at these wonders, for, though the incidents might be called small, the purposes of the Most High are great and venerable in all his works; and also the works of our most prudent Queen were great, no matter of what kind they might have been. And who is so presumptuous as to ignore the importance of knowing how much of God's essence and perfections are manifest in the existence of all the creatures? How important it is to seek Him and find Him, to bless Him and magnify Him in all his creatures, as admirable, powerful, generous and holy? Why should it not be our duty to imitate Mary, who overlooked no time, place or occasion, to attain this object? And how also shall our ungrateful forgetfulness, not be confounded, and our hardness of heart not be softened? How can our listless heart fail to be aroused, when we see ourselves reprehended and urged for very shame to thankfulness by the irrational creatures? Merely for the slight participation of the Divinity that consists in bare existence, they proclaim his praises without intermission; whereas we men, who are made to the image and likeness of God, furnished with the powers of knowing Him and enjoying Him eternally, forget Him so far as not even to know Him, and

instead of serving Him, offend Him! Thus it comes that in
no wise can men be preferred to the brute animals, since they
have become worse than the brutes (Ps. 48, 13).

Words of the Queen

THE VIRGIN MARY SPEAKS TO SISTER MARY OF AGREDA

187. My daughter, thou hast received my instruction until
now in order to desire and strive after the heavenly science,
which I wish thee so earnestly to acquire and which shall
teach thee to understand profoundly, what decorous reverence is due to God. I remind thee once more, that this
science is very hard to learn and little coveted by men on
account of their ignorance; for thence, to their great loss, it
arises that, in conversing with the Most High or rendering
Him service or worship, they fail to form a worthy concept of
his infinite greatness, and to free themselves from the darksome images of their earthly occupations, which make them
torpid and carnal, unworthy and unfit for the magnificent
intercourse with the supernal Deity. And this ill-bred coarseness entails another disorder: namely, that whenever they
converse with their neighbors, they do it without order,
measure or discretion, become entangled in their outward
actions, and losing the memory and presence of their Creator
in the excitement of their passions, are completely entangled
in what is earthly.

188. I desire therefore, my dearest, that thou By from this
danger and learn the science, of the immutable being and
infinite attributes of God. In such a way must thou study
Him and unite thyself to Him, that no created being will
come between thy soul and the true and highest Good. At all
times and in all places, occupations and operations thou must
keep Him in sight, without releasing Him from the intimate
embrace of thy heart (Cant. 3, 4). Therefore I command thee

to treat Him with a magnanimous heart, with decorum and reverence, with deep felt fear of the soul. And whatever pertains to his divine worship, I desire that thou handle with all attention and care. Above all in order to enter into his presence by prayer and petitions, free thyself from all sensible and earthly images. And since human frailty cannot always remain constant in the force of love, nor always experience the sweet violence of its movements on account of its earthly nature, thou shouldst seek other assistance, such as will help thee toward the same end of finding thy God. Such help, for instance, is afforded by his praise in the beauty of the heavens and of the stars, in the variety of the plants, in the pleasant vista of the fields, in the forces of the elements, and especially in the exalted nature of the angels and in the glory of his saints.

189. But bear continually in mind especially this particular caution, not to seek any earthly alleviation in any event or in any labor which thou art to undergo, nor to indulge in any diversion coming from human creatures; and especially not in those coming from men, for an account of thy naturally weak and yielding character, so much adverse to giving pain, thou placest thyself in danger of exceeding and overstepping the limit of what is allowed or just, following, more than is proper for the religious spouses of my most holy Son, thy sensible likings. The risks of this negligence all the human creatures incur; for if full reins are given to frail human nature, it will not give heed to reason, not to the true light of the Spirit; but, forgetting them entirely, it will blindly follow the impulse of its passions and pleasures. Against this general danger is provided the enclosure and retirement of the souls consecrated to my Son and Lord, in order to cut off the root of those unhappy and disgraceful occasions for those religious, who would willingly seek them and entangle themselves in them. Thy recreations, my dearest, and those of thy

sister religious, must be free from such danger and deadly poison. Seek always those, which thou shalt find in the secret of thy breast and in the chamber of thy Beloved, who is faithful in consoling the sorrowful and in assisting the afflicted.

Chapter XV

MOST HOLY MARY IS INFORMED OF THE WILL OF THE LORD, THAT SHE VISIT HOLY ELISABETH; SHE ASKS SAINT JOSEPH FOR PERMISSION TO GO, REMAINING SILENT ABOUT ALL THAT HAD HAPPENED TO HER.

190. By the words of the heavenly messenger, the archangel Gabriel, most holy Mary had been informed, that her cousin Elisabeth (who was held to be sterile) had conceived a son and that She was already in the sixth month of her pregnancy. Afterwards, in one of the intellectual visions, the Most High revealed to Her, that in a miraculous birth, Elisabeth would bring forth a son, who would be great before the Lord (Luke 1, 15) ; a Prophet and the Forerunner of the incarnate Word; also other great mysteries of the holiness and of the personality of saint John were revealed to Her. On this same occasion and on others the heavenly Queen was informed, that it would be agreeable and pleasing to the Lord, if She would visit her cousin, in order that as well Elisabeth as also the child in her womb might be sanctified by the presence of their Redeemer; for his Majesty was anxious to communicate the benefits of his coming into the world and his merits to his Precursor, in order to make of him as it were the well seasoned first fruit of his Redemption.

191. At the news of this sacramental mystery the most prudent Virgin, with admirable jubilee of spirit, rendered

thanks to the Lord for such great condescension and favor vouchsafed to the soul of the Precursor and Prophet and to his mother Elisabeth. Signifying her readiness to fulfill the divine pleasure, She spoke to his Majesty and said: "Most high Lord, beginning and cause of all good, let thy name be eternally glorified, acknowledged and praised by all the nations. I, the least of thy creatures, give thee humble thanks for the liberal kindness, which thou wishest to show to thy servant Elisabeth and to the son of her womb. If it is according to the promptings of thy condescension, that I serve thee in this work, I stand prepared, my Lord, to obey eagerly thy divine mandates." The Most High answered Her: "My Dove and my Beloved, elect among creatures, truly I say to thee, that on account of thy intercession and thy love I will, as a Father and most liberal God, take care of thy cousin Elisabeth and of the son, who is to be born of her: I will choose him as my Prophet and as the Precursor of the Word, which is made man in thee; I will look upon them as belonging to thee and intimately connected with thyself. Therefore I wish, that my and thy Onlybegotten go to see the mother, in order to free the son from the chains of the first sin and in order that, before the common and ordinary time decreed for other men, his voice and praise may sound up to my ears (Cant. 2, 14), and that the mysteries of the Incarnation and Redemption may be revealed to his sanctified soul. Therefore I wish thee to visit Elisabeth; for We three Persons of the blessed Trinity have chosen her son for great deeds conformable to our pleasure."

192. To this command of the Lord the most obedient Mother responded: "Thou knowest, my Lord and God, that all the desires of my heart seek but thy divine pleasure and that I wish to fulfill diligently whatever Thou commandest to thy humble servant. Allow me, my God, to ask permission from my husband Joseph and that I make this journey ac-

cording to his will and direction. And in order that I may not diverge from what is thy pleasure, do Thou govern me during that journey in all my actions, direct my footsteps to the greater glory of thy name (Ps. 118, 113). Accept therefore the sacrifice, which I bring in going out in public and in leaving my cherished retirement. I wish to offer more than my desires, God and King of my soul, I hope to be made able to suffer all that will conduce to thy greater service and pleasure purely for thy love, so that the longings of my soul may not remain entirely unfulfilled."

193. When our great Queen came out of this vision, She called upon the thousand angels of her guard, who appeared to Her in bodily forms, and told them of the command of the Most High. She asked them to assist Her with careful solicitude in this journey, to teach Her how to fulfill all the commands according to the greater pleasure of the Lord, to defend Her and guard Her from dangers so that She might conduct Herself in all things during that journey in the most perfect manner. The holy princes, with wonderful devotion, offered to obey and serve Her. In the same manner the Mistress of all prudence and humility was wont to act also on other occasions. For though She was Herself more wise and more perfect in her deeds than the angels, yet because She was yet in the state of pilgrimage and endowed with a nature lower than that of the angels, She was always solicitous to attain the plenitude of perfection by consulting and asking for the aid of her guardian angels, though they were her inferiors in sanctity. Under their direction, as also by the promptings of the holy Spirit, all her human actions were well disposed and well ordered. The heavenly spirits obeyed Her with alacrity and punctuality, such as was proper to their nature and due to their Queen and Lady. They held sweet intercourse and delightful colloquy with Her, and alternately with Her they sang highest songs of praise and adoration of

the Most High. At other times they conversed about the supernal mysteries of the incarnate Word, the hypostatic union, the sacrament of the Redemption, the triumphs to be celebrated by Him, the fruits and blessings accruing there from to mortals. It would necessitate lengthening out this work too much, if I were to write all that has been revealed to me about these conversations.

194. The humble Spouse proceeded immediately to ask the consent of saint Joseph for executing the mandate of the Most High, and, in her consummate prudence, She said nothing of these happenings, but simply spoke to him these words: "My lord and spouse, by the divine light it was made known to me, that through condescension of the Most High the prayer of my cousin Elisabeth, the wife of Zacharias, has been heard; she has conceived a son, though she was sterile. Since she has obtained this singular blessing, I hope that through God's infinite bounty, her Son will greatly please and glorify the Lord. I think that on this occasion I am under obligation to visit her and converse with her on certain things for her consolation and spiritual encouragement. If this is according to thy liking, my master, I will perform it with thy permission, for I am entirely subject to thy will and pleasure. Consider then what is best for me and command what I am to do."

195. This prudent silence of the most holy Mary, so full of humble subjection, was very agreeable to the Lord; for She showed Herself thereby worthy and capable of receiving the deposit of the great sacraments of the King (Tob. 12, 7). Therefore, and on account or the confidence in his fidelity with which She proceeded, his Majesty disposed the most pure heart of saint Joseph, giving him his divine light to act conformably to his will. This is the reward of the humble, who ask for counsel: that they will find it with certainty and security (Eccli, 32, 29). It is also the peculiar prerogative of a

holy and discreet zeal to be able to give prudent advice to those that ask. Full of this holy counsel saint Joseph answered our Queen: "Thou knowest already, my Lady and Spouse, that my utmost desires are to serve Thee with all diligence and attention; for I am bound to have this confidence in thy great virtue, that Thou wilt not incline toward anything, which is not according to the greater pleasure and glory of the Most High; and this is my belief also in regard to this journey. Lest thy making this journey alone and without the company of thy husband cause surprise I will gladly go with Thee and attend to thy wants on the way. Do Thou appoint the day on which we shall depart together."

196. The most holy Mary thanked her prudent spouse Joseph for his loving solicitude and for his attentive cooperation with the will of God in whatever he knew to be for his service and honor. They both concluded to depart immediately on their visit to the house of saint Elisabeth (Luke 1, 39), and prepared without delay the provisions, which consisted merely in a little fruit, bread and a few fishes, procured by saint Joseph. In addition to these he borrowed an humble beast of burden, in order to carry their provisions and his Spouse, the Queen of all creation. Forthwith they departed from Nazareth for Judea; the journey itself I will describe in the following chapter. On leaving their poor dwelling the great Mistress of the world knelt at the feet of her spouse Joseph and asked his blessing in order to begin the journey in the name of the Lord. The saint was abashed at the rare humility of his Spouse, with which He had already been impressed by experience on so many other occasions. He hesitated giving Her his benediction; but the meek and sweet persistence of the most holy Mary overcame his objections and he blessed Her in the name of the Most High. The heavenly Lady raised her eyes and her heart to God, in order to direct her first steps toward the fulfillment of the divine

pleasure and willingly bearing along in her womb the Onlybegotten of the Father and her own, for the sanctification
of John in that of his mother Elisabeth.

Words of the Queen

THE VIRGIN MARY SPEAKS TO SISTER MARY OF AGREDA

197. My dearest daughter, many times I have confided and
manifested to thee the love burning within my bosom: for I
wish that it should be ardently re-enkindled within thy own,
and that thou profit from the instruction, which I give thee.
Happy is the soul, to which the Most High manifests his
holy and perfect will; but more happy and blessed is he, who
puts into execution, what he has learned. In many ways God
shows to mortals the highways and pathways of eternal life:
by the Gospels and the holy Scriptures, by the Sacraments
and the laws of the holy Church, by the writings and examples of the saints, and especially, by the obedience due to the
guidings of its ministers, of whom his Majesty said: "Whoever hears you, hears Me;" for obeying them is the same as
obeying the Lord himself. Whenever by any of these means
thou hast come to the knowledge of the will of God, I desire
thee to assume the wings of humility and obedience, and, as
if in ethereal flight or like the quickest sunbeam, hasten to
execute it and thereby fulfill the divine pleasure.

198. Besides these means of instruction, the Most High
has still others in order to direct the soul; namely, He intimates his perfect will to them in a supernatural manner, and
reveals to them many sacraments. This kind of instruction is
of many and different degrees; not all of them are common
or ordinary to all souls; for the Lord dispenses his light in
measure and weight (Wis. 11, 21). Sometimes He speaks to
the heart and the interior feelings in commands; at others, in
correction, advising or instructing: sometimes He moves the

heart to ask Him; at other times He proposes clearly what He desires, in order that the soul may be moved to fulfill it; again He manifests, as in a clear mirror, great mysteries, in order that they may be seen and recognized by the intellect and loved by the will. But this great and infinite Good is always sweet in commanding, powerful in giving the necessary help for obedience, just in his commands, quick in disposing circumstances so that He can be obeyed, notwithstanding all the impediments which hinder the fulfillment of his most holy will.

199. In receiving this divine light, my daughter, I wish to see thee very attentive, and very quick and diligent in following it up in deed. In order to hear this most delicate and spiritual voice of the Lord it is necessary, that the faculties of the soul be purged from earthly grossness and that the creature live entirely according to the spirit; for the animal man does not perceive the elevated things of the Divinity (I Cor. 2, 14). Be attentive then to his secrets (Is. 24, 16) and forget all that is of the outside; listen, my daughter, and incline thy ear; free thyself from all visible things (Ps. 44, 11). And in order that thou mayest be diligent, cultivate love; for love is a fire, which does not have its effect until the material is prepared; therefore let thy heart always be disposed and prepared. Whenever the Most High bids thee or communicates to thee anything for the welfare of souls, or especially for their eternal salvation, devote thyself to it entirely; for they are bought at the inestimable price of the blood of the Lamb and of divine love. Do not allow thyself to be hindered in this matter by thy own lowliness and bashfulness; but overcome the fear which restrains thee, for if thou thyself art of small value and usefulness, the Most High is rich (I Pet. 1, 18), powerful, great, and by Himself performs all things (Rom 10, 12). Thy promptness and affection will not go

without its reward, although I wish thee rather to be moved entirely by the pleasure of thy Lord.

Chapter XVI

THE JOURNEY OF THE MOST HOLY MARY ON HER VISIT TO
SAINT ELISABETH AND HER ENTRANCE INTO THE HOUSE
OF ZACHARIAS.

200. "And Mary rising up in those days," says the sacred text,
"went into the hill country with haste, into a city of Judea"
(Luke 1, 39). This rising up of our heavenly Queen signified
not only her exterior preparations and setting out from
Nazareth on her journey, but it referred to the movement of
her spirit and to the divine impulse and command which
directed Her to arise interiorly from the humble retirement,
which She had chosen in her humility. She arose as it were
from the feet of the Most High, whose will and pleasure She
eagerly sought to fulfill, like the lowliest handmaid, who
according to the word of David (Ps. 122, 2) keeps her eyes
fixed upon the hands of her Mistress, awaiting her commands. Arising at the bidding of the Lord She lovingly
hastened to accomplish his most holy will, in procuring
without delay the sanctification of the Precursor of the
incarnate Word, who was yet held prisoner in the womb of
Elisabeth by the bonds of original sin. This was the purpose
and object of this journey. Therefore the Princess of heaven
arose and proceeded in diligent haste, as mentioned by the
Evangelist saint Luke.

201. Leaving behind then the house of her father and forgetting her people (Ps. 44, 11), the most chaste spouses, Mary and Joseph, pursued their way to the house of Zacharias in mountainous Judea. It was twenty six leagues distant from Nazareth, and the greater part of the way was very rough and broken, unfit for such a delicate and tender Maiden. All the convenience at their disposal for the arduous undertaking was a humble beast, on which She began and pursued her journey. Although it was intended solely for her comfort and service, yet Mary, the most humble and unpretentious of all creatures, many times dismounted and asked her spouse saint Joseph to share with Her this commodity and to lighten the difficulties of the way by making use of the beast. Her discreet spouse never accepted this offer; and in order to yield somewhat to the solicitations of the heavenly Lady, he permitted her now and then to walk with him part of the way, whenever it seemed to him that her delicate strength could sustain the exertion without too great fatigue. But soon he would again ask Her, with great modesty and reverence, to accept of this slight alleviation and the celestial Queen would then obey and again proceed on her way seated in the saddle.

202. Thus alleviating their fatigue by humble and courteous contentions, the most holy Mary and saint Joseph continued on their journey, making good use of each single moment. They proceeded alone, without accompaniment of any human creatures; but all the thousand angels, which were set to guard the couch of Solomon, the most holy Mary, attended upon them (Cant. 3, 7). Although the angels accompanied them in corporeal form, serving their great Queen and her most holy Son in her womb, they were visible only to Mary. In the company of the angels and of saint Joseph, the Mother of grace journeyed along, filling the fields and the mountains with the sweetest fragrance of her pres-

ence and with the divine praises, in which She unceasingly occupied Herself. Sometimes She conversed with the angels and, alternately with them, sang divine canticles concerning the different mysteries of the Divinity and the works of Creation and of the Incarnation. Thus ever anew the pure heart of the immaculate Lady was inflamed by the ardors of divine love. In all this her spouse saint Joseph contributed his share by maintaining a discreet silence, and by allowing his beloved Spouse to pursue the flights of her spirit; for, lost in highest contemplation, he was favored with some understanding of what was passing within her soul.

203. At other times the two would converse with each other and speak about the salvation of souls and the mercies of the Lord, of the coming of the Redeemer, of the prophecies given to the ancient Fathers concerning Him, and of other mysteries and sacraments of the Most High. Something happened on the way, which caused great wonder in her holy spouse Joseph: he loved his Spouse most tenderly with a chaste and holy love, such as had been ordained in Him by the special grace and dispensation of the divine love itself (Cant. 2, 4); in addition to this privilege (which was certainly not a small one) the saint was naturally of a most noble and courteous disposition, and his manners were most pleasing and charming; all this produced in him a most discreet and loving solicitude, which was yet increased by the great holiness, which he had seen from the beginning in his Spouse and which was ordained by heaven as the immediate object of all his privileges. Therefore the saint anxiously attended upon most holy Mary and asked her many times, whether She was tired or fatigued, and in what he could serve Her on the journey. But as the Queen of heaven already carried within the virginal chamber the divine fire of the incarnate Word, holy Joseph, without fathoming the real cause, experienced in his soul new reactions, proceeding from the words

and conversations of his beloved Spouse. He felt himself so inflamed by divine love and imbued with such exalted knowledge of the mysteries touched upon in their conversations, that he was entirely renewed and spiritualized by this burning interior light. The farther they proceeded and the more they conversed about these heavenly things, so much the stronger these affections grew, and he became aware, that it was the words of his Spouse, which thus filled his heart with love and inflamed his will with divine ardor.

204. So great were these new sensations, that the prudent Joseph could not help but pay the greatest attention to them. Although he knew that all this came to him through the mediation of most holy Mary, and although it was a wonderful consolation to him, that She was the cause, he meditated upon it without curiosity, and, on account of his great modesty, he did not dare to ask Her any questions. The Lord having ordained it thus, for it was not yet time, that he should know the sacrament of the King, which was already completed in her virginal womb. The heavenly Princess beheld the interior of her spouse, knowing all that passed within his soul; and in her prudence She reflected how it would naturally be unavoidable, that he should come to know of her pregnancy; for there would be no possibility of concealing it from her most beloved and chaste spouse. The great Lady did not know at the time, how God would arrange this matter; yet, although She had not received any' intimation or command to conceal this mystery, her heavenly prudence and discretion taught Her that it would be proper to conceal it as a great sacrament, greater than all other mysteries. Therefore She kept it secret, saying not a word about it to her husband, neither after the message of the angel, nor during this journey, nor later on, during the anxieties occasioned to saint Joseph at becoming aware of her pregnancy.

205. O admirable discretion and prudence more than human! The great Queen resigned Herself entirely to the divine Providence, hoping that God would arrange all things; yet She felt anxiety and pain, at the thought of what her husband might think, and of her inability to do anything in order to dissipate his anxiety. This anxiety was increased by the attentive care and service, lavished by him upon Her with so much love and affection; since his faithful services certainly deserved a corresponding return on her part as far as was prudently possible. Therefore, in loving solicitude and in pursuance of her desires to solve this coming difficulty, She prayed to the Lord, asking Him to grant his divine assistance and guidance to saint Joseph, when it should arrive. In this state of suspense, in which She found Herself, her Highness performed great and heroic acts of faith, hope and charity, of prudence, humility, patience and fortitude, imbuing all her activity with the plenitude of holiness and reaching in all things the summit of perfection.

206. This journey was the first pilgrimage begun by the divine Word, four days after He had entered the world; for his most ardent love would not suffer any longer delay or procrastination in enkindling the fire, which He came to scatter in the world (Luke 12, 49), and in beginning his justification of mortals with his Precursor. This haste He communicated also to his holy Mother, in order that She might arise without delay and fly on her visit to Elisabeth (Luke 1, 39). The most heavenly Lady on this occasion served as the coach of the true Solomon; but much more richly adorned and more elegant, as Solomon himself infers in the canticles (Cant. 3, 9). Therefore this journey was glorious and occasioned great joy to the Onlybegotten of the Father. For He traveled at his ease in the virginal chamber of his Mother, enjoying the sweet tokens of her love. At the time She alone was the archive of this Treasure, the secretary

of so great a sacrament, and She adored Him, blessed and admired Him, spoke and listened to Him, and answered Him; She reverenced Him and thanked Him for Herself and for all the human race, much more than all the men and the angels together.

207. In the course of the journey, which lasted four days, the two holy pilgrims, Mary and Joseph, exercised not only the virtues which were interior and had God for their immediate object, but also many other outward acts of charity toward their neighbors; for Mary could not remain idle at the sight of want. They did not find the same hospitable treatment at all the inns of the road; for some of the innkeepers, being more rude, treated them with slight consideration in accordance with their natural disposition; others received them with true love inspired by divine grace. But the Mother of mercy denied to no one such help as She could administer; and therefore, whenever She could decently do so, She hastened to visit and hunt up the poor, infirm and afflicted, helping them and consoling them, and curing their sicknesses. I will not stop to relate all that happened on the way, but will only mention the good fortune of a poor sick girl, whom our great Queen found in passing through a town on the first day of her journey. She was moved to tenderest compassion at the sight of her grievous illness; and, making use of her power as Mistress of the creatures, She commanded the fever to leave the maiden and the humors to recompose and reduce themselves to their natural state and condition. At this command and at the sweet presence of the purest Mother, the sick maiden was suddenly freed and healed from her pains of body and benefited in soul; so that afterwards She lived more and more perfectly and attained the state of sanctity; for the image of the Authoress of her happiness remained stamped within her memory and her heart was enkindled with a great love toward the heavenly Lady, alt-

hough She never again saw Her, nor was the miracle ever made public.

208. Having pursued their journey four days, the most holy Mary and her spouse arrived at the town of Juda, where Zachary and Elisabeth then lived. This was the special and proper name of the place, where the parents of saint John lived for a while, and therefore the Evangelist saint Luke specifies it, calling it Juda, although the commentators have commonly believed that this was not the name of the town in which Elisabeth and Zacharias lived, but simply the name of the province, which was called Juda or Judea; just as for the same reason the mountains south of Jerusalem were called the mountains of Judea. But it was expressly revealed to me that the town was called Juda and that the Evangelist calls it by its proper name; although the learned expositors have understood by this name of Juda the province, in which that town was situated. This confusion arose from the fact that some years after the death of Christ the town Juda was destroyed, and, as the commentators found no trace of such a town, they inferred that saint Luke meant the province and not a town; thus the great differences of opinion in regard to the place, where most holy Mary visited Elisabeth, are easily explained.

209. As holy obedience has enjoined upon me the duty of clearing up these doubts, on account of the strange inconsistency in the sayings of learned men, I will also add to what I have already said, that the house in which the visitation took place was built upon the very spot on which now the faithful pilgrims, who travel to or live in the holy Land, venerate the divine mysteries transacted during the visit. Although the town of Juda itself, where the house of Zacharias stood is ruined, the Lord did not permit the memory of the venerable locality in which those great mysteries transpired, and which were hallowed by the footsteps of most

holy Mary, of Christ our Lord, and of the Baptist as well as of his holy parents, to be blotted out and effaced from the memory of men. Therefore it was by divine influence, that the ancient Christians built up those churches and restored the holy places, in order to preserve by the agency of divine light the traditional truth and to renew the memory of the admirable sacraments. Thus we ourselves, the faithful of our times, can enjoy the blessing of venerating and worshipping the sacred localities, proclaiming and confessing our Catholic faith in the works of our Redemption.

210. For the better understanding of these things let it be remembered that after the demon had become aware on Calvary that Christ our Lord was God and the Redeemer of men, he sought with incredible fury to blot out the remembrance of Him from the land of the living, as Jeremias says (Jer. 11, 19) ; and the same is to be said of the memory of his most holy Mother. Thus he managed to have the most holy Cross hidden and buried under ground and to have it delivered as spoil of war to the Persians; and in the same way he procured the ruin and obliteration of many holy places. On this account the holy angels carried back and forth so many times the venerable and holy house of Loretto; for the same dragon who pursued the heavenly Lady (Apoc. 12, 13), had already excited the minds of the inhabitants of that land to tear down and raze to the ground that most sacred oratory, which had been the workshop of the Most High in the mystery of the Incarnation. The same astute hatred of the enemy urged him to blot out the town of Juda, aided partly by the negligence of the inhabitants, who gradually died off, partly also by untoward events and happenings. Yet the Lord did not allow all traces of the house of Zachary to be effaced or obliterated, on account of the sacraments, which were there enacted.

211. This town was distant from Nazareth, as I have said, twenty-six leagues, and about two leagues from Jerusalem, and it was situated in that part of the Judean mountains, where the stream Sorec takes its rise. After the birth of saint John and the return of the most holy Mary and her spouse Joseph to Nazareth, saint Elisabeth received a divine revelation that a great calamity and slaughter impended over the infants of Bethlehem and its vicinity. And though this revelation was indeterminate and unclear, it nevertheless induced the mother of saint John to betake herself with Zacharias, her husband, to Hebron, which was eight leagues more or less from Jerusalem; for they were rich and noble, and they had dwellings not only in Juda and Hebron, but they had houses and possessions also in other places. When the most holy Mary and Joseph were on their way flying from Herod to Egypt (Matth. 2, 14) after the birth of the Word and some months after the birth of saint John, saint Elisabeth and Zacharias were in Hebron. Zacharias died four months after our Lord was born, which was ten months after the birth of his son John. It seems to me I have now sufficiently solved this doubt, and it ought to be evident that the house of the Visitation was neither in Jerusalem, nor in Bethlehem, nor in Hebron, but in the town called Juda. I saw that this is the true explanation, which was made known to me by divine light together with the other mysteries of this heavenly history; afterwards, when I was constrained by obedience to ask about this matter, a holy angel again made the same declaration to me.

212. It was at this city of Juda and at the house of Zacharias that most holy Mary and Joseph arrived. In order to announce their visit, saint Joseph hastened ahead of Mary and calling out saluted the inmates of the house, saying: "The Lord be with you and fill your souls with divine grace." Elisabeth was already forewarned, for the Lord himself had

informed her in a vision that Mary of Nazareth had departed to visit her. She had also in this vision been made aware that the heavenly Lady was most pleasing in the eyes of the Most High; while the mystery of her being the Mother of God was not revealed to her until the moment, when they both saluted each other in private. But saint Elisabeth immediately issued forth with a few of her family, in order to welcome most holy Mary, who, as the more humble and younger in years, hastened to salute her cousin, saying: "The Lord be with you, my dearest cousin," and Elisabeth answered: "The same Lord reward you for having come in order to afford me this pleasure." With these words they entered the house of Zacharias and what happened I will relate in the following chapter.

Words of the Queen

THE VIRGIN MARY SPEAKS TO SISTER MARY OF AGREDA

213. My daughter, whenever the creature holds in proper esteem the good works and the services, which the Lord commands for his glory, it will feel within itself great facility of operation, great sweetness in undertaking them, and a readiness and alacrity in continuing and pursuing them. These different feelings then give testimony of their being truly useful and commanded by God. But the soul cannot experience these affections, if it is not altogether devoted to. the Lord, keeping its gaze fixed upon his divine pleasure, hearing of it with joy, executing it with alacrity and forgetting its own inclination and conveniences. The soul must be like the faithful servant, who seeks to do only the will of his master and not his own. This is the manner of obeying, which is fruitful and which is due from an the creatures to their God and much more from an the religious, who explicitly promise this kind of obedience. In order that thou, my

dearest, mayest attain to it perfectly, remember with what esteem David in many places speaks of the precepts (Ps. 118), of the sayings and of the justifications of the Lord; and remember the effects, which they caused in that Prophet and even now in the souls. He says that they make the infants wise (Ps. 18, 8), rejoice the heart of men (Ps. 18, 9), that they enlighten the eyes of the soul, so that they become a most brilliant light for its footsteps (Ps. 118, 105) that they are more sweet than honey (Ps. 18, 11), more desirable and more estimable than the most precious stones. This promptitude and subjection to the divine will and to his laws made David so conformable to the heart of God. These are the kind of souls his Majesty seeks for his servants and friends (I Kings 13, 14, Acts 13, 22).

214. Attend therefore, my daughter, with a solicitude to the works of virtue and perfection, which thou knowest to be desirable in the eyes of the Lord. Despise none of them nor withdraw from any of them and cease not to exercise them, no matter how violently thy inclinations and thy weakness should oppose their exercise. Trust in the Lord and proceed to put them into execution, and soon his power will overcome all difficulties. Soon thou wilt also know by happy experience how light is the burden and how sweet is the yoke of the Lord (Matth. 11, 13). He did not deceive us when He spoke those words, as might be argued by the tepid and the negligent, who in their torpidity and distrust, tacitly repudiate the truth of this statement. I wish also that thou, in order to imitate me in this perfection, take notice of the favor, which the divine condescension vouchsafed me in furnishing me with a most sweet love and affection for the creatures as participators in the divine goodness and existence. In this love I sought to console, alleviate and enliven all the souls; and by a natural compassion I procured all spiritual and corporeal goods for them; to none of them, no matter how

great sinners they might have been, did I wish any evil; on the contrary I was urged by the great compassion of my tender heart to procure for them eternal salvation. From this also arose my anxiety concerning the grief, which was to grow out of my pregnancy to my spouse saint Joseph; for to him I owed more than to all other creatures. Tender compassion filled my heart, especially for the suffering and the infirm, and I tried to obtain some relief for all. In these virtues then I wish that thou, making use of the knowledge of them given to thee, most prudently imitate me.

Chapter XVII

THE SALUTATION GIVEN TO SAINT ELISABETH BY THE
QUEEN OF HEAVEN. AND THE SANCTIFICATION OF JOHN.

215. When the most holy Mother Mary arrived at the house
of Zacharias, the Precursor of Christ had completed the sixth
month of his conception in the womb of saint Elisabeth. The
body of the child John had already attained a state of great
natural perfection; much greater than that of other children,
on account of the miracle of his conception by a sterile
mother and on account of the intention of the Most High to
make him the depositary of greater sanctity than other men
(Matth. 11, 11). Yet at that time his soul was yet filled with
the darkness of sin, which he had contracted in the same way
as the other children of Adam, the first and common father
of the human race; and as, according to the universal and
general law, mortals cannot receive the light of grace before
they have issued forth to the light of the sun (Rom. 5, 7) ; so,
after the first, the original sin contracted by our nature, the
womb of the mother must serve as a dungeon or prison for
all of us, who have laden upon ourselves this guilt of our
father and head, Adam. Christ our Lord resolved to anticipate this great blessing in his Prophet and Precursor by
conferring the light of his grace and justification upon him
six months after his conception by saint Elisabeth, in order

that he might be as well in holiness, as he was in his office of Precursor and Baptist.

216. After the first salutation of Elisabeth by the most holy Mary, the two cousins retired, as I have said at the end of the preceding chapter. And immediately the Mother of grace saluted anew her cousin saying:

"May God save thee, my dearest cousin, and may his divine light communicate to thee grace and life" (Luke 1, 40). At the sound of most holy Mary's voice, saint Elisabeth was filled by the Holy Ghost and so enlightened interiorly, that in one instant she perceived the most exalted mysteries and sacraments. These emotions, and those that at the same time were felt by the child John in the womb of his mother, were caused by the presence of the Word made flesh in the bridal chamber of Mary's womb, for, making use of the voice of Mary as his instrument, He, as Redeemer, began from that place to use the power given to Him by the eternal Father for the salvation and justification of the souls. And since He now operated as man, though as yet of the diminutive size of one conceived eight days before, He assumed, in admirable humility, the form and posture of one praying and beseeching the Father. He asked in earnest prayer for the justification of his future Precursor and obtained it at the hands of the blessed Trinity.

217. Saint John was the third one for whom our Redeemer made special petition since his presence in the womb of his mother. His Mother was the first for whom He gave thanks and prayed to the Father; next in order was her spouse, saint Joseph, for whom the incarnate Word offered up his prayers, as we have said in the twelfth chapter; and the third one was the Precursor saint John, whom the Lord mentioned by name in his prayers to the Father. Such was the great good fortune and privilege of saint John, that Christ our Lord presented to the eternal Father the merits of his Passion and

Death to be endured for men; and in view thereof He requested the sanctification of this soul. He appointed and set apart this child as one who is to be born holy as his Precursor and as a witness of his coming into the world (John I, 7); as one who was to prepare the hearts of his people in order that they might recognize and receive Him as the Messias. He ordained that for such an exalted ministry the Precursor should receive all the graces, gifts and favors which are befitting and proportionate to his office. All this the Father granted just as the Onlybegotten had requested it of Him.

218. This happened before the most holy Mary had put her salutation into words. At the pronunciation of the words mentioned above, God looked upon the child in the womb of saint Elisabeth, and gave it perfect use of reason, enlightening it with his divine light, in order that he might prepare himself by foreknowledge for the blessings which he was to receive. Together with this preparation he was sanctified from original sin, made an adopted son of God, and filled with the most abundant graces of the Holy Ghost and with the plenitude of all his gifts; his faculties were sanctified, subjected and subordinated to reason, thus verifying in himself what the archangel Gabriel had said to Zacharias; that His son would be filled with the Holy Ghost from the womb of his mother (Luke 1, 17). At the same time the fortunate child, looking through the walls of the maternal womb as through clear glass upon the incarnate Word, and assuming a kneeling posture, adored his Redeemer and Creator, whom he beheld in most holy Mary as if enclosed in a chamber made of the purest crystal. This was the movement of jubilation, which was felt by his mother Elisabeth as coming from the infant in her womb (Luke 1, 44). Many other acts of virtue the child John performed during this interview, exercising faith, hope, charity, worship, gratitude, humility, devotion and all the other virtues possible to him

there. From that moment he began to merit and grow in sanctity, without ever losing it and without ever ceasing to exercise it with all the vigor of grace.

219. Saint Elisabeth was instructed at the same time in the mystery of the Incarnation, the sanctification of her own son and the sacramental purpose of this new wonder. She also became aware of the virginal purity and of the dignity of the most holy Mary. On this occasion, the heavenly Queen, being absorbed in the vision of the Divinity and of the mysteries operated by it through her most holy Son, became entirely godlike, filled with the clear light of the divine gifts which She participated; and thus filled with majesty saint Elisabeth saw Her. She saw the Word made man as through a most pure and clear glass in the virginal chamber, lying as it were on a couch of burning and enlivened crystal. The efficacious instrument of all these wonderful effects was the voice of most holy Mary, as powerful as it was sweet in the hearing of the Lord. All this force was as it were only an outflow of that which was contained in those powerful words: "Fiat mihi secundum verbum tuum," by which She had drawn the eternal Word from the bosom of the Father down to her soul and into her womb.

220. Filled with admiration at what She saw and heard in regard to these divine mysteries, saint Elisabeth was wrapt in the joy of the Holy Ghost; and, looking upon the Queen of the world and what was contained in Her, she burst forth in loud voice of praise, pronouncing the words reported to us by saint Luke: "Blessed are Thou among women and blessed is the fruit of thy womb. And whence is this to me, that the Mother of my Lord should come to me? For behold as soon as the voice of thy salutation sounded in my ears, the infant in my womb leaped for joy, and blessed art Thou, that has believed, because those things shall be accomplished, that were spoken to Thee by the Lord." In these prophetic words

saint Elisabeth rehearsed the noble privileges of most holy Mary, perceiving by the divine light what the power of the Lord had done in Her, what He now performed, and what He was to accomplish through Her in time to come. All this also the child John perceived and understood, while listening to the words of his mother; for she was enlightened for the purpose of his sanctification, and since he could not from his place in the womb bless and thank her by word of mouth, she, both for herself and for her son, extolled the most holy Mary as being the instrument of their good fortune.

221. These words of praise, pronounced by saint Elisabeth were referred by the Mother of wisdom and humility to the Creator; and in the sweetest and softest voice She intoned the Magnificat as recorded by saint Luke (Ch. 1,46–55).

46. My soul doth magnify the Lord;

47. And my spirit hath rejoiced in God my Saviour.

48. Because He hath regarded the humility of his handmaid; for behold from henceforth all generations shall call me blessed.

49. Because He that is mighty hath done great things to me; and holy is his name.

50. And his mercy is from generation unto generation to them that fear Him.

51. He hath shewed might in his arm; He hath scattered the proud in the conceit of their heart.

52. He hath put down the mighty from their seat and hath exalted the humble.

53. He hath filled the hungry with good things; and the rich He hath sent empty away.

54. He hath received Israel, his servant, being mindful of his mercy;

55. As He spoke to our fathers, to Abraham and his seed forever.

222. Just as saint Elisabeth was the first one who heard this sweet canticle from the mouth of most holy Mary, so she was also the first one who understood it and, by means of her infused knowledge, commented upon it. She penetrated some of the great mysteries, which its Authoress expressed therein in so few sentences. The soul of most holy Mary magnified the Lord for the excellence of his infinite Essence; to Him She referred and yielded all glory and praise (I Tim. 1, 17), both for the beginning and the accomplishment of her works. She knew and confessed that in God alone every creature should glory and rejoice, since He alone is their entire happiness and salvation (II Cor. 10, 17). She confessed also the equity and magnificence of the Most High in attending to the humble and in conferring upon them his abundant spirit of divine love (Ps. 137, 6). She saw how worthy of mortals it is to perceive, understand and ponder the gifts that were conferred on the humility of Her, whom all nations were to call blessed, and how all the humble ones, each one according to his degree, could share the same good fortune. By one word also She expressed all the mercies, benefits and blessings, which the Almighty showered upon Her in his holy and wonderful name; for She calls them altogether "great things" since there was nothing small about anything that referred to this great Queen and Lady.

223. And as the mercies of the Most High overflowed from Mary's plenitude to the whole human race, and as She was the portal of heaven, through which they issued and continue to issue, and through which we are to enter into the participation of the Divinity; therefore She confessed, that the mercy of the Lord in regard to Her is spread out over all the generations, communicating itself to them that fear Him. And just as the infinite mercies raise up the humble and seek out those that fear God; so also the powerful arm of divine justice scatters and destroys those who are proud in the mind

of their heart, and hurls them from their thrones in order to set in their place the poor and lowly. This justice of the Lord was exercised in wonderful splendor and glory upon the chief of all the proud, Lucifer and his followers, when the almighty arm of God scattered and hurled them (because they themselves precipitated themselves) from their exalted seats which befitted their angelic natures and their graces, and which they occupied according to the original (Isaias 14; Apoc. 12) decree of the divine love. For by it He intended that all should be blessed (I Tim. 2, 4) while they, in trying to ascend in their vain pride to positions, which they neither could attain nor should aspire to, on the contrary cast themselves from those which they occupied (Isaias 14, 13). In their arrogance they were found opposed to the just and inscrutable judgments of the Lord, which scattered and cast down the proud angel and all his followers (Apoc. 12, 8). In their place were installed the humble of heart through the mediation of most holy Mary, the Mother and the treasure house of his ancient mercies.

224. For the same reason this divine Lady says and proclaims that God enriches the needy, filling them with the abundance of his treasures of grace and glory; and those that are rich in their own estimation and presumptuous arrogance, and those who satisfy their heart with the false goods, which the world esteems as riches and happiness, the Most High has banished and does banish from his presence, because they are void of the truth, which cannot enter into hearts filled and occupied with falsehood and deceit. He received his servants and his children, the people of Israel, remembering his mercies in order to teach them, wherein prudence, truth and understanding (Bar. 3, 14), wherein free and abundant life and nourishment, wherein the light of the eyes and peace consists. He taught them the way of prudence and the hidden paths of wisdom and discipline, which is

concealed from the princes of the gentiles, and is not known to the powerful, who dominate over the beasts of the earth and entertain themselves and play with the birds of the air and heap up treasures of gold and silver. Nor can the sons of Agar and the inhabitants of Ternan, who are the wise and the proudly prudent of this world, ever attain this wisdom. But to those that are sons of the light (Galat. 3, 7), and who are sons of Abraham by faith, hope and obedience, the Most High distributes it; for in this manner has it been promised to his posterity and his spiritual children, made secure by the blessed and happy Fruit of the virginal womb of the most holy Mary.

225. Saint Elisabeth looking upon Mary the Queen of creation understood these hidden mysteries; and not only those, which I am able to express here, did this fortunate matron understand, but many more and greater sacraments, which my understanding cannot comprehend; nor do I wish to dilate upon all that have been shown to me, lest I unduly extend this history. But the sweet discourses and conversations, which these two holy and discreet ladies held with each other, reminded me of the two seraphim, which Isaias saw above the throne of the Most High, repeating the divine and always new canticle: Holy, holy, etc., while they covered their head with one pair of wings, their feet with another, flew with the third pair (Isaias 6, 2). It is certain that the inflamed love of these two holy women exceeded that of all the seraphim, and Mary by Herself loved more than they all together. They were consumed in the flame of divine love, extending the two wings of their hearts in order to manifest to each other their love and in order to soar into the most exalted intelligence of the mysteries of the Most High. With two more wings of rarest knowledge they covered their faces; because both of them discussed and contemplated the sacrament of the King (Tob. 12, 7), guarding its secrets within

themselves all their lives; also because they restrained their discourse and subjected it to their devoted faith, without giving scope to proud inquisitiveness. They also covered the feet of the Lord and their own with the third pair of seraphic wings, because they were lowered and annihilated in their own humble estimation of themselves at the sight of such great Majesty. Moreover since most holy Mary enclosed within her virginal womb the God of majesty himself, we can with reason and with literal truth say, that She covered the seat where the Lord sat enthroned.

226. When it was time to come forth from their retirement, saint Elisabeth offered herself and her whole family and all her house for the service of the Queen of heaven. She asked Her to accept, as a quiet retreat, the room which she herself was accustomed to use for her prayers, and which was much retired and accommodated to that purpose. The heavenly Princess accepted the chamber with humble thanks, and made use of it for recollecting Herself and sleeping therein, and no one ever entered it, except the two cousins. As for the rest She offered to serve and assist Elisabeth as a handmaid, for She said, that this was the purpose of visiting her and consoling her. O what friendship is so true, so sweet and inseparable, as that which is formed by the great bond of the divine love! How admirable is the Lord in manifesting this great sacrament of the Incarnation to three women before He would make it known to anyone else in the human race! For the first was saint Anne, as I have said in its place; the second one was her Daughter and the Mother of the Word, most holy Mary; the third one was saint Elisabeth, and conjointly with Her, her son, for he being yet in the womb of his mother, cannot be considered as distinct from her. Thus "the foolishness of God is wiser than men," as saint Paul says.

227. The most holy Mary and Elisabeth came forth from their retirement at nightfall, having passed a long time together; and the Queen saw Zacharias standing before Her in his muteness, and She asked him for his blessing as from a priest of the Lord, which the saint also gave to Her. Yet, although She tenderly pitied him for his affliction, She did not exert her power to cure him, because She knew the mysterious occasion of his dumbness; yet She offered a prayer for him. Saint Elisabeth, who already knew the good fortune of the most chaste spouse Joseph, although he himself as yet was not aware of it, entertained and served him with great reverence and highest esteem. After staying three days in the house of Zacharias, however, he asked permission of his heavenly Spouse Mary to return to Nazareth and leave Her in the company of saint Elisabeth in order to assist her in her pregnancy. The holy husband left them with the understanding that he was to return in order to accompany the Queen home as soon as they should give him notice; saint Elisabeth offered him some presents to take home with him; but he would take only a small part of them, yielding only to their earnest solicitations, for this man of God was not only a lover of poverty, but was possessed of a magnanimous and noble heart. Therewith he pursued his way back to Nazareth, taking along with him the little beast of burden, which they had brought with them. At home, in the absence of his Spouse, he was served by a neighboring woman and cousin of his, who, also when most holy Mary was at home, was wont to come and go on the necessary errands outside of the house.

Words of the Queen

THE VIRGIN MARY SPEAKS TO SISTER MARY OF AGREDA

228. My daughter, in order that thy heart may be ever more and more inflamed with the desire of gaining the grace and friendship of God, I wish very much that thou grow in the knowledge of the dignity, excellence and happiness of a soul, that has been endowed with this privilege; however, remember that it is so admirable and of so great a value that thou canst not comprehend it, even if I would explain it to thee; and much less canst thou express it in words. Look upon the Lord and contemplate Him by means of the divine light, which thou receivest, and then thou wilt understand that the Lord performs a greater work in justifying a soul than in having created all the orbs of heaven and the whole earth with all the beauty and perfection contained within them. And if on account of the wonders which creatures are able in part to perceive in these works by the senses, they are impressed with the greatness and power of God, what would they say and think if they could see with the eyes of their soul the preciousness and beauty of grace in so many creatures, who are capable of receiving them?

229. There are no terms of human language equal to the task of expressing what participations and perfections of God are contained in sanctifying grace. It is little to say that it is more pure and spotless than the snow; more refulgent than the sun; more precious than gold or precious stones, more charming, more amiable and pleasing than all the most delightful feasts and entertainments, and more beautiful than all that in its entirety can be imagined or desired by the creatures. Take notice also of the ugliness of sin, in order that by the opposite thou mayest come to so much the better understanding of the beauty of grace; for neither darknesses, nor rottenness, nor the most horrible, the most dreadful, nor

the foulest of creatures can ever be compared to sin and to its ugliness. The martyrs and saints understood much of this mystery (Heb. 11, 36), who in order to secure the beauty of grace and preserve themselves from the ruin of sin, did not fear fire, nor wild beasts, nor the sword, nor torments, nor prisons, ignominies, pains, afflictions, nor death itself, nor prolonged and perpetual suffering; for to escape all these must be counted for little or nothing, and must scarcely be thought of in comparison with one degree of grace, which souls may attain, even though they be the most abject of the whole world. All this the men, who esteem and seek after the fugitive and apparent beauty of creatures, are ignorant of; and whatever does not present to them this deceitful beauty, is for them vile and contemptible.

230. Thou perceivest therefore something of the greatness of the blessing, which the incarnate Word conferred upon his Precursor in the womb of his mother; and because saint John recognized it, he leaped for joy and exultation in the womb of his mother. Thou wilt also see what thou thyself must do and suffer in order to attain this happiness, and in order not to lose, or in the least impair this most precious beauty by any fault, nor retard its consummation by any imperfection, no matter how small. I wish that in imitation of my cousin Elisabeth, thou do not enter into any friendship with any human creatures, except those, with whom thou canst and shouldst converse about the works of the Most High and of his mysteries, and with whom thou canst learn to pursue the true path of his divine pleasure. Although thou art engaged in important undertakings and works, do not forget or omit thy spiritual exercises and the strictness of a perfect life; for this must not only be preserved and watched over, when all things go smoothly, but also under the greatest adversity, difficulty and labor; for imperfect human nature takes occasion of the slightest circumstance to relax its vigilance.

Chapter XVIII

MOST HOLY MARY ARRANGES THE ORDER OF HER DAILY
EXERCISES IN THE HOUSE OF ZACHARIAS; SOME INCIDENTS
IN HER INTERCOURSE WITH SAINT ELISABETH.

231. When the Precursor John had been sanctified and saint
Elisabeth, his mother, had been endowed with such great
gifts and blessings, and when thus the principal object of
Mary's visit was fulfilled, the great Queen proceeded to
arrange her daily life in the house of Zacharias; for her occupations could not be uniformly the same as those She was
accustomed to in her own house. In order to direct her desire
by the guidance of the Holy Ghost She retired and placed
Herself in the presence of the Most High, asking Him as
usual to guide Her and direct Her in that which She was to
do during her stay in the house of his servants Elisabeth and
Zacharias; so that She might in all things be pleasing to Him
and fulfill entirely his pleasure. The Lord heard Her petition
and answered Her saying: "My Spouse and my Dove, I will
direct all thy actions and I will direct thy footsteps in the
fulfillment of my service and pleasure, and I will make
known to thee the day on which I wish thee to return to thy
home. In the meanwhile remain in the house of my servant
Elisabeth and converse with her. As for the rest, continue thy
exercises and prayers, especially for the salvation of men, and
pray also, that I withhold my justice in dealing with their

incessant offenses against my bounty. Conjointly with thy prayers thou shalt offer to Me the Lamb without spot (1 Pet. 1, 19) which thou bearest in thy womb and which takes away the sins of the world (John 1, 291). Let these now be thy occupations."

232. In conformity with this instruction and new mandate of the Most High, the Princess of heaven ordered all her occupations in the house of her cousin Elisabeth. She rose up at midnight in accordance with her former custom, spending the hours in the continued contemplation of the divine mysteries and giving to waking and sleep the time, which most perfectly and exactly agreed with the natural state and conditions of her body. In labor and repose She continued to receive new favors, illuminations, exaltation and caresses of the Lord. During these three months She had many visions of the Divinity, mostly abstractive in kind. More frequent still were the visions of the most holy humanity of the Word in its hypostatic union; for her virginal womb, in which She bore Him, served Her as her continual altar and sanctuary. She beheld the daily growth of that sacred body. By this experience and by the sacraments, which every day were made manifest to Her in the boundless fields of the divine power and essence, the spirit of this exalted Lady expanded to vast proportions. Many times would She have been consumed and have died by the violence of her affections, if She had not been strengthened by the power of the Lord. To these occupations, which were concealed from all, She added those, which the service and consolation of her cousin Elisabeth demanded, although She did not apply one moment more to them, than charity required. These fulfilled, She turned immediately to her solitude and recollection, where she could pour out the more freely her spirit before the Lord.

233. Not less solicitous was She to occupy Herself interiorly, while She was engaged for many hours in manual

occupations. And in all this the Precursor was so fortunate that the great Queen, with her own hands, sewed and prepared the swaddling clothes and coverlets in which he was to be wrapped and reared; for his mother Elisabeth, in her maternal solicitude and attention, had secured for saint John this good fortune, humbly asking this favor of the heavenly Queen. Mary with incredible love and subjection complied with her request in order to exercise Herself in obedience to her cousin, whom She wished to serve as the lowest handmaid; for in humility and obedience most holy Mary always surpassed all men. Although saint Elisabeth sought to anticipate Her in much that belonged to her service, yet, in her rare prudence and wisdom, Mary knew how to forestall her cousin, always gaining the triumph of humility.

234. In this regard a great and sweet competition arose between the two cousins, which was very pleasing to the Most High and wonderful in the sight of the angels; for saint Elisabeth was very solicitous and attentive in serving our Lady and great Queen, and in commanding also the same service to be rendered Her by all the inmates of the house. But She, who was the Teacher of virtues, most holy Mary, being still more attentive and eager to serve, met and diverted the anxieties of her cousin, saying: "My dear cousin, I find my consolation in being commanded and in obeying during all my life; it is not good that thy love should deprive me of the comfort I feel therein; since I am the younger one, it is proper that I serve not only thee, as my mother, but all in thy house; deal with me as with thy servant as long as I am in thy company." Saint Elisabeth answered: "My beloved Lady, it beseems much more that I obey Thee and that Thou command and direct me in all things; and this I ask of thee with greater justice. For if Thou, the Mistress, wishest to exercise humility, I on my part owe worship and reverence to my God and Lord, whom Thou bearest in thy virginal womb,

and I know that thy dignity is worthy of all honor and reverence." And the most prudent Virgin rejoined: "My Son and Lord did not choose me for his Mother, in order that I receive reverence as mistress; for his kingdom is not of this world (Joan 18, 36), nor did He come into it in order to be served; but to serve (Matth. 20, 28), and to suffer, and to teach obedience and humility to mortals (Matth. 11, 29), condemning fastidiousness and pride. Since therefore his Majesty teaches me this and the Highest calls Himself the ignominy of men (Ps, 21, 22), how can I, who am his slave and do not merit the company of creatures, consent that thou serve me, who art formed according to his image and likeness?" (Gen. 1, 27).

235. Saint Elisabeth still insisted and said: "My Mistress and Protectress, this is true for those, who do not know the sacrament which is enclosed in Thee. But I, who have without merit been informed by the Lord, will be very blamable in his eyes, if I do not give Him in Thee the veneration which is due to Him as God, and to Thee as his Mother; for it is just that I serve Both, as a slave serves his masters." To this the most holy Mary answered: "My dear sister, this reverence which thou owest and desirest to give, is due to the Lord, whom I bear within my womb, for He is the true and highest Good and our Redeemer. But as far as I am concerned, who am a mere creature and among creatures only a poor worm, look upon me as I am in myself, although thou shouldst adore the Creator, who chose my poor self as his dwelling. By his divine enlightenment thou shalt give unto God, what is due to Him, and allow me to perform that which pertains to me, namely to serve and to be below all. This I ask of Thee for my consolation and in the name of the Lord, whom I bear within me."

236. In such blessed and happy contentions most holy Mary and her cousin Elisabeth passed some of their time. But

the divine prudence of our Queen caused in Her such an alertness and ingenuity in matters concerning humility and obedience, that She never failed to find means and ways of obeying and of being commanded. However, during all the time in which She stayed with saint Elisabeth, all this was done in such a way that both according to their condition treated with the highest respect the sacrament of the King which had been entrusted to their knowledge, and which was deposited in the most holy Mary. This high respect in Mary was such as befitted the Mother and the Mistress of all virtue and grace, and in Elisabeth, such as was worthy of the prudent matron, so highly enlightened by the holy Spirit. By this light she wisely directed her behavior in regard to the Mother of God, yielding to her wishes and obeying Her in whatever she could, and at the same time reverencing her dignity, and in it, her Creator. In her inmost heart she made the intention that if she were obliged to give any command to the Mother of God, she would do it only in order to obey and satisfy her wishes; and whenever she did it, she asked permission and pardon of the Lord, at the same time never ordering anything by direct command, but always by request; and she would use greater earnestness only in such things as were conducive to Mary's convenience, as for instance, that She take some sleep or nourishment. She also asked Mary to make a few articles for her with her own hands; Mary complied, but saint Elisabeth never made use of them, except to preserve them with the greatest veneration.

237. In this way most holy Mary put into practice the doctrine of the eternal Word who humiliated Himself so far, that, being the form of the eternal Father, the figure of his substance, true God of the true God, He nevertheless assumed the form and condition of a servant (Heb. I, 3, Philip 2, 6, 7). This Lady was the Mother of God, Queen of all creation, superior in excellence and dignity to all creatures,

and yet She remained the humble servant of the least of them; and never would She accept homage and service as if due to Her, nor did She ever exalt Herself, or fail to judge of Herself in the most humble manner. What shall we now say of our most execrable presumption and pride? Since, full of the abomination of sin, we are so senseless as to claim for ourselves with dreadful insanity the homage and veneration of all the world? And if this is denied us, we quickly lose the little sense which our passions have left us. This whole heavenly history bears the stamp of humility, and is a condemnation of our pride. And since it is not my office to teach or correct, but to be taught and to be corrected, I beseech and pray all the faithful children of light to place this example before their eyes for our humiliation.

238. It would not have been difficult for the Lord to preserve his most holy Mother from such extreme lowliness and from the occasions in which She embraced it; He could have exalted Her before creatures, ordaining that She be renowned, honored and respected by all; just as He knew how to procure homage and renown for others as Assuerus did for Mardocheus. Perhaps, if this had been left to the judgment of men, they would have so managed that a Woman more holy than an the hierarchies of heaven, and who bore in her womb the Creator of the angels and of the heavens, should be surrounded by a continual guard of honor, withdrawn from the gaze of men and receiving the homage of all the world; it would have seemed to them unworthy of Her to engage in humble and servile occupations, or not to have all things done only at her command, or to refuse homage, or not to exercise fullest authority. So narrow is human wisdom, if that can be called wisdom, which is so limited. But such fallacy cannot creep into the true science of the saints, which is communicated to them by the infinite wisdom of the Creator, and which esteems at their just weight and price these

honors without confounding the values of the creatures. The Most High would have denied his beloved Mother much and benefited Her little, if He had deprived and withdrawn from Her the occasion of exercising the profoundest humility and had instead exposed Her to the exterior applause of men. It would also be a great loss to the world to be without this school of humility and this example for the humiliation and confusion of its pride.

239. From the time of her receiving the Lord as her Guest in her house, though yet in the womb of the Virgin Mother, the holy Elisabeth was much favored by God. By the continued conversation and the familiar intercourse with the heavenly Queen in proportion as she grew in the knowledge and understanding of the mysteries of the Incarnation, this great matron advanced in all manner of sanctity, as one who draws it from its very fountain. A few times She merited to see most holy Mary during her prayers, ravished and raised from the ground and altogether filled with divine splendor and beauty, so that she could not have looked upon her face, nor remain alive in her presence, if she had not been strengthened by divine power. On these occasions, and at others whenever she could be witness of them without attracting the attention of most holy Mary, she prostrated herself and knelt in her presence, and adored the incarnate Word in the virginal temple of the most holy Mother. All the mysteries which became known to her by the divine light and by the intercourse with the great Queen, saint Elisabeth sealed up in her bosom, being a most faithful depositary and prudent secretary of that which was confided to her. Only with her son John and with Zacharias, during the short time in which he lived after the birth of his son, saint Elisabeth conversed to some extent concerning those sacraments which had become known to all. But in all this she acted as a courageous, wise and very holy woman.

Words of the Queen

THE VIRGIN MARY SPEAKS TO SISTER MARY OF AGREDA

240. My daughter, the favors of the Most High and the knowledge of his divine mysteries, in the attentive souls, engender a kind of love and esteem of humility, which raises them up with a strong and sweet force, like that which causes fire to ascend, like the gravity which causes a stone to fall, each of them striving to reach its own and natural sphere. This is done by the true light, which places the creature in the possession of a clear knowledge of its own self and attributes the graces to the proper source, whence all perfect things come (James 1, 17); and thus it brings all things into correct balance. And this is the most proper order of right reason which overthrows and as it were exerts violence against the false presumption of mortals. On account of this presumption of pride the heart, wherein it lives, cannot strive after contempt, nor bear it, nor can it suffer a superior over itself, and is offended even at equals; it violently opposes all in order to place itself alone above all fellow creatures. But the humble heart is abased in proportion to the benefits it received, and in its interior quietly grows a desire or an ardent hunger for self-abasement and for the last place; it is violently disturbed in not finding itself esteemed as the inferior of all and in being deprived of humiliation.

241. In me, my dearest, thou wilt find exhibited the practical application of this doctrine; since none of the favors and blessings, which the right hand of the Most High lavished upon me, were insignificant. Yet never was my heart inflated with presumption above itself (Ps. 110, 1), nor did it ever know anything else than to desire to be abased and occupy the last place among all creatures. The imitation of this I desire especially of thee; let thy ambition be to take the last place, to live in subjection to all others; abased and consid-

ered as useless, in the presence of the Lord and of men, thou must judge thyself as less than the dust of the earth itself. Thou canst not deny, that in no generation has anyone been more favored than thou, and no one has merited these favors less than thou. How then wilt thou make any return for this great debt of gratitude if thou dost not humiliate thyself below all others and more than all the sons of Adam; and if thou dost not awaken within thyself exalted and loving sentiments concerning humility? It is good to obey the prelates and instructors, therefore do it always. But I desire that thou go much farther, and that thou obey the most insignificant of thy fellow beings in all that is not sinful, and in such a way, as if thou wert obeying the highest of thy superiors; and I desire that in this matter thou be very earnest, as I was during my earthly life.

242. Thou must, however, be circumspect in regard to the obedience to thy inferiors, so that they may not, knowing of thy anxiousness to obey in all things, seek to induce thee to obey in things unseemly and unbecoming. Thou canst do much good by giving them the good and orderly example of obedience, without causing them to lose any of their subjection and without derogating from thy authority as their superioress. If any disagreeable accident or injury should happen, which affects thee alone, accept it gladly, without so much as moving thy lips in self defense, or making any complaints. Whatever is an injury to God do thou reprehend without mixing up any of thy own grievances with those of his Majesty; for thou shouldst never find any cause for self defense, but always be ready to defend the honor of God. But neither in the one nor the other, allow thyself to be moved by disorderly anger and passion. I wish also, that thou use great prudence in hiding and concealing the favors of the Lord, for the sacrament of the King is not to be lightly manifested (Tob. 12, 7), nor are carnal men capable or worthy of the

mysteries of the Holy Ghost (I Cor. 2, 14). In all things imitate and follow me, since thou wishest to be my beloved daughter; this thou wilt attain by obeying me and thou wilt induce the Almighty to strengthen and direct thy footsteps to that which I desire to accomplish in thee. Do not resist Him, but dispose and prepare thy heart sweetly and quickly to obey his light and grace. Let grace not be void in thee (II Cor. 6, 1), but labor diligently and let thy actions be performed in all perfection.

Chapter XIX

OF SOME CONVERSATIONS, WHICH MOST HOLY MARY HELD WITH HER ANGELS IN THE HOUSE OF SAINT ELISABETH, AND OF OTHERS, WHICH SHE HELD WITH HER COUSIN.

243. The plenitude of the wisdom and grace of most holy Mary, being of such immense capacity, could not remain idle at any point of time, nor in any place or occasion. For it gave forth the plenitude of all perfection; active at all times and seasons to the fullest extent of duty and possibility, without ever falling short of the holiest and the most excellent in virtue. And as in all places She acted the part of a pilgrim on earth and of an inhabitant of heaven, and as She herself was the intellectual and most glorious heaven, the living temple, in which God himself had made his habitation; so She also carried with Her her own oratory and sanctuary and in this respect there was for Her no difference between her own house and that of her cousin saint Elisabeth, nor could any other place, time or occupation be a hindrance to Her in this regard. She was placed above all things and without any outside claim She incessantly devoted Herself to the influence of the love, which was continually in her sight. Yet at the same time She conversed with the creatures at opportune times and treated with them according as occasion required, giving as much attention to them, as the most prudent

Mistress could fittingly spare for each in particular. And as her most frequent conversings during the three months, in which She remained in the house of Zacharias, were with saint Elisabeth and with the holy angels of her guard, I shall relate in this chapter something of that which formed the subject of her conferences with them, and also mention other things, which happened in her intercourse with the saint.

244. When She was left alone and free to Herself our heavenly Princess passed many hours ravished and elevated in divine contemplations and visions. Sometimes during these trances, sometimes outside of them, She was accustomed to converse with her angels about the sacraments and mysteries of her interior love. One day, soon after She had arrived at the house of Zacharias, She spoke to them in the following manner: "Heavenly spirits, my guardians and companions, ambassadors of the Most High and luminaries of his Divinity, come and strengthen my heart, which is captured and wounded by his divine love; for it is afflicted with its own limitations in that it cannot properly respond to the obligations which are known to it and which dictate its desires. Come, ye supernal princes, and praise with me the admirable name of the Lord and let us magnify his holy judgments and operations. Help this poor little worm to praise its Maker, who condescends kindly to look upon its insignificance. Let us talk of the wonders of my Spouse; let us discuss the beauty of my Lord, of my beloved Son! Let my heart find relief in uniting its inmost aspirations to your own, my friends and companions; for you do know the secrets of my Treasure, which the Lord has deposited within me in the narrowness of so fragile and constrained a vase. Great are these sacraments and admirable these mysteries; and I contemplate them with sweet affection, but their supernal greatness overwhelms me, the profundity and the greatness of my love overpowers me even while they inflame my heart. In the ardor of my soul I

cannot rest satisfied and I find no repose; for my desires surpass all that I can accomplish and my obligations are greater than my desires; I am dissatisfied with myself, because I do not exert myself as much as I desire, because I do not desire to accomplish as much as I should, and because I find myself continually falling short and vanquished by the greatness of the returns which are due. Ye heavenly seraphim, listen to my loving anxieties; I am fallen sick with love (Cant 2, 5). Open to me your bosoms, whence the beauty of my God is flashed forth, in order that the splendors of his light and the visions of his loveliness may replenish the life, which wastes away in his love."

245. "Mother of our Creator and our Mistress," answered the holy angels, "Thou possessest truly the Almighty and our highest Good. Since Thou hast Him so closely bound to Thee and art his true Spouse and Mother, rejoice in Him and keep Him with Thee for all eternity. Thou art the Spouse and the Mother of the God of love, and as in Thee is the only cause and fountain of life, no one shall live with Him as Thou, our Queen and Mistress. But do not seek to find repose in a love so inflamed; for thy state and condition of a pilgrim do not permit thy love to attain the repose of perfect consummation, nor will it cease to aspire to new and greater increase of merit and triumph. Thy obligations surpass without comparison those of all the nations; but they are to increase and grow continually; never will thy so vastly inflamed love equal its Object, since It is eternal and infinite and without measure in its perfection; Thou shalt always be happily vanquished by its greatness; for no one can comprehend It; only He himself comprehends Himself and loves Himself in the measure, in which He deserves to be loved. Eternally, o Lady, shalt Thou find in Him more to desire and more to love, since that is required by the essence of his greatness and of our beatitude."

246. In these colloquies and conferences the fire of divine love was more and more enkindled in the heart of most holy Mary; in Her was exactly fulfilled the command of the Lord (Levit. 6, 12), that in his tabernacle and on his altar should burn continually the fire of the holocaust and that the priest of the ancient law should see to its perpetual nourishment and maintenance. This precept was executed to the letter in the most holy Mary, for in Her were jointly contained the altar and the new Highpriest, Christ our Lord, who nourished and augmented its flame day by day, by administering new material in favors, blessings, graces and communications of his Divinity; while the exalted Lady on her part, contributed her ceaseless exertions, which were ineffably enhanced in value by the continual flow of the graces and sanctity of the Lord. From the moment in which this Lady entered into the world, this conflagration of his divine love took its rise, in order never to be extinguished on this altar through all the eternities of God himself. For as lasting as this eternity and as continuous was and will be the fire of this living sanctuary.

247. At other times She spoke and conversed with the holy angels, when they appeared to Her in human forms, as I have said in several places. Most frequently this conversation turned about the mystery of the incarnate Word; and in this She manifested so profound a knowledge in citing the holy Scriptures and the Prophets that She caused wonder even in the angels. On one occasion in speaking to them of these venerable sacraments, She said: "My lords, servants of the Most High and his friends, my heart is pierced and torn by arrows of grief, when I meditate on what the sacred Scriptures say of my most holy Son or what Isaias and Jeremias wrote (Gen. 22, 2; Isai. 33, 2; Jerem. 11, 18) concerning the most bitter pains and torments in store for Him. Solomon says (Wis. 2, 20), that they shall condemn Him to a most ignominious death and the Prophets always speak in weighty

and superlative terms of his Passion and Death, which all are to be fulfilled in Him. O were it the will of his Majesty that I live at that time in order to offer myself to die instead of the Author of my life! My soul is sorely afflicted in the consideration of these infallible truths and that my God and my Lord should come forth from my womb only in order to suffer. O who will guard Him and defend Him against his enemies! O tell me, ye heavenly princes, by what services or by what means can I induce the eternal Father to divert the rigor of his justice upon me, in order that the Innocent, who cannot have any guilt upon Him, may be freed from punishment? Well do I know that in order to satisfy the infinite God for the offenses of men, the satisfaction of the incarnate God is required; but by his first act my most holy Son has merited more than all the human race can lose or demerit by its offenses. Since this is sufficient, tell me, is it not possible that I die in order to relieve Him from his death and torments? My humble desires will not be annoying to my God, and my anxieties will not be displeasing to Him. Yet, what am I saying? And to what lengths do sorrow and love drive me, since I must be subject in all things to the divine will and its perfect fulfillment?"

248. Such and like colloquy the most holy Mary held with her angels, especially during the time of her pregnancy. The holy spirits met all her anxieties and comforted her with great reverence, consoling Her by renewing the memory of the very sacraments, which She already knew and by reminding Her of the reasonableness and propriety of the death of Christ for the salvation of the human race, for the conquest of the demons and spoliation of their power, for the glory of the eternal Father and the exaltation of the most holy and highest Lord his Son (Tim. 2, 14). So great and exalted were the mysteries touched upon in these discourses of the Queen with the holy angels, that neither can the human tongue

describe, nor our capacity comprehend them in this life. When we shall enjoy the Lord we shall see what we cannot at present conceive. From this little which I have said, our piety can help us to draw conclusions in regard to others much greater.

249. Saint Elisabeth was likewise much versed and enlightened in the divine Scriptures, and much more so since the Visitation; and therefore our Queen conversed with Her concerning these heavenly mysteries, which were known and understood by the matron, instructing and enlightening her by heavenly teachings; for through her intercession Elisabeth was enriched with many blessings and gifts of heaven. Many times she wondered at the profound wisdom of the Mother of God, and blessed Her over and over again, saying: "Blessed art Thou, my Mistress and Mother of my Lord, among all womankind (Luke 1, 42); and may the nations know and magnify thy dignity. Most fortunate art Thou on account of the rich Treasure, which Thou bearest in thy virginal womb. I tender to Thee my humble and most affectionate congratulations for the joy with which thy spirit shall be filled, when Thou shalt hold in thy arms the Son of justice and nurse Him at thy virginal breasts. Remember me thy servant, O Lady, in that hour and offer my heart in sacrifice to thy most holy Son, my true and incarnate God. O who shall merit to serve Thee from now on and attend upon Thee! But if I am unworthy of this good fortune, may I enjoy that of being borne in thy heart; for I fear (not without cause) that mine will be torn asunder, when I must part from Thee." Many other sentiments of sweetest and most tender love saint Elisabeth uttered in her personal intercourse with the most holy Mary; and the most prudent Lady consoled her, strengthened and enlivened her by her divinely efficacious reasonings. These so exalted and heavenly dealings of Mary were diversified by many other acts of humility and

self-abasement in serving not only her cousin Elisabeth, but also the servants of her house. Whenever She could find an occasion, She swept the house of her relative, and always her oratory at regular times; and with the servants She washed the dishes, and performed other acts of profound humility. Let no one think it strange that I particularize in these small matters; for the greatness of our Queen has made them of importance for our instruction and in order that knowing of them, our pride may vanish and our vileness may come to shame. When saint Elisabeth learnt of the humble services, performed by the Mother of piety, She was deeply moved and tried to prevent them; and therefore the heavenly Lady concealed them from her cousin wherever it was possible.

250. O Queen and Mistress of heaven and earth, my Protectress and Advocate, although Thou art the Teacher of all sanctity and perfection, lost in astonishment at thy humility, I dare, O my Mother, to ask Thee: how was it possible that, knowing of the Onlybegotten of the Father within thy virginal womb, and wishing in all things to conduct Thyself as his Mother, thy greatness should abase itself to such lowliness, as sweeping the floor and similar occupations; since, according to our notions, Thou couldst, on account of the reverence due to thy most holy Son, easily have excused Thyself without failing against the duties of thy most perfect Motherhood. My desire is, O Lady, to understand how thy Majesty was governed in this matter.

Words of the Queen

THE VIRGIN MARY SPEAKS TO SISTER MARY OF AGREDA

251. My daughter, in order to solve thy difficulty more explicitly than as already noted down in the foregoing chapter, thou must remember that no occupation or exterior act pertaining to virtue, no matter how lowly it may be, can, if it

is well-ordered, impede the worship, reverence and exaltation of the Creator of all things; for these acts of virtue do not exclude one another; but they are all compatible with one another in the creature, and much more in me, who lived in the continual presence of the highest Good without ever losing It out of sight by exterior activity. Labored and re-membered God in all my actions, referring them all to his greater glory; and the Lord himself, who orders and creates all things, despises none of them, nor is He offended, or irritated by their smallness. The soul that loves Him, is not disconcerted by any of these little things in his divine pres-ence; for it seeks and finds Him as the beginning and the end of all creatures. And because terrestrial creatures cannot exist without these humble performances and without others that are inseparable from our lowly condition and the preserva-tion of our nature, it is necessary to understand this doctrine well, in order that we may be governed by it. For if we engage in these thoughts and occupations without reference to their Creator, they will cause many and great interruptions in the practice of virtue and in our merits, as well as in the right use of interior advantages. Our whole life will be blameworthy and full of reprehensible defects, little removed from the earthliness of creatures.

252. According to this doctrine thou must so regulate thy terrestrial occupations, whatever they may be, that thou do not lose thy time, which can never be recovered. Whether thou eat, labor, rest, sleep, or watch, in all times and places, and in all occupations, adore, reverence and look upon thy great and powerful Lord, who fills all things and conserves all things (I Cor. 10, 3; Matth. 11, 29). I wish also that thou pay special attention to that which moved and incited me most to perform all acts of humility; namely, the thought that my divine Son came in the guise of humility in order to teach the world this virtue in word and example, to inculcate

the hate of vanity and pride and rooting out its seed sown by Lucifer among mortals in the first sin. His Majesty gave me such a deep knowledge of how much He is pleased with this virtue, that in order to be allowed to perform only one of the acts mentioned by thee, such as sweeping the floor or kissing the feet of the poor, I would have been ready to suffer the greatest torments of the world. Thou wilt never find words to express the love for humility which I had, nor to describe its excellence and nobility. In the Lord thou wilt know and understand what thou canst not describe in words.

253. But write this doctrine in thy heart and observe it as the rule of thy life; continue to exercise thyself in the contempt of all things belonging to human vanity, and esteem them as odious and execrable in the eyes of the Most High. But in connection with this humility of thy life, let thy thoughts always be of the noblest and thy conversation in heaven and with the angelic spirits (Philip 3, 20) ; deal with them and converse with them in order to obtain new light concerning the Divinity and the mysteries of Christ my most holy Son. With creatures let thy intercourse be such as will continually increase thy fervor and serve thee as means of advancing and profiting by means of humility and divine love. In thy own mind assume the lowest place beneath all creatures, so that when the occasion and the time of exercising the acts of humility arrive, thou mayest be found prompt and willing to exercise them. Only then wilt thou be the mistress of the passions, if first thou hast acknowledged thyself in thy heart as the least and weakest and most useless of all the creatures.

Chapter XX

SOME SPECIAL FAVORS WHICH MOST HOLY MARY CON
FERRED UPON SEVERAL PERSONS IN THE HOUSE OF ZACH
ARIAS.

254. It is a well known quality of love to be active as the fire
in works of kindness, wherever it finds occasion; and this is
especially true of the fire of spiritual love; for it will reach out
in search of material, as soon as this falls short. The Master
has taught lovers of God so many ways and methods of
pursuing virtue, that there is no need of remaining idle. And
as love is not blind nor insane, it knows well the qualities of
the noble object it aims at. Its only concern is that not all
men love it properly; and thus it seeks to communicate this
love without strife or envy. We know that the love of all the
other saints, though most fervent and holy, appears limited
in comparison with that of most holy Mary. Yet if their love
is admirable and powerful, inciting them to vast works of zeal
for souls, what immense works then must not the love this
great Queen have accomplished for the benefit of her fellowmen, since She was the Mother of the divine love (Eccli,
24, 24), and since She carried with her the true and living
fire that was to enkindle the world? (Luke 12, 49). Let all the
mortals learn from this heavenly history how much they owe
to the love of this Lady. Although it will be impossible to
notice all the particular instances of the benefits conferred on

the souls by Her, nevertheless, in order that from some of them, many more may be inferred, I will relate a few that our Queen conferred while in the house of her cousin Elisabeth.

255. One of the servants in that house was of perverse inclination, restless, subject to anger, and accustomed to swear and curse. With all these vices and disorders, she still knew how to make herself agreeable to her masters, but at the same time she was so given over to the power of the demon that this tyrant could easily induce her to throw herself into all sorts of miseries and mistakes. For fourteen years many devils surrounded and accompanied her without intermission in order to make certain the capture of her soul. Only when this woman came into the presence of the Mistress of heaven, most holy Mary, these enemies withdrew; for, as I have said in other places, the virtue issuing from our Queen tormented them, and especially during that time when She carried within her virginal repository the powerful God and Lord of all virtues. As on the one hand this woman was freed from her cruel exactors, being released from the evil influences of their company, and as on the other hand she experienced within her the beneficial effects of the sweet vision and intercourse of the Queen, she began to be much attracted and moved toward Mary and she sought to be in her presence and offered to serve Her with much affection, striving to pass all the time possible with Her and watching Her with reverence; for among her distorted inclinations she had also a good one, which was a natural kindness and compassion for the needy and the humble, so that she was naturally drawn toward them and ready to do them good.

256. The heavenly Princess, who saw and knew all the inclinations of this woman, the state of her conscience, the danger of her soul and the malice of the demons against her, turned upon her an eye of mercy and watched her with the love of a mother. Although her Majesty knew that the com-

pany and the interference of the demons was a just punishment for the sins of this woman, yet She interceded for her
and obtained for her pardon, remedy and salvation. She
commanded the demons, in virtue of the authority conceded
to Her, to leave this creature and not dare to disturb her or
molest her thenceforth. As they could not resist the sway of
our great Queen, they yielded and fled in highest consternation, not knowing how to account for such power of the
most holy Mary. They conferred about it in astonishment
and indignation, saying: "Who' is this Woman, that exerts
such dominion over us? Whence does such strange power
come, which enables Her to perform all that She wishes?"
The demons therefore conceived new wrath and indignation
against Her, who had crushed their heads (Gen. 3, 15). The
happy woman, however, was snatched from their claws.
Mary admonished her, corrected her, and taught her the way
of salvation, and changed her into a woman of kind and
meek disposition. She persevered therein during all her life,
being well aware, that all this had come to her through the
hands of our Queen; although she did not know nor penetrate into the mystery of her dignity, she remained humbly
thankful and lived a holy life.

257. Not in a better state than this servant was another
woman living in the neighborhood of the house of Zacharias,
who as a neighbor was wont to come and listen to the conversation of the family of saint Elisabeth. She lived a licen-
tious life, far from honorable, and when she heard of the
arrival of our great Queen in that town, of her modesty and
retirement, she spoke of Her lightly and with some curiosity:
"Who is this Stranger, that has come as a guest of our neighbors, and who gives Herself such holy and recollected airs?"
In the vain and inquisitive desire of spying out novelty, as is
customary with such kind of people, she managed to get
sight of the heavenly Lady and scrutinized her dress and her

countenance. Her intention was impertinent and presumptuous; but far different the effect: for having succeeded in scrutinizing most holy Mary, she left with a wounded heart: the presence and the sight of the Queen transformed her into a new woman. Her inclinations were altogether changed, and without knowing by what efficacious influence the change came about, she felt its power and began to shed abundant floods of tears in deep felt sorrow for her sins. Merely on account of having fixed her attentive gaze in curiosity upon the Mother of virginal purity, this happy woman received in return the love of chastity and was freed from the sensual habits and inclinations of her former life. In that very hour she sorrowfully retired to weep over her wicked life. Whenever later on she desired to converse with the Mother of grace, her Highness, in order to confirm her, permitted it. For as Mary knew what had happened and as She bore within Her the origin of grace, the Sanctifier and Justifier by whose power She fulfilled her office of Advocate of sinners She received her with maternal kindness, admonished and instructed her in virtue, dismissing her strengthened and confirmed for perseverance in her new life.

258. In this manner our great Lady performed many works and caused many admirable conversions in a great number of souls; although it was done in silence and hidden to all. The whole family of saint Elisabeth and Zacharias were sanctified by her intercourse and conversation, Those who were just, experienced new increase of gifts and favors; those that were not, She justified and enlightened by her intercession; all of them were captured by reverential love of Her so completely, that each one strove to obey Her and acknowledge Her as mother, as protectress and as a consolation in all their necessities. The mere privilege of seeing Her, without any words, was sufficient to produce all these effects; yet She was careful not to omit whatever seemed necessary to

obtain this end. As She penetrated the secrets of all hearts and knew the state of each one's conscience, She knew how to apply the opportune medicine. Sometimes, not always, the Lord manifested to Her the final end of those She met: informing Her, which were chosen and which were reprobate, predestined for happiness or foreknown as damned. At sight of both one and the other her heart broke forth in admirable flashes of most perfect virtue: for when She knew of any that were just and predestined, She bestowed upon them many blessings, which She also does now in heaven, and the Lord looked with favor upon her beneficence. Exerting incredible and prayerful diligence She asked Him to preserve them in his grace and friendship. Whenever She saw anyone in sin, She asked from the bottom of her heart for his justification and ordinarily She also obtained it. But if it happened to be one of the reprobate, She wept bitterly and humiliated Herself in the presence of the Most High for the loss of that image and work of the Divinity; She redoubled her heartfelt prayers, offerings and humiliations in order that no others might damn themselves, and her whole being was one flame of divine love, which never rested nor reposed in accomplishing great things.

Words of the Queen

THE VIRGIN MARY SPEAKS TO SISTER MARY OF AGREDA

259. My dearest daughter, within two limits, as if within two extremes, all the harmony of thy powers and wishes must move. They are: to preserve thyself in the grace and friendship of God, and to seek the same good fortune for others. In this let all thy life and activity be consumed. For such high purpose I wish that thou spare no labor, beseeching the Lord and offering thyself in sacrifice unto death, accepting actually all that is opportune and possible. Although, in order to

solicit the good of souls, thou need not make any great ado before creatures, since that is not appropriate to thy sex; yet thou must seek and prudently apply all the hidden means, that are most efficacious within thy knowledge. If thou wilt be my daughter and a spouse of my most holy Son, consider that the possessions of our house are the rational creatures, which He acquired as a rich prize at the cost of his life (I Cor. 6, 20) and of his blood; for through their own disobedience they were lost to Him (Gen. 3, 6), after He had created and selected them for Himself.

260. Hence whenever the Lord sends to thee, or throws in thy way, a needy soul and makes thee aware of its state, labor faithfully to assist it. Pray and weep with heartfelt and fervent love, that God may furnish the remedy for such great and dangerous evil, and do not neglect any means, divine or human, as far as thou art concerned, in order to obtain the salvation of eternal life for the soul entrusted to thee. By means of the prudence and moderation which I have taught thee, thou must not grow weary in admonishing, nor in praying for that which will benefit that soul; and in all secrecy continue thy labor in its behalf. Likewise I wish, that whenever it is necessary, thou command the demons in the powerful name of the Almighty and my own, to depart and leave in peace the souls oppressed by them; and as all this is to be done in secret, thou canst in all propriety animate and encourage thyself to this kind of work. Remember that the Lord has placed thee, and will place thee in a position to exercise this doctrine. Do not forget it, nor fail in understanding, how much thou art bounden to his Majesty to use care and solicitude in extending the possessions of thy Father's house. Do not rest until thou accustom thyself to do this with all diligence (Phil. 4, 13). Fear not, for thou canst do all in Him that strengthens thee; and his power will strengthen thy arm to do great things (Prov. 31,27).

Chapter XXI

SAINT ELISABETH ASKS THE QUEEN OF HEAVEN TO ASSIST
AT HER CONFINEMENT AND IS ENLIGHTENED CONCERN-
ING THE BIRTH OF JOHN.

261. Already two months had passed since the coming of the
Princess of heaven into the house of holy Elisabeth; and the
discreet matron was even now filled with grief at the thought
of the departure and of the absence of the Mistress of the
world. She dreaded the loss of so great a blessing as her
presence was, and with reason, since she knew, that it could
not come within the range of human merits; in her holy
humility she scrutinized her heart, fearing lest any fault of
hers might be the cause of the setting of that beautiful moon
and of the Sun of justice within the virginal Womb. Sometimes She wept and sighed in private, because she could find
no means of prolonging their stay, which had shed much
clear light of grace in her soul. She asked the Lord with many
tears to inspire her Cousin, the most holy Lady Mary, not to
forsake her; at least, not to withdraw so soon her sweet
company. She served Her with great reverence and solicitude
and studied to oblige Her. It is no wonder, that so saintly,
attentive and prudent a woman should ask for that which
even the angels coveted. For in addition to the divine light,
which she had received from the Holy Ghost concerning the
supreme dignity and sanctity of the Virgin Mother, she had

the personal experience of her most sweet intercourse and conversation, and all this combined had ravished her heart, so that without divine aid, she could not have survived the parting, after once having known and conversed with the blessed Lady.

262. In order to find some consolation, saint Elisabeth resolved to open her heart to the heavenly Lady, who was, however, not ignorant of her sorrow; and she said to Her in great submission and humility: "Cousin, dear Lady, on account of the respect and consideration, with which I am bound to serve Thee, I have not until now dared to speak of my desire and of the sorrow in my heart; give me now the permission to relieve it by making them known. The Lord has condescended in his mercy to send Thee hither, in order that I might have the unmerited blessing of conversing with Thee and of knowing the mysteries, which his divine Providence has entrusted to Thee, my Mistress. Unworthy I am to praise Him eternally for this favor (Dan. 3, 53). Thou art the living temple of his glory, the ark of the Testament, containing the Manna, which is the food of the angels (Heb. 9, 4). Thou art the tablet of the true law, written in his own Being (Ps. 77,25). I appreciate in my lowliness how rich his Majesty has made me, that without my merit I should entertain in my own house the Treasure of heaven and Her, whom He has chosen as his Mother among all women. I justly fear that I displease Thee and the Fruit of thy womb by my sins, and that therefore thou wilt forsake thy slave, withdrawing the great blessing, which I now enjoy. Possibly, if it be thy pleasure, I might have the happiness of serving Thee and remaining with Thee all the rest of my life. If it is a hardship for Thee to return to thy dwelling, it will be most convenient for Thee to stay in my house. I f Thou wilt call thy holy spouse Joseph and live with him here as my masters, I will serve you with affectionate readiness of heart. Although I do

not merit what I ask, I beseech Thee-not to despise my humble petition, since the Lord can surpass by his mercies all my merits and desires."

263. The most holy Mary heard with sweetest complacency the petition of her cousin Elisabeth and answered her: "Dearest friend of my soul, thy holy wishes are acceptable in the eyes of the Most High. I also thank thee from my heart; but in all our undertakings and resolves it is necessary that we conform to the divine will and entirely subject ourselves to it. Although this is the duty of all creatures, thou knowest, that it is my duty before all others, since by the power of his arm He has raised me from the dust and in boundless love has looked upon me (Luke 1,53). All my words and movements must be guided by the divine will of my Lord and Son and I must not desire anything except what is according to his pleasure. Let us present to his Majesty thy desires, and whatever He in his goodness shall ordain, that let us execute. I must also obey my spouse Joseph, for without his order and consent, I can neither decide upon my occupations, nor upon my dwellingplace; it is just, my dearest, that we obey our superiors."

264. Saint Elisabeth yielded to the persuasive words of the Princess of heaven and answered with humble submission: "My Lady, I am ready to obey thy will and revere thy teaching. I wish only once more to commend to Thee my sincere affection and heartfelt devotion to thy service. If my wishes cannot be fulfilled and are contrary to the will of God, I desire at least, if possible, that Thou, my Queen, do not forsake me until my son shall come forth to the light; in order that, just as within my womb he has adored and recognized his Redeemer in thy own, so he may enjoy his divine presence and enlightenment before any other creature and that he may receive thy blessing for the first advances in life (Prov. 16, 9) by the presence of Him, who is to direct his

footsteps. And do Thou, the Mother of grace, present Him to the Creator and obtain from his goodness the perseverance in that grace, which he received at the sound of thy sweetest voice, when it carne to my unworthy ears. Let me behold my child in thy arms, where the God, who made and preserves heaven and earth, is likewise to rest (Is. 42, 5). Let not thy maternal kindness be strained or diminished by my sins; deny not this consolation to me, nor to my son this great happiness, which as a mother I ask and unworthily desire for him."

265. Most holy Mary did not wish to refuse and She promised to pray the Lord for the fulfillment of this request of her cousin, asking her at the same time to unite her prayers with hers in order to know his most holy will. Accordingly the two mothers of the two most holy Sons born into the world betook themselves to the oratory of the heavenly Princess and presented their petitions to the Most High. Most pure Mary fell into an ecstasy, wherein She was enlightened anew concerning the mysterious life and the dignity of the Precursor and concerning his work in preparing the hearts of men for the reception of their Redeemer and Teacher, and She made known to saint Elisabeth these sacraments in as far as it was proper. She was informed of the great sanctity of her saintly cousin, also, that she had only a short while to live and that Zacharias would die before her. The kind Mother lovingly besought the Lord to assist her at her death and to fulfill her wishes in regard to her son. In regard to the other fond desires, the most prudent Virgin made no request, for in her heavenly wisdom She immediately saw, that to live always in the house of her cousin was not advisable, nor according to the will of the Most High.

266. To these petitions his Majesty answered: "My Spouse and my Dove, it is my pleasure that thou assist and console my servant Elisabeth at her childbirth, which is to be

very soon; for there are only eight days left before that event. After her son shall be circumcised, thou shalt return to thy home with thy spouse Joseph. After his birth thou shalt offer to Me my servant John in pleasing sacrifice; and continue, my Beloved, to pray to Me for the salvation of souls." Saint Elisabeth united her prayers with those of the Queen of heaven and earth, beseeching the Lord to command his Mother and Spouse not to forsake her during her confinement. During this prayer the Lord revealed to her, that her confinement was close at hand, and informed her also of many other things for her relief and consolation in her anxiety.

267. Most holy Mary issued from her trance and, having finished their prayer, the two mothers conferred upon the nearness of the confinement of saint Elisabeth as made known to them by the Lord; and anxious to make sure of her good fortune, the holy matron asked our Queen:

"My Lady, pray tell me, whether I shall have the happiness of thy assistance at my impending confinement?" Her majesty answered: "My beloved cousin, the Most High has heard our prayers and deigned to command me to assist on that occasion. This I will do, not only remaining till then, but also until the circumcision of thy child, which will take place in fifteen days." At this resolve of the most holy Mary the joy of her cousin was renewed; she acknowledged this great favor in humble thankfulness to the Lord and to the holy Queen. Thus rejoiced and enlivened by mutual conferences, the holy matron began to prepare for the birth of her son and for the departure of her exalted Cousin.

Words of the Queen

THE VIRGIN MARY SPEAKS TO SISTER MARY OF AGREDA

268. My daughter, whenever our desires arise from loving affection and are accompanied by a good intention, the Most High is not offended at our making them known, as long as it is done with submission and resignation to the dispositions of his divine Providence. When the soul presents itself before the Lord with such sentiments, He looks upon it as a Father and grants to it what is proper, withholds what is improper or does not conduce to its true welfare. The desire of my cousin to remain with me all her life arose from a pious and praiseworthy zeal; but it was not in harmony with the plans of the Most High, by which He had already arranged the conduct, travels and events of my life. Though the Lord denied her this request He was not displeased, but granted her whatever would not hinder the decrees of his infinite wisdom and whatever would benefit her or her son John. On account of the love shown toward me by the mother and son, and on account of my intercession, the Almighty enriched them with many blessings and favors. For to ask Him with upright intention and through my mediation, is always the most efficacious means of moving his Majesty.

269. I wish that thou offer up all thy petitions and prayers in the name of my most holy Son and my own; and be assured without doubt, that they will be heard, if they are joined with the upright intention of pleasing God. Look upon me with loving affection as thy Mother, thy refuge and thy help; trust thyself to my devoted love, and remember, my dearest, that my desire for thy greater good urges me to teach thee the means of obtaining great blessings and favors of divine grace at the most liberal hands of God. Do not make thyself unfit for them, nor hinder them by thy timidity. And if thou wishest to induce me to love thee as my much be-

loved daughter, rouse thyself to a fulfillment of what I tell thee and manifest to thee. Toward this direct thy careful efforts, resting satisfied only when thou hast labored hard to put my teachings into practice.

Chapter XXII

THE BIRTH OF THE PRECURSOR OF CHRIST AND WHAT THE LADY MARY DID ON THIS OCCASION.

270. The hour for the rising of the morning star, which was to precede the clear Sun of justice and announce the wished-for day of the law of grace, had arrived (John 5, 35). The time was suitable to the Most High for the appearance of his Prophet in the world; and greater than a prophet was John, who pointing out with his finger the Lamb (John 1, 29), was to prepare mankind for the salvation and sanctification of the world. Before issuing from the maternal womb the Lord revealed to the blessed child the hour in which he was to commence his mortal career among men. The child had the perfect use of his reason, and of the divine science infused by the presence of the incarnate Word. He therefore knew that he was to arrive at the port of a cursed and dangerous land, and to walk upon a world full of evils and snares, where many are overtaken by ruin and perdition.

271. On this account the great child was as it were in a state of suspense and doubt: for on the one hand, nature having nourished his body to that state of perfection, which is proper to birth, he recognized and felt, in addition to the express will of God, the compelling forces of nature which urged him to leave the retreat of the maternal womb. On the

other hand he contemplated the dangerous risks of mortal life. Thus he hesitated between the fear of danger and the desire to obey. And he debated within himself: "If I meet this danger of losing God, whither shall it lead me? How can I safely converse with men, of whom so many are enveloped in darkness and wander from the path of life? I am in the obscurity of my mother's womb, but I must leave it for a more dangerous darkness. I was imprisoned here, since I received the light of reason; but more must I dread the unrestrained freedom of mortals. But let me, o Lord, fulfill thy will and enter the world; for to execute it is always best. To know that my life and my faculties shall be consumed in thy service, highest King, will make it easier for me to come forth to the light and begin life. Bestow, O Lord, thy blessing for my passage into the world."

272. By this prayer the Precursor of Christ merited new graces and blessings at his birth. The fortunate child knew by the indwelling of God in his mind, that he was sent to perform great things and was assured of the necessary help. Before describing this most happy birth, I will try to explain the scriptural dates concerning it. It must be remembered, that the miraculous pregnancy of saint Elisabeth lasted nine days less than nine months. For on account of the fecundity miraculously restored to a barren woman, the fruit conceived matured for parturition in this shorter time. When the angel Gabriel announced to most holy Mary, that her cousin was in the sixth month of her pregnancy, it must be understood to mean, that eight or nine days were still wanting for the completion of the sixth month. I have also said in chapter sixteen that the heavenly Lady departed on the fourth day after the incarnation of the Word for her visit to saint Elisabeth. Saint Luke does not say, that most holy Mary departed immediately, but "in those days," and though She went "in

haste," yet she consumed four days on her journey, as said in the same chapter (No. 207).

273. I likewise reminded the reader, that when the Evangelist says, that holy Mary remained about three months in the house of saint Elisabeth, there were only two or three days missing; for in all respects the Evangelist was exact in his words. Accordingly most holy Mary, our Lady, was present not only at the confinement of saint Elisabeth and at the birth of John, but also at the naming and circumcision of saint John, as I will now show. Counting eight days after the incarnation of the Word, our Lady arrived at the house of Elisabeth on the evening of the second of April, if we reckon according to our solar months; adding thereto three months less two days, we have the first of July, the eighth day of the birth of saint John, and early next day most holy Mary departed on her return to Nazareth. Saint Luke mentions the return of our Queen before he speaks of the birth of saint John, although this happened before She returned. The sacred text anticipates the mention of the journey, in order to have done with it, and not to interrupt the thread of the narrative of the Precursor's birth. This is what I was told to write down in explanation of the text.

274. Her time approaching, saint Elisabeth felt the child in motion as if he wanted to place himself on his feet; but he was merely following the ordinary course of nature and the dictates of obedience. Some moderate pains overtook the mother and she informed the Princess Mary. But she did not call Her to be present at the birth, because reverence for the dignity of Mary and for the Fruit within her womb, prudently withheld her from asking, what might not seem befitting. Nor was the great Mistress in the same room, but She sent her the coverings and swaddling-clothes, which She had made for the fortunate child. Presently thereafter he was born, very perfect and complete in shape, and by the freedom

from impure matter showed signs of the purity of his soul. He was wrapped in the coverings sent by Mary, which therefore had already been great and venerable relics. Shortly after, when saint Elisabeth had composed herself, most holy Mary, at the command of the Lord, issued from her oratory, in order to pay her visit to the mother and child and give them her blessing.

275. At the request of his mother the Queen received in her arms the new-born child and offered him as a new oblation to the eternal Father and his Majesty, well pleased, accepted it as the first-fruits of the Incarnation and of the divine decrees. The most blessed child, full of the Holy Ghost, acknowledged his sovereign Queen, showing Her not only interior, but outward reverence by a secret inclination of his head, and again he adored the divine Word, which was manifested to him in her womb by an especial light. And as he also was aware, that he was privileged before all men, the grateful child performed acts of fervent thanksgiving, humility, love and reverence of God and of his Virgin Mother. The heavenly Queen, in offering him to the eternal Father, pronounced this prayer for him: "Highest Lord and Father, all holy and powerful, accept in thy honor this offering and seasonable fruit of thy most holy Son and my Lord. He is sanctified by the Onlybegotten and rescued from the effects of sin and from the power of thy ancient enemies. Receive this morning's sacrifice, and infuse into this child the blessings of thy holy Spirit, in order that he may be a faithful minister to Thee and to thy Onlybegotten." This prayer of our Queen was efficacious in all respects, and She perceived how the Lord enriched this child, chosen as his Precursor; and She also felt within Herself the effects of these admirable blessings.

276. While the Queen of the Universe held the infant in her arms, She was for a short time secretly wrapt in sweetest

ecstasy; during it She offered up this prayer for the child, holding it close to the same breast where the Onlybegotten of the Eternal and her own was soon to rest. This was the singular prerogative of the great Precursor, granted to none among the saints. Therefore it is not surprising, that the angel called him great in the eyes of the Lord; for before he was born, the Lord visited and sanctified him, and being born, he was placed on the throne of grace; he was embraced by the arms, which were to enfold the incarnate Word God, and thereby excited in the sweetest Mother of God the entrancing desire of holding within them the Son of the Most High, filling Her with delightful affections for his Precursor, the new-born child. Saint Elisabeth, being divinely informed of these sacraments, beheld her wonderful child in the arms of Her, who was his Mother in a more exalted sense than she herself, she being his mother only, as to his natural being, while most holy Mary held that position as to his existence in the order of grace. All this caused a most sweet tie of affection between the most blessed women and in the child, who likewise was enlightened in regard to these mysteries. By the motions of his tender body he manifested the joy of his spirit, clinging to the heavenly Lady and seeking to attract her caresses and to remain with Her. The sweetest Lady fondled him, but with such majestic moderation, that She did not kiss him, as his age would have permitted; for She preserved her most chaste lips intact for her most holy Son. Nor did She look intently into his face, directing all her intention to the holiness of his soul. So great was the prudence and modesty of the great Queen of heaven in the use of her eyes, that She would scarcely have known him by sight.

277. When the birth of John became known, all the relations and acquaintances, as saint Luke says, gathered to congratulate saint Zacharias and Elisabeth, for his house was

rich, noble and honored in the whole province and their piety attracted the hearts of all that knew them. Having known them so many years without children and being aware of the sterility and advanced age of Elisabeth, all were stirred to amazement and joyful wonder, and they looked upon the birth of the child rather as a miracle than as a natural event. The holy priest Zacharias remained mute and unable to manifest his joy by word of mouth; for the hour of his miraculous cure had not arrived. But, freed of his incredulity, he showed his joy in other ways and he was full of affectionate gratitude and praise for the rare blessing, which he had now witnessed with his own eyes. His behavior we shall describe in the next chapter.

Words of the Queen

THE VIRGIN MARY SPEAKS TO SISTER MARY OF AGREDA

278. My dearest daughter, do not be surprised, that my servant John feared and hesitated to come into the world. Life can never be loved by the ignorant devotee of the world in the same degree, as the wise, in divine science, abhor and fear its dangers. This science was eminently possessed by the Precursor of my most holy Son; hence knowing of the loss which threatened, he feared the risk. But, since he that knows and dreads the treacherous seas of this world, sails so much the more securely over their unfathomed depths, it served him in good stead for entering securely into the world. The fortunate child began his career with such disgust and abhorrence of all earthly things, that his horror never abated. He made no peace with the flesh (Mark 6, 17), nor partook of its poison, nor allowed vanity to enter his senses nor obstruct his eyes; in abhorrence of the world and of worldly things, he gave his life for justice. The citizen of the true Jerusalem cannot be in peace or in alliance with Babylon; nor is it

possible to enjoy at the same time the grace of the Most High and the friendship of his declared enemies; for no one can serve two hostile masters, nor can light and darkness, Christ and Beliel, harmonize (Matth. 4, 4).

279. Guard thyself, my dearest, against those living in darkness and the lovers of the world more than against fire; for the wisdom of the sons of this world is carnal and diabolical, and their ways lead to death. In order to walk the way of truth, even at the cost of the natural life, it is necessary to preserve the peace of the soul. Three dwelling-places I point out for thee to live in, from which thou must never intentionally come forth. If at any time the Lord should bid thee to relieve the necessities of thy fellow creatures, I desire that thou do not lose this refuge. Act as one who lives in a castle surrounded by enemies, and who perchance must go to the gate to transact necessary business. He acts with such wariness, that he will pay more attention to safeguard his retreat and shield himself, than to transact business with others, being always on the watch and on guard against danger. So must thou live, if thou wishest to live securely; for doubt not, that enemies more cruel and poisonous than asps and basilisks surround thee.

280. Thy habitations shall be the Divinity of the Most High, the humanity of my most holy Son, and thy own interior. In the Divinity thou must live like the pearl in its shell, or like the fish in the sea, allowing thy desires and affections to roam in its infinite spaces. The most holy humanity shall be the wall, which defends thee; and his bosom shall be the place of thy rest, and under his wings shalt thou find refreshment (Ps. 16, 8). Thy own interior shall afford thee peaceful delight through the testimony of a good conscience (Cor. 2, 12), and it will, if thou keep it pure, familiarize thee with the sweet and friendly intercourse of thy Spouse. In order that thou mayest be aided therein by

retirement of the body, I desire that thou remain secluded in thy choir or in thy cell, leaving it only, when obedience or charity make it inevitable. I will tell thee a secret: there are demons, whom Lucifer has expressly ordered to watch for the religious, who come forth from their retirement, in order to beset them and engage them in battle and cause their fall. The demons do not easily go into the cells, because there they do not find the occasions afforded by conversations and the use of the senses, wherein they ordinarily capture and devour their prey like ravenous wolves. They are tormented by the retirement and recollection of religious, knowing that they are foiled in their attempts, as long as they cannot entice them into human discourse.

281. It is also certain that ordinarily the demons have no power over souls, unless they gain entrance by some venial or mortal fault. Mortal sin gives them a sort of direct right over those who commit it; while venial sin weakens the strength of the soul and invites their attacks. Imperfections diminish the merit and the progress of virtue, and encourage the enemy. Whenever the astute serpent notices that the soul bears with its own levity and forgets about its danger, it blinds it and seeks to instill its deadly poison. The enemy then entices the soul like a little heedless bird, until it falls into one of the many snares from which there seems to be no escape.

282. Admire then, my daughter, what thou hast learned by divine enlightenment and weep in deepest sorrow over the ruin of so many souls absorbed in such dangerous tepidity. They live in the obscurity of their passions and depraved inclinations, forgetful of the danger, unmoved by their losses, and heedless of their dealings. Instead of fearing and avoiding the occasions of evil, they encounter and seek for them in blind ignorance. In senseless fury they follow their pleasures, place no restraint on their passionate desires, and care not

where they walk, even if to the most dangerous precipices. They are surrounded by innumerable enemies, who pursue them with diabolical treachery, unceasing vigilance, unquenchable wrath and restless diligence. What wonder then, that from such extremes, or rather from such unequal combat, irreparable defeats should arise among the mortals? And that, since the number of fools is infinite, the number of the reprobate should also be uncountable, and that the demon should be inflated by his triumphs in the perdition of so many men? May the eternal God preserve thee from such a misfortune; and do thou weep and deplore that of thy brethren, continually asking for their salvation as far as is possible.

Chapter XXIII

THE GOOD COUNCIL AND INSTRUCTION, WHICH MOST
HOLY MARY GAVE TO SAINT ELISABETH AT HER REQUEST;
SAINT JOHN IS CIRCUMCISED AND RECEIVES HIS NAME;
ZACHARIAS PROPHESIES.

283. After the birth of the Precursor of Christ the return of
most holy Mary was unavoidable; and although the prudent
Elisabeth had found consolation in resigning herself to the
divine will, she could not restrain her desire of securing for
herself the good counsel and instruction of the Mother of
wisdom. Therefore She spoke to Her and said: "My Mistress
and Mother of the Creator, I know, that Thou art preparing
to leave me and that I am to be deprived of thy loving intercourse, help and protection. I beseech Thee, my Cousin,
furnish me with some good counsel, which will help me to
conform all my actions to the greater pleasure of the Most
High. In thy virginal womb Thou bearest Him, who is the
Corrector of the wise and the fountain of light (Wis. 7, 15);
through Him Thou canst communicate it to all. Let some of
the rays, which illumine thy purest soul fall upon thy servant,
in order that I may be enlightened in the paths of justice,
until I arrive at the vision of the God of gods in Sion." (Ps.
22, 3.)

284. These words of saint Elisabeth moved the most holy
Mary to tender compassion and She spoke words that served

her cousin as celestial guidance for the rest of her life. This, She said, would be of short duration; but the Most High would take care of her child, and She herself had prayed for him to the Almighty. Although it is not possible to record all the sweet words of counsel, which the heavenly Lady spoke to saint Elisabeth before her departure, I will write down some of them, as far as I have understood them and as far as they can be reproduced by our insufficient language. Most holy Mary said: "My beloved cousin, the Lord has selected Thee for the fulfillment of most exalted mysteries. He has condescended to enlighten thee concerning them and wishes, that I should open to thee my heart. Thy name is written within it for remembrance before his Majesty. I wilt not forget the devoted kindness with which thou hast treated me, the most useless of creatures; and from my most holy Son and Lord I hope thou shalt receive a plentiful reward."

285. "Keep thy mind and spirit fixed on high and by the light of divine grace preserve the vision of the unchangeable and infinite being of God and the remembrance of his immense goodness, which moved Him to create out of nothing all the intellectual creatures in order to bestow upon them his glory and his gifts of grace. The extreme mercy of the Most High, in favoring us more than all other creatures with his knowledge and light, ought to incite us to make up by our thankfulness for the blind ingratitude of mortals, who are so far removed from acknowledging and praising their Creator. This shall be our task, that we keep our hearts free and unhindered in our advance toward the last end. Therefore, my beloved, I charge thee to keep it unhampered and unburdened of all earthly things, free from even such as pertain to thy possessions, in order that, void of earthly hindrances, it may attend to the divine calls. Hope in the coming of the Lord (Luke 12, 36), so that when He arrives, thou mayest answer his call joyfully and not with convulsive violence at

the thought of leaving thy body and all earthly things. Now, while it is time to suffer and earn the crown, let us gain merit and hasten to be united intimately with our true and highest God."

286. "As long as thy husband Zacharias lives, seek to love, serve and obey him with especial earnestness. Look upon thy miraculous child as a continual sacrifice to his Creator; in God and for God thou canst love him as a mother; for he shall be a great Prophet, and in the spirit of Elias he shall defend the honor of the Most High and exalt his name. My most holy Son, who has chosen him for his Precursor and for the harbinger of his coming, will favor him with the special gifts of his right hand (Matth. 11, 9) and make him great and wonderful among the nations, manifesting to the world his great sanctity."

287. "See that the holy name of thy God and the Lord of Abraham, Isaac and Jacob be honored and reverenced by all thy house and family (Tob. 4). Above all be anxiously careful to relieve the needs of the poor, as far as is possible; enrich them with the temporal goods so lavishly given to thee by thy God; 'show a like generosity to the needy, knowing that these earthly goods are more theirs than yours, since we are the children of the heavenly Father to whom all things belong. It is not proper, that the child of a rich father should live in superfluity, while his brethren live in poverty and need. In this thou canst make thyself especially pleasing to the Good of undying mercy. Continue in thy former practices and follow out thy plans of still greater charity, since Zacharias has given this work into thy hands. With his permission thou canst be generous. Confirm thy hopes in all the tasks imposed upon thee by the Lord, and with thy fellow beings practice kindness, humility and patience in the joy of thy soul, although some of them will give thee occasion to increase thy crown of merit. Bless God eternally for having

manifested to thee his exalted mysteries and pray for the salvation of souls with unabated love and zeal. Pray also for me, that his Majesty may govern and guide me worthily to preserve the sacrament confided by his goodness to so lowly and poor a servant as I am. Send for my husband in order that I may have his company while returning to Nazareth. In the meanwhile prepare for the circumcision of thy child and call him John; for this name was given to him according to an unchangeable decree of the Most High."

288. These counsels of most holy Mary together with other words of eternal life produced in the heart of saint Elisabeth such divine affections, that for a time, she was lost in the exalted teachings and sentiments of these heavenly doctrines and made mute by the force of the spiritual light infused into her. For the Lord, by means of the living words of his most pure Mother, enlivened and renewed the heart of his servant. When the flow of her tears had moderated, she answered: "My Mistress and Queen of the universe, speech fails me in alternate sorrow and consolation. Hear Thou the words of my inmost heart, which my tongue cannot express. My affections shall witness, what my lips leave unspoken. May the Lord, who is the enricher of our poverty, return to Thee the favor Thou showest me. I beseech Thee, who art the fountain of all my help and the source of all my blessings, to obtain for me the grace to fulfill thy counsels and to bear the great sorrow of losing thy company."

289. Then they bespoke the arrangements for the circumcision of the child, for the time appointed by the law was approaching. Complying with the custom observed among the Jews, especially among the more distinguished, many relatives and other acquaintances of the house of Zacharias began to gather, in order to resolve upon the name to be given to the child; for, in addition to the ordinary preparations and consultations concerning the name to be given to a

son, the high position of Zacharias and Elisabeth and the news of the miraculous fecundity of the mother naturally suggested the existence of some great mystery to the minds of all their relations. Zacharias was still dumb, and therefore it was necessary that saint Elisableth should preside at this meeting. Over and above the high esteem which she inspired, she now exhibited such evident signs of the exalted renewal and sanctification of her soul, which resulted from the knowledge of the mysteries and from the intercourse with the Queen of heaven, that all her relatives and friends noticed the change. For even in her countenance she exhibited a kind of effulgence which made her mysteriously attractive and was the reflection of the Divinity, in whose presence she lived.

290. At this meeting was present also the heavenly Lady Mary, for Elisabeth had earnestly besought Her, and had even compelled Her by a sort of reverent and humble command. The great Lady obeyed, but She begged the Most High not to make known any of her great privileges, lest She draw upon Herself the applause or veneration of others. The desire of the most Humble among the humble was granted. And as the world persists in ignoring those who fail to use ostentation, nobody took particular notice of Her except saint Elisabeth, who looked upon Her with outward and inward reverence and who knew, that on Her depended the success of this consultation. As is recorded in the Gospel of saint Luke, some of those present in the meeting suggested that the infant be named after his father: but the prudent mother, seconded by the most holy Mary, said: "My son must be named John." Her relatives objected, that none of their family bore that name; for the names of illustrious forefathers were always held in great esteem, and were preferred in order to incite their bearers to the imitation of ancestral virtues. Saint Elisabeth again expressed herself to the effect, that the child should be called John.

291. The relatives then appealed by signs to Zacharias, who, being unable to speak, asked for a pen and declared his will by writing upon the tablet: "Johannes est nomen ejus." "John is his name." At the same time most holy Mary, making use of her power over all nature, commanded the dumbness to leave him, his tongue to be loosened, as the moment had arrived when it should bless the Lord. At this heavenly command he found himself freed from his affliction, and, to the astonishment and fear of all present, he began to speak, as narrated by the Evangelist. What I say here is not adverse to the Gospel narrative; for, although it is there related, that the angel foretold Zacharias that he should remain mute until his message should be fulfilled, yet God, when He reveals any decree of his will, absolutely unfailing as they are, does not always reveal the means or the manner of their fulfillment, foreseen by Him in his infinite foreknowledge. Thus the archangel announced to Zacharias the punishment of his unbelief, but he did not tell him that he should be freed from it by the intercession of most holy Mary, although this also had been foreseen and decreed.

292. Therefore, just as the voice of our Lady Mary was the instrument for the sanctification of the child John and his mother, so her secret mandate and her intercession had the effect of loosening the tongue of Zacharias, filling him with the holy Spirit and the gift of prophecy. Hence he broke forth in the words (Luke 1, 68–79) :

68. "Blessed be the Lord God of Israel; because He hath visited and wrought the redemption of his people:

69. And hath raised up an horn of salvation to us, in the house of David his servant:

70. And he hath spoken by the mouth of his holy prophets, who are from the beginning;

71. Salvation from our enemies, and from the hands of all that hate us:

72. To perform mercy to our fathers, and to remember his holy testament,

73. The oath, which he swore to Abraham our father, that he would grant to us,

74. That being delivered from the hand of our enemies, we may serve him without fear,

75. In holiness and justice before him, all our days.

76. And thou, child, shalt be called the prophet of the Highest: for thou shalt go before the face of the Lord to prepare his ways:

77. To give knowledge of salvation to his people: unto the remission of their sins:

78. Through the bowels of the mercy of our God, in which the Orient from on high hath visited us:

79. To enlighten them that sit in darkness, and in the shadow of death: to direct our feet into the way of peace."

293. In the divine canticle of the Benedictus Zacharias embodied all of the highest mysteries, which the ancient prophets had foretold in a more profuse manner concerning the Divinity, Humanity and the Redemption of Christ, and in these few words he embraces many great sacraments. He also understood them by the grace and light, which filled his spirit, and which raised him up in the sight of all that had come to attend the circumcision of his son; for all of them were witnesses to the solving of his tongue and to his divine prophecies. I will hardly be able to give an explanation of the deep meaning of these prophecies, such as they had in the mind of that holy priest.

294. "Blessed be the Lord God of Israel," he says, knowing that the Most High could have saved his people and given them eternal salvation merely by desiring it or speaking one word, but He exerted not only his power, but showed also his immense goodness and mercy, the Son of the eternal Father himself coming down to visit his people and to be-

come their Brother in the human nature; their Teacher by his example and doctrine, their Redeemer by his life, passion and death of the Cross. At these words Zacharias understood the union of the two natures in the person of the Word and in heavenly clearness he saw this mystery realized in the virginal bridal-chamber of the most holy Mary. He understood also the exaltation of the Humanity by the triumph of the God-man, in earning the salvation of the human race according to the promises made to David and his ancestors (II Kings 7, 12; Ps. 131, 11). He understood that the same promise had been made to the whole world by the prophecies of the Saints and Patriarchs from the beginning. For from the first creation God commenced to direct the course of nature and grace toward his coming into the world, and to ordain all his works since the time of Adam toward this same blessed end.

295. He understood that the Most High in this manner provided for us the means of obtaining grace and eternal life lost by our enemies in their pride and stubborn disobedience, which hurled them into hell; and the seats which would have been theirs, if they had been obedient, were reserved for the obedient among the mortals. He saw however since then the enmity which the serpent had conceived against God was now turned against men, because we were decreed and enshrined in the eternal mind according to his divine will (Apocalypse 12, 17); how Adam and Eve, our first parents, having fallen from his friendship and grace, were not given over to chastisement, like the rebellious angels, but were raised to a state of hope (Wisdom 10, 2); and that, in order to assure their descendants of his mercy, God provided the prophecies and figures of the old Testament, which were to be fulfilled in the coming of the Redeemer and Savior. To make this promise still more certain it was made to Abraham under an oath, affirming that he would be the father of all his people and of all the children of the faith (Gen. 22, 16).

Assured of this stupendous and vast blessing, namely that of receiving his own Son made man, we may serve God free from the fear of our enemies; for by our adoption and regeneration they are already overcome and subdued through our Redeemer (Gal. 4, 5).

296. In order that we may understand what the Word has earned for us in restoring to us this liberty in the service of God, he says: that He has renewed the world in sanctity and justice, and founded the new law of grace for all the days of this world, and for the time of life given to each of the children of the Church. In it they not only can, but they should live in holiness and justice. And as Zacharias saw in his son John the beginning of all these sacraments, he turns to him and congratulates him, because of the dignity and sanctity of his office, saying: And thou, child, shalt be called a prophet of the Most High; for thou shalt go before his face, namely his Divinity, and prepare his ways by spreading the light of his coming, and giving notice to the people of the Jews concerning eternal life, which is Christ our Lord, the promised Messias (Mark 1, 41). Thus might they dispose themselves by the baptism of penance for the remission of their sins and become convinced that the Messias has come to take away not only their sins, but those of the whole world (John 1, 29); since it is through his mercy and on account of his merits (Tit. 3, 5) that He visits us, by descending from the bosom of the eternal Father and by being born as man. He it was that brought light to those who had lost the truth for so many ages, who were sitting in darkness and in the shadows of death. He it was who by his own example taught us to direct our steps toward the true peace, which we were awaiting.

297. Much more clearly than I can explain, Zacharias perceived these mysteries in their plenitude and depth, and expressed them in his prophecies. Some of those present were

likewise enlightened, becoming aware that the time of the Messias and of the fulfillment of the ancient prophecies was at hand. Full of astonishment at these unexpected wonders and prodigies, they exclaimed:

"Who shall this child be, since the hand of the Most High is in him so marvelous and powerful?" In accordance with the letter of the law, and with the concurrence of his father and mother, the child was then circumcised and named John; and the report of these wonders spread through all the mountains of Judea.

298. Queen of the universe, I admire the wonderful works wrought through thy intervention by the arm of the Lord in his servants Elisabeth, John and Zacharias. At the same time I reflect on the different courses pursued by divine Providence and on thy rare discretion. Thy most sweet voice served the son and the mother as an instrument of sanctification, filling them with the Holy Ghost, and this remained hidden; then again thy secret prayer and command solved the tongue of Zacharias, and this was manifested to all the bystanders, revealing the effects of God's grace in the holy priest. I cannot find the reason for this diversity, and therefore I make known to Thee my ignorance, so that Thou mayest instruct me as my Teacher.

Words of the Queen

THE VIRGIN MARY SPEAKS TO SISTER MARY OF AGREDA

299. For two reasons, my daughter, the divine effects wrought through me by my Son in saint John and Elisabeth were concealed, while those in Zacharias were manifest. First, because Elisabeth spoke out clearly in praise of the incarnate Word and of me; yet at the time it was not proper that either this mystery or my dignity should be openly known; the coming of the Messias was to be manifested by other more

appropriate means. Secondly, not all hearts were so well
prepared as that of Elisabeth for receiving such precious and
unprecedented seed of divine knowledge, nor would they
have welcomed such sacramental revelation with due reverence. On the other hand it was more becoming that Zacharias in his priestly dignity should proclaim what was then to be
made known; for the beginnings of the heavenly light would
be accepted more readily from him than from saint Elisabeth,
especially while he was present. That which she said, was
reserved to bring forth its effects in due time. Although the
words of God have their own inherent force; yet the more
sweet and acceptable manner of communicating with the
ignorant and the unskilled in divine mysteries is by means of
the priest.

300. Likewise it was proper that the dignity and honor of
the priesthood should receive its due; for the Most High
holds the priests in such esteem, that if He finds them in the
right disposition, He exalts them and fills them with his
Spirit in order that the world may venerate them as his
chosen and anointed ones. Moreover the wonders of the
Lord run less risk in priests, even when they are more openly
revealed to them. If they live up to their dignity, their works
in comparison with those of the other creatures, are like those
of the angels and of the seraphim. Their countenance should
be resplendent, like that of Moses, when he came forth from
converse with the Lord (Exod. 34,29). At least they should
deal with the rest of men in such a manner that they be
honored and revered as next to God. I desire that thou
understand, my dearest, that the Most High is greatly incensed against the world in this matter: as well against the
priests as against laymen. Against the priests because, forgetting their exalted dignity, they debase themselves by a contemptible, degraded and scandalous life, giving bad example
to the world by mixing up with it to the neglect of their

sanctification. And against the laymen, because they act with a foolhardy presumption toward the anointed of the Lord whom, though of imperfect and blameworthy lives, they ought to honor and revere as taking the place or Christ, my most holy Son, on earth.

301. On account of this reverence due to the priesthood my behavior toward saint Zacharias was different from that toward Elisabeth. For, although the Lord wished, that I should be the instrument, by which the gifts of the holy Spirit should be communicated to both; yet I saluted Elisabeth in such a manner, that I at the same time showed a certain authority, exerting my power over the original sin of her son; for at my words this sin was forgiven him, and both mother and son were filled with the Holy Ghost. As I had not contracted original sin and was exempt from it, I possessed dominion over it on this occasion: I commanded as the Mistress, who had triumphed over it by the help of the Lord (Gen. 3, 5), and who was no slave of it, as all the sons of Adam, who sinned in him (Rom. 5, 12). Therefore the Lord desired that, in order to free John from the slavery and chains of sin, I should command over it as one who never was subject to its bondage. I did not salute Zacharias in this authoritative way, but I prayed for him, observing the reverence and decorum due to his dignity and my modesty. I would not have commanded the tongue of the priest to be loosened, not even mentally and secretly, if the Most High had not enjoined it upon me, intimating at the same time, that the defect of speech hardly suited his office, for a priest should stand ready to serve and praise the Almighty with all his powers. In regard to the respect due to priests I will tell thee more on another occasion; let this suffice at present for the solution of thy doubt.

302. But from my instruction today learn especially to seek direction in the way of virtue and of eternal life in all thy

intercourse with men, be they above or below thee in dignity. Imitate therein me and my cousin Elisabeth, with due discretion asking all to direct thee and guide thee; for in return for such humility the Lord will provide thee with secure counsel and divine light for exercising thy discreet and sincere love of virtue. Drive away, or do not allow thyself to be influenced by even the least breath of flattery and avoid the conversations which expose thee to it; for such deceitful pleasure darkens the light and perverts the unsuspecting mind. The Lord is so jealous of the souls especially beloved by Him, that He will immediately turn away from them if they find pleasure in the praises of men and seek to recompense themselves by their flatteries; since by this levity they become unworthy of his favors. It is not possible to unite in a soul the adulations of the world and the caresses of the Most High. For these latter are sincere, holy, pure, and lasting: they humiliate, cleanse, pacify and illumine the heart; while on the other hand the flatteries of creatures are vain, fleeting, deceitful, impure and false, issuing from the mouths of those who are all liars (Ps. 115, 11); and whatever is deceitful is a work of the enemy.

303. Thy Spouse, my dearest daughter, does not wish thy ears to be enthralled by deceitful earthly talk, nor contaminated by the flatteries of the world. Therefore I desire that thou keep them closed and well guarded against all these poisonous influences. If thy Lord is pleased to speak to thy heart the words of eternal life, it is proper that thou thyself be deaf and lifeless to all that is earthly. All else should be to thee a deadly torment in comparison with the caresses of his love. Remember that thou owest Him the perfection of thy love, and that all hell will combine against thee, in order to ensnare thee by thy natural tenderness to be sweet and loving toward creatures, and less grateful to the eternal God. Watch

over thyself, and see that thou resist this unfaithfulness, trusting in thy beloved Master and Spouse.

Chapter XXIV

MOST HOLY MARY LEAVES THE HOUSE OF ZACHARIAS AND
RETURNS TO HER HOME IN NAZARETH.

304. At the call of Elisabeth, the most fortunate of husbands,
saint Joseph, had come in order to attend most holy Mary on
her return to her home in Nazareth. On arriving at the house
of Zacharias he had been welcomed with indescribable
reverence and devotion by saint Elisabeth and Zacharias; for
now also the holy priest knew that he was the guardian of the
sacramental treasures of heaven, though this was yet unknown to the great patriarch saint Joseph himself. His heavenly Spouse received him in modest and discreet jubilation,
and, kneeling before him, She, as usual, besought his blessing, and also his pardon, for having failed to serve him for
nearly three months during her attendance upon her cousin
Elisabeth. Though She had been guilty of no fault, not even
of an imperfection in thus devotedly fulfilling the will of God
in conformity with the wishes of her spouse, yet, by this
courteous and endearing act of humility, She wanted to repay
her husband for the want of her consoling companionship.
The holy Joseph answered that as he now again saw Her, and
again enjoyed her delightful presence, he was relieved of the
pain caused by her absence. In the course of a few days they
announced the day of their departure.

305. Thereupon the princess Mary took leave of the priest Zacharias. As he had already been enlightened by the Lord concerning her dignity, he addressed Her with the greatest reverence as the living sanctuary of the Divinity and humanity of the eternal Word. "My Mistress," he said, "praise and bless eternally thy Maker, who in his infinite mercy has chosen Thee among all his creatures as his Mother, as the sole Keeper of all his great blessings and sacraments. Be mindful of me, thy servant, before thy Lord and God, that He may lead me in peace through this exile to the security of the eternal peace which we hope for, and that through thee I may merit the vision of his Divinity, which is the glory of the saints. Remember also, O Lady, my house and family, and especially my Son John, and pray to the Most High for thy people."

306. The great Lady knelt before him and in profound humility asked him to bless Her. This Zacharias hesitated to do and instead asked Her to give him her blessing. But nothing could overcome the humility of Her who was the Teacher of that virtue and of all holiness; and therefore She importuned the priest for his blessing until he yielded to the impulse of the divine light. In the words of holy Scripture, he said to Her: "The right arm of the almighty and true God assist Thee always, and deliver Thee from all evil (Ps. 120, 7). Possess thou the grace of His unfailing protection, and be filled with the dew of heaven and with the fruits of the earth, and let Him give Thee abundance of bread and wine (Gen. 27, 28) ; let the nations serve Thee and let the generations worship Thee, since Thou art the tabernacle of God (Eccl. 24, 12); be Thou the Mistress of thy brethren, and let the sons of thy mother kneel in thy presence. Those that praise and bless Thee shall be honored and blessed; and those that bless and extol Thee not shall be cursed. In Thee let all

nations know their God (Judith 13, 31), and through Thee let the name of the most high God of Jacob be glorified."

307. In return for this prophetic blessing, most holy Mary kissed the hand of the priest and asked him to forgive Her the faults committed in his house. The saintly old man was much moved by these parting words of the most pure and amiable of creatures, and ever thereafter bore hidden within him the memory of the mysteries revealed to him concerning the most holy Mary. Only once, when he was present at a meeting of the priests in the temple, who were congratulating him on account of the birth of his son and the restoration of his speech, he was moved by the excess of his joy and he answered them: "I believe firmly that the Most High has visited us and has already sent us the promised Messias, who will redeem his people." But he spoke no further of what he really knew of the mystery. The holy priest Simeon, however, who was present and heard these words, was seized with great joy of spirit and by divine impulse exclaimed: "Let not, O Lord God of Israel, thy servant depart from this valley of misery before he has seen thy salvation and the Redeemer of his people." To this prayer he afterwards alluded when, at the presentation of infant God in the temple, He received Him into his arms, as we shall see later on. Until that event took place he desired more and more ardently to see the incarnate Word.

308. Leaving Zacharias in tears, Mary betook Herself to her cousin Elisabeth. As She was a cousin of Mary, of a tender heart, and as She had enjoyed so many days of sweet intercourse, and had received so many favors of the Mother of grace, she was almost overcome with grief at the mere thought of now losing the source whence so many blessings had flown and were yet to flow, if she could only retain it. Hence, when the time for taking leave of the Mistress of heaven and earth finally arrived her heart was torn with

sorrow, and she could say only a few words amid her copious tears and sighs revealing her inmost soul. The serene Queen, being superior to all inordinate movements of the natural passions, in affable modesty spoke to Elisabeth: "My beloved cousin, do not grieve so much over my departure, since the charity of the Most High, in whom I truly love thee, knows no distance of time or place. In Him I behold thee, and I keep thee in my mind; and thou also wilt find me in that same presence. Short is the time of our bodily separation, since all the days of human life are so fleeting (Job 14, 5), and if we gain the victory over our enemies we shall very soon see ourselves and enjoy ourselves in the celestial Jerusalem, where there is no sorrow, no weeping, no separation (Apoc, 21, 4). In the meanwhile thou wilt find all blessings in the Lord and also me thou wilt find and possess in Him. He will remain in thy heart and console thee." Our most prudent Queen said no more to allay the grief of saint Elisabeth; instead She knelt down at her feet and asked her blessing, and her pardon for what might have been disagreeable in her intercourse with her; nor would Mary yield to the protests of Elisabeth until her petition was granted. Elisabeth then insisted on her part and asked the blessing of the heavenly Lady in return, and not wishing to deny her this consolation, most holy Mary complied.

309. The Queen visited also the child John, received him in her arms and bestowed upon him many mysterious blessings. The wonderful infant by divine dispensation spoke to the Virgin, although in a low and infantile voice: "Thou art the Mother of God himself, the Queen of all creation, the Keeper of the ineffable Treasure of heaven, my help and protection: grant me, thy servant, thy blessing, and may thy intercession and favor never fail me." Three times he kissed the hand of the Queen of heaven; likewise he adored the incarnate Word in her virginal Womb, and asked Him for

his benediction and grace. The infant God manifested his pleasure and benevolence toward his Precursor, while the most happy Mother Mary beheld and understood all that was passing. In all things She acted with the plenitude of divine science, venerating all these mysteries according to their proper import; for She responded with a magnanimous heart to all the works of his divine wisdom (II Mach. 2, 9).

310. The whole household of Zacharias had been sanctified by the presence of most holy Mary and of the incarnate Word in her womb; all its inmates had been edified by her example, instructed by her conversations and teachings, and sweetly affected by her intercourse and modest behavior. While She had drawn toward Herself all the hearts of that happy family, She also merited and obtained for them from her most holy Son the plenitude of celestial gifts. Holy Joseph was held in high veneration by Zacharias, Elisabeth and John; for they had come to know his high dignity before he himself was yet aware of it. The blessed Patriarch, happy in his Treasure, the full value of which as yet he did not know, took leave of all and departed for Nazareth: what happened on the way I will narrate in the following chapter. But before they began their journey most holy Mary, on bended knees, besought saint Joseph to bless Her, as She was accustomed to do on such occasions, and after She had received his blessing, they betook themselves on their journey.

Words of the Queen

THE VIRGIN MARY SPEAKS TO SISTER MARY OF AGREDA

311. My daughter, the happy souls which God has chosen for his intimate friendship and perfection must keep themselves in continual readiness and peace, in order to perform all that his Majesty may ordain without hesitation or delay.

That is what I did when the Most High commanded me to leave the beloved retreat of my house and betake myself to Elisabeth; likewise, when he ordered me to return. I obeyed in all these things with joyful alacrity; and although I had received so many benefits from Elisabeth and her family and so many tokens of love and friendship, as thou hast seen, yet, knowing the will of the Lord, I set aside all obligation and my own inclination and followed them only so far as was strictly demanded by charity and compassion, and in so far as the promptest obedience to the divine command permitted.

312. My dearest daughter, how wilt thou not hasten to obtain this true and perfect resignation as soon as thou knowest its vast value! How pleasing it is in the eyes of the Lord, and how profitable for thy soul! Labor then to attain it in imitation of me, as I have already so often invited thee and urged thee. The greatest hindrances toward its attainment are the leanings and special likings to earthly things; for these make the soul unworthy of the caresses of the Lord and of knowing fully his will. And even if the soul knows his will, the base love of unworthy things will keep the soul from fulfilling it; for on account of its inclinations, it will be wanting in the ready and joyful obedience required by the Lord. Take notice of this danger, my daughter, and do not allow any particular affection to enter into thy heart, for I wish that thou be well versed and perfect in this art of divine love, and that thy obedience be that of an angel, and thy love that of a seraphim. Thus show thyself in all thy actions, for to this my love urges thee, and thus art thou taught by the knowledge and light imparted to thee.

313. I do not say that thou must do away with all sensible feeling, for that is not naturally possible to the creature; but whenever thou meetest adverse happenings, or when thou art deprived of what is useful, necessary or agreeable thou must bear it with joyful resignation and give praise to the Lord,

because his will is being fulfilled in thy regard. By seeking only his pleasure, and considering all else as of passing moment, thou wilt gain a quick and easy victory over thyself, and thou wilt seek all occasions to humiliate thyself under the mighty hand of the Lord (I Pet. 5, 6). I also exhort thee to imitate me in my esteem and veneration of the priests, and that thou always ask their blessing before speaking to them and in leaving them. Do this also in regard to the Most High before beginning any work. Toward thy superiors always show thyself devoted and submissive. If any married women come to seek thy advice, exhort them to be obedient to their husbands (Tit. 5, 2), peacefully subjecting themselves, living retired in their houses and carefully fulfilling their obligations toward their families. Tell them not to give themselves up entirely to their occupations, nor to lose themselves in their daily cares on pretext of necessity; for much more must be trusted to the goodness and liberality of God than to one's own immoderate bustle and activity. In whatever happened to me in my condition, thou wilt find true instruction and example; and my whole life will be an example of perfection for the guidance of souls, and therefore I will not need to give thee further direction.

Chapter XXV

THE JOURNEY OF MOST HOLY MARY FROM THE HOUSE OF
ZACHARIAS TO HER HOME IN NAZARETH.

314. Returning from the town of Juda to Nazareth the most
holy Mary, the living tabernacle of God, pursued her way
through the mountains of Judea in the company of her most
faithful spouse saint Joseph. Although the Evangelists do not
make mention of any haste in this journey homeward, such
as is recorded by saint Luke and occasioned by the special
mystery connected with it, yet the great Princess made also
this return journey with great expediency, on account of the
events which awaited Her at home. All the journeys of this
heavenly Lady were a mystical counterpart of her spiritual
and interior advances. For She was the true tabernacle of the
Lord, which was to find no definite resting-place in this
mortal pilgrimage (I Par. 17, 5); on the contrary, progressing
daily from one stage to another and to higher condition of
wisdom and grace, She continually pushed forward on her
pilgrimage to the promised land (Numb. 7, 89); and She
bore continually with Her on her journey the true propitiato-
ry, whence She drew ceaseless increase of her gifts and acquired for us eternal salvation.

315. The great Queen and saint Joseph again consumed
four days in their return journey, as they had done on their

coming. On the way they maintained the same divine conversations, and they experienced events similar to those
already mentioned in chapter sixteenth. In the ordinary
practices of humility, in which they vied with each other, our
Queen always came out victorious, except when saint Joseph
called obedience to his aid; because She considered obedience
the greater humility. As She was already in her third month
of pregnancy, She was more attentive and careful in her
journey; not that her pregnancy caused her any difficulties,
for it was on the contrary a most sweet alleviation of any
hardships. But this careful and prudent Mother was filled
with the consciousness of her Treasure; for She beheld day by
day the natural growth of the body of her most holy Son in
her virginal womb. Notwithstanding the ease and lightness of
her pregnancy, She nevertheless was subject to the exertion
and the fatigue of the journey; for the sovereign Lady made
no use of her privileges to diminish her sufferings, but She
gave free scope to the fatigues and inconveniences of travel in
order to be in all things our teacher and the faithful image of
her most holy Son.

316. As the divine Fruit of her womb was naturally of the
most perfect growth, and as She was Herself of the most
comely and well-proportioned shape without any defect
whatever, it was natural that her condition should become
noticeable, and She knew that it would be impossible to
conceal it much longer from her husband. Already She began
to look upon him with greater tenderness and compassion in
view of the shock which his love would feel on noticing her
condition. Gladly would She have turned it aside if She had
known that such was the will of God. But the Lord gave Her
no intimation of his will in these anxious thoughts; for He
had ordained that the event should come about in such a way
as to increase his glory and the merits both of saint Joseph
and of the Virgin Mother. Nevertheless the great Lady

besought his Majesty to fill the heart of her spouse with patience and wisdom, and to assist him with grace, that he might act in this conjuncture according to the divine pleasure. For She was convinced that it would occasion him great grief to see her pregnant.

317. In the course of the journey the Mistress of the world performed some wonderful works, although always in secret. It happened that when they arrived at a place not far from Jerusalem some people from another town came to the same hostelry. They brought with them a young woman seeking a cure for her sickness in the larger and more populous city. She was known to be very sick, but no one knew what was her sickness or the cause of it. This woman had lived a very virtuous life. On this account the enemy, who knew her character and her advanced virtues, began to direct his attacks especially against her, as he always does against the friends of God, since he considers them his own enemies. He caused her to commit some sins and, in order to force her from one abyss into another, he tempted her with despondent thoughts and disorderly grief at her fall. Having thus upset her judgment this dragon found entrance into her body, and now he, with many other demons, had possession of her. I have already said in the first part that the infernal dragon, when he saw in heaven the woman clothed with the sun (Apoc. 12, 1), conceived a great wrath against all virtuous women. Of her progeny are all those that follow Mary, as may be judged from that same chapter of the Apocalypse. On this account he exerted all his arrogance and tyranny in the possession of the body and soul of this afflicted woman.

318. The heavenly Princess saw her in the tavern and knew of her affliction, which was unknown to the others. Moved by her motherly pity, She begged her most holy Son to give health of body and soul to the unfortunate woman. Perceiving that the divine will was inclined to mercy, She

used her power as Queen and commanded the demons instantly to leave this creature never to return. Moreover, She banished them to the infernal depths, their lawful and appropriate dwelling. This command of our great Queen and Lady was not given vocally, but mentally, in such a way as to be perceptible to the impure spirits. It was so powerful that Lucifer and his companions hastened to leave that body and hurl themselves into the infernal darkness. The fortunate woman was freed and seized with wonder at the unhoped-for delivery; and in her inmost heart she was drawn toward the most pure and holy Lady. She looked upon Her with an especial veneration and love, thereby deserving two other favors. One was that she was filled with a most sincere sorrow for her sins; the other, that the evil effects or traces of the demoniacal possession under which she had suffered were effaced. She was aware that the mysterious Stranger, whom she had so fortunately met on her way was concerned in the heavenly blessing. She therefore spoke to Her, and our Queen answered with words that went straight to the heart; She exhorted her to perseverance and also merited it for her during the rest of her life. Her companions likewise recognized the miracle; but they attributed it to their promise of bringing her to the temple of Jerusalem and of offering some gift for her. This promise they fulfilled, praising God, but remaining ignorant of the source of their good fortune.

319. Vast and furious was the wrath of Lucifer when he found himself and his demons dispossessed and cast out from their abode by the mere word of this woman Mary. Full of wrathful astonishment, he exclaimed: "Who is this weak Woman, that commands us and oppresses us with so much power? What new surprise is this, and how can my pride stand it? We must hold a council and see how we can unite to destroy Her." Since I will say more of their doings in the next chapter, I leave them to their wrathful designs. Our

pilgrims in the meanwhile came to another tavern, the master of which was a man of bad habits and character; and as a beginning of his happiness, God ordained that he should receive most holy Mary and Joseph with a good will and marks of kindness. He showed them more courtesy and good services than he was accustomed to show to others. In order to return his hospitality with still greater kindness the great Queen, who knew the sad state of his interior, prayed for him, justifying his soul and causing him to change his life. Her prayers had also the effect of adding to his worldly possession, for on account of the small favor done to his heavenly guests, God increased them from that time on. Many more miracles the Mother of grace wrought in this journey, for all her doings were divine (Cant. 4, 13), and all who were of proper disposition were sanctified by meeting Her. They finished their journey at Nazareth, where the Princess of heaven set her house in order and cleaned it with the assistance of her holy angels, for they vied with Her in humility and were anxious to serve and honor Her by taking part in these humble occupations. The holy Joseph applied himself to his ordinary daily work, providing for the sustenance of the Queen; and his trusting heart was not deceived in Her (Prov, 31, 11). She girded Herself with new strength for the mysteries which She awaited, and She put forth her hands to valiant deeds, enjoying in her soul the undimmed vision of the Treasure of her womb and, connected with it, incomparable delights and blessings. Thus She continued to gain vast merits and made Herself unspeakably pleasing to God.

Words of the Queen

THE VIRGIN MARY SPEAKS TO SISTER MARY OF AGREDA

320. My daughter, the faithful souls and children of the Church, who know God, must make no distinction of time, place or occasions in the practice of faith and the other virtues connected with it. For God is present in all things and fills them with his infinite being (Jer. 23, 24), and in all places and circumstances faith will enable them to see and adore Him in spirit and in truth (John 4, 22). Just as preservation follows upon creation, and as breathing follows upon life, and just as there is no intermission in the breathing, nourishment and growth of man until the end is reached: so the rational creature, after having been regenerated by faith of grace, must never interrupt the course of the spiritual life, continually pursuing works of life by faith, hope and charity in all places and at all time (James 2, 26). On account of their forgetfulness and carelessness, the children of men, and especially the members of the Church, possess the life of faith as if they had lost it, allowing it to die for want of charity. These are the ones who have received in vain this their new soul, as David says, because they neglect it as if they had never obtained it (Psalm 23, 4).

321. I desire, my dearest, that thy spiritual life be just as continual as thy natural life. Thou must continue to lead a life such as is required by the grace and gifts of the Most High, believing and hoping in the Lord, loving, praising and adoring Him in spirit and in truth, no matter what changes there may be in time, occupation or place, He is in all things and He wishes to be loved and served by all rational creatures. I therefore charge thee that whenever souls come to thee full of this forgetfulness of their faults, and harassed by the demons, thou pray for them with lively faith and confidence. If the Lord does not always fulfill what thou desirest

and what they ask, He will follow his own secret counsel, and thou wilt have pleased Him by having acted as a true spouse and daughter. If thou faithfully followest my instructions, I assure thee that He will confer upon thee many special privileges for the benefit of souls. Consider what I did at the sight of souls displeasing to the Lord, and how zealously I worked for all, and for some in particular. To imitate and oblige me, do thou likewise work and pray for those whose interior becomes known to thee through the Lord or through other means; admonish them with prudence, humility and resignation; for the Almighty does not desire thee to proceed noisily, nor that the results of thy labors be always manifest, but that they remain hidden. In this He conforms Himself to thy naturally retiring disposition and to thy desires, and He seeks what is most secure for thee. And, although thou must pray for all souls, yet thou must pray more earnestly for those whom the divine will points out to thee.

Chapter XXVI

THE DEMONS HOLD A MEETING IN HELL IN ORDER TO
TAKE COUNSEL AGAINST MOST HOLY MARY.

322. At the instant of the incarnation of the Word, as I said
in chapter eleventh (140), Lucifer and all hell felt the power
of the right arm of the Almighty which hurled them to the
deepest of the infernal caverns. There they remained overwhelmed for some days, until the Lord in his admirable
providence allowed them to come forth from this captivity,
the cause of which they did not know. The great dragon then
arose and scoured the earth, spying everywhere for new
developments to which he might attribute the rout which he
and all his satellites had experienced. This search the proud
prince of darkness would not trust entirely to his companions, but he himself issued forth in their company to course
about upon the globe, seeking with the most cunning malice
to find what he wanted. He spent in this search three months
and finally returned to hell just as ignorant of the true cause
as when he had come forth. For the great mysteries of heaven
were not intelligible to him at that time, because the darkness
of his malice did not permit him either to rejoice in their
wonderful effects or to glorify and bless their Author. This
was reserved to us men, for whom Redemption was inaugurated.

323. The enemy of God was very much confused and aggrieved, without knowing how to account for it. In order to discuss the matter, he called together all the infernal hosts, without excusing or permitting a single one of the demons to be absent. In this convention, from a place of vantage, he addressed the meeting in this manner: "You well know, my subjects, with what great anxiety I, ever since God has cast us out from his dwelling and deprived us of our might, have sought to avenge myself and tried to destroy the power of the Almighty. Although I cannot do anything to injure Him, I have spared no time or exertion in extending my dominion over men whom He loves. By my own strength I have peopled my reign (Job 41, 25) and many nations and tribes obey and follow me (Luke 4, 6). Day by day I draw toward myself innumerable souls, depriving them of the knowledge and possession of God, in order that they may not enjoy the happiness which we have lost. I ensnare them to these eternal pains which we suffer, since they will follow my teachings and guidance: on them I will wreak the vengeance which I have conceived against their Creator. But all this appears of small consequence to me in the face of the sudden overthrow which we have experienced; for an attack so powerful and ruinous has not happened to us since we were hurled from heaven. I must acknowledge that as well your as my power has met a serious shock. This new and extraordinary defeat must have some new cause, and our weakness, I fear, is the beginning of our ruin."

324. "This matter will require renewed diligence, for my fury is unquenchable and my vengeance remains insatiable. I have scoured the whole earth, observed all its inhabitants with great care, and yet I have found nothing notable. I have watched and persecuted all the virtuous and perfect women who are of the race of Her whom we saw in heaven, and whom I expected to meet among them. But I find no sign of

her having as yet been born; for I do not find one who possesses the marks of Her who is to be the Mother of the Messias. A Maiden whom I feared on account of her great virtues, and whom I persecuted in the temple, is already married; and therefore She can not be the one we look for, since Isaiah says She is to be a Virgin (Is. 7, 14). Nevertheless I fear and detest this Maiden, since such a virtuous Woman might give birth to the Mother of the Messias or to some great prophet. To this hour I have not been able to overcome Her in anything, and of Her life I understand less than of that of others. She has always valiantly resisted me, as She eludes my memory; or remembering Her, I cannot approach Her. I have not yet been able to decide whether these difficulties in regard to Her are miraculous, or arise from my forgetfulness, or whether they are simply the consequences of the contempt in which I hold such an insignificant Maiden. But I will consider this matter; for recently we could not resist the power of her command, by which we were dispossessed of our right to dwell in those persons from whom She drove us. This certainly requires satisfaction, and She merits my wrath solely on account of what She has shown Herself to be on these occasions. I resolve to persecute Her and overcome Her, and do you yourselves assist me in this enterprise with all your strength and malice; and those who will distinguish themselves in this conquest shall receive great rewards at my hands."

325. The whole infernal rabble, which had listened attentively to Lucifer, praised and approved his intentions, and they told him not to worry over this Woman, for She would easily be overcome and he should not be without his triumphs over Her, since his power was so great and ruled all the world (John 14, 30). Then they set about discussing the means of entrapping most holy Mary, supposing Her to be a woman of distinguished and remarkable virtue and holiness,

but not the Mother of the incarnate Word; for at that time, as I have said, the demons were ignorant of the hidden sacrament connected with Her. Accordingly Lucifer and his companions in malice immediately entered upon a mighty conflict with the heavenly Princess, thus making it possible for Her to crush the head of the infernal dragon many times (Gen. 3, 15). Yet, though this was a great battle, and one of the most remarkable conflicts of her life, She fought another one later on after the Ascension of her most holy Son into heaven. Of this I will speak in the third part of this history. It was very remarkable, because Lucifer at that time already knew Her as the Mother of God. Saint John speaks of it in the twelfth chapter of the Apocalypse, as I will explain in its place.

326. In dispensing the mysteries of the Incarnation the providence of the Most High was most admirable, and so it is even yet in the government of the Catholic Church. There is no doubt that it is befitting the strong and sweet providence of God to hide many things from the demons, which are better unknown to them; as well because they are unworthy of knowing the sacred mysteries (for the reason given above in number 318), as also because the divine power becomes more manifest in keeping the demons in subjection. But it is especially necessary that they remain in ignorance in order that the works of God in the Church and his sacraments may take their course in greater peace; also in order that the unmeasured wrath of the demons may be more effectively curbed by not allowing them to proceed according to their malice. Although the Almighty could always repress and restrain the devils by force, yet He proceeds in this matter according to what is most appropriate to his infinite goodness. On this account the Lord concealed from these enemies the dignity of the most holy Mary and the wonderful manner of her pregnancy, as well as her virginal integrity

before and after the birth; and He concealed it still more effectively by giving her a husband. Likewise they were uncertain of the Divinity of Christ our Lord until the moment of his Death; only then they saw that they had been deceived and misled in regard to many mysteries of the Redemption. Instead of inciting the Jews to inflict upon Him the most cruel death, they would have sought to prevent it, and they would have tried to retard our Redemption by making known to the world that Christ is the true God. Therefore, when saint Peter confessed Him as such, Christ forbade him and the rest of the Apostles to make it known to anybody (Matth. 16, 20). Although, on account of the miracles He wrought and the exorcisms which He performed (Luke 8,28), they almost began to suspect Him to be the Messias, and called Him Son of God; yet his Majesty would not allow them to publish it about. Nor did they call Him so with certain conviction. For their suspicions subsided when they saw our Lord despised and fatigued: they could never penetrate the mystery of the Savior's humility and their inflated pride kept them in darkness.

327. Since Lucifer then did not know the dignity of Mary the Mother of God at the time of this persecution, fierce as it was, it was not so terrible as the one She suffered later on, when He knew who She was. If in this present occasion he had known that She was the One whom he had seen in heaven clothed with the sun and (Apoc. 12, 1) that She was to crush his head (Gen. 3, 15), he would have been lashed into devouring fury and consumed in fiery wrath. If they were so fearfully enraged at the mere thought of her sanctity and perfection, it is certain, that, had they known her greatness, they would, as far as would be allowed them, have disturbed the whole universe, in order to make an end of Her. However, since they on the one hand were ignorant of the mysteries of the heavenly Lady and other hand felt the

effects of her extreme virtue and sanctity, they were on this occasion thrown into confusion and doubt, asking each other: who this Woman could be, against whom they saw their power dwindle into insignificance? And whether perhaps She was not the one who was to hold first place among creatures?

328. Others judged that She could not possibly be the Mother of the Messias, for whom men were waiting; for besides having a husband, She with her husband belonged to the poorest, humblest, and the most insignificant people in this world: they had wrought no public miracles or prodigies, nor had they attracted the esteem or reverence of any of their fellowmen. As Lucifer and his associates are so proud, they could not persuade themselves that such extreme humility and self-debasement can consort with the dignity of Mother of God. Lucifer thought that God in his power would not choose for Himself what the devil had considered unworthy of his own dignity, which he knew was beneath that of the Almighty. In short, he was deceived by his own arrogance and giddy pride, for these are the vices which are most apt to darken the intellect and to drag the will to ruin. On this account Solomon says, that their own malice has made them blind (Sap. 2, 21), in order that they might not know that the eternal Word was to make use of such means in order to destroy the arrogance and haughtiness of the dragon. For his thoughts were distant from those of the Almighty farther than the earth is distant from heaven (Is. 55, 9). He thought that God would come from heaven into the world with great show of strength and opposition, humiliating by his power the proud princes and monarchs, which the demon had filled with his own arrogance; and so well had he succeeded, that many, who reigned before the time of Christ, were inflated with such pride and presumption, as to have lost their common sense and to have forgotten that they were mortal and

earthly. Lucifer judged of all these things according to his own vanity and according to his own method of proceeding against the works of the Lord.

329. But the infinite Wisdom took measures beyond all the calculations of Lucifer: for He came to conquer him not only by his Omnipotence, but by humility, meekness, obedience and poverty, which are the weapons of his warfare (II Cor. 10, 4); far from Him are the empty show and vanity maintained by the riches of the world. He came disguised and hidden in the outward appearance of lowliness; He chose a poor Mother. All that the world values, He came to despise, teaching the true science of life in word and example. Thus the devil found himself deceived and overcome by the very things that were most repugnant and unbearable to him.

330. In ignorance of all these mysteries Lucifer spent some days in spying out and reconnoitering the natural condition of most holy Mary, her character, temperament, inclinations, the tranquility, evenness and considerateness of her conduct; but the enemy could discover no flaw. Seeing the perfection and sweetness of all that concerned Her, and that She was like an impregnable wall, he returned to his demons and laid before them the great difficulty of tempting Her. All of them projected mighty plans of attack, encouraging each other in trying to solve the difficulties. Of the execution of these designs, of the glorious triumphs of the heavenly Princess over all her enemies, and of the foiling of all their damned and malicious counsels, I will speak in the following chapter.

Words of the Queen

THE VIRGIN MARY SPEAKS TO SISTER MARY OF AGREDA

331. My daughter, I wish that thou be very cautious and watchful in regard to the ignorance and darkness, by which

the demon commonly ensnares mortals and makes them forget their eternal salvation and the continual danger of its loss through his persecutions. Men are lost in forgetful rest and sleep, as if there were no vigilant and powerful enemies. This dreadful carelessness arises from two causes: on the one hand men are so taken up with their earthly and sensible being (I Cor. 2, 14), that they do not feel any other evils except those concerning the animal nature in them; all that is interior is harmless in their estimation. On the other hand, since the princes of darkness are invisible and unperceived by any of the senses (Ephes, 6, 12) and since carnal men neither touch, nor feel, nor see them, they forget the fear of them. Yet for this very reason they ought to be more attentive and careful, since invisible enemies are more cunning and adroit in injuring us by their treachery. So much the more certain is the danger, the more concealed it is, and so much the more deadly are the wounds, the less they are felt and recognized.

332. Listen, my daughter, to most important truths concerning eternal life. Attend to my counsels, follow my instructions and receive my warnings; for if thou pass them by unheeded, I will cease to speak to thee. Hear what thou hast not until now known of the disposition of these enemies. I wish to make known to thee that no intellect, nor any tongue of man or angels can describe the wrath and fury which Lucifer and his demons entertain against mortals just because they are images of God and because they are capable of enjoying Him for all eternity. The Lord alone can comprehend the wicked malice of these proud and rebellious spirits against his holy name and against his worship. If these foes were not restrained by his almighty arm they would in one moment destroy the world; they would like famishing lions, like wild beasts and fierce dragons, dispatch all mankind and tear them to pieces. Now however the most kind Father of all mercies wards off and curbs their wrath and He bears his

little children in his arms in order that they may not fall a prey to these hellish wolves.

333. Consider then, as seriously as thou canst, whether anything deserves greater pity, than to see so many men misled into danger and made forgetful of it; how some of them cast themselves into it on account of their lightheartedness, some of them for trivial reasons, others for a short and instantaneous pleasure, others through negligence, and yet others on account of their inordinate appetites, tearing themselves away from the places of refuge, in which the Almighty has placed them, to fall into the hands of such cruel and furious enemies; and not only to feel their fury for an hour, a day, a month, a year, but to suffer indescribable and unmeasured torments for all eternity. Thou shouldst be filled with fear and wonder, my daughter, to see such horrible and dreadful foolishness among the impenitent mortals and to see even the faithful, who have come to know and confess all this by faith, so far lose their understanding and allow themselves to be so insanely blinded by the devil that they neither regard nor avoid this danger.

334. In order that thou mayest fear it and preserve thyself the better, remember that this dragon knows thee and lurks about thee ever since the hour of thy creation and entrance into this world. Night and day he restlessly prowls about seeking some chance of capturing thee as a prize. He observes thy natural inclinations and also the gifts of the Lord, in order to combat thee with thy own weapons. He charges other demons with thy ruin and promises reward to those that are more diligent in securing it. They weigh thy actions carefully, watch thy footsteps, and work zealously to lay snares for thee in all thy undertakings. I desire thee to meditate on these truths in the Lord, who will show thee whither they lead; compare them afterwards with thy own experience and thou wilt understand, whether thou hast any occasion

for sleep in the midst for such dangers. Although this watchfulness is important for all the woman-born, it is more necessary to thee than to others for especial reasons: and if I do not mention them all to thee now, do not doubt, that thou must live with great vigilance and caution. It suffices to remind thee of thy soft and yielding nature, which thy enemies will strive to make use of for thy destruction.

Chapter XXVII

THE LORD PREPARES MOST HOLY MARY TO MEET LUCIFER
IN BATTLE AND THE DRAGON BEGINS TO PERSECUTE HER.

335. The eternal Word, already made man in the womb of
Mary the Virgin, and possessing Her as his Mother, was
aware of the designs of Lucifer, not only through the uncre-
ated knowledge of his Godhead, but also by the created
knowledge of his humanity. He prepared the defense of his
tabernacle, which was more estimable in his sight than all the
rest of the creatures. In order to clothe the invincible Lady
with new strength against the foolhardy daring of the treacherous dragon and his hosts, the most holy humanity of
Christ, rose up as it were in an attitude of defense in the
virginal chamber of Mary in order to meet and offer battle to
the princes of darkness. In this position He prayed to the
Father and asked Him to renew his favors and graces in
Mary, in order that She might with added strength crush the
head of the ancient serpent, that this Woman might humiliate and overcome him, frustrate his designs and all his powers, and that She come forth triumphant and victorious over
hell to the glory and praise of God and of his virginal Mother.

336. The prayer of Christ our Lord was punctually fulfilled in the most blessed Trinity. Then, in an indescribable

manner, her most holy Son was shown to Mary in her virginal womb. In this vision the plenitude of graces and unspeakable gifts were vouchsafed to Her. Illumined anew with additional light of wisdom She recognized the highest and most hidden mysteries impossible to describe. She understood especially that Lucifer had prepared vast designs of pride against the glory of the Lord; and that his arrogance rose up to drink the pure waters of Jordan (Job 40, 18). The Most High, informing Her of these things, said to Her:

"My Spouse and my Dove, the infernal dragon thirsts with such wrath against my holy name and all those that adore it, that he wishes to drag toward him all without exception and with daring presumption he tries to blot out my name from the land of the living. I wish thee, my Beloved, to come to the defense of my cause and of my holy name, by giving battle to the cruel enemy; and I will be with thee in battle, since I am in thy virginal womb. I wish that thou confound and destroy the enemies before I appear in the world; for they are convinced that the Redemption of the world is nigh and therefore they desire to gain over and ruin all souls without exception, before the world is redeemed. I trust this victory to thy fidelity and love. Do thou battle in my name, just as I in thee, against this dragon and ancient serpent" (Apoc. 12, 9).

337. These words of the Lord and the knowledge of these secrets so moved the heart of the heavenly Mother, that I cannot find expression for that which then happened. When She understood, that her most holy Son wished Her to defend the honor of the Most High, She was so inflamed with divine love and filled with such invincible fortitude, that, if each one of the demons would have been an entire hell and filled with the fury of all its inmates, they altogether would have been only like a few weak ants, compared to the incomparable strength of this our valiant Leader. All of them

She would have vanquished and destroyed by the smallest part of her virtues and of her zeal for the honor and glory of the Lord. And her divine Protector and Helper ordained this glorious triumph of his most holy Mother over hell, in order that the arrogance of his enemies might no longer lord it over us nor rest assured of being able to destroy the world. But He wished to hasten its Redemption and put us mortals under obligation not only to the inestimable love of his most holy Son, but also to Mary, our heavenly Defender and Reparatrix, She was to issue forth to battle, stop his progress, vanquish and suppress him, placing mankind on a proper footing for the reception of their Redeemer.

338. O sons of men, dull and slow of heart! How is it that you do not heed such admirable blessings? Who is man, that Thou shouldst honor and favor Him thus (Ps. 8, 5), O most high King! Thy own Mother and our Mistress Thou sendest out to labor and combat in our defense! Who ever heard of similar happenings? Who has ever shown such force and ingenuity of love? Where is our intellect? Who has deprived us of the use of reason? What hardness of heart is this? What has drawn us into such vile ingratitude? What shameful conduct of men, who, while they claim to love and honor Her so much, are guilty of such low and infamous ingratitude as to forget such an obligation? The true nobility and honor of the sons of Adam would rather seem to consist in thanking Her incessantly and sacrificing their lives in gratitude!

339. The obedient Mother, offering Herself to battle with Lucifer for the honor of her most holy Son, of the holy Trinity and our own, answered Him that had commanded Her, saying: "My Lord and highest Good, from whom I have received my being and all the grace and light which I possess: to Thee I belong entirely, and Thou, Lord, hast condescended to be my Son. Do with thy servant, what shall be to thy

greater glory and pleasure. For if Thou art in me, and I in Thee, who shall be powerful enough to resist thy will? I shall be the instrument of thy almighty arm: give me thy strength and come with me, and let us go forth to battle against the dragon with all his followers." In the meanwhile Lucifer issued from the meeting, now filled with such hateful spite against Her, that he considered the perdition of all the other souls as of small consequence. If we could know the fury of satan as it is in reality, we would understand better what God says to holy Job, that he counts steel as straw and bronze as rotten wood (Job 41, 18). Such was the wrath of the dragon against most holy Mary; and such it is even now against the souls; for if he esteemed the most holy, the invincible and most strong Woman to be no more than a dried up leaf, what will he do to sinners, who like empty and decaying reeds do not withstand him? (Ephes. 6, 16). Living faith alone and humility of heart are the double armor which enable them to procure glorious victory.

340. In order to begin his battle Lucifer brought with him the seven legions with their seven principal leaders whom after the fall from heaven he had appointed to tempt men to the seven capital sins (Apoc. 12). Each of these seven squadrons he charged with the duty of exerting their utmost strength against the immaculate Princess. The invincible Lady was occupied in prayer, when the Lord permitted the first legion of devils to begin the battle by tempting Her to the sin of pride, to which special work they had been appointed. They sought to approach the heavenly Queen by trying to cause changes in her natural passions and inclinations, for this is the ordinary way in which the demons find access to other mortals; and they thought that She was infected in the same way as other men with passions disordered by sin. They could not however come as close to Her as they wished, for they were repelled by the fragrance of her

virtues and holiness, which tormented them more than the
fire which consumes them. In spite of this obstacle and
although the very sight of most holy Mary pierced them with
raging torments, they nevertheless ignored their pains and
lashed themselves into furious and ungovernable wrath in
their obstinate endeavors to approach nearer to Her and exert
upon Her their cursed and damnable influence.

341. The most holy Mary, who was alone and left only to
her natural forces, stood prepared for the assault of those
countless demons; yet She by Herself was as formidable and
terrible (Cant. 6, 3) to them as many armies in battle array.
They presented themselves before Her (Ps. 118, 85) in the
most horrid masks and with wicked lies. But the sovereign
Queen, teaching us how to conquer, did not change her
position nor was moved interiorly or exteriorly, nor did She
show any emotion of fear in her countenance. She took no
notice of them, nor attended to them any more than if they
had been the weakest ants. She despised them with an invincible and magnanimous heart; for this kind of battle, as it is a
battle of virtues, is not accompanied by the extremes of noise
and excitement, but is fought in all tranquillity, in outward
and inward peace and modesty. Just as little could She be
moved by the passions and the appetites; for these were not
in subservience to the devil in our Queen. In Her they were
all swayed by reason, and this again was subject to God, since
none of her faculties had been cast into disorder by the first
sin, as in the rest of the children of Adam. Therefore the
arrows of these enemies, as David says, were like those of
little children (Ps. 63, 8), and their armories were like those
which were without ammunition. Only to themselves were
they harmful, for their weakness only brought upon them
confusion. Although they were not aware of the innocence
and the original justice of most holy Mary and therefore did
not understand that She was not to be injured by the com-

mon temptations; yet by the Majesty of her bearing and her constancy they could conjecture their ill-success and how She despised them. Their efforts were not of the least avail; for, as says the Apostle in the Apocalypse (Apoc. 12, 18) and as I have mentioned in the first part (1–129), the earth helped the Woman, who was clothed with the sun, when the dragon opened upon Her the flood of his impetuous temptations; meaning thereby, that the earthly body of this Lady had not been vitiated in its faculties and passions, as those of others, who had been touched by sin.

342. The demons then assumed corporeal shapes of the most horrible and dreadful kind; and they began to emit fearful howls, roaring with terrible voices, pretending to rush upon Her and threatening destruction; they shook the earth and the house, striving also by other furious assaults to frighten and disturb the Princess of the world; so that at least in this, or in making Her desist from prayer they might seem victorious. But the invincible and magnanimous heart of most holy Mary was not disturbed, nor moved in the least. It must be remembered, that in order to enter upon this battle, the Lord left Her entirely to the resources of her own faith and virtue. He suspended the effects of the other favors and privileges, which She was wont to enjoy at other times. The Most High wished it so, in order that the triumph of his Mother might be more glorious and honorable; besides this there were the other reasons, which God has in allowing the souls to be tempted in this manner. His judgments are unsearchable and unknowable (Rom. 11, 33). At times the great Lady would repeat: "Who is like unto God, that lives in the highest and looks upon the humble in heaven and on earth?" (Ps. 112, 5). By these words She routed the hosts that opposed Her.

343. Then these hungry wolves laid aside their terrible shapes: they assumed sheeps' clothing, transforming them-

selves into angels of light, resplendent and beautiful. Approaching the heavenly Lady, they said: "Thou hast conquered, Thou hast conquered, we come to attend on Thee and reward thy fortitude and invincible courage." Surrounding Her, they protested their friendship in flattering and deceitful terms. But the most prudent Lady withdrew within Herself, suspended all the activity of her senses and, raising Herself above Herself (Thren. 3, 28) by means of the infused virtues, adored the Lord in spirit and in truth (J no. 4, 23). Despising all the snares of these evil tongues and their deceitful lies, She spoke to her most holy Son: "My Lord and Master, Light of light and my Strength, in thy help alone do I place all my confidence and the exaltation of thy holy name. All those that speak otherwise I abjure, abhor and detest." But the doers of evil persevered in their insane attempts against the Mother of knowledge and continued to extol beyond the skies Her, who had humiliated Herself beneath the lowest of creatures. They protested that they wished to exalt Her above all women and confer upon Her an exquisite favor: they would select Her in the name of the Lord for the Mother of the Messias, and they assured Her that her holiness would be greater than that of the Patriarchs and Prophets.

344. Lucifer himself was the author of this new plot and his malice is here made known for a warning to other souls. But it was ridiculous to offer to Mary, the Queen of heaven, a dignity already her own. They themselves were ensnared and deceived, not only in offering what they neither knew nor were able to give, but also in being ignorant of the sacrament of the King so intimately connected with the most blessed Woman, whom they persecuted. Nevertheless the iniquity of the dragon was great, because he knew that he could not fulfill what he promised. He tried to spy out whether perhaps our blessed Lady held that dignity, or

whether She would give him some signs, by which he could conjecture it. Most holy Mary was aware of this double-dealing of Lucifer, and admirably met it with a quiet firmness. She answered the deceitful flatteries by quietly continuing her prayer and adoring the Lord. Prostrated upon the floor She humiliated Herself, confessing Herself as the most despicable of creatures, more despicable than the dust under her feet. By this humble prayer and prostration She cut off the presumptuous pride of Lucifer as long as this temptation lasted. As for the rest which happened, the cunning of the demons, their cruelty and lying deceits on this occasion, it seemed to me, that I should not relate all, nor that I should expatiate on all that has been shown to me; let this much suffice for our instruction; for not all can be trusted to the ignorance of weak and earthly creatures.

345. Dismayed and routed, the first host of enemies retired and gave way to the second. These were to tempt Her, who was the most poor of human kind, to the sin of avarice. They offered to Her great riches, gold, silver, and most precious gems and in order that these might not seem empty promises, thy placed before Her a great quantity of these riches, although they were only apparent; for they thought that they could exert greater influence on her will by actually presenting these objects before Her. They accompanied this offer with many deceitful words and told Her that God had sent Her all this for distribution among the poor. When they saw that all this had no effect upon Her, they changed their tactics and urged, that since She was so holy, it was a great wrong that She should remain so poor. It was more reasonable that She possess these riches, than that they remain in the hands of wicked sinners, for this would be an injustice and a disarrangement of the divine Providence that the just be visited with poverty, while God's wicked enemies abound in riches and affluence.

346. In vain the net is spread before the eyes of the bird in its flight, says the wise man. This was true of all the temptations of our sovereign Queen; but the malice of the serpent was much more preposterous in regard to this temptation of avarice, for this Phoenix of poverty was so far removed from the earth, and winged her flight so far above that of even the seraphim, that such a vile and contemptible snare was entirely in vain. The most prudent Lady, although She possessed divine wisdom, never undertook to argue with these enemies, as in truth nobody should; for they battle against the manifest truth and will not admit defeat, even when they must acknowledge its effects. The most holy Mary made use of some words of the holy Scriptures and repeated them with serene humility. On this occasion She selected the words of the 118th Psalm: "Haereditate acquisivi testimonia tua in aeternum," "I have acquired for my heritage and for my riches the keeping of thy testimonies and thy laws, my Lord" (Ps. 118, 112). She made use of many other passages, gratefully praising and blessing the Most High, because He had created and preserved Her without her merits. In this most wise manner She rejected and overcame the second temptation, to the confusion and torment of these agents of iniquity.

347. Then advanced the third legion, led on by the prince of impurity who assails the weakness of the flesh. These made so much the greater efforts, because they foresaw more clearly the improbability of success; and in truth they gained less than all the others, if one may speak of more or less in these different temptations of the Virgin Mary. They tried to suggest to Her vile images and to produce before her eyes unspeakable monstrosities. But all their efforts vanished in midair; for the most pure Virgin, as soon as She had recognized the first signs of this vice, withdrew entirely within Herself and suspended all the activity of her senses. Thus not

even the shadow of a suggestion or indecent image could enter her thoughts, since none of her faculties were in action. With the most ardent longing She renewed many times her vow of chastity in the presence of the Lord, and She merited more on this occasion than all the virgins that ever existed or will exist in this world. The Almighty furnished Her with such virtue, that in comparison the sudden expulsion of the cannon ball from the cannon, is but a poor image of the force with which these enemies were repelled from the presence of most holy Mary when they sought to touch her purity by their temptations.

348. The fourth legion undertook to test her meekness and patience, seeking to move this mildest Dove to anger. This temptation was most annoying, for the demons overturned the whole house: they broke and shattered everything contained therein, and in such a manner as to cause the greatest amount of annoyance to the most meek Lady; but her holy angels soon repaired all the damage. Foiled in this attempt, the demons assumed the shapes of some women known to the serenest Princess. They flew at Her with greater wrath and fury than if they had been real women; they added outrageous insults, dared to threaten Her, and took possession of things most necessary. But all these were only despicable tricks in the eyes of Her that knew them; for none of their pranks and assaults escaped the penetration of the most holy Mary. She disregarded them altogether and despised them entirely, without giving any signs of being moved or influenced by them. The demons then chose a real woman of a disposition adapted to their purposes, whom they influenced by diabolical art against the Princess of heaven. For this purpose one of the demons assumed the shape of an acquaintance of this Woman and began to tell her that this Mary, the wife of Joseph, had slandered her in her presence

and had accused her of many gross faults, which this demon invented for the occasion.

349. The deceived woman, who was naturally very much inclined to anger, hastened furiously to our meekest Lamb and hurled at Her the vilest accusations and insults. She, however, allowing the angry woman to pour out her wrath gradually began to speak to her in words so humble and sweet, that She changed her entirely, appeased and softened her heart. When She had thus brought her about, She consoled and admonished her against the wiles of the devil. As this woman was poor, Mary added some alms and dismissed her in peace. Thus also this attempt was foiled, just as were many others, by which Lucifer tried to irritate our meekest Dove and bring her into discredit. The Most High always defended the honor of his most holy Mother, making use of her own perfection in virtue and of her prudence and humility, so that the devil could never succeed in harming her good name in the least. She always acted so prudently and with so much meekness and wisdom, that the multitude of the hellish attempts were totally ineffectual. The tranquility and meekness of the sovereign Lady during these temptations of the dragon caused the admiration of the angels. Even the demons were full of astonishment, (though of a different kind), at seeing such behavior in a mere creature and that a woman; for never had they seen the like.

350. The fifth legion followed with temptations to gluttony. Although the ancient serpent did not bid our Queen to turn stones into bread (Matth. 4, 3) as he afterwards presumed to do with her most holy Son (for he had not seen Her do such great wonders, since they had been withheld from his know ledge), yet he tempted Her like the first woman with the pleasures of the taste (Gen. 1). They placed before Her a great feast, in order to incite and mislead her appetite by outward allurance; they tried to influence the

humors of her body, so as to cause in Her a counterfeit hunger and they used other means to attract her attention to what they were offering. But all their labor was in vain and without effect; for from all these material and earthly things the noble heart of our Princess was as far removed as heaven is from earth. Just as little did She use her senses in order to enjoy the pleasures of taste, yea She never even took notice of them; for in all things She had set Herself to counteract what our first mother Eve had done. Eve incautiously and heedlessly had looked upon the beauty of the tree of knowledge and upon its sweet fruit, and then had reached out her hand to eat, thus beginning our woe. Not so most holy Mary, who withdrew and locked up her senses, although She was in no such danger as Eve. Our first mother was overcome for our perdition, while our Queen conquered for our rescue and salvation.

351. Much dismayed by the discomfitures of the preceding hosts, the spirits of envy approached. Though they could not estimate the full perfection of the deeds of the Mother of sanctity, they nevertheless felt her invincible strength. They had seen Her so unmovable that they almost despaired of enticing Her to any of their wicked purposes. Nevertheless the insatiate hatred of the dragon and his inmeasurable pride would not yield; they laid new plots in order to provoke the Lady most beloved of the Lord and of men to envy in others what She Herself possessed and even what She abhorred as useless and dangerous. They drew up a long list of natural blessings possessed by others and denied to Her. And as they thought that supernatural gifts would move Her more, they mentioned great spiritual favors and blessings, which the Almighty had conferred upon others and not upon Her. But how could these lying representations move Her, who was the Mother of all the graces and gifts of heaven? For the blessings of all the creatures taken together were less than her

single privilege of being the Mother of the Author of grace. Precisely because his Majesty had so favored Her and because the fire of his charity burned within Her, She ardently desired, that the hand of the Most High enrich and favor her fellowmen so much the more. How then could envy find room, where charity abounded? (I Cor. 13,4). But the fierce enemies would not desist. They pictured to the Queen the apparent happiness of those, who in their riches and good fortune, considered themselves happy and exalted in this world. They induced several persons to approach most holy Mary and describe to Her the consolation of being rich and well to do. As if this deceitful happiness of mortals had not been condemned so often in holy Scriptures (Ps. 48), and as if contempt of riches had not been the very science and doctrine, which the Queen of heaven and her most holy Son had come to exemplify in their lives for the benefit of the whole world!

352. Those persons, who came to our heavenly Mother, were exhorted by Her to use the temporal goods and riches well and to give thanks for them to the Author of all good. She Herself fulfilled this duty, making up for the habitual ingratitude of men. Although the most humble Lady judged Herself unworthy of the least of blessings of the Most High; yet Her own sanctity and exalted dignity in point of fact gave witness to the words of holy Scriptures saying in her name; "With me are glorious riches and justice. For my fruit is better than gold and precious stone" (Prov. 8, 18). "In me is all grace of the way and the truth, in me is all hope of life and of virtue" (Eccli. 24, 25). In this exalted excellence of virtue She conquered all her enemies, astonishing and confusing them by this new experience. For they were made to feel that where they had exerted their greatest force and their deepest cunning, they gained least and experienced the greatest repulse.

353. Nevertheless the demons stubbornly persisted and proceeded with the seventh temptation, which was that of idleness. They sought to cause in Her a corporeal indisposition, or a feeling of weakness and fatigue, accompanied by dejection of spirit. This is a trick of satan little known and under its cover the sin of laziness causes much ruin among souls and prevents much progress in virtue. They suggested moreover that She postpone some exercises on account of weariness in order to be able to perform them so much the better after having rested. This too is one among many other tricks of satan, and we do not often discover it or know what to do against it. They also sought maliciously to hinder the most holy Lady in some exercises by means of human creatures, whom they sent to visit Her at unseasonable times, trying to impede the performance of some of her holy exercises and occupations at the time and hour set for them. But all these delusions were detected by the most prudent and alert Princess. She evaded them by her wise precautions, without permitting the enemy to succeed in any of them and acting in all things up to the standard of the most exquisite perfection. Her enemies were obliged to desist, hopelessly foiled and repulsed. Lucifer was full of rage against his companions and against himself. But in their fury and insane pride, they resolved to make one more general assault upon Mary, as I will relate in the following chapter.

Words of the Queen

THE VIRGIN MARY SPEAKS TO SISTER MARY OF AGREDA

354. My daughter, although thou hast only very briefly summed up my lengthy battle against temptations, I wish that from what thou hast written and from what thou knowest otherwise concerning these things, thou learn the manner of resisting and overcoming the powers of hell. The surest

way of fighting the demon is to despise him, looking upon him as the enemy of the Most High, who has lost all fear of God and all hope of good; who in his stubbornness has deprived himself of all means of recovery and is without sorrow for his wickedness, Relying on this indubitable truth thou shouldst show thyself far superior to him, exalted and unflinching in thy thoughts, and treat him as a contemner of the honor and worship of his God. Knowing that thou art defending so just a cause, do not let thy courage sink; but resist and counteract him with great strength and valor in all his attempts, as if thou wert fighting at the side of the Lord himself; for there is no doubt that his Majesty assists all those that enter loyally into his battles. Thou art truly in good hope and in the way of eternal life glory, as long as thou laborest faithfully for thy Lord and God.

355. Remember then, that the demons detest and abominate that which thou desirest and lovest, namely the honor of God and thy eternal felicity; and that they are striving to deprive thee of that which they cannot restore to themselves. God has reprobated the demon, while He offers to thee his grace, his virtues and his strength in order to overcome his and thy enemy and to procure for thee the happy end of eternal peace; only thou must work faithfully and keep the commandments of the Lord. The arrogance of the dragon is great (Is. 16,6), yet his weakness is greater; and he does not represent more than a weak atom in the face of the divine power. Yet as his cunning and malice far exceed that of mortals (Job 41, 21), it is not advisable to allow the soul to bandy words with him, whether he is present invisibly or visibly; for from his darksome mind, as from a smoking furnace, issue the shadows of confusion, obscuring the judgments of mortals; if they listen to him, he will fill their minds with deceits and darkness, so that they will neither recognize the truth and the beauty of virtue, nor the vileness of his

poisonous falsehoods. Thus the souls will be made unable to distinguish the precious from the worthless, life from death, truth from error (Jer. 15, 19), and they easily fall into the clutches of this fierce and wicked dragon.

356. In temptation let it be thy invariable course not to attend to anything which he proposes, not to listen, not to argue with him concerning aught. If thou canst withdraw and place thyself at a distance, so as not to perceive or recognize his wicked attempts, so much the more secure thou wilt be for thus looking upon him only at a distance. The demon always seeks to prepare the way for his deceits, especially in souls which he fears will resist his entrance unless he can thus facilitate his approach. He is accustomed to begin by causing sorrow or dejection of heart, or he makes use of other trickery or snares, by which he diverts or withdraws the soul from the love of the Lord; then he comes with his poison, concealed in the golden cup in order to diminish the horror of the soul. As soon as thou noticest in thyself any of these signs, (for thou hast thy experience, obedience and instructions for a guide), I wish that with the wings of the dove thou direct thy flight to the high refuge of the Almighty (Ps. 54, 7), calling upon Him for aid and proffering the merits of my most holy Son. To me also shouldst thou fly for protection as I am thy Mother and Teacher, and to thy devoted angels, and to all the rest of thy advocates in the Lord. Quickly close up thy senses and consider thyself as dead to them, or as a soul already belonging to the other life, whither the jurisdiction and the exacting tyranny of the serpent does not reach. Occupy thyself so much the more earnestly in the exercise of the virtue contrary to the vice to which he tempts thee, and especially in acts of faith, hope and love, which dispel cowardice and doubt, and weaken the influence of discouragement and fear in the human heart.

357. The arguments for overcoming Lucifer thou must seek in God alone; and do not disclose them to your enemy, lest he meet thee with fallacies and confusing pretense. Besides knowing it to be dangerous, esteem it as unworthy of thee to argue with him openly, or to pay particular attention to him, who is not only the enemy of thy Beloved but also of thee. Show thyself superior to him and highmindedly apply thyself to the practice of all virtues. Be content with this treasure and withdraw thyself; for the most skillful battle of the sons of God consists in flying farthest from evil. The devil is proud and is deeply hurt by contempt; in the presumption of his arrogance and vanity he desires above all the attention of men. On this account he is so persistent in pursuing us step by step; for in his deceitfulness he cannot rely upon the force of truth, but on his persistent counterfeiting of the good and the true. As long as this slave of wickedness is not despised, he never believes himself discovered and he continues, like an importunate fly, to buzz about the spot tainted by the greatest corruption.

358. Not less warily must thou conduct thyself, when thy enemy makes use of other creatures for thy destruction. This he does in two ways: either leading them on to immoderate love, or to undue dislike or hatred. As soon as thou noticest a disorderly affection in those with whom thou conversest, observe the same precaution as in flying from the demon; yet with this difference, that while thou hatest him as thy enemy, thou consider the others as God's creatures to whom thou must not deny the consideration due to them on account of his Majesty. But in as far as withdrawing from them is concerned, act as if they were thy enemies; for in regard to the service, which the Lord requires of thee and in regard to thy present condition, it is the devil who operates in these persons toward separating thee from thy God and from thy duty. If on the other hand they hate and persecute thee,

answer them with meekness and love, praying for them with intimate affection of thy heart (Matth. 5,44). If it should be necessary, soothe the wrath of thy persecutors with sweet words, and undeceive those who are led astray by false reports. Do this not in order to excuse thyself, but in order to pacify thy brothers and for their inward and outward peace; thus thou wilt at one and the same time conquer thyself and those who hate thee. In order to be well practiced in this way of acting it is necessary to cut off the very roots of the capital sins, to tear them out, and to die to the movements of the appetites. For in these appetites the seven capital vices to which the devil leads men, are rooted, and in these disorderly and undisciplined passions he sows the germs of the seven sins.

Chapter XXVIII

LUCIFER WITH ALI. HIS SEVEN LEGIONS PERSISTS IN TEMPT-
ING MOST HOLY MARY; SHE CONQUERS THE DRAGON AND
CRUSHES HIS HEAD.

359. Even if the prince of darkness and wickedness had now
retreated, his exorbitant pride would have been sufficiently
discomfited and humiliated by the victories, which had been
gained by the Queen of heaven. But as, even if vanquished,
he continues to rise up against God with insatiate malice, he
did not acknowledge his defeat (Ps, 73, 23). Finding himself
conquered, and conquered so completely by an apparently
insignificant and weak Woman, though he and his hosts had
overcome so many valiant men and high-minded women, his
fury raged onward, though in smothered flames of wrath.
God had permitted the enemies to become aware of the
pregnancy of the most holy Mary, though leaving them
under the impression, that it was entirely a natural process;
for the Divinity of the Child and other mysteries connected
with It always remained hidden to these enemies. Hence they
persuaded themselves that this was not the promised Messias,
since they held this Child to be a man like the rest of the
human race. This error also confirmed them in the mistake
that most holy Mary was not the Mother of the Word (Gen.
3, 15): Both of whom were to crush the head of the dragon.
Yet they were persuaded that of a Woman so valiant and

victorious, some man of distinguished sanctity would be born. The great dragon, convinced of this, conceived against the fruit of the most holy Mary that vast fury mentioned in the twelfth chapter of the Apocalypse and referred to in this history, and he awaited the birth of her Son in order to devour Him.

360. Whenever Lucifer directed his looks toward this Child enclosed in the womb of the most holy Mary, he felt a mysterious power oppressing him. Although his presence seemed to cause only a certain weakening and deadening of his strength; yet this was sufficient to enrage him and to make him seek by all means the destruction of this suspicious Child and of his victorious Mother. Assuming the most fearful shapes of fiercest bulls and terrible dragons or of other monsters, he sought to approach Her without ever being able to succeed. He rushed upon Her, but found himself repulsed, without knowing by whom or how. He struggled like a wild beast in chains and gave forth awe-inspiring howls, which, if God had not prevented their being heard, would have terrified the world and would have frightened many men to death. He shot forth from his mouth fire and fumes of sulphur mixed with poisonous spittle. All this the heavenly Princess Mary saw and heard, without being moved more than if She saw a gnat. He caused disturbances in the air, upon the earth, or in her house, disarranging and overthrowing it in all its parts; but most holy Mary still remained unmoved, retaining her inward and outward tranquillity and peace and showing Herself invincibly superior to all his attempts.

361. Lucifer, finding himself thus vanquished, opened his most impure mouth and set in motion his lying and defiled tongue. He loosened the floodgates of his malice and spouted forth in the presence of the heavenly Empress all the heresies and infernal falsehoods of the sects, which he and his associ-

ates spread through the world. For after they had been hurled from heaven and after they were informed that the divine Word was to assume human flesh in order to be the Chief of a race, which He would replenish with graces and celestial teachings, the dragon resolved to concoct falsehoods and heresies, in opposition to all the truths concerning the knowledge, love and worship of the Most High. In this occupation the demons consumed many years before the coming of Christ, the Lord of the world; and all this poisonous deceit Lucifer, the ancient serpent, had stored up within himself. Now he poured it out in the presence of the Mother of truth and purity; hoping to infect Her by all the falsehoods, which He had conceived against the truth of God up to that day.

362. They are not fit to be described here, even less so than some of the temptations indicated in the last chapter; for it would be dangerous not only for the weak souls, but even the strongest must fear the pestilential breath of Lucifer, who on this occasion exhaled all his deceitful malice. According to what I saw, I believe doubtlessly, that there was no error, idolatry or heresy known to have existed in the world to this day, which this dragon did not vomit forth in the hearing of the sovereign Mary. Therefore the Church can truly congratulate Mary on account of her victories, affirming of Her, that She by Herself has smothered and extinguished all the heresies of the whole world (Office B. V. M.). Thus in truth our victorious Sulamite, armed with her virtues advanced like an army in battle array (Cant. 7, 1) to confound, overwhelm and destroy the infernal hosts. All their falsehoods, and each one in particular, She refuted, contradicting, detesting and anathematizing all of them with invincible faith and sublime constancy. She proclaimed the various truths opposed to his falsehoods, magnifying the Lord by means of them as true, just and holy. She broke out into

songs of praise, in which his virtues and doctrines were extolled as true, holy, immaculate and altogether praiseworthy. In fervent prayer She besought the Lord to humiliate the arrogance of the demons by preventing them from spreading so freely their poisonous errors through the world, and asking Him to diminish the influence of the false teachings, which they had already sowed and which they were yet allowed to sow among men.

363. On account of this victory of the great Queen and on account of her prayers, I perceived that the Most High in justice set narrower bounds to the demons, so that they would not be able to scatter the seeds of error as much as they intended and as much as the sins of men would merit. Although their sins are the cause of so many heresies and sects unto this day, yet they would have caused many more, if most holy Mary had not crushed the head of the dragon by such great victories, by her prayers and petitions. I have been informed of a great mystery, which affords us consolation in this conflict of the holy Church against her wicked enemies. Namely, on account of this triumph of most holy Mary and on account of another, which She gained over the demons after the Ascension of our Lord (Part III, 528), the Almighty, in reward of her battles, decreed, that through her intercession and virtue all the heresies and sects of the world against the holy Church were to be destroyed and extinguished. The time appointed for this blessing was not made known to me; probably, the fulfillment of this decree is dependent upon some tacit and unknown condition. Yet I am sure, that if the Catholic princes and their subjects would seek to please this great Queen of heaven and betake themselves to her intercession as being their especial Patroness and Protectress, and if they would direct all their influence and riches, all their power and sovereignty toward the exaltation of the faith and the honor of God and of purest Mary (for this may perhaps

be the condition imposed), they would be as it were the instruments, by which the infidels would be refuted and vanquished, the sects and errors infesting the world would be repressed, and splendid and magnificent victories would be gained for the Catholic truth.

364. Before the birth of Christ our Redeemer it seemed to Lucifer (as was intimated in the foregoing chapter) that his coming was retarded by the sins of the world. In order to prevent his coming altogether he sought to increase this hindrance by multiplying the aberrations and crimes of mortals. This iniquitous pride of the devil the Lord confounded by the magnificent triumphs of his most holy Mother. After the Birth and the Death of the Redeemer, the malicious dragon sought to hinder and divert the fruits of his blood and redemption. For this purpose he began to sow and spread the errors, which after the times of the Apostles have afflicted and do now afflict the Church. The victory over this infernal malice was likewise left by Christ in the hands of his most holy Mother: for She alone could merit, and did merit, such a victory. Through Her idolatry was extinguished by the preaching of the Gospel; through Her were brought to naught the ancient sects of Arius, Nestorius and Pelagius and of others; She it was that instigated the zeal and solicitude of kings, princes, fathers, and doctors of the holy Church. Hence, how can it be doubted, if the Catholic princes, both of the Church and of the state, would use the proper diligence, aiding as it were this heavenly Lady, that She on her part would not fail to help them, conferring upon them happiness in this life and in the next, and cutting down all the heresies of the world? For this very purpose the Lord has so enriched so greatly as well the Church as the Catholic reigns and monarchies. If it were not for this purpose, it were better that they remain poor. It was not proper that all the results of the Gospel should be obtained through miracles,

but through natural means, obtainable by the proper application of riches. But it is not for me to judge whether they fulfill this obligation or not. I have only to report what the Lord himself has made known to me: that those who hold the titles of honor and sovereignty conferred by the Church, without coming to her aid and defense and without applying their riches toward preventing the waste of the blood of Christ our Savior, are usurpers and unjust possessors of those titles: for in this very thing should the difference between Christian and infidel princes consist.

365. Coming back to my subject, I say that the Most High, in his infinite foresight, well knew the iniquity of the dragon, and that in the pursuit of his wrath against the Church he would bring to disorder many of the faithful, striking down the stars of the heaven of the militant church, namely the faithful, and thus seeking to rouse still more the divine justice and diminish the fruits of the Redemption. The highest Lord in immense kindness resolved to meet this danger that threatened the world. In order that He might be moved in this by so much the greater equity and for the greater glory of his name, He arranged that the most holy Mary should oblige Him to give this help. She alone was worthy of the privileges, gifts and prerogatives by which She was to overcome the world; and this most eminent Lady alone was capable of such an enterprise as to draw toward Her the heart of God by her holiness, purity, merits and prayers. For the greater exaltation of the divine power He wished it to be known through all the eternities that He had conquered Lucifer and all his followers through means of a mere Creature and a Woman, just as the devil had cast down the whole human race by another woman, and that there was none other to whom this salvation of the Church and whole world could be worthily credited. On account of these and other reasons apparent to us in faith, the Almighty gave into

the hands of our victorious Chieftainess the sword for cutting off the head of the infernal dragon; a power never to be diminished in Her, and with which She defends and assists the militant Church according to the labors and necessities of coming centuries.

366. While Lucifer with his infernal legions in visible forms persisted in his unhappy attempts, the most serene Mary never looked upon them nor paid any attention to them, although by the permission of God She heard the uproar. Since the hearing cannot be so easily stopped as the sight, She took precaution, lest what She heard should enter her imagination or interior faculties. Nor did She deign to speak to them otherwise than to command them to stop their blasphemies. And this command was so powerful that it forced the demons to press their mouths to the earth, while She in the meanwhile sang great canticles of praise and glory in honor of the Most High. This intercourse of her Majesty with God and her profession of the divine truths, was likewise so oppressive and painful to them that they began to attack each other like ravenous wolves, or like rabid dogs; every action of the Empress Mary was for them a burning shaft, and everyone of her words a flame of fire more dreadful than hell itself. This is not an exaggeration for the dragon and his followers really strove to fly and escape from the presence of most holy Mary; while the Lord, in order to enhance the triumph of his Mother and Spouse and confound entirely the pride of Lucifer, detained them by a secret force. His Majesty permitted and ordained that the demons themselves should humiliate themselves so far as to ask the heavenly Lady to command them to go and be driven from her presence, which they had sought. Accordingly She commanded them to return to the infernal regions. There they lay prostrate for a time, while the great Vanquisher Mary remained absorbed in divine praise and thanksgiving.

367. When by the permission of the Lord Lucifer rose from his defeat, he returned to the conflict, selecting for his instrument some of the neighbors of the holy spouses, and sowing among them and their wives the hellish seed of discord concerning temporal interests. For this purpose the demon took the shape of a woman known to them all and telling them that they should not disagree among themselves, since the source of all their differences was none other than Mary, the wife of Joseph. The woman, whose shape the demon took, held the esteem and regard of all these persons, and therefore her words were so much the more weighty. Although the Lord did not allow the good name of his most holy Mother to suffer in any important point, yet He permitted, that for her greater glory and merit, all these deceived persons should give Her an opportunity of exercising her patience on this occasion. They betook themselves in a body to the house of saint Joseph and in his presence they called forth most holy Mary and spoke very harshly to Her, accusing Her of disturbing their homes and their peace. This event was painful to the most innocent Lady, on account of the worry occasioned to saint Joseph, who had already noticed the increase of her virginal womb, and who, as She had perceived, was already troubled by the thoughts beginning to arise in his heart. Nevertheless, in her prudence and wisdom, She sought to meet this disturbance with humility, and overcome it by patience and lively faith. She did not defend Herself, nor fall back on the faultlessness of her conduct; on the contrary, She humiliated Herself and begged Her ill-informed neighbors to pardon Her, if in anything She had offended them. With sweet and wise words She enlightened and pacified them, making them understand that none of them had committed any offense against the others. Satisfied by her explanations and edified by the humility of her answer, they peacefully withdrew to their houses, while the

demon fled, not being able to endure such great sanctity and heavenly wisdom.

368. Saint Joseph remained somewhat pensive and sad, and he began to give way to conjecture, as I will relate in the following chapters (Nos. 375 to 394). The demon, although he was ignorant of the chief cause of the troubled thoughts of saint Joseph, wished to profit by the occasion (for he allows none to escape him), in order to disquiet him still more. But doubting whether his dissatisfaction did not arise from a certain disgust at his poverty and his lowly habitation, the demon hesitated between two different courses. On the one hand he suggested a feeling of restlessness to saint Joseph, irritating and disgusting him against his poverty; and on the other hand he tried to persuade him that Mary, his Spouse, devoted too much time to her meditations and prayers, and led a too negligent and leisurely life, instead of exerting Herself to improve their poor circumstances. But saint Joseph, upright and magnanimous of heart, readily despised and rejected such considerations. The solicitude with which he was secretly filled in regard to the pregnancy of his Spouse easily smothered all other anxieties. The Lord, leaving him in the beginning to these anxious thoughts, freed him from the temptations of the demon through the intercession of the most holy Mary. For She was very attentive to all that passed within the heart of her most faithful spouse. She therefore besought her most holy Son to relieve him of these assaults, and to be satisfied with the service which he rendered to God in enduring the sorrow of seeing Her pregnant.

369. The Most High ordained that the Princess of heaven should still farther prolong this great battle with Lucifer. He permitted him and all his legions in one general assault to strain all their forces and exert all their malice, so that the demons might find themselves entirely crushed and vanquished. The heavenly Lady was to achieve the greatest

triumph that ever was gained, or could be gained, over hell
by a mere creature. These legions of wickedness arrived in all
their hellish array to present themselves before the heavenly
Queen, and with indescribable fury. Uniting all the scheming
plots, of which they had until now availed themselves separately, and adding what little they could, they advanced to
make a universal onslaught. But I will not detain myself in
describing it specially, as nearly all can be understood from
what has been described in the two preceding chapters. She
met them all and awaited their fearful onslaught with the
same tranquillity, high-mindedness and serenity, as if She
had been in the position of the highest choirs of the angels
seated on their secure and unassailable thrones. No strange or
improper emotion could disturb the serenity of her heavenly
interior, although the menacing terrors, illusions and falsehoods of all hell were poured forth in torrents by the dragon
against this strong and unconquered Woman, most holy
Mary.

370. While She thus in the midst of this conflict exercised
heroic acts of all the virtues against her enemies, She was
made aware of the adorable decree of the Most High, that
She should humiliate and crush the pride of the dragon by
her great dignity as Mother of God. Rising up in ardent and
invincible valor, She turned toward the demons and spoke to
them: "Who is like unto God, who dwells on high?" And
repeating these words, She added: "Prince of darkness,
author of sin and death, in the name of the Most High I
command thee to become mute, and with thy legions to cast
thyself into the infernal caverns, where thy place is appointed
to thee, and whence thou shalt not come forth until the
promised Messias shall vanquish thee and crush thee, or until
He otherwise permit." The heavenly Empress shone forth in
the light and splendor of heaven; and, as the proud dragon
made a pretence of resisting Her command, She directed

upon him the full force of her power. His resistance drew
upon him. so much the greater pain, humiliation and torment, since such he thereby merited before all the other
demons. Together they fell into the abyss and remained fixed
in its lowest caverns, as had happened to them at the time of
the Incarnation, and as I will describe further on at the
temptation and at the death of Christ our Lord (No. 130,
999, 1421). And when this dragon afterwards engaged in his
last battle with this Queen, which is described in the third
part of this history (Part III, 452 seq.), this heavenly Lady
vanquished him so completely that through Her and her
most holy Son his head was entirely crushed. In that final
battle his strength was so weakened and ruined that if human
creatures do not deliver themselves into the hands of his
malice they can very easily resist and overcome him with the
divine grace.

371. Then the Lord himself appeared to his most holy
Mother, and in reward of her glorious victories He communicated to Her new gifts and privileges; Her thousand guardian angels visibly presented themselves with innumerable
hosts of others, and sang to Her new canticles of praise in
honor of the Most High and of Herself. And with celestial
concord of sweet and audible voices they sang of Her, that
which the holy Church figuratively sings of the triumph of
Judith: "Thou art all beautiful, Mary our Lady, and there is
no stain of sin in Thee; Thou art the glory of the heavenly
Jerusalem; Thou art the honor of the people of God; Thou
art She, who magnifies his name, the Advocate of sinners,
who defendest them against their proud enemy ! O Mary!
Thou are full of grace and of all perfection." The heavenly
Lady was filled with glad jubilee, praising the Author of all
good and acknowledging Him as the source of all She possessed. Whereupon She began to pay more particular atten-

tion to the well-being of her spouse, as I shall relate in the following chapter of the fourth book.

Words of the Queen

THE VIRGIN MARY SPEAKS TO SISTER MARY OF AGREDA

372. My daughter, the silence which the soul should maintain when the invisible enemies advance with their specious reasonings, should not prevent it from imposing silence upon them in the name of the Most High, and from commanding them to leave its presence in confusion. Therefore I desire this to be thy prudent behavior when they assault thee; for there is no other defense so powerful against the dragon than to be conscious of the power which we possess as children of God, and to use the advantage which this confidence gives us by exercising our dominion and superiority over the infernal spirits (Matth. 6, 9). For the whole aim of Lucifer, after he had fallen from heaven, consists in enticing souls from their Creator and in sowing the seed of discord, by which he hopes to separate from the heavenly Father his adopted children, and the spouses of Christ from their Bridegroom. Whenever he perceives that a soul is united with his Creator and in living communion with its head Christ, he tries to surpass himself in his furious attempts at persecuting it; his envy arouses the utmost exertion of his deceitfulness and malice for its destruction. But as soon as he sees that he cannot succeed in his attempts, because the soul takes refuge in the unfailing and unassailable protection of the Most High, he weakens in his attempts and begins to writhe in exquisite torments. If the soul, thus strengthened with the authority of God's truth, despises and casts him out, there is no creeping worm or ant so weak as that giant of iniquitous pride.

373. By this most true doctrine thou must comfort and strengthen thyself, when, according to the decree of the

Almighty, thou meetest tribulations and art surrounded by the sorrows of death in temptations such as I have suffered. For they afford thy Spouse the best occasion of verifying thy fidelity by experience. Therefore love must not be satisfied merely with mere protestations of affection without looking for more valuable fruit; for the desire which costs nothing is not a sufficient proof of love in a soul, nor of its proper esteem of the good which it pretends to hold dear and love. If thou wishest to give a satisfactory proof of thy love to thy Spouse, show thyself invincible in thy trust in Him also then when thou findest thyself most afflicted and forsaken by human aid; confide in the Lord thy God, and hope in Him, if necessary, against hope (Rom. 4, 18). For He does not slumber, nor does He sleep, who calls Himself the protection of Israel (Ps, 120, 4). In due time He will command the waves and the wind, and restore tranquillity (Matth. 8,26).

374. Thou must be much more wary, my daughter, in the beginning of the temptations; for there is then greater danger lest the soul, yielding to the concupiscent or the irascible passions, by which the light of reason is obscured and darkened, allow itself to be thrown into confusion. As soon as the demon notices such a state of mind he will raise a whirlwind of dust in the faculties. His fierceness is so immeasurable and implacable that it will then increase in fury. He will add flame to flame, thinking that the soul has no one to defend and rescue it from his hands (Ps. 120, 11). With the force of his temptations increases also the danger of failing in the necessary resistance, since the soul has commenced to yield in the very beginning. All this I make known to thee, in order that thou mayest fear the danger of being remiss in guarding against the first approaches of the demon. Do not incur it in what is so important. Thou shouldst continue in the even tenor of thy duties in every temptation; keeping up the sweet and devout union with the Lord and preserving thy prudent

and loving intercourse with thy neighbors, thou shouldst forestall by prayer and by restraint of thy feelings the disorder which the enemy seeks to bring about in thy soul.

CITY OF GOD PART II

THE INCARNATION

BOOK IV

Describing the Anxieties of Saint Joseph on Account of the Pregnancy of Most Holy Mary, the Birth of Christ our Lord, His Circumcision, the Adoration of the Kings, the Presentation of the Infant Jesus In the Temple, the Flight Into Egypt, the Death of the Holy Innocents, and the Return to Nazareth.

Chapter I

SAINT JOSEPH BECOMES AWARE OF THE PREGNANCY OF HIS
SPOUSE, THE VIRGIN MARY, AND IS FILLED WITH ANXIETY,
AS HE KNOWS THAT HE HAD NO PART IN IT.

375. The divine pregnancy of the Princess of heaven had
advanced to its fifth month when the most chaste Joseph, her
husband, commenced to notice the condition of the Virgin;
for on account of the natural elegance and perfection of her
virginal body, as I have already remarked (No. 115), any
change could not long remain concealed and would so much
the sooner be discovered. One day, when saint Joseph was
full of anxious doubts and saw Her coming out of her oratory, he noticed more particularly this evident change, without
being able to explain away what he saw so clearly with his
eyes. The man of God was wounded to his inmost heart by
an arrow of grief, unable to ward off the force of evidence,
which at the same time wounded his soul. The principal
cause of his grief was the most chaste, and therefore the most
intense love with which he cherished his most faithful
Spouse, and in which he had from the beginning given over
to Her his whole heart. Moreover, her charming graces and
incomparable holiness had captured and bound to Her his
inmost soul. As She was so perfect and accomplished in her
modesty and humble reticence, saint Joseph, besides his
anxious solicitude to serve Her, naturally entertained the

loving desire of meeting a response of his love from his Spouse. This was so ordained by the Lord, in order that by the desire for this interchange of affection he might be incited to love and serve Her more faithfully.

376. Saint Joseph fulfilled this obligation as a most faithful spouse and as the guardian of the sacrament, which as yet was concealed from him. In proportion as he was solicitous in serving and venerating his Spouse, and loving Her with a most pure, chaste, holy and just love, in so far also increased his desire of finding a response to his affection and service. He never manifested or spoke of this desire, as well on account of the reverence elicited by the humble majesty of his Spouse as also because the more than angelic purity, conversation and intercourse of the Virgin with him had given him no apprehension in this regard. But when he found himself thus unexpectedly in the face of this disclosure, where the clear evidence of his senses allowed no denial, his soul was torn asunder by sorrowful surprise. Yet, though overwhelmed by the evidence of this change in his Spouse, he gave his thoughts no greater liberty than to admit what his eyes could not fail to perceive. For, being a holy and just man (Matth. 1, 19), although he saw the effect, he withheld his judgment as to the cause. Without doubt, if the saint had believed that his Spouse had any guilt in causing this condition, he would have died of sorrow.

377. Besides all this was the certainty of his not having any part in this pregnancy, the effects of which were before his eyes; and there was the inevitable dishonor which would follow as soon as it would become public. This thought caused so much the greater anxiety in him, as he was of a most noble and honorable disposition, and in his great foresight he knew how to weigh the disgrace and shame of himself and his Spouse in each circumstances. The third and most intimate cause of his sorrow, and which gave him the

deepest pain, was the dread of being obliged to deliver over his Spouse to the authorities to be stoned (Lev. 20, 10), for this was the punishment of an adulteress convicted of the crime. The heart of saint Joseph, filled with these painful considerations, found itself as it were exposed to the thrusts of many sharp-edged swords, without any other refuge than the full confidence which he had in his Spouse. But as all outward signs confirmed the correctness of his observations, there was no escape from these tormenting thoughts, and as he did not dare to communicate about his grievous affliction with anybody, he found himself surrounded by the sorrows of death (Ps. 17, 5), and he experienced in himself the saying of the Scriptures, that: "Jealousy is hard as hell" (Cant. 8, 6).

378. When he attempted to follow out these thoughts in solitude, grief suspended his faculties. If his thoughts touched upon the wrong, which his senses led him to suspect, they melted away as the ice before the sun, or vanished like the dust before the wind, as soon as he remembered the well-tried holiness of his modest and circumspect Spouse. If he tried to suspend the workings of his chaste love, he could not; for She continued to present Herself to his thoughts as the most worthy object of his love, and the hidden truth of her fidelity had more power of attracting his love than the deceitful appearances of infidelity to destroy it. The strong and sure bond which truth, reason and justice had woven about her fidelity could not be broken. He found no suitable occasion of opening his mind to his heavenly Spouse, nor did her serene and heavenly equanimity seem to invite him to such an explanation. Although he could not but admit the change in her shape, yet he could not conceive how her purity and holiness could be compatible with any failing such as this change might indicate. For it seemed impossible to him to connect such a sin with One who manifested such

chastity, tranquillity and holy discretion, and such united harmony of all graces and virtues in her daily life.

379. In the midst of these tormenting anxieties the holy Spouse Joseph appealed to the tribunal of the Lord in prayer and placing himself in his presence, he said: "Most high Lord and God, my desires and sighs are not unknown to Thee. I find myself cast about by the violent waves of sorrow (Ps, 31. 10) which through my senses have come to afflict my heart. I have given myself over with entire confidence to the Spouse whom thou hast given me. I have confided entirely in her holiness; and the signs of this unexpected change in Her are giving rise to tormenting and fearful doubts lest my confidence be misplaced. Nothing have I until now seen in Her which could give occasion for any doubt in her modesty and her extraordinary virtue; yet at the same time I cannot deny that She is pregnant. To think that She has been unfaithful to me, and has offended Thee, would be temerity in view of such rare purity and holiness: to deny what my own eyes perceive is impossible. But it is not impossible that I die of grief, unless there is some mystery hidden beneath it which I cannot yet fathom. Reason proclaims Her as blameless, while the senses accuse Her. She conceals from me the cause of her pregnancy, while I have it before my eyes. What shall I do? We both have come to an agreement concerning our vows of chastity, and we have both promised to keep them for thy glory; if it could be possible that She has violated her fidelity toward Thee and toward me, I would defend thy honor-and would forget mine for love of Thee. Yet how could She preserve such purity and holiness in all other things if She had committed so grave a crime in this? And on the other hand, why does She, who is so holy and prudent, conceal this matter from me? I withhold and defer my judgment. Not being able to penetrate to the cause of what I see, I pour out in thy presence my afflicted soul (Ps, 141, 3), God of Abra-

ham, Isaac and Jacob. Receive my tears as an acceptable sacrifice; and if my sins merit thy indignation, let thy own clemency and kindness move Thee not to despise my excruciating sorrow. I do not believe that Mary has offended Thee; yet much less can I presume that there is a mystery of which I, as her Spouse, am not to be informed. Govern Thou my mind and heart by thy divine light, in order that I may know and fulfill that which is most pleasing to Thee."

380. Saint Joseph persevered in this kind of prayer, adding many more affectionate petitions; for even though he conjectured that there must be some mystery in the pregnancy of the most holy Mary hidden from him, he could not find assurance therein. This thought had no greater force to exculpate most holy Mary than the other reasons founded upon her holiness; and therefore the idea that the most holy Queen might be the Mother of the Messias did not come to his mind. If at times he drove away his conjectures, they would return in greater number and with more urgent force of evidence. Thus he was cast about on the turbulent waves of doubt. From sheer exhaustion he would at times fall into a condition of mind wherein he could find neither an anchor of certainty for his doubts, nor tranquillity for his heart, nor any standard by which he could direct his course. Yet his forbearance under this torment was so great that it is an evident proof of his great discretion and holiness, and that it made him worthy of the singular blessing which awaited him.

381. All that passed in the heart of saint Joseph was known to the Princess of heaven, who penetrated into its interior by the light of her divine science. Although her soul was full of tenderness and compassion for the sufferings of her spouse, She said not a word in the matter; but She continued to serve him with all devotion and solicitude. The man of God watched Her without outward demonstration,

yet with a greater anxiety than that of any man that ever lived. The pregnancy of most holy Mary was not burdensome or painful to Her; but as the great Lady in serving him at table or any other domestic occupations, necessarily disclosed her state more and more openly, saint Joseph noticed all these actions and movements and with deep affliction of soul verified all his observations. Notwithstanding his being a holy and just man, he permitted himself to be respected and served by the most holy Virgin after their espousal, claiming in all things the position of head and husband of the family, though with rare humility and prudence. As long as he was ignorant of the mystery of his Spouse he judged it right, within befitting limits, to show his authority in imitation of the ancient Fathers and Patriarchs. For he knew that they demanded subjection and prompt obedience of their wives, and he did not wish to. She served him on her knees, and although this somewhat consoled saint Joseph, yet on the other hand, it was also a cause for new grief. For thus he only saw the motives of love and esteem multiplied and still remained uncertain whether She had been untrue or not. The heavenly Lady offered up continual prayers for him and besought the Most High to look upon him and console him; as for the rest She submitted all to the will of his Majesty.

383. Saint Joseph could not entirely conceal his cruel sorrow, and therefore he often appeared to be in doubt and sad suspense. Sometimes, carried away by his grief, he spoke to his heavenly Spouse with some degree of severity, such as he had not shown before. This was the natural effect of the affliction of his heart, not of anger or vengeful feelings; for these never entered his thoughts, as we shall see later. The most prudent Lady, however, never lost the sweetness of her countenance, nor showed any feeling; but merely redoubled her efforts to relieve her husband. She served at table, offered him a seat, administered food and drink, and if, after all these

services, which She performed with incomparable grace, saint Joseph urged Her to sit down, he could convince himself more and more of her pregnancy. There is no doubt that all this was one of the greatest trials not only of saint Joseph, but of the Princess of heaven, and that it greatly manifested the most profound humility and wisdom of her most holy soul. The Lord thereby gave Her an opportunity of exercising and proving all Her virtues; for He had not only not commanded Her to conceal the sacrament of her pregnancy, but contrary to his usual manner of proceeding, He had not even manifested to Her his pleasure in any way. It seemed as if God had left this whole matter in her hands and entrusted it all to the wisdom and virtue of his chosen Spouse, without giving Her special enlightenment of help. The divine Providence afforded the most holy Mary and her most faithful Spouse an opportunity to exercise in a heroic manner the gifts and graces which He had infused into them, and delighted, (according to our way of speaking), in the faith, hope and love, in the humility, patience, peace and tranquillity of these two hearts in the midst of their grievous affliction. In order to increase their glory and furnish to the world an example of holiness and prudence, and in order to hear the sweet cries of his most holy Mother and of her most chaste spouse, He became as it were deaf to their prolonged invocations and delayed answering them until his own opportune and fitting time.

Words of the Queen

THE VIRGIN MARY SPEAKS TO SISTER MARY OF AGREDA

384. My dearest daughter, most exalted are the thoughts and intentions of the Lord; his Providence with souls is sweet and powerful and He is admirable in the government of them all, especially of his friends and chosen ones. If mortals would

strive to know the loving care for their direction and advancement, as shown by this Father of mercies (Matth. 6, 5), they would be relieved and would not be involved in such irksome, useless and dangerous anxieties, living in perpetual toils and vain trust in the help of creatures. For they would resign themselves without hesitation to the infinite wisdom and love, which, with paternal sweetness and gentleness would watch over all their thoughts, words and actions and all things necessary for them. I do not wish thee to be ignorant of this truth, but to understand how the Lord from all eternity bears in his mind all the predestined of the different times and ages; and that by the invincible force of his infinite wisdom and goodness He continually disposes and prepares all the blessings useful to them, so that the end desired for them may be attained.

385. Hence it is very important for the rational creature to allow itself to be led by the hand of the Lord and leave all to the divine disposition; for mortal men are ignorant of their ways and of the goal to which they lead. In their ignorance they should not presume to chose, lest they make themselves guilty of great temerity and incur the danger of damnation. But if they resign themselves with all their heart to the divine Providence of God, acknowledging him as their Father and themselves as his children and creatures, his Majesty will constitute Himself as their Protector, Helper and Director; and He will assume these offices with such love that He wishes to call heaven and earth to witness how much He considers it his affair to govern his own and direct those who trust and resign themselves into his hands. If God were capable of grief, or of jealousy like men, it would be aroused in Him at seeing creatures claiming a part in the providing for the welfare of souls and that souls should seek to supply their necessities from other quarters independently of Him (Wis. 12, 13). Mortals would not be so ignorant of this truth

if they would study what happens between a father and his children, a husband and his wife, one friend and another, a prince and his well-loved and honored subject. All that these do is nothing in comparison with the love which God had for his children, and that which He can do and will do for them.

386. Yet although men in general believe this truth, no one can fully estimate the love of God and its effects on those souls who resign themselves entirely to his will. Nor canst thou, my daughter, manifest what thou knowest, nor shouldst thou; but thou must not lose sight of it in the Lord. His Majesty says, that not a hair of his elect shall perish, because He keeps account of them (Luke 21, 18). He directs their footsteps toward eternal life and keeps them from death. He observes their labors, lovingly corrects their defects, favors their desires, forestalls their anxieties, defends them in anger, rejoices them in peace, strengthens them in battle, assists them in tribulation. His wisdom is at their service against deceit, his goodness for their sanctification. As He is infinite, whom none can hinder or resist, He executes what He wishes, and He wishes to be entirely at the service of the just, who are in his grace and trust themselves wholly to Him. Who could ever measure the number and greatness of the blessings which He would shower upon a heart prepared to receive them!

387. If thou, my dearest, wishest to attain to gain this good fortune, imitate me with true solicitude and apply thyself from now on to establish in thee a true resignation in the divine Providence. If He sends thee tribulations, sorrows and labors, accept and embrace them with tranquillity of soul, with patience, lively faith and hope in the goodness of the Most High, who always provides that which is the most secure and profitable for thy salvation. Chose nothing for thyself, since God knows thy ways; trust thyself to the heav-

enly Father and Spouse, who will shield and assist thee with most faithful love. Study also My works, since they are known to thee; and remember that, excepting the labors of my most holy Son, the greatest suffering of my life was to see the tribulations of my spouse saint Joseph, and his grief in the matter which thou hast described.

Chapter II

THE ANXIETIES OF SAINT JOSEPH INCREASE; HE RESOLVES
TO LEAVE HIS SPOUSE, AND HE BETAKES HIMSELF TO PRAY-
ER ON THIS ACCOUNT.

388. In his tormenting doubts the most upright heart of saint
Joseph sometimes prudently tried to find relief and ease for
his sorrow by reasoning for himself and persuading himself
that the pregnancy of his Spouse was as yet doubtful. But this
self-deception vanished more and more every day on account
of the increasing evidence of that state in the most holy
Virgin. As this vain and fleeting consolation failed him more
and more and finally changed into complete conviction as
her pregnancy advanced, the glorious saint found no haven
of refuge in his anxieties. In the meanwhile the heavenly
Princess grew in loveliness and in perfect freedom from all
bodily failings. Her charming beauty, healthfulness and
gracefulness visibly increased before his eyes. All this only
nourished the anxieties and the torments of his most chaste
love, so that his interior was involved by the turbulent waves
of his loving sorrow in unutterable confusion and he was
finally stranded on the shores of a sea of grief by the over-
powering evidence of his senses in regard to the pregnancy of
Mary. Although his spirit was always conformed to the will
of God, yet his flesh in his weakness felt the excess of his
interior trouble, which at last reached such a point that he

knew not any more which way to turn. The strength of his body was broken and vanished away, not by a definite disease, but in weakness and emaciation. These effects of his profound sorrow and melancholy became openly visible in his countenance. Moreover, as he suffered all this alone without seeking relief or lessening his sorrow by communication with others, as is customary with the afflicted, his suffering grew to be so much the more serious and incurable.

389. In the meanwhile the sorrow which filled the heart of the most holy Mary was equally great. Yet, although her sorrow exceeded all bounds, the capacity of her generous and magnanimous soul was much greater and therefore She could conceal her grief more completely, and occupy her faculties in the loving care of saint Joseph, her spouse. Her sorrow therefore only incited Her to attend so much the more devotedly to his health and comfort. Nevertheless, as the inviolable rule of the actions of the most prudent Queen was to perform all in the fullness of wisdom and perfection, She continued to conceal the mystery about the disclosure of which She had received no command. Though She alone could relieve her spouse by an explanation, She withheld it in reverence and faithfulness due to the sacrament of the heavenly King (Tob. 12, 7). As far as She herself was concerned, She exerted her utmost powers; She spoke to him about his health, She asked what She could do to serve him and afford him help in the weakness which so mastered him. She urged him to take some rest and recreation, since it was a duty to yield to necessity and repair the weakened strength, in order to be able to work for the Lord afterward. Saint Joseph observed all the actions of his heavenly Spouse, and, pondering over such virtue and discretion and feeling the effects of her intercourse and presence, he said:

"Is it possible that a Woman of such habits, and in whom such graces of the Lord are manifest, can bring over me such affliction? How can this prudence and holiness agree with these open signs of her infidelity to God and to me, who love Her so much? If I conclude to send Her away, or to leave Her, I lose her most loving company, all my comfort, my home and my tranquility. What blessing equal to Her can I find if I withdraw from Her? What consolation, if this one fails? But all this weighs less than the infamy connected with this sad misfortune, and that I should come to be looked upon as her accomplice in crime. That this event remain concealed is not possible; since time will reveal all, even if I strive now to hide it. To pass as the author of this pregnancy will be a vile deceit and a blotch on my good name and conscience. I cannot recognize it as caused by me, nor can I ascribe it to any other source known to me. Hence, what am I to do in this dire stress? The least evil will be to absent myself and leave my house before her delivery comes upon Her; for then I would be still more confused and afflicted. I would then be obliged to live in my own house with a child not my own, without being able to find any outlet or expedient."

390. The Princess of heaven, becoming aware of the resolve of her spouse saint Joseph to leave Her and absent himself, turned in great sorrow to her holy angels and said to them: "Blessed spirits and ministers of the highest King, who raised you to felicity which you enjoy, and by his kind Providence accompany me as his faithful servants and as my guardians, I beseech you, my friends, to present before God's clemency the afflictions of my spouse Joseph. Beseech the Lord to look upon him and console him as a true Father. And you also, who so devotedly obey his words, hear likewise my prayers; in the name of Him who is infinite, and to whom I am to give human shape in my womb, I pray, beseech and supplicate you, that without delay you assist and relieve my most faithful spouse in the affliction of his heart

and drive from his mind and heart his resolve of leaving me."
The angels which the Queen selected for this purpose obeyed
immediately and instilled into the heart of saint Joseph many
holy thoughts, persuading him anew that his Spouse Mary
was holy and most perfect, and that he could not believe
anything wrong of Her; that God was incomprehensible in
his works, and most hidden in his judgments (Ps. 33, 19);
that He was always most faithful to those who confide in
Him, and that He would never despise or forsake them in
tribulation.

391. By these and other holy inspirations the troubled
spirit of saint Joseph was somewhat quieted, although he did
not know whence they came; but as the cause of his sorrow
was not removed, he soon relapsed, not finding anything to
assure and soothe his soul, and he returned to his resolve of
withdrawing and leaving his Spouse. The heavenly Queen
was aware of this and She concluded that it was necessary to
avert this danger and to insist in earnest prayer on a remedy.
She addressed Herself entirely to her most holy Son in her
womb, and with most ardent affection of her soul She
prayed:

"Lord and God of my soul, with thy permission, although
I am but dust and ashes (Gen. 18,27), I will speak in thy
kingly presence and manifest to Thee my sighs, that cannot
be hidden from Thee (Ps. 37, 10). It is my duty not to be
remiss in assisting the spouse whom I have received from thy
hand. I see him overwhelmed by the tribulation, which Thou
hast sent him, and it would not be kind in me to forsake him
therein. If I have found grace in thy eyes, I beseech Thee,
Lord and eternal God, by the love which obliged Thee to
enter into the womb of thy servant for the salvation of mankind, to be pleased to console thy servant Joseph and dispose
him to assist me in the fulfillment of thy great works. It
would not be well that I, thy servant, be left without a hus-

band for a protection and guardian. Do not permit, my Lord
and God, that he execute his resolve and withdraw from me."

392. The Most High answered Her: "My dearest Dove, I
shall presently visit my servant Joseph with consolation; and
after I shall have manifested to him by my angel the sacrament, which is unknown to him, thou mayest speak openly
about all that I have done with thee, without the necessity of
keeping silent thenceforward in these matters. I will fill him
with my spirit and make him apt to perform his share in
these mysteries. He will assist Thee in them and aid Thee in
all that will happen." With this promise of the Lord, most
holy Mary was comforted and consoled, and She gave most
fervent thanks to the same Lord, who disposes all things in
admirable order, measure and weight. For besides the consolation, which the relief from this anxiety afforded Her, She
also knew well how proper it was that the spirit of saint
Joseph be tried and dilated by this tribulation before the
great mysteries should be entrusted to his care.

393. In the meanwhile saint Joseph was anxiously debat-
ing within himself concerning the proper course of action,
for he had borne his tribulation already for two months; and
now, overcome by the greatness of it, he argued with himself:
I do not find a better way out of these difficulties than to
absent myself. I confess that my Spouse is most perfect and
exhibits nothing but what shows Her a saint; but after all She
is pregnant and of it I cannot fathom the mystery. I do not
wish to injure Her reputation of holiness by involving Her in
the punishment of the law; yet at the same time I cannot
stand by and witness the consequences of her pregnancy. I
will leave her now, and commit myself to the providence of
the Lord, who governs me." He then resolved to depart
during that night, and in order to prepare for his journey he
packed some clothes and other trifles into a small bundle.
Having also claimed some wages due to him for his work, he

retired to rest with the intention of leaving at midnight. But on account of the strangeness of his undertaking, and because he was in the habit of commending his intentions to God in prayer, after he had come to this resolve he spoke to the Lord: "Highest and eternal God of our fathers Abraham, Isaac and Jacob, Thou true and only refuge of the poor and afflicted, the grief and tribulation of my heart are well known to thy clemency. Thou knowest also, O Lord (although I am unworthy), that I am innocent of that which causes my sorrow, and Thou likewise art aware of the infamy and danger consequent upon the condition of my Spouse. I do not believe Her an adulteress, because I see in Her great virtue and perfection; yet I certainly see Her pregnant. I do not know by whom or how it was caused; and therefore I find no way to restore my peace. In order to choose the least evil I will withdraw from Her and seek a place where no one knows me and, resigning myself to thy Providence, I will pass my life in a desert. Do not forsake me, my Lord and eternal God, since I desire solely thy honor and service."

394. Saint Joseph prostrated himself on the ground and made a vow to go to the temple of Jerusalem and offer up a part of the small sum of money which he had provided for his journey, in order that God might help and protect Mary his Spouse from the calamities of men and free Her from all misfortune; for great was the uprightness of that man of God, and the esteem in which he held the heavenly Lady. After this prayer he composed himself for a short sleep with the intention of departing in secret and at midnight from his Spouse. During this sleep, however, happened what I will relate in the next chapter. The great Princess of heaven, (assured by the divine promise), observed from her retirement all that saint Joseph was preparing to do; for the Almighty showed it to Her. And hearing the vow, which he made for her welfare, and seeing the small bundle and the

poor provision he prepared for his journey, She was filled with tender compassion and prayed anew for him, giving praise and thanks to the Lord for his Providence in guiding the actions of men beyond all human power of comprehension. His Majesty so ordained events, that both most holy Mary and saint Joseph should be brought to the utmost reach of interior sorrow. For besides the merits of this prolonged martyrdom they would gain the admirable and precious blessing of the divine consolation deserved thereby. Although the great Lady persevered in the belief and hope of a seasonable intervention of the Lord, and therefore remained silent in order not to reveal the sacrament, concerning the disclosure of which the King had given Her no command; yet She was much afflicted by the resolve of saint Joseph to leave Her; because She reflected upon the great inconvenience of being alone, without a companion and a protector, on whom She could rely for consolation and support in the natural order; for She well knew that She could not expect all to proceed according to the supernatural and miraculous. Yet all her sighs could not prevent Her from exercising the most exalted virtues with a magnanimous spirit, such as patience in bearing her afflictions and the suspicions of saint Joseph and its results; prudence, in withholding the disclosure of the mystery on account of its greatness; silence, in signalizing Herself as a woman who knew how to refrain from speaking about that which so many human reasons urged Her to make known; forbearance and humility, in silently submitting to the suspicions of saint Joseph. Many other virtues did She exercise in this trouble in a wonderful manner; by which She taught us to hope in the Almighty for our deliverance in the greatest tribulations.

Words of the Queen

THE VIRGIN MARY SPEAKS TO SISTER MARY OF AGREDA

395. My daughter, the example of my silence, which thou hast been writing about, should teach thee to use it as a guide in thy treatment of the favors and sacraments of the Lord, namely that thou keep them concealed within thy heart. Although it might at times seem useful to reveal them for the consolation of some soul, thou must not act upon this opinion without having first consulted God in prayer, and then thy superiors. For these spiritual matters must not be made dependent upon human feeling, which are so much subject to the passions and inclinations of nature. There is always great danger of considering that to be an advantage which is harmful, and a service to God, what is injurious. It is not given to eyes of the flesh and blood (I Cor. 2, 14) to discern the interior movements, so as to decide which of them are divine and caused by grace, or which are human, engendered by the disorderly affections. Although there is great difference between these two kinds of affections and their causes, nevertheless, if the creature is not highly enlightened and dead to its passions, it cannot recognize this difference, nor separate the precious from the vile (Jer. 15, 19). This danger is greater when some temporal or human motive is mixed up with or underlies our actions; for then our natural selflove is wont to creep in and take away discretion and supervision of heavenly and spiritual things, leading on to many sudden and dangerous falls.

396. Let it therefore be to thee as a rule always to be followed that thou reveal nothing to anyone except to thy spiritual guide, unless I command otherwise. Since I have constituted myself thy Teacher, I will not fail to give thee advice and direction in this and in all other things, lest thou stray from the path appointed to thee by the will of my most

holy Son. Yet I admonish thee to appreciate highly all the favors and revelations of the Most High. Preserve them with a magnanimous heart; esteem them, give thanks for them, and put them to practice in preference to anything else, especially in preference to anything originating from thy own inclinations. The reverential fear of God bound me to silence, having (as was proper) such a high regard for the Treasure deposited in me. Notwithstanding the natural feeling of love and obligation toward my master and spouse saint Joseph, and in disregard of the sorrow and compassion for his afflictions, of which I so desired to free him, I hid the secret of my state in silence, preferring the pleasure of the Lord to all these, and leaving to Him the defense of my cause. Learn also from this never to defend thyself against accusations, no matter how innocent thou mayest be. Oblige the Lord to do it by confiding in his love. Charge thy reputation to his account; and in the meanwhile overcome by patience and humility, by sweet and kind words, those who have offended thee. Above all things I admonish thee never to judge evil of anyone, even if thou seest with thy own eyes the outward warrants of thy judgment; for perfect and sincere charity will teach thee to find a prudent evasion and excuse for all faults of thy neighbor. God has placed my spouse, saint Joseph, as a shining example for such a course of action, since no one had more evident proofs of evil, and no one was more discreet in deferring his judgment. For in the law of discreet and holy charity it must be held as prudence, not temerity, to suspect higher causes, as yet unseen, rather than to judge and condemn our neighbors for faults in which his guilt is not clearly evident. I do not give thee special instructions for those that are in the state of matrimony, since they can derive them manifestly from the whole course of my life. But from the above instruction all can profit, although just now I have in view thy own advancement, because I desire it with especial love. Hear me, daughter, and fulfill my counsels and follow these my words of eternal life.

Chapter III

THE ANGEL OF THE LORD SPEAKS TO SAINT JOSEPH IN HIS
SLEEP AND MAKES KNOWN TO HIM THE MYSTERY OF THE
INCARNATION—HIS BEHAVIOR THEREAFTER.

397. The sorrow of jealousy keeps such vigilant watch in
those that are beset by it, that very often it not only awakens
them from sleep, but drives away altogether the refreshment
of slumber. Nobody ever suffered this sorrow in the same
degree as saint Joseph, although, if he, had known the truth,
nobody ever had less occasion. He was endowed with exalted
light and knowledge, so that he could penetrate to the abyss
of the incalculable sanctity and perfection of his heavenly
Spouse. As the reasons which urged him to resign the possession of such great blessing were inexorable, it naturally
followed that the knowledge of what he was to lose should
add to the sorrow of parting therefrom. Hence, what saint
Joseph suffered in this regard exceeds all that ever was endured by any man; for no one ever equaled him in the loss,
and no one could so value and estimate it. Besides, there was
a great difference in the zeal and jealousy of this faithful
servant of God and the jealousies of others in like troubles.
For jealousies create in the vehement and ardent lover a great
anxiety to preserve and prevent loss of the loved object; and
to this anxiety is naturally added the pain caused by the fear
lest the loved one be alienated by others. This kind of feeling

or sorrow is commonly called jealousy. In those who have disorderly passions, and who, for want of prudence or other virtues, yield to them, it usually causes the different feelings of wrath, fury, envy toward the person loved, or against the rival who impedes the return of love, be it a well-ordered love or not. Then arise the storms of suspicion and conjecture in the imagination, engendered by these passions; the tempests of alternate desire and abhorrence; of loving affection and vain regret. Thus the irascible and concupiscent faculties are in perpetual strife, without any regard for the demands of reason or prudence; for this kind of sorrow confounds the understanding, perverts reason, and rejects prudence.

398. In saint Joseph this disorder was not infected with all these faults, nor could they find room in him, on account both of his own exalted holiness and that of his Spouse; for in Her he could find no fault to exasperate him, nor had he any suspicion that her love had been captured by anyone else, against whom or toward whom his envy might be aroused in defense. The jealousy of saint Joseph was founded entirely in his own great love for Her, in a certain conditional doubt or suspicion lest his Spouse had not entirely responded to his own love; for he found no such strong reasons against, as he did for his mistrust. A greater uncertainty was not necessary in his case in order to cause such vehement sorrows; for in the possession of a spouse, no rival can be tolerated. Hence, the chaste marital love of our saint, which filled his whole heart, was sufficient to cause in him the most vehement grief at the least appearance of infidelity, or danger of losing this most perfect, most beautiful and delightful object of all his desires and thoughts. For if love is in possession of such just motives, strong and unbreakable are the bonds and chains with which it captivates the heart and most powerful is the dominion which it exercises; especially when there are no imperfections to weaken it. Our Queen exhibited nothing

which either in the spiritual or in the natural order was calculated to diminish or moderate this love in her holy spouse, but only what tended to blow it into greater flame on many occasions and for many reasons.

399. Full of this sorrow, which had now become an intolerable pain, saint Joseph, after saying the prayer above mentioned, composed himself for a short sleep, assured that he would wake up at the right time to leave his home at midnight, and, as he thought, without the knowledge of his Spouse. The heavenly Lady awaited the intervention of God, asking it of Him in most humble prayer. For She knew that the tribulation of her troubled spouse had reached such a high point, that the time of God's merciful assistance must have arrived. The Most High sent his archangel Gabriel, in order to reveal to him during his sleep the mystery of the Incarnation and Redemption in the words recorded in the gospel. It might cause some wonder, (and such was caused in me), why the archangel spoke to saint Joseph in his sleep and not while awake; since the mystery was so high, and so difficult to comprehend, especially in the present afflicted and troubled state of his mind; while this same mystery was made known to others, not while they were asleep, but awake.

400. In these operations of course, the last reason is always the divine will itself, just, holy and perfect. However, as far as I have understood, I will partly mention some other reasons in explanation. The first reason is, that saint Joseph was so prudent, filled with such heavenly light, and had such high conception of our most holy Lady, the blessed Mary, that it was not necessary to convince him by strong evidence, in order to assure him of her dignity and of the mysteries of the Incarnation; for in hearts well-disposed the divine inspirations find easy entrance. The second reason is, because his trouble had its beginning in the senses, namely in seeing with

his eyes the pregnancy of his Spouse; hence it was a just retribution, that they, having given occasion for deception or suspicion, should as it were be deadened or repressed by the privation of the angelic vision. The third reason is as it were a sequence of this last one: saint Joseph, although he was guilty of no fault, was under the influence of his affliction and his senses were so to say deadened and incapacitated for the sensible perception and intercourse of the angel. Therefore it was befitting, that the angel deliver this message to him at a time, when the senses, which had been scandalized, were inactive and suspended in their operations. Thus the holy man might afterwards, regaining their full use, purify and dispose himself by many acts of virtue for entertaining the operation of the holy Spirit, which had been entirely interrupted by his troubles.

401. Hence will be also understood, why God spoke to the ancient Fathers oftener during sleep than happens to the faithful ones of the evangelical law; for in the new law revelation in sleep is less frequent than direct intercourse with angels, which affords a more efficient mode of communication. The explanation of this fact is this: since according to the divine ordainment the greatest impediment and obstacle of a more familiar intercourse and converse of the souls with God and his angels is the commission of sins, even venial sins or even only imperfections, it follows, that, after the divine Word became man and conversed with mortals, the senses and all our faculties are purified day by day by the sanctifying use of sensible Sacraments, by which men in some degree are spiritualized and elevated, their torpid faculties aroused and made apt for participation in the divine influences. This blessing we owe in a greater degree to the blood of Christ our Lord than the ancients; for by its efficiency we are made partakers of his holiness through the Sacraments, wherein we receive the effects of special graces, and in some of them even

a spiritual character, which destines and prepares us for Most High ends. But whenever the Lord in our times spoke or speaks in sleep, He excludes the operations of the senses, as being unfit and unprepared to enter into the spiritual nuptials of his communications and divine influences.

402. It will also appear from this doctrine, that, in order to receive the hidden favor of the Lord, men must not only be free from guilt and possess merits and grace, but that they be also in peace and tranquillity of spirit; for if the republic of the faculties is in disturbance (as it was in saint Joseph), the soul is not in a fit condition to receive such exalted and delicate influences as are implied by the visits and the caresses of the Lord. It is not at all uncommon, that, no matter how much tribulations and afflictions increase the merits of the soul (as were those of saint Joseph, the spouse of the Queen), they nevertheless hinder the divine operations. For in suffering them the soul is involved in a conflict with the powers of darkness, while this kind of blessing consists in the possession of light; and therefore the vision of darkness, even if only in order to ward it off, is not in harmony with the vision of God or the angels. But in the midst of the conflict and the battle of temptations, which may be compared to a dream in the night, the voice of the Lord is nevertheless wont to be heard and perceived through the ministry of the angels, just as it happened to saint Joseph. He heard and understood all that saint Gabriel said: that he should not be afraid to remain with his Spouse Mary (Matth. 1,20,21), because what She bore in her womb, was the work of the holy Spirit; that She would give birth to a Son, who should be called Jesus and who was to be the Savior of his people; that in all this should be fulfilled the prophecy of Isaias, who said (Is. 7, 14): A Virgin shall conceive and shall bring forth a Son, who was to be called Emmanuel, God with us. Saint Joseph did not see the angel by imaginary image, he heard only the interior

voice and he understood the mystery. The words of the angel imply, that saint Joseph had in his mind already resolved to sever his connection with most holy Mary; for he was told to receive Her again without fear.

403. Saint Joseph awoke with the full consciousness, that his Spouse was the true Mother of God. Full of joy on account of his good fortune and of his inconceivable happiness, and at the same time deeply moved by sudden sorrow for what he had done, he prostrated himself to the earth and with many other humble, reverential and joyful tokens of his feelings, he performed heroic acts of humiliation and of thanksgiving. He gave thanks to the Lord for having revealed to him this mystery and for having made him the husband of Her, whom God had chosen for his Mother, notwithstanding that he was not worthy to be even her slave. Amid these recognitions and these acts of virtue, the spirit of saint Joseph remained tranquil and apt for the reception of new influences of the holy Spirit. His doubts and anxieties of the past few months had laid in him those deep foundations of humility, which were necessary for one who should be entrusted with the highest mysteries of the Lord; and the remembrance of his experiences was to him a lesson which lasted all his life. The holy man began to blame himself alone for all that had happened and broke forth in the following prayer: "0 my heavenly Spouse and meekest Dove, chosen by the Most High for his dwelling-place and for his Mother: how could thy unworthy slave have dared to doubt thy fidelity? How could dust and ashes ever permit itself to be served by Her, who is the Queen of heaven and earth and the Mistress of the universe? How is it, that I have not kissed the ground which was touched by thy feet? Why have I not made it my most solicitous care to serve Thee on my knees? How will I ever raise my eyes in thy presence and dare to remain in thy company or open my lips to speak to Thee? O my Lord and

God, give me grace and strength to ask her forgiveness; and move her heart to mercy, that She do not despise her sorrowful servant according to his guilt. Ah woe is me! Since She is full of light and grace and She bears within Herself the Author of light, all my thoughts were open to her sight, also that I had in my mind actually to leave Her; hence it will be temerity on my part to appear in her presence. I now recognize my rude behavior and my gross error; since even with such great holiness before my eyes I gave way to unworthy thoughts and doubts concerning her fidelity, which I did not deserve. And if in punishment thy justice had permitted me to execute my presumptuous resolve, what would now be my misfortune? Eternally be thanked, Most High Lord for such great blessing! Assist me, most powerful King, to make some kind of reparation. I will go to my Spouse and Lady, confiding in her sweetness and clemency; prostrate at her feet I will ask her pardon, so that for her sake, Thou, my eternal Lord and God, mayest look upon me with the eyes of a Father and mayest pardon my gross error."

404. The holy spouse now left his little room, finding himself so happily changed in sentiments since the time he had composed himself for sleep. As the Queen of heaven always had kept Herself in retirement, be did not wish to disturb her sweet contemplation, until She herself desired. In the meantime the man of God unwrapped the small bundle, which he had prepared, shedding many tears with feelings quite different from those with which he had made it up. Weeping, he began to show his reverence for his heavenly Spouse, by setting the rooms in order, scrubbing the floors, which were to be touched by the sacred feet of most holy Mary. He also performed other chores which he had been accustomed to leave to the heavenly Lady before he knew her dignity. He resolved to change entirely his relation toward Her, assume for himself the position of servant and leave to

Her the dignity of Mistress. From that day on arose a wonderful contention between the two, which of them should be allowed to show most eagerness to serve and most humility. All that happened with saint Joseph the Queen of heaven saw, and not a thought or movement escaped her attention. When the time arrived, the saint approached the oratory of her Highness, and She awaited him with sweetest kindness and mildness, as I will describe in the following chapter.

Words of the Queen

THE VIRGIN MARY SPEAKS TO SISTER MARY OF AGREDA

405. My daughter, in what thou hast understood of this chapter, thou hast a sweet motive for praising the wonderful ways of God's wisdom in afflicting and again consoling his servants and chosen ones; from both the one and the other, He most wisely and kindly draws for them increase of merit and glory. Besides this doctrine, I wish that thou receive another one, most important for thy direction, and for the narrow pathway, which the Most High has assigned to thee. It is this, that thou strive with all thy might to preserve thyself in tranquillity and interior peace, without allowing thyself to be deprived of it by any troublesome event of this life whatever, and by always keeping in mind the example and instruction contained in this part of the life of my spouse saint Joseph. The Most High does not wish to see the creatures disturbed by afflictions, but that they gain merit; not that they lose courage, but that they test their own power when aided by grace. Although the more violent temptations are wont to close the haven of exalted peace and knowledge of God, and although they ground the creature more firmly in the knowledge of its own lowliness; yet if the soul loses its interior tranquillity and equilibrium, it will make itself unfit for the visit of the Lord, for hearing his voice, and for being

raised up to his embraces. The Majesty of God does not come in a stormcloud (III. Reg. 19,12), nor will the rays of this supreme Sun of justice shine, when calm is not reigning in the soul.

406. If then the want of this tranquillity so hinders the pure intercourse of the Most High, it is clear that sins are a still greater hindrance to this great blessing. I desire that thou be very attentive to this doctrine and that thou do not presume to allow any disregard of it in any operation of thy faculties. Since thou hast so often offended the Lord, call upon his mercy, weep and wash thyself from thy sins with copious tears; remember that, under pain of being condemned as unfaithful, thou art obliged to watch over thy soul and preserve it for an eternal resting-place of the Almighty, pure, clean and undisturbed; so that thy God may possess it and find in it a worthy habitation (I Cor. 2, 16). The harmony of thy faculties and feelings is to be like that of the music of soft and delicate instruments; in which the more delicate the harmony, so much the greater is the danger of discord and so much the greater must be the care to preserve the instruments from all gross contact. For even the atmosphere infected by earthly tendencies is sufficient to disturb and spoil the powers of the soul thus consecrated to God. Labor therefore to live a careful life and to keep full command over thy faculties and operations. If at any time thou art disturbed or disconcerted in maintaining this order, strive to attend the divine light, making use of it without fear or hesitation and working with it whatever is most perfect and pure. In this I point out to thee the example of my spouse saint Joseph, who believed the angel without a moment's hesitation and immediately with prompt obedience executed his commands; find thereby he merited to be raised to great reward and dignity. If he humiliated himself so deeply after having had such great, though only apparent reasons for

anxiety and without even having sinned in what he did, how must thou, a mere worm of the earth, acknowledge thy littleness and humble thyself to the dust, weeping over thy negligences and sins, in order that the Most High may look upon thee as a Father and as a Spouse

Chapter IV

SAINT JOSEPH ASKS PARDON OF THE MOST HOLY MARY, HIS
SPOUSE, AND THE HEAVENLY LADY CONSOLES HIM WITH
GREAT PRUDENCE.

407. The husband of Mary, saint Joseph, now better informed, waited until his most holy Spouse had finished her
contemplation, and at the hour known to him he opened the
door of the humble apartment which the Mother of the
heavenly King occupied. Immediately upon entering the holy
man threw himself on his knees, saying with the deepest
reverence and veneration: "My Mistress and Spouse, true
Mother of the eternal Word, here am I thy servant prostrate
at the feet of thy clemency. \ For the sake of thy God and
Lord, whom Thou bearest in thy virginal womb, I beseech
Thee to pardon my audacity. I am certain, O Lady, that
none of my thoughts is hidden to thy wisdom and to thy
heavenly insight. Great was my presumption in resolving to
leave Thee and not less great was my rudeness in treating
Thee until now as my inferior, instead of serving Thee as the
Mother of my Lord and God. But Thou also knowest that I
have done all in ignorance, because I knew not the sacrament
of the heavenly King and the greatness of thy dignity, although I revered in Thee other gifts of the Most High. Do
not reflect, my Mistress, upon the ignorance of such a lowly
creature, who, now better instructed, consecrates his heart

and his whole life to thy service and attendance. I will not rise from my knees, before being assured of thy favor, nor until I have obtained thy pardon, thy good will and thy blessing."

408. The most holy Mary, hearing the humble words of saint Joseph, experienced diverse feelings. For with tender joy in the Lord She saw how apt he was to be entrusted with the sacraments of the Lord, since he acknowledged and venerated them with such deep faith and humility. But She was somewhat troubled by his resolve of treating Her henceforth with the respect and self abasement alluded to in his words; for the humble Lady feared by this innovation to lose the occasions of obeying and humiliating Herself as a servant of her spouse. Like one, who suddenly finds herself in danger of being deprived of some jewel or treasure highly valued, most holy Mary was saddened by the thought that saint Joseph would no longer treat Her as an inferior and as subject to him in all things, having now recognized in Her the Mother of the Lord. She raised her holy spouse from his knees and threw Herself at his feet, although he tried to hinder it, and said: "I myself, my master and spouse, should ask thee to forgive me and thou art the one who must pardon me the sorrows and the bitterness, which I have caused thee; and therefore I ask this forgiveness of thee on my knees, and that thou forget thy anxieties, since the Most High has looked upon my desires and afflictions in divine pleasure."

409. It seemed good to the heavenly Lady to console her spouse, and therefore, not in order to excuse Herself, She added: "As much as I desired, I could not on my own account give thee any information regarding the sacrament hidden within me by the power of the Almighty; since, as his slave, it was my duty to await the manifestation of his holy and perfect will. Not because I failed to esteem thee as my lord and spouse did I remain silent: for I was and always will

be thy faithful servant, eager to correspond to thy holy wishes
and affection. From my inmost heart and in the name of the
Lord, whom I bear within me, I beseech thee not to change
the manner of thy conversation and intercourse with me.
The Lord has not made me his Mother in order to be served
and to command in this life, but in order to be the servant of
all and thy slave, obeying thy will in all things. This is my
duty, my master, and outside of it I would lead a life without
joy and full of sorrow. It is just that thou afford me the
opportunity of fulfilling it, since so it was ordained by the
Most High. He has furnished me with thy protection and
devoted assistance, in order that I may live securely in the
shade of thy provident solicitude and with thy aid rear the
Fruit of my womb, my God and my Lord." With these
words and others most sweet and persuasive most holy Mary
consoled and quieted saint Joseph, and he raised Her from
her knees in order to confer with Her upon all that would be
necessary for this purpose. Since on this occasion the heavenly Lady was full of the Holy Ghost and moreover bore within
Her, as his Mother, the divine Word, who proceeds from the
Father and the Holy Ghost, saint Joseph received special
enlightenment and the plenitude of divine graces. Altogether
renewed in fervor of spirit he said:

410. "Blessed art Thou, Lady, among all women, fortunate and preferred before all nations and generations. May
the Creator of heaven and earth be extolled with eternal
praise, since from his exalted kingly throne He has looked
upon Thee and chosen Thee for his dwelling-place and in
Thee alone has fulfilled the ancient promises made to the
Patriarchs and Prophets. Let all generations bless Him: for in
no one has He magnified his name as He has done in thy
humility; and me, the most insignificant of the living, He has
in his divine condescension selected for thy servant." In these
words of praise and benediction saint Joseph was enlightened

by the Holy Ghost, in the same manner as saint Elisabeth, when she responded to the salutation of our Queen and Mistress. The light and inspiration, received by the most holy spouse was wonderfully adapted to his dignity and office. The heavenly Lady, upon hearing the words of the holy man, answered in the words of the Magnificat, as She had done on her visit to saint Elisabeth, and She added other canticles. She was all aflame in ecstasy and was raised from the earth in a globe of light, which surrounded Her and transfigured Her with the gifts of glory.

411. At this heavenly vision saint Joseph was filled with admiration and unspeakable delight; for never had he seen his most blessed Spouse in such eminence of glory and perfection. Now he beheld Her with a full and clear understanding, since all the integrity and purity of the Princess of heaven and mystery of her dignity manifested themselves to him. He saw and recognized in her virginal womb the humanity of the infant God and the union of the two natures of the Word. With profound humility and reverence he adored Him and recognized Him as his Redeemer, offering himself to his Majesty. The Lord looked upon him in benevolence and kindness as upon no other man, for He accepted him as his foster-father and conferred upon him that title. In accordance with this dignity, He gifted him with that plenitude of science and heavenly gifts which Christian piety can and must acknowledge. I do not dilate upon this vast excellence of saint Joseph made known to me, because I would extend this history beyond the prescribed bounds.

412. However, if it was a proof of the magnanimity of the glorious saint Joseph and a clear evidence of his great sanctity, that he did not wear away and die of the grief sustained at the thought of the loss of his beloved Spouse, it is yet more astonishing, that he was not overwhelmed by the unexpected joy of this revelation of the true mystery connected with his

Spouse. In the former he proved his high sanctity; but in the latter he showed himself worthy of gifts, such which, if the Lord had not expanded his heart, he could neither have been capable of receiving nor could he have outlived to bear in the joy of his spirit. In all things he was renewed and elevated, so as to be able to treat worthily Her, who was the Mother of God himself and his Spouse, and to co-operate with Her in the mystery of the Incarnation and in taking care of the Word made man, as I shall relate farther on. In order that he might be still more apt and so much the more recognize his obligation to serve his heavenly Spouse, it was also made known to him, that all the gifts and blessings came to him because of Her: those before his espousal, because he had been selected for her husband, and those afterward, because he had won and merited this distinction. He also perceived with what prudence the great Lady had acted toward him, not only in serving him with such inviolate obedience and profound humility, but also in consoling him in his affliction, soliciting for him the grace and assistance of the. Holy Ghost, hiding her feelings with such discretion, tranquilizing and soothing his sorrow, thus fittingly disposing him for the influence of the divine Spirit. Just as the Princess of heaven had been the instrument for the sanctification of saint John the Baptist and his mother, so She also was instrumental in procuring for saint Joseph the plenitude of graces in still greater abundance. All this the most faithful and fortunate man understood and for it, as a most faithful servant, was proportionately thankful.

413. These great sacraments and many others connected with our Queen and her spouse saint Joseph, the sacred Evangelists passed over in silence, not only because they wished to treasure them in their hearts, but also because neither the humble Lady nor saint Joseph had spoken of them to anyone. Nor was it necessary to mention these

wonders in the life of Christ our Lord, which they wrote in order to establish our belief in the new Church and the law of grace; for such things might give rise to many inconveniences among the heathens in their first conversion. The admirable providence of God, in his hidden and inscrutable judgments, reserved these secrets for a more suitable time foreseen in divine wisdom. He wished that, after the Church had been already established and the Catholic faith well grounded. the faithful, standing in need of the intercession, the assistance and protection of their great Queen and Lady should draw, from the knowledge of these mysteries, new and old treasures of grace and consolation (Matth. 13, 52). Perceiving by new enlightenment what a loving Mother and powerful Advocate they had in heaven with her most holy Son, to whom the Father has given the power to judge (John 5, 52), let them flee to Her for help as to the only and sacred refuge of sinners. Let the tribulations and the tears of the Church themselves give witness, whether such times of affliction have not come upon us in our days; for never were her trials greater than now, when her own sons, reared at her breast, afflict her, seek to destroy her, and dissipate the treasures of the blood of her Spouse with a greater cruelty than was done by her most embittered enemies. In this crying need, when the blood, shed by her children calls heavenward, and much more loudly, the blood of our high Priest Christ (Heb. 12, 24) trodden under foot and polluted under pretext of justice, resounds in anguish, what are the most faithful children of the Church doing? Why are they so speechless? Why do they not call upon most holy Mary? Why do they not invoke her aid and urge Her to help? What wonder if help is delayed, since we postpone seeking Her and acknowledging Her as the true Mother of God? I give witness, that great mysteries are enclosed in this City of God and that in lively faith we should confess and extol them.

They are so great, that the deeper insight into them is reserved for the time after the general resurrection, when all the saints will know them in the Most High. But in the meanwhile let the pious and faithful souls acknowledge the condescension of this their most loving Queen and Lady in revealing some of the great and hidden sacraments through me, a most unworthy instrument; for I, in my weakness and insignificance, could be induced to attempt this work only by the repeated command and encouragement of the Mother of piety, as was stated several times.

Words of the Queen

THE VIRGIN MARY SPEAKS TO SISTER MARY OF AGREDA

414. My daughter, my objective in revealing to thee in this history so many sacraments and secrets, both those which thou hast written and many others, which thou art unable to manifest, is, that thou use them as a mirror of my life and as an inviolable rule of action for thy own. All of them should been graven in the tablets of thy heart and I recall to thy mind the teachings of eternal life, I, thereby complying with my duty as thy Teacher. Be ready to obey and fulfill all commands as a willing and careful pupil; let the humble care and watchfulness of my spouse saint Joseph, his submission to divine direction and his esteem for heavenly enlightenment, serve thee as an example. For only because his heart had been well disposed and prepared for the execution of the divine will, was he entirely changed and remodeled by the plenitude of grace for the ministry assigned to him by the Most High. Let therefore the consciousness of thy faults serve thee as a motive to submit in all humility to the work of God, not as a pretext to withdraw from the performance of that which the Lord desires of thee.

415. However, I wish on this occasion to reveal to thee the just reproach and indignation of the Most High against mortals; so that, comparing the conduct of other men with the humility and meekness, which I exercised toward my spouse saint Joseph, thou mayest understand it better in divine enlightenment. The cause of this reproach, which the lord and I have to make against men, is the inhuman perversity of men in persisting to treat each other with so much want of humility and love. In this they commit three faults, which displease the Most High very much and which cause the Almighty and me to withhold many mercies. The first is, that men, knowing that they are all children of the same Father in heaven (Is. 64, 8), works of his hands, formed of the same nature, graciously nourished and kept alive by his Providence, reared at the same table of divine mysteries and Sacraments, especially of his own body and blood, nevertheless forget and despise all these advantages, concentrating all their interest upon earthly and trivial affairs, exciting themselves without reason, swelling with indignation, creating discords, quarrels, indulging in detractions and harsh words, sometimes rising up to most wicked and inhuman vengeance or mortal hate of one another. The second is, that, when through human frailty and want of mortification, incited by the temptation of the devil, they happen to fall into one of these faults, they do not at once seek to rid themselves of it nor strive to be again reconciled, as should be done by brothers in the presence of a just judge. Thus they deny Him as their merciful Father and force Him to become the severe and rigid Judge of their sins; for no faults excite Him sooner to exercise his severity than the sins of revenge and hate. The third offense, which causes his great indignation, is, that sometimes, when a brother comes in order to be reconciled, he that deems himself offended will not receive him and asks a greater satisfaction than that which he knows would be

accepted by the Lord, and which he himself offers as satisfaction to God's Majesty. For all of them wish that God, who is most grievously offended, should receive and pardon them, whenever they approach Him with humility and contrition; while those that are but dust and ashes, ask to be revenged upon their brothers and will not content themselves with the satisfaction, which the Most High himself readily accepts for their own sins.

416. Of all the sins, which the sons of the Church commit, none is more horrible than these in the eyes of the Most High. This thou wilt readily understand by the divine light and in the vigor of God's law, which commands men to pardon their brethren, although they may have offended seventy times seven. And if a brother offend many times every day, as soon as he says that he is sorry for it, the Lord commands us to forgive the offending brother as many times without counting the number. And those that are not willing to forgive, He threatens with severest punishment on account of the scandal, which they cause. This can be gathered from the threatening words of God himself: Woe to him from whom scandal comes and through whom scandal is caused! It were better for him, if he fell into the depths of the sea with a heavy millstone around his neck. This was said in order to indicate the danger of this sin and the difficulty of obtaining deliverance therefrom, which must be compared to that of a man dropping into the sea with a grinding-stone around his neck. It also points out that the punishment is the abyss of eternal pains (Matth. 18,9). Therefore the command of my most holy Son is good advice to the faithful, that they rather permit their eyes to be torn out and their hands chopped off, than allow themselves to fall into this crime of scandalizing the little ones.

417. O my dearest daughter! How thou must bewail the wickedness and evils of this sin with tears of blood! That is

the sin, which grieves the Holy Ghost (Eph. 4, 30), affords proud triumphs to the demons, makes monsters of rational creatures, and wipes out in them the image of the eternal Father! What thing more unbecoming, or hateful and monstrous, than to see creatures of the earth, the food of worms and corruption, rise up against one another in pride and arrogance? Thou wilt not find words strong enough to describe this wickedness, in order to persuade mortals to fear it and guard against the wrath of the Lord (Matt. 3, 7). But do thou, dearest, preserve thy heart from this contagion, stamp and engrave in it the most useful doctrine for thy guidance. Never think for a moment, that in offending thy neighbor or scandalizing him in this way, the guilt can be small, for all these sins are weighty in the sight of God. Place a damper on all thy faculties and feelings in order to observe most strictly the rules of charity toward all creatures of the Most High. To me also afford this pleasure, since I wish thee to be most perfect in this virtue. I impose upon thee as my most vigorous precept, that thou give offense neither in thought, word or deed to any of thy neighbors; and that thou prevent any of thy subjects, and, as far as thou canst, any other person in thy presence from injuring their neighbor. Meditate well on this, as I ask it of thee, my dearest; for it is a doctrine most divine and least understood by mortals. Serve thyself with the only remedy against these passions: namely, with the compelling example of my humility and meekness, the effect of the sincere love not only toward my spouse, but toward all the children of the heavenly Father; for I esteemed them and looked upon them as redeemed and bought for a great price (I Pet. 1, 18). With true fidelity and ingenious charity watch over thy religious. The divine Majesty is offended grievously by anyone who does not fulfill this command expressly inculcated and called a new one by my Son (John 15, 12); but He is roused to incomparably greater indignation against religious persons, who offend against it. Among these there are many, who should distinguish themselves as perfect children of the Father and Teacher of this virtue; nevertheless they cast it aside and thereby become more odious and detestable in his sight than worldly persons.

Chapter V

SAINT JOSEPH RESOLVES TO DEVOTE HIMSELF ENTIRELY TO
THE SERVICE OF MOST HOLY MARY; THE BEHAVIORS OF
HER MAJESTY, AND OTHER PARTICULARS OF THE LIFE OF
MARY AND JOSEPH.

418. The most faithful Joseph, after being informed of the
mystery and sacrament of the Incarnation, was filled with
such high and befitting sentiments concerning his Spouse,
that, although he had always been holy and perfect, he was
changed into a new man. He resolved to act toward the
heavenly Lady according to a new rule and with much greater reverence, as I will relate farther on. This was conformable
to the wisdom of the saint and due to the excellence of his
Spouse; for saint Joseph by heavenly enlightenment saw well,
that he was the servant and She the Mistress of heaven and
earth. In order to satisfy his desire for honoring and reverencing Her as the Mother of God, whenever he passed Her or
spoke to Her alone, he did it with great external veneration
and on bended knees. He would not allow Her to serve him,
or wait upon him, or perform any other humble services,
such as cleaning the house or washing the dishes and the like.
All these things the most happy spouse wished to do himself,
in order not to derogate from the dignity of the Queen.

419. But the heavenly Lady, who among the humble was
the most humble and whom no one could surpass in humili-

ty, so managed all these things, that the palm of victory in all
these virtues always remained with Her. She besought saint
Joseph not to bend the knees to Her, for though this worship
was due to the Lord whom She carried in her womb, yet as
long as He was within unseen by anyone no distinction was
externally manifest between his and her own person. The
saint therefore allowed himself to be persuaded and conformed to the wishes of the Queen of heaven; only at times,
when She was not looking, he continued to give this worship
to the Lord whom She bore in her womb, and also to Her as
his Mother, intending thereby to honor Both according to
the excellence of Each. In regard to the other works and
services, a humble contention arose between them. For saint
Joseph could not overcome his conviction as to the impropri-
ety of allowing the great Queen and Lady to perform them,
and therefore he sought to be beforehand with such household duties. His heavenly Spouse was filled with the same
eagerness to seize upon occasions in advance of saint Joseph.
As however he busied himself in these duties during the time
which She spent in contemplation, he frustrated her continual desire of serving him and of performing all the duties of
the household, which She considered as belonging to Her as
a servant. In her affliction on this account, the heavenly Lady
turned to the Lord with humble complaints, and besought
Him to oblige saint Joseph not to hinder Her in the exercise
of humility, as She desired. As this virtue is so powerful
before the divine tribunal and has free access, no prayer
accompanied by it is small. Humility makes all prayers
effective and inclines the immutable Being of God to clemency. He heard Her petition and He ordered the angel
guardian of the blessed husband to instruct him as follows:
"Do not frustrate the humble desires of Her who is supreme
over all the creatures of heaven and earth. Exteriorly allow
Her to serve thee and interiorly treat Her with highest rever-

ence, and at all times and in all places worship the incarnate Word. It is his will, equally with that of the heavenly Mother, to serve and not to be served, in order to teach the world the knowledge of life and the excellence of humility. In some of the work thou canst assist Her, but always reverence in Her the Lord of all creation."

420. Instructed by this command of the Most High, saint Joseph permitted the heavenly Princess to exercise her humility and so both of them were enabled to make an offering of their will to God: most holy Mary, by exercising the deepest humility and obedience toward her spouse in all her acts of virtue which She performed without failing in the least point of perfection; and saint Joseph by obeying the Almighty with a holy and prudent embarrassment, which was occasioned by seeing himself waited upon and served by Her, whom he had recognized as his Mistress and that of the world, and as the Mother of his God and Creator. In this manner the prudent saint made up for the humility, which he could not practice in the works now consigned to his Spouse. This arrangement seemed to humiliate him more and filled him with a greater reverential fear. In this fear he observed most holy Mary, always bearing in mind the Treasure of her virginal womb and adoring, magnifying and praising the Lord. A few times, in reward of his holiness and reverence, or for the increase of both, the infant God manifested Himself to him in a wonderful manner: he saw Him in the womb of his purest Mother enclosed as it were in the clearest crystal. The sovereign Queen conversed with the glorious saint concerning the Incarnation; because She did not need to be so reserved in her heavenly words since he had been enlightened and instructed in the sublime sacraments of the hypostatic union of the divine and human natures in the virginal chamber of his Spouse.

421. No human tongue can reproduce the celestial words and conversations of the most holy Mary and the blessed Joseph. I will adduce some of them in the following chapters, as far as I know how. Yet, who call declare the effects wrought in the sweet and devout heart of this saint in seeing himself not only constituted the husband of Her who was the true Mother of his Creator, but in finding himself also served by Her as if She was the humblest slave, while at the same time he beheld Her raised in sanctity and dignity above the highest seraphim and inferior only to God? If the divine right hand enriched with blessings the house of Obededom for having sheltered for a few months the figurative ark of the old Testament (I Par. 13, 14), what blessings did He not shower upon saint Joseph, to whom He entrusted the true ark and the Lawgiver himself enshrined in Her? Incomparable was the good fortune and happiness of this saint! Not only because he had with him in his house the living and true ark of the new Testament, the altar, the sacrifice, and the temple, all left in his charge: but also because he cared for them worthily and as a faithful servant (Matth. 24, 45), constituted by the Lord himself over his family to provide for all their necessities in the right time as a most faithful dispenser (Os. 14, 20). Let all generations and peoples acknowledge and bless him, let them extol his merits; since the Most High has favored none other in the same degree. I, an unworthy and poor worm, in the light of such venerable sacraments, exalt and magnify this Lord God, confessing Him as holy, just, merciful, wise and admirable in the disposition of all his great works.

422. The humble but blessed house of Joseph contained three rooms, which occupied nearly all its space and formed the exclusive dwelling place of the two Spouses; for they kept neither a man nor a maid-servant. In one of the rooms saint Joseph slept, in another he worked and kept the tools of his

trade of carpentering; the third was ordinarily occupied by the Queen of heaven and was also her sleeping room. It contained a couch made by the hands of saint Joseph. This arrangement they had observed since their espousal and from the day on which they had come to this, their dwelling. Before knowing the dignity of his Spouse and Lady, saint Joseph rarely went to see Her; for while She kept her retirement he was engaged in his work, unless some affair made it absolutely necessary to consult Her. But after he was informed of his good fortune, the holy man was more solicitous for her welfare, and in order to renew the joy of his heart he began to come often to the retreat of the sovereign Lady, visiting Her and receiving her commands. But he always approached Her with extreme humility and reverential fear, and before he spoke to Her, he was careful to note in what She was engaged. Many times he saw Her in ecstasy raised from the earth and resplendent with most brilliant light; at other times in the company of her angels holding celestial intercourse with them; and at other times, he found Her prostrate upon the earth in the form of a cross, speaking to the Lord. Her most fortunate spouse was a participator in these favors. But whenever he found the great Lady in these occupations and postures, he would presume no farther than to look upon Her with profound reverence; and thereby he merited sometimes to hear the sweetest harmony of the celestial music, with which the angels regaled their Queen, and perceived a wonderful fragrance which comforted him and filled him entirely with jubilation and joy of spirit.

423. The two holy spouses lived alone in their house, for as I have said, they had no servants of any kind, not only on account of their humility, but in order more fittingly to hide from any witnesses the wonders, which passed between them and which were not to be communicated to outsiders. Likewise the Princess of heaven did not leave her dwelling, except

for very urgent causes in the service of God or her fellow-men. Whenever anything was necessary She asked that fortunate neighbor, who as I have said had served saint Joseph during the absence of Mary in the house of Zacharias. This woman received such a good return from Mary, that not only she herself became most holy and perfect, but her whole household and family was blessed by the help of the Queen and Mistress of the world. She was visited by most holy Mary in some of her sicknesses and with her family was copiously enriched by the blessings of heaven.

424. Never did saint Joseph see his heavenly Spouse asleep, nor did he of his own experience know whether She ever slept, although he besought Her to take some rest, especially during the time of her sacred pregnancy. The resting-place of the Princess was the low couch, which I said had been constructed by saint Joseph; and on it were the coverings which served Her during her brief and holy sleep. Her undergarment was a sort of tunic made of cotton, but softer than the ordinary or common cloth. This tunic She never changed from the time since She left the temple, nor did it wear out or grow old or soiled, and no person ever saw it, nor did saint Joseph know that She wore that kind of a garment; for he never saw any other part of her clothing except the outside garments, which were open to the view of other persons. Those were of a gray color, as I have said (Part I. No. 400), and these only and her head-coverings were the garments, which the Queen changed now and then; not because they were soiled, but because, being visible to all, She wished to avoid notice by such strange sameness of outward appearance. Nothing that She wore upon her most pure and virginal body became soiled or worn; for She neither per-spired, nor was She subject to the punishments, which are laid upon the sin-impregnated bodies of the children of Adam. She was in all respects most pure and the works of her

hands were like crystal ornaments; and with the same purity She cared for the clothes and other necessities of saint Joseph. The food of which She partook, was most limited in kind and quantity; but She partook of some every day and in company of her spouse; she never ate meat, although he did, and She prepared it for him. Her sustenance was fruit, fishes, and ordinarily bread and cooked vegetables; but of all these She partook in exact measure and weight, only so much as was necessary for the nourishment of the body and the maintaining of the natural warmth without any superfluities that could pass over into excess of harmful corruption; the same rule She observed in regard to drink, although Her fervent acts of love often caused a superabundance of preter-natural ardor. This rule, as to the quantity of her nourish-ment, She followed during her whole life, although as to the kind of food She adapted Herself to the various circumstanc-es demanding a change, as I shall relate further on.

425. In all things the most pure Mary exhibited consum-mate perfection, without any fault or want of grace; and all her actions both in the natural and the supernatural order reached the pinnacle of excellence. But words fail me in describing it: for I am never satisfied, seeing how far short these words fall of that which I perceive and how much more excellence this sublime Creature possesses than I can express. Continually I am grieved by my insufficiency and dissatisfied with my limited terms and descriptions, fearing lest I pre-sume more than I should in striving to do that which so far exceeds my powers. But the force of obedience inspires me with I do not know what sweet strength, which dispels my hesitancy and impels my backwardness, encouraging me to face the greatness of my undertaking and the smallness of my ability. I work under obedience, and through it I hope to make great gains. It will also serve me as an excuse.

Words of the Queen

THE VIRGIN MARY SPEAKS TO SISTER MARY OF AGREDA

426. My daughter, in the school of humility, which my whole life affords thee, I wish that thou be studious and diligent; and this should be thy first and principal care, if thou wishest to enjoy the sweet embraces of the Lord, assure thyself of his favor and possess the treasures of light, which are hidden to the proud (Matth. 11, 25). For without the trusty foundation of humility such treasures cannot be confided to any man. Let all thy ambition be to humble thyself in thy own estimation and thought, so that in thy exterior actions thou mayest truly exhibit this humility of thy interior. It must be a subject of confusion and a spur of humility for thee and for all the souls to have the Lord as their Father and Spouse, to see, that the presumption and pride of worldly wisdom is more powerful in its devotees, than humility and true self-knowledge is in the children of light. Consider the watchfulness, the untiring study and care of ambitious and aspiring men. Look upon their struggle to be esteemed in the world, their strivings never at rest, though so vain and worthless; how they conduct themselves outwardly according to the false notions which they have of themselves; how they pretend to be what they are not, and how they exert themselves to obtain through these false pretenses the treasures, which, though only earthly, they do not deserve. Hence it should be a cause of confusion and shame to the good, that deceit should urge on the sons of perdition with greater force than truth urges the elect; that the number of those, who in the world are anxious to strive in the service of their God and Creator, should be so small in comparison with the number of those who serve vanity; that there should be so few of the elect, though all are called (Matth. 20. 16).

427. Seek therefore, my daughter, to make progress in this science of humility and to gain for thyself the palm of victory in this virtue in the midst of the children of darkness; in opposition to their pride, study what I did in order to overcome darkness in this world by the pursuit of humility. In this the Lord and I desire thee to be very wise and proficient. Never miss an occasion of exercising humility and allow no one to deprive thee of such works; and if occasions of humility fail thee and are scarce, seek after them and ask God to send them to you; for it pleases his Majesty to see such kind of anxiety and ambition in what He desires so much. For the sake of this divine complacency alone, thou, as a daughter of his house, as his domestic and as his spouse, shouldst be solicitous and anxious for acts of humility; for in this, human ambition itself will teach thee not to be negligent. Observe how a woman in her house and family conducts herself in order to benefit and advance her family, and how she loses no chance of advancing it; nothing seems too much for her, and if anything, no matter how small it is, goes to loss (Lucas. 15, 8) she becomes much excited. All this is the effect of worldly covetousness, and there is certainly no reason, that the wisdom of heaven be less fruitful or less careful in the gifts received. Therefore I desire thee to allow no carelessness or forgetfulness concerning what so much concerns thee, and to lose no occasion of practicing humility and laboring for the glory of the Lord; but do thou seek and strive after his gifts and draw merits from them as a faithful daughter and spouse. Then wilt thou find grace in the eyes of the Lord and in mine, according to thy desire.

Chapter VI

SOME OF THE SAYINGS AND CONVERSATIONS OF THE MOST
HOLY MARY AND JOSEPH REGARDING DIVINE THINGS;
OTHER WONDERFUL EVENTS.

428. Before saint Joseph had been instructed in the mystery
of the Incarnation, the Princess of heaven made use of opportune occasions for reading to him some of the passages of
holy Scriptures, especially from the Prophets and from the
Psalms. As a most wise Teacher She also explained them to
him, and her holy spouse who was indeed capable of the
exalted truths contained therein, asked Her many questions,
wondering at and consoling himself with the heavenly answers of his Spouse; and thus both of them alternately
praised and blessed the Lord. But after he had himself become instructed in the great sacrament, he conversed with
our Queen, as with one, who was Herself to be the Coadjutrix of the admirable works and mysteries of our Redemption. For now they could more openly and clearly discuss the
divine prophecies and oracles concerning the conception of
the Word through a Virgin-Mother, of his birth, his bringing
up, and his most holy life. All these things her Highness
discussed and explained, delineating beforehand the course of
action, which they were to pursue, when the longed-for day
of the birth of the Child should have arrived, when She
should hold Him in her arms, nourish Him at her breast

with virginal milk, and when the holy spouse himself should share in this greatest of mortal blessedness. Only of his Passion and Death, and of the sayings of Isaias and Jeremias, the most prudent Queen spoke more rarely; for as her spouse was of a most kind and tender heart, She thought it best not to dilate upon or anticipate that which he himself remembered of the sayings of the ancient writers concerning the coming and the sufferings of the Messiah. The most prudent Virgin also waited until the Lord should grant more particular revelation of what was to happen, or until She herself would know better the divine will in this respect.

429. Her most faithful and blessed husband was wholly inflamed by her sweet words and conversations, and with tears of joy he said to the heavenly Spouse: "Is it possible, that in thy most chaste arms I shall see my God and Redeemer? That I shall hear him speak, and touch Him, and that my eyes shall look upon his divine face, and that the sweat of my brow shall be so blessed as to be poured out in his service and for his sustenance? That He shall live with us, and that we shall eat with Him at the same table, and that we shall speak and converse with Him? Whence comes to me this good fortune which nobody can ever deserve? O how much do I regret that I am so poor! Would I possessed the richest palaces for his entertainment and many treasures to offer Him I" And the sovereign Queen answered: "My master and spouse, there is abundant reason that thy desires extend to all things possible for the reception of thy Creator; but this great God and Lord does not wish to enter into the world in the pomp of ostentatious riches and royal majesty. He has need of none of these (Ps. 15,2), nor does He come from heaven for such vanities. He comes to redeem the world and to guide men on the path of eternal life (John 10, 10) ; and this is to be done by means of humility and poverty; in these He wishes to be born, live and die, in order to destroy

in the hearts of men the fetters of covetousness and pride, which keep them from blessedness. On this account He chose our poor and humble house, and desired us not to be rich in apparent, deceitful and transitory goods, which are but vanity of vanities and affliction of spirit (Eccles. 1, 24) and which oppress and obscure the understanding."

430. At other times the saint asked the most pure Lady to teach him the nature and essence of virtues, especially of the love of God, in order that he might know how to behave toward the Most High become man and in order that he might not be rejected as a useless and incapable servant. The Queen and Teacher of virtues complied with these requests and explained to him the nature of true virtues and the manner of exercising them in all perfection. But in these discourses She proceeded with so much humility and discretion that She did not appear as the Teacher of her spouse, though such She was; but She managed to give her information under the guise of conversation or in addressing the Lord, or at other times asking questions of saint Joseph, which of themselves suggested the information. In all circumstances She knew how to preserve her most profound humility, without permitting even the least gesture not in accordance with it. These alternate discourses or readings from the holy Scriptures they interrupted by manual labor as occasion required. Not only was the hard and tiresome labor of saint Joseph lightened by the admirable words of sympathy of our Lady, but in her rare discretion She also knew how to add instruction, so that his manual labor became more an exercise of virtue than a work of the hands. The mildest Dove, with the prudence of a most wise virgin, administered her consolations by pointing out the most blessed fruits of labor. In Her estimation She held Herself unworthy of being supported by her spouse, and She felt Herself in continual debt to the sweat of saint Joseph, as one who is receiving a

great alms and most generous gift. All these considerations
caused in Her sentiments of deepest obligation, as if She were
the most useless creature on earth. Therefore, though She
could not assist the saint in his trade, since that was above the
strength of women and unbecoming the modesty and retirement of the heavenly Queen; yet in all that was befitting Her
She served Him as an humble handmaid, since her discreet
humility and thankfulness would not suffer any less return
for the faithful services of saint Joseph.

431. Among other wonderful happenings in connection
with his intercourse with most holy Mary during these days
of her pregnancy, saint Joseph one day saw many birds
flocking around Her in order to pay their respect to the
Queen and Mistress of all creatures. They surrounded Her as
if to form a choir and raised up their voices in songs of sweet
harmony not less wonderful than their visit to the heavenly
Lady. Saint Joseph had never seen this wonder until that day
and, full of admiration and joy, he said to his sovereign
Spouse; "Is it possible, my Mistress, that these simple birds
and irrational creatures should understand and fulfill their
obligations better than I? Surely it is reasonable, that if they
recognize, serve and reverence Thee according to their powers, that Thou allow me to perform that which in duty I am
bound to do." The most pure Virgin answered him; "My
master, in the behavior of these little birds the Creator offers
us a powerful motive worthily to employ all our strength and
faculties in his praise, just as they recognize and acknowledge
their Creator in my womb. I, however, am but a creature and
therefore I deserve no veneration, nor is it right that I accept
it; it is my duty to induce all creatures to praise the Most
High, since He has looked upon me, his handmaid, and has
enriched me with the treasures of the divinity" (Luke 1, 48).

432. It happened also not a few times that the heavenly
Lady and her spouse found themselves so poor and destitute

of means that they were in want of the necessaries of life; for they were most liberal in their gifts to the poor, and they were never anxious to store up beforehand food or clothing, as is wont with the children of this world in their faint-hearted covetousness (Matth. 6, 25). The Lord so disposed things that the faith and patience of his most holy Mother and of saint Joseph should not be vain, for this indigence was a source of incomparable consolation to our Lady, not only because of her love of poverty, but also on account of her astonishing humility. She considered Herself unworthy of the sustenance of life, and that She above all others should suffer the want of it. Therefore She blessed the Lord for this poverty as far as it affected Her, while She asked the Most High to supply the needs of saint Joseph, as being a just and holy man and well worthy of this favor of the Almighty. The Lord did not forget his poor entirely (Ps. 73, 19), for while He permitted them to exercise virtues and gain merits, He also gave them nourishment in opportune time (Ps. 144, 15). This his Providence provided in various ways. Sometimes He moved the hearts of their neighbors and acquaintances to bring some gratuitous gift or pay some debt. At other times, and more ordinarily, saint Elisabeth sent them assistance from her home; for ever since She had harbored in her house the Queen of heaven this devoted matron insisted on sending them a gift from time to time, which the humble Princess always acknowledged by sending in return some work of her hands. On some occasions, for the greater glory of the Most High, the blessed Lady availed Herself of the power given to Her as the Mistress of all creation; then She would command the birds of the air to bring some fishes from the sea, or fruits of the field, and they would fulfill her commands to the point; sometimes they would bring also bread in their beaks, which the Lord had furnished them. Many times the most fortunate spouse saint Joseph was a witness to all these happenings.

433. Also in other necessities they were on some occasions succored by the holy angels in an admirable manner. In order properly to understand some of the great miracles which happened through the ministry of the angels to most holy Mary and Joseph, it is necessary to take into account the magnanimity and generous faith of the saint, for these virtues were so great in him that not even the shadow of covetousness, or greediness, could find entrance into his soul. Although he labored for others, as did also his heavenly Spouse, yet never did they ask for any wages, or set a price on their work, asking payment therefore they performed all their work not for gain, but in obedience to a request or for charity, leaving the payment of wages entirely in the hands of their employers and accepting it not as a just return for their labors, but as a freely given alms. This is the perfection of sanctity, which saint Joseph learnt from the heavenly example given to him in his house by the most holy Virgin. Owing to this circumstance, that he was not paid for his work, it happened sometimes that they were in total want of food and sustenance until the Lord would provide for them. One day it came to pass that the hour set for their meal passed without their having anything in the house to eat. They persevered in prayer until very late, giving thanks to the Lord for this privation, and hoping that He would open his all-powerful hand (Ps. 144, 16). In the meanwhile the holy angels prepared the meal and placed upon the table some fruit, and whitest bread and fishes, also especially a sort of preserve or jelly of wonderful and nourishing sweetness. Then some of the angels went to call their Queen, and others called saint Joseph her spouse. Each came forth from their separate retirement and, perceiving the regalement provided by heaven, they thanked the Most High in tears of fervent

gratitude and partook of the food; and afterwards they broke out in exalted songs of praise of the Almighty.

434. Many other similar events came to pass almost daily in the house of most holy Mary and her spouse; for as they were alone and as there was no need of hiding these wonders from witnesses, the Lord did not hesitate to perform them for his beloved, who were entrusted with co-operation in the most wonderful of all the works of his powerful arm, I wish merely to remark, that when I say Mary sang canticles of praise, either She by Herself or in company with saint Joseph or the holy angels, new songs are meant, such as saint Anne sang, the mother of Samuel, or Moses, Ezechias and other Prophets, when they were visited by great blessings of the Lord. If all the canticles (Kings 2, 1; Deut. 32, 1, etc.) which the Queen of heaven composed and sang would have been recorded, there would be a large volume of them, the contents of which would excite unheard of wonder in this world.

Words of the Queen

THE VIRGIN MARY SPEAKS TO SISTER MARY OF AGREDA

435. Much-beloved daughter, I wish that the science of the Lord be many times renewed in thee, and that thou acquire the knowledge of the voice (Wis. 1, 7), so that thou mayst know, (and let also mortals know), the dangerous deceit and perverse estimation in which they, as lovers of falsehood, hold the temporal and visible goods (Ps. 4, 4). How many men are not fascinated by their unbounded greed? All of them ordinarily stake their hopes on gold and material riches; and in order to increase them, they exert all the forces of their natural being. Thus they spend all the time of their life, which was given them in order to gain eternal rest and happiness, in these vanities. They lose themselves in these dark labyrinths and mazes, as if they knew nothing of God

and of his Providence; for they do not think of asking Him for that which they desire, and do not moderate their desires in such a way as will dispose them to ask and hope for what they desire at his hands. Thus they lose all, because they confide in the lying and deceitful prospects of their own efforts. This blind greed is the root of all evils (I Tim. 6, 20) ; for the Lord, incensed at such great perversity, permits the mortals to be entangled in the vile slavery of avarice, in which their understanding is darkened and their will hardened. Soon the Most High, for greater punishment, withdraws his kindly care as from creatures so detestable and denies them his paternal protection, thus letting them fall into what is the deepest misfortune that can befall man in this life.

436. Although it is true that nothing can hide itself from the eyes of the Lord (Ps. 138, 6), yet when the transgressors and enemies of his law offend Him, they forfeit the kind attention and care of his Providence and are left to their own desires (Ps. 80, 13). They cease to experience the paternal foresight shown toward those who trust in the Lord. Those that confide in their own efforts and in the gold, which they can touch and feel, will reap the fruit of their hopes. But just as far as the divine Essence and Power is distant from the lowliness and limitation of mortals, so far also the results of human covetousness are distant from the help and protection of eternal Providence shown to the humble who trust in it (Ps. 17, 31). Upon these his Majesty looks with kindest love, delights in them, nourishes them at his breast, and attends to their wishes and wants. I and my holy spouse Joseph were poor, and at times we suffered great wants; but none of them were powerful enough to engender within our hearts the contagion of avarice. We concerned ourselves entirely with the glory of the Most High, relying wholly on his most faithful and tender care. This was what pleased Him so much, as thou hast understood and written; since He sup-

plied our wants in various manners, even commanding the angels to help us and prepare for us our nourishment.

437. I do not wish to say that the mortals should yield to laziness and negligence; on the contrary it is just that all should labor (Ps. 48, 7), and doing nothing is also a great and very reprehensible fault. Neither leisure nor solicitude must be disorderly; nor should the creature trust in his own strength; nor should he smother the divine love in anxiety; nor seek more than is necessary for a temperate life. Neither should he fear that the divine Providence will fail to supply what is necessary, nor should he be troubled or lose hope when the Creator seems to delay his assistance. In the same way he that is in abundance should not (Eccli, 31, 8) lay aside all exertion and forget that he is a man subject to labor and travail. Thus riches as well as poverty must be attributed to God and made use of in a holy and legitimate way for the glory of the Creator and Ruler of all things. If men would observe this rule of action nobody would be without the assistance of the Lord, who is a true Father, and neither would the poor be led into sin by poverty, nor the rich by prosperity. Of thee, my daughter, I require the practice of these rules, and through thee I wish to inculcate them on other mortals. Thou must especially impress this doctrine upon all thy subjects, telling them not to be troubled or faint-hearted because of the wants they suffer, nor inordinately solicitous about their eating or clothing (Matth. 6, 25), but that they confide in the Most High and in his Providence. For if they correspond to his love, I assure them that they shall never suffer from the want of what is necessary. Exhort them also to let their words and conversations continually turn about holy and divine things, engaging in the praise and exaltation of the Lord according to the teachings of the Bible and holy writings. Let their conversations be in heaven (Philip 3,20) with the Most High, and with me,

who am their Mother and Superior, and let it be with the angels, imitating them in holy love.

Chapter VII

THE MOST HOLY MARY PREPARES THE SWADDLING CLOTHES AND THE LINENS FOR THE DIVINE INFANT WITH ARDENT LONGINGS TO SEE IT BORN.

438. The divine pregnancy of the Mother of the eternal Word had already far advanced. Although She knew that the necessary coverings and linens for the time of her parturition must be provided, She wished to proceed in all things with the fullness of heavenly prudence. Therefore, fulfilling all requirements of an obedient and faithful handmaid, She presumed to arrange nothing without the permission and consent of the Lord and of her holy spouse. Although She could have acted for Herself in such matters as pertained to her office of chosen Mother and of her most holy Son, She would not undertake anything without speaking to saint Joseph. Therefore She said to him: "My master, it is time that we prepare the things necessary for the birth of my most holy Son. Although his Majesty wishes to be treated as one of the children of men, humiliating Himself and suffering with them, yet it is just that we acknowledge Him as our God and as our true King and Lord by rendering Him our devoted service, and by making careful provision for his wants as an infant. If thou give me permission I will begin to prepare the coverings and linens for his protection and shelter. I have already woven with my own hands a piece of linen which

may serve as his first swaddling-clothes; and do thou, my master, seek to procure some woolen cloth of a soft texture and an humble color from which I may prepare other coverings; and later on I will weave a seamless tunic appropriate for Him. In order to avoid any mistake, let us offer special prayers asking his Highness to govern and direct us in the right way, so that we may know his will and fulfill his pleasure."

439. "My Spouse and Lady," answered saint Joseph, "if it were possible to serve with my own heart-blood my Lord and God and thus fulfill thy commands, I would be willing to shed it amid most atrocious torments; and as I cannot do this, would that I had great riches to buy the most costly textures in order to offer them to Thee on this occasion. Do Thou give thy orders as Thou seest fit, for I will serve Thee as thy servant." Both of them betook themselves to prayer, and each separately heard the answer of the Lord, repeating what the sovereign Queen had already heard many times, and, which now was said in her hearing and that of saint Joseph: "I have come from heaven to the earth in order to exalt humility and discredit pride, to honor poverty and contemn riches, to destroy vanity and establish truth, and in order to enhance worthily the value of labor. Therefore it is my will that exteriorly you treat Me according to the humble position which I have assumed, as if I were the natural child of both of you, and that interiorly you acknowledge Me as the Son of my eternal Father, and bestow the reverence and love due to Me as the Man-God."

440. Encouraged by this divine voice to seek the wisest course in the rearing of the infant God, most holy Mary and Joseph conferred with each other in what way they might conceal the most noble and perfect worship which was ever given to the true God by his creatures, beneath the treatment which in the eyes of the world was due to a natural child of

them both; for this was to be the opinion of the world, and such a conduct the Lord himself had enjoined upon them. Having therefore come to an agreement they lived up to this command of the Lord in such perfection that they were the admiration of all heaven; and further on I will say more of this (Nos. 506, 508, 536, 545). They both concluded that according to the limited means allowed them by their poverty they were to expend whatever they could afford in the service of the infant God without going into excess or failing in anything; for the sacrament of the King was to be concealed in humble poverty, though at the same time they wished to exercise their burning love as far as was possible. Saint Joseph, in exchange for some of his work, accepted two pieces of woolen cloth such as his heavenly Spouse had described; the one white, the other mulberry-colored mixed with grey, both of them of the best quality he could find. Of these the heavenly Queen made the first little dresses of her most holy Son, while She prepared the swathing clothes and shirts from the piece of linen which She herself had spun and woven. Being woven by such hands, it was a most delicate piece of cloth. She had commenced work upon it from the day of her entrance into their house at Nazareth; for She had intended it for the temple as a present. Although it could now serve for another much higher purpose, nevertheless, She offered whatever remained of it after She had completed the furnishings of the infant God as a gift to the temple of Jerusalem, according to her original intention. All the articles and coverings necessary for her divine Infant the great Lady prepared with her own hands, and while She sewed and trimmed them She shed tears of ineffable devotion remaining continually on her knees. Saint Joseph gathered such flowers and herbs as he could find from which, together with other aromatic materials, the zealous Mother extracted fragrant essences. With these She sprinkled the sacred vestments of the Victim of sacrifice which She awaited; then She folded and laid them away in a chest, in which She afterwards took them along with Her, as I shall relate farther on.

441. All these doings of the Princess of heaven are to be thought of and estimated not as being without life, nude and bare as I here represent them, but of incomparable grace and loveliness, full of sanctity and exalted merit, of a greater perfection than human intellect can comprehend; because She performed all these works as the Mother of wisdom, and as the Queen of all virtues. In preparing for the appearance of the most holy humanity of her Son in this world, She celebrated the dedication of the living temple of God. The sovereign Queen understood better than all the rest of creation the ineffable greatness of the mystery of the Incarnation of a God and of his coming into the world. Not in a spirit of doubt, but inflamed by love and veneration, She repeated many times the words of Solomon when he built the temple: "How is it possible that God should dwell with men on earth? If all the heavens, and the heaven of heavens cannot comprehend Thee, how can this human body contain Thee, which is formed in my womb?" But if the temple of Solomon, which served only as a place in which God should hear the prayers within it, was built and dedicated with such lavish expenditure of gold, silver, treasures and sacrifices, what should not the Mother of the true Solomon do for the building up and the dedication of the living temple (Colos. 2, 9) where was to dwell the plenitude of the true Divinity, the eternal and incomprehensible God? All these innumerable sacrifices and treasures of the figurative temple, most holy Mary duplicated not in gold, silver, or rich texture, since God sought no such riches in the living temple, but in heroic virtues and in canticles of praise, by which She fructified and extolled the graces and gifts of the Most High. She offered up the sacrifice of her burning love, and ransacked all the holy

writings for hymns, canticles and psalms to praise and magnify this mystery, adding thereto the expression of her own exalted sentiments. In a mystical and yet altogether real manner She fulfilled the ancient figures and types by her virtues and by her interior and her exterior acts. She called upon and invited all the creatures to praise their God, to give honor and glory to their Creator, and place the hope of their sanctification in his coming into the world. In many of these exercises the most fortunate and blessed Joseph, her spouse, took part.

442. No human tongue can describe, and no created understanding can reach the sublime height of merit which the Princess of heaven attained, and the degree of pleasure and complacency which they afforded the Most High. If the least degree of grace, which any creature merits by an act of virtue, is more valuable than all the created universe, what treasures of grace did She not gain, whose acts exceeded in value not only all the sacrifices, offerings and holocausts of the old law and all the merits of the human race, but far excelled also those of the highest seraphim? The loving extremes of the heavenly Lady in hoping to look upon her Son and true God, to receive Him in her arms, nourish Him at her breast, tend Him with her own hands, converse with Him and serve Him, and adore Him made man from her own flesh, reached such a pass that in the ardors of love She would have breathed forth her spirit and have been consumed if She had not been preserved from dissolution, assisted and strengthened by the miraculous intervention of that same God. Yes, many times would She have lost her life, if it had not been preserved by her most holy Son; for many times She saw Him in her virginal womb and with divine clearness She saw his humanity united to his Divinity, observed the interior acts of that most holy Soul, the conditions and postures of his body, the prayers offered up by Him for Her, for saint

Joseph, for all the human race and especially for the predestined. All these and other mysteries were open to Her, and in perceiving them She was altogether inflamed with the desire of imitating and exalting Him, since She bore within Her the devouring fires which illumine yet do not consume (Exod. 3, 2).

443. Amidst this conflagration of divine love She spoke sometimes to her most holy Son: "My sweetest Love, Creator of the universe, when shall my eyes enjoy the light of thy divine countenance? When shall my arms be consecrated as the altar of the Victim, which is awaited by the eternal Father? When shall I kiss the earth trodden by thy divine feet, and when shall I as thy Mother gain the coveted kiss of my Beloved (Cant. 1, 1) so that I may inhale thy own Spirit from the flow of thy breath? When shalt Thou, the inaccessible light, the true God of the true God, Light of the Light (John 1, 9), manifest Thyself to us mortals, after so many ages of concealment from our view? When shall the children of Adam, laden with the guilt of their sins, know their Redeemer (Baruch 3, 38), see their salvation, welcome in their midst their Teacher, their Brother and their true Father? O Light of my soul, my strength, my Beloved, for whom dying I live! Son of my womb, how can I fulfill the office of a Mother, since I know not how to fulfill the duties, nor merit the name of even a slave? How shall I be able to treat Thee worthily, who am a vile and insignificant, poor worm? How can I serve and administer to Thee, since Thou art sanctity itself and infinite goodness, and I only dust and ashes? How can I dare to speak before Thee, or stand in Thy presence? Do Thou, Master of my being, who hast chosen me, the little one among the other daughters of Adam, govern my conduct, direct my desires and inflame my affections, in order that I may please Thee with all my powers! And what shall I do, my only Delight, since Thou art to issue from my womb

into the world in order to suffer affronts and death for the human race, if at the same time I shall not be allowed to die with Thee and accompany Thee in thy sacrifice? Since Thou art my life and my being, let the same cause and motive that brings about thy Death bring about also mine; for they are united as if they were one and the same. Less than thy Death will suffice to save the world, yes thousands of worlds; let me die instead of Thee, and let me suffer thy ignominies, while Thou, by thy love and light, sanctify the world and enlighten the darkness of mortals, and if it is not possible to revoke the decree of the eternal Father, which requires that Redemption be abundant (Ephes, 2, 4) and thy excessive charity be satisfied, look graciously upon my desires and let me take part in: all the labors of thy life, since Thou art my Son and Lord."

444. The variety of these and other sweetest sentiments of love uttered by the Queen made Her most beautiful in the eyes (Esth. 2,9) of the Prince of the eternities, who was enshrined in the virginal chamber of her womb. All her interior movements were conformable to the actions of that most sacred and deified Humanity; for as a worthy Mother of such a Son She closely observed them as models for her imitation. Sometimes the infant God would place Himself on his knees in order to pray to the Father or assume the position of one crucified, as if in order to exercise Himself therein beforehand. From that retirement (as even now from the highest throne in heaven) He looked upon and comprehended, by the science of his most holy soul, all that He knows even at this day, and no creatures of the present, past, or future, with all their thoughts and actions, was hidden from his view. To all things He attended as the Lord and Redeemer. Since these mysteries were manifest also to his heavenly Mother and since She was also endowed with all the graces and gifts necessary for acting in concert with Him, She brought forth such great fruits of sanctity, that no human

words can ever describe them. But if we were not perverted in our judgments, and if we were not hardened as stone, we would find it impossible, at the sight and experience of these vast and admirable works, to remain untouched by loving sorrow and thankful acknowledgment.

Words of the Queen

THE VIRGIN MARY SPEAKS TO SISTER MARY OF AGREDA

445. The lesson of this chapter, my daughter, should be, that thou bear in mind with what reverence thou must handle all the things consecrated and devoted to the divine service; and at the same time estimate how reprehensible is the irreverence with which the ministers of the Lord offend in their disregard for the sacred objects. They should not forget or slight the indignation of his Majesty against them for the gross discourtesy and ingratitude, which they ordinarily show by handling the sacred ornaments and objects of worship without attention and respect. And much greater is the anger of the Lord against those who possess the incomes or stipends of his most sacred blood, if they waste and squander them in vile vanities and indecent profanities. They seek for their sustenance and convenience what is most costly and valuable, while for the honor and worship of the Lord they are satisfied with what is most cheap, common and ordinary. When this happens, especially in regard to the linens, which touch the body and blood of my most holy Son, such as corporals and purificators, I wish thee to understand that the holy angels, that assist at the most exalted and sublime sacrifice, are as it were struck with horror and cover their eyes at the sight, full of astonishment that the Most High bears with them and suffers such boldness and presumption. Although not all offend in this, yet there are many; and few distinguish themselves in outward respect and care at the divine cult, or treat

the sacred objects with due reverence; they are the smaller number and even they do not all have the pure intention, not observing this due respect out of reverence, but out of vanity and for other human ends. Thus they who adore and worship their Creator in the spirit of truth and with a pure and upright intention have become very scarce.

446. Consider, my dearest, what should be our sentiments when, on the one hand, we reflect on the incomprehensible being of God, who in his goodness has created us for his honor and worship, establishing this as the very law of our nature and of all the created universe, and when, on the other hand, we see with what ingratitude men correspond to the gifts of the most liberal Creator by withholding from his service the very things intended for it, reserving for their own vanities the most costly and valuable and applying for their Creator only the most valueless and despicable of this world. This fault is little thought of and recognized, and therefore I wish not only that thou deplore it with true sorrow, but also that thou make reparation for it as far as possible during the time in which thou art superioress. Give to the Lord of the best, and instruct thy religious that they attend with a sincere and devout heart to the keeping in order and the cleaning of the sacred articles; and this not only for their own convent, but also by seeking to furnish other poor churches with the corporals and vestments of which they stand in need. Let them be convinced that the Lord will repay their holy zeal for his worship, and that He will relieve their poverty and the necessities of their convent like a Father, and that thereby it will never become poorer. This is the most appropriate occupation and legitimate business of the spouses of Christ, and in this they ought to consume their time which may remain after fulfilling the obligations of the choir and other duties of obedience. If all the religious would busy themselves purposely in these honorable, praiseworthy and agreeable

occupations they would never suffer any want and they would maintain an angelic existence in this life. Because they do not attend to this service of the Lord, many of them, forsaken by the hand of the God, turn toward the dangerous levities and distractions, which on account of their vileness, I do not wish thee to describe or consider except to deplore them from thy heart and to avert such displeasure and offense against God.

447. But because I have especial reason to look with favor upon the inmates of thy convent, I wish that, in my name and by my authority, thou admonish and lovingly urge them always to live retired and dead to the world, with unbroken forgetfulness of all that passes within it; that among themselves their conversation be of heaven, and that above all they preserve intact the mutual peace and love, to which I have exhorted thee so often (Philip 3, 20). If they obey me in this I offer them my protection, and I will constitute myself their Mother, their help and defense in the same way as I am thine, and I will also promise them my continual and efficacious intercession with my most holy Son, if they do not displease me. For this purpose thou shouldst exhort them to continual love and devotion toward me, engrafting it in their hearts; in being thus faithful they will attain all that thou wishest for them, and much more, for I will obtain it for them. In order that they may occupy themselves with joy and alacrity in preparing things for the divine worship, and gladly undertake all that pertains to it, remind them of all that I did in the service of my most holy Son and of the temple. I desire thee to understand that the holy angels were full of admiration at the zeal, careful attention and neatness with which I took charge of all that belonged to the service of my Son and Lord. This loving and reverent anxiety caused me to prepare all that was necessary for his rearing up beforehand, so that I was never in want of anything necessary for clothing Him

and administering to his comfort (as some have thought); for my prudence and love would not permit any negligence or inadvertence in this regard.

Chapter VIII

THE EDICT OF CESAR AUGUSTUS IS PUBLISHED, COMMAND-
ING ALL SUBJECTS OF THE EMPIRE TO REGISTRATE; AND
WHAT SAINT JOSEPH DID WHEN HE HEARD OF IT.

448. It had been decreed by the immutable will of Providence that the Onlybegotten of the Father should be born in
the town of Bethlehem (Mich. 5, 2), and accordingly it had
been foretold by the Saints and Prophets of foregone ages
(Jerem. 10, 9) ; for the decrees of the absolute will of God are
infallible, and since nothing can resist them (Esther 13, 9),
sooner would heaven and earth pass away than that they fail
of accomplishment (Matth. 24, 35). The fulfillment of this
immutable decree the Lord secured by means of an edict of
Caesar Augustus for the whole Roman empire, ordering the
registration or enumeration of all the world, as saint Luke
says (Luke 2, 1). The Roman empire at that time embraced
the greater part of what was then known of the earth and
therefore they called themselves masters of the world, ignoring all the other nations. The object of this census was to
make all the inhabitants acknowledge themselves as vassals of
the emperor, and to pay a certain tax to their temporal lord;
for this registration every one was to go to his native city in
order to be inscribed. This edict was also proclaimed in
Nazareth and came to the hearing of saint Joseph while he
was on some errand. He returned to his house in sorrowful

consternation and informed his heavenly Spouse of the news which had spread about concerning the edict. The most prudent Virgin answered: "Let not this edict of our temporal ruler cause thee any concern, my master and spouse, for all that happens to us is ordained by the Lord and King of heaven and earth; and in all events his Providence will assist and direct us (Eccli, 22, 28). Let us resign ourselves into his hands and we shall not be disappointed."

449. Most holy Mary was capable of being entrusted with all the mysteries of her most holy Son and She knew of the prophecies and their fulfillment; hence, also, that the Onlybegotten of the Father and her own was to be born in Bethlehem, a Stranger and an Unknown. But She said nothing of this to saint Joseph; for without being commissioned by the Lord She would reveal none of his secrets. All that She was not commanded to reveal She concealed with admirable prudence, notwithstanding her desire of consoling her most faithful and holy spouse. She wished to entrust Herself to his direction and arrangement without acting the part of those who are wise in their own conceit, as Wisdom warns us (Prov, 3, 7). They therefore conferred with each other about the course to be pursued; for already the pregnancy of the heavenly Lady was far advanced and her parturition was approaching. Saint Joseph said: "Queen of heaven and earth and my Mistress, if Thou hast no order to the contrary from the Almighty, it seems to me necessary that I go alone. Yet, although this order refers only to the heads of families, I dare not leave Thee without assistance, nor could I live without Thee, nor would I have a moment's peace away from Thee; for my heart could not come to any rest without seeing Thee. Thy heavenly delivery is too imminent to ask Thee to go with me to Bethlehem, whither this edict calls us; and I fear to place Thee in any risk, as well on account of thy condition as also on account of my poverty. If thy delivery should

happen on the way, amid inconveniences, which I could not alleviate, I would be heartbroken. These are the anxious thoughts which trouble me. I pray Thee, Lady, present them before the Most High and beseech Him to grant me my desire of not being separated from Thee."

450. His humble Spouse obeyed saint Joseph and although She was not ignorant of the divine will, yet She would not omit this act of obedience as a most submissive Spouse. She presented to the Lord the fervent wishes of saint Joseph and received the following answer:

"My dearest Dove, yield to the wishes of my servant Joseph in what he proposes. Accompany him on the journey. I shall be with Thee and I shall assist Thee with paternal love in the tribulations which Thou shalt suffer for my sake; although they shall be very great, my powerful arms will make Thee come forth glorious from all of them. Thy footsteps will be beautiful in my sight (Cant. 7, 1), do not fear, since this is my will." Then the Lord gave to the holy guardian angels, in the presence of the heavenly Mary, a new and special command and precept, that they serve Her during this journey with particular care and solicitude, as befitted the magnificent mysteries that should be transacted. Beside the thousand angels which served ordinarily as her guard, the Lord commanded another nine thousand to attend on their Queen and Mistress, and serve as a guard of honor ten thousand strong from the first day of her journey. This they did as most faithful servants of the Lord, as I shall say later on (Nos. 456, 489, 616, 622, 631, 634). The great Queen was renewed and strengthened with new enlightenment for the troubles and tribulations which would be occasioned by the persecution of Herod and other happenings at the birth of the infant God (Matth. 2, 16). Her invincible heart being thus prepared, She offered Herself to the Lord without any disquietude and gave thanks for all that He should choose to do and arrange in regard to these future events.

451. She returned from this heavenly interview to saint Joseph, and announced to him the will of the Most High, that She accede to his wishes and accompany him on his journey to Bethlehem. Joseph was filled with new consolation and delight; acknowledging the great favor conferred upon him by the right hand of the Most High, he gave thanks with fervent acts of gratitude and humility; and, addressing the heavenly Spouse, he answered: "My Lady, source of my happiness and good fortune, the only cause of grief in this journey will now be the hardships which Thou must undergo because I have no riches to procure Thee the conveniences which I would like to furnish for thy pilgrimage. But we shall find relations, acquaintances and friends of our family in Bethlehem; I hope they will receive us hospitably, and there thou canst rest from the exertions of the journey, if the Lord will dispose as I thy servant would wish." Thus the holy spouse saint Joseph lovingly planned; but the Lord had already pre-arranged all things in a way unknown to him; and therefore he experienced so much the greater bitterness of disappointment when all his loving expectations failed, as we shall see. Most holy Mary said nothing to saint Joseph of what She knew the Lord had decreed concerning the heavenly Birth, although She well knew that it would be different from what he expected She rather encouraged him, saying:

"My spouse and my master, I accompany thee with much pleasure, and we will make this journey as poor people in the name of the Lord: for the Most High will not despise poverty, which He came to seek with so much love. Relying on his protection and assistance in our necessities and labors, we will proceed with confidence. Do thou, my master, place to his account all thy difficulties."

452. They at the same time resolved upon the day of their departure, and Joseph diligently searched in the town of Nazareth for some beast of burden to bear the Mistress of the world. He could not easily find one because so many people were going to different towns in order to fulfill the requirements of the edict of the emperor. But after much anxious inquiry saint Joseph found an unpretentious little beast which, if we can call such creatures fortunate, was the most fortunate of all the irrational animals; since it was privileged not only to bear the Queen of all creation and the blessed fruit of her womb, the King of kings and the Lord of lords, but afterwards to be present at his Birth (Isaias 1, 3) ; and since it gave to its Creator the homage denied to Him by men, as I shall relate (No. 485). They provided the articles for the journey, which would last five days. The outfit of the heavenly travelers was the same as that which they had provided for their previous journey to the house of Zacharias on their visit to Elisabeth. They carried with them bread, fruit and some fishes, which ordinarily composed their nourishment. As the most prudent Virgin was enlightened regarding their protracted absence, She made use of prudent concealment in taking along the linens and clothes necessary for her heavenly delivery, for She wished to dispose all things according to the exalted intents of the Lord and in preparation for the events which She expected. Their house they left in charge of some neighbor until they should return.

453. The day and hour for their departure for Bethlehem arrived and, because of the reverence with which the most faithful and fortunate Joseph had begun to treat his sovereign Spouse, he diligently and anxiously sought to do all in his power to please Her; he besought Her with great affection to make known to him all her wishes and to call his attention to all that he might forget in regard to her pleasure, convenience and comfort, or that might please the Lord whom She bore

in her womb. The humble Queen thanked him for his loving attention, and referring it to all the glory and service of her most holy Son, She consoled and animated him to meet courageously the hardships of the journey, assuring him anew that the Almighty was pleased with his affectionate solicitude. She also informed him of the will of his Majesty that they meet with patience and joy of heart the hardships of poverty on their way. In order to begin her journey the Empress of heaven knelt at the feet of saint Joseph and asked him for his blessing. Although the man of God shrunk from such a request and strenuously objected on account of the dignity of his Spouse, She nevertheless remained victorious in her humility and prevailed upon him to give Her his benediction. Saint Joseph complied with great timidity and reverence, and immediately cast himself at her feet in a flood of tears, asking Her to present him anew to her most holy Son, and obtain for him divine pardon and grace. Thus prepared they started from Nazareth for Bethlehem in midwinter, which made the journey more painful and difficult. But the Mother of God, who bore eternal Life within Her, attended solely to the divine activities and colloquies of the Lord, observing Him in the virginal chamber of her womb, imitating Him in his works, and giving Him more delight and honor than all the rest of creatures taken together.

Words of the Queen

THE VIRGIN MARY SPEAKS TO SISTER MARY OF AGREDA

454. My daughter, in all thy discourse on my life, and in each of the chapters and mysteries so far rehearsed, thou wilt find the admirable providence of the Most High and his fatherly love toward me, his humble servant. Although human capacity cannot fully penetrate and estimate the admirable works of such high wisdom, yet it must venerate it

with all its powers, and must seek to participate in the favors which the Lord showed me, by striving to imitate me. For mortals must not think that only for my sake and in me God wished to show Himself as holy, powerful and infinitely good. It is certain that if any or all of the souls would entrust themselves to the direction and government of this Lord they would soon experience that same fidelity, punctuality and most sweet efficacy with which his Majesty arranged all things that touched upon his honor and service in my life. They would likewise taste those delightful and divine emotions which I felt in relying upon his most holy will; nor would they fail to receive the abundance of his gifts, which are enclosed as in an infinite ocean within his Divinity. And just as the waters of the ocean rush forth wherever they find a suitable opening, so the graces and blessings of the Lord overflow upon rational creatures, when they are well-disposed and do not hinder their course. This truth is hidden to mortals because they do not stop to ponder and consider the works of the Almighty.

455. I desire thee to study this truth, to write it within thy heart, and to learn from my own actions the secret workings of thy own interior so that thou understand what goes on within thee; also that thou practice ready obedience and subjection to others, always preferring the good counsels of others to thy own insight and judgment. Thou must carry this to such a point that, in order to obey thy superiors and thy spiritual directors, thou take no notice of what thou foreseest will happen contrary to their expectations; just as I, when I knew that what my holy spouse Joseph expected would not happen on our journey to Bethlehem. And even when some equal or inferior command thee such things, be silent and hide thy better foreknowledge; perform all that is no sin or imperfection. Listen to all with attention and silence so that thou mayest learn; in speaking be very slow

and reserved, for in this consist prudent and careful inter-course. Always bear in mind that thou ask the blessing of the Lord for all that thou wishest to undertake, in order that thou mayest not wander from what is pleasing to Him. Whenever thou hast an opportunity, ask also the permission and blessing of thy spiritual father and director, so that thou mayest not fall short of the greatest merits and perfections in thy works, and in order that thou mayest also give me the pleasure, which I desire of thee.

Chapter IX

THE JOURNEY OF MOST HOLY MARY FROM NAZARETH TO BETHLEHEM IN THE COMPANY OF THE HOLY SPOUSE JOSEPH AND OF THE HOLY GUARDIAN ANGELS.

456. The most pure Mary and the glorious saint Joseph departed from Nazareth for Bethlehem alone, poor and humble in the eyes of the world. None of the mortals thought more of them than what was warranted by their poverty and humility. But O the wonderful sacraments of the Most High, hidden to the proud, and unpenetrated by the wisdom of the flesh! They did not walk alone, poor or despised, but prosperous, rich and in magnificence. They were most worthy of the immense love of the eternal Father and most estimable in his eyes. They carried with them the Treasure of heaven, the Deity itself. The whole court of the celestial ministers venerated them. All the inanimate beings recognized the living and true Ark of the Testament (Josue 3, 16) more readily than the waters of the Jordan recognized its type and shadow, when they courteously laid open and free the path for its passage and for those that followed it. They were accompanied by the ten thousand angels, which as mentioned (No. 450), were appointed by God himself as the servants of her Majesty during that whole journey. These heavenly squadrons marched along as their retinue in human forms visible to the heavenly Lady, more refulgent than so

many suns. She herself walked in their midst better guarded and defended than the bed of Solomon, surrounded by the sixty valiant ones of Israel, girded with their swords (Cant. 3, 7). Besides these ten thousand angels there were many others, who descended from heaven as messengers of the eternal Father to his Onlybegotten made man in his most holy Mother, and who ascended from earth as their ambassadors with messages and treaties from them to the heavenly Father.

457. In the midst of this royal retinue, hidden from the gaze of men, most holy Mary and Joseph proceeded on their way secure that their feet would not be bruised by the stone of tribulation (Ps. 40, 12), since the Lord had commanded his angels to be their defense and watchfulness. This command the most faithful ministers, as vassals of their great Queen, fulfilled with wonder and delight, seeing centered in a mere Creature such great sacraments, such perfections, and immense treasures of the Divinity, and seeing in Her all this distinction united to dignity and grace far exceeding their own angelic capacity. They composed new songs in honor of the Lord, whom they saw reclining as the highest King of glory, on his throne of gold (Cant. 3, 9) ; and in honor of the heavenly Mother, who was like his living and incorruptible chariot, or like the fertile ear of corn of the promised land, enclosing the living grain (Lev. 23, 10); or like the rich merchant ship, which brings the grain to the house of bread, in order that dying in the earth it might be multiplied for heaven (John 12, 24). Their journey lasted five days, for on account of the pregnancy of his Spouse, saint Joseph shortened each day's journey. The sovereign Queen experienced no darkness of night on the way; for a few times, when their travel extended beyond nightfall the holy angels spread about such effulgence as not all the lights of heaven in their noontide splendor would have thrown forth in the clearest heavens. This light and vision of the angels also saint Joseph

enjoyed at those times; then all of them together would form celestial choirs, in which they and the two holy travelers alternated in singing wonderful hymns and canticles of praise, converting the fields into new heavens. During this whole journey the Queen was rejoiced by the sight of her resplendent ministers and vassals and by the sweet interior conversation held with them.

458. With these wonderful favors and delights, however, the Lord joined some hardships and inconveniences, which the divine Mother encountered on the way. For the concourse of people in the taverns, occasioned by the imperial edict, was very disagreeable and annoying to the modest and retiring Virgin-Mother and her spouse. On account of their poverty and timid retirement they were treated with less hospitality and consideration than others, especially the well-to-do; for the world judges and usually confers its favors according to outward appearance and according to personal influence. Our holy pilgrims were obliged repeatedly to listen to sharp reprimands in the taverns, at which they arrived tired out by their journey, and in some of them they were refused admittance as worthless and despicable people. Several times they assigned to the Mistress of heaven and earth some corner of the hallway; while at others She did not fare even so well, being obliged to retire with her husband to places still more humble and unbecoming in the estimation of the world. But in whatever places She tarried, how contemptible so ever it might be considered, the courtiers of heaven established their court around their supreme King and sovereign Queen. Immediately they surrounded and enclosed them like an impenetrable wall, securing the bridal chamber of Solomon against the terrors of the night. Her most faithful spouse Joseph, seeing the Mistress of heaven so well guarded by the angelic hosts, betook himself to rest and sleep; for to this She urged him on account of the hardships

of travel. She, however, continued her celestial colloquies with the ten thousand angels of her retinue.

459. Solomon, in the Canticles, describes in diverse metaphors and similitudes many great mysteries of the Queen of heaven, but in the third chapter he refers more particularly to what happened to the heavenly Mother in her pregnancy and during this journey. During this time was fulfilled to the letter all that is said of the couch of Solomon (Cant. 3, 7), of his chariot and of his golden bed, of the guard, which was stationed around it enjoying the divine vision; also all the other sayings, which are contained in those prophecies. What I have pointed out will suffice to make them understood, and they should excite our admiration of the wonderful sacraments of God's activity for the good of man. Who is there among mortals whose heart is not softened? Or who is so proud as not to be abashed? Or so careless as not to be filled with wonder at such miraculous extremes? The infinite and true God hidden and concealed in the virginal womb of a tender Maiden, full of grace and beauty, innocent, pure, sweet, pleasing and amiable in the eyes of God and of men, surpassing all that the Lord God has ever or shall ever create! To see this great Lady, bearing the treasure of the Divinity, despised, persecuted, neglected, and cast out by the blind ignorance and pride of the world! And on the other hand, while She is thus pushed aside into the last places, to see Her loved and esteemed by the triune God, regaled by his caresses, served by his angels, revered, defended and assisted with the greatest anxiety and watchfulness! O children of men, slow and hard of hearts! (Ps. 4, 3). How deceitful are your ways and how erroneous is your judgment in esteeming the rich and despising the poor (James 2, 2), exalting the proud and humiliating the lowly, applauding the braggarts and casting out the just! Blind is your choice and full of error your judgment, and you will find yourselves frustrated in all

your desires. Ambitiously you seek riches and treasures, and you find yourself in poverty beating the air; if you had received the true ark of God, you would have been blessed by the hand of the Almighty, like Obededom (II Kings, 6, 11) ; but because you have treated it unworthily, many of you have experienced the punishment of Oza.

460. The heavenly Lady observed and knew the secrets of the different souls of those She met, penetrating into the very thoughts and conditions of each, whether of grace or of guilt in their different degrees. Concerning many souls She also knew whether they were predestined or reprobate, whether they would persevere, fall, or again rise up. All this variety of insight moved Her to the exercise of heroic virtues as well in regard to the ones as to the others. For many of them She obtained the grace of perseverance, for others efficacious help to rise from their sin to grace; for others again She prayed to the Lord with affectionate tears, feeling intensest sorrow for the reprobate, though She did not pray as efficaciously for them. Many times, worn out by these sorrows, much more than by the hardships of travel, the strength of her body gave way; on such occasions the holy angels, full of refulgent light and beauty, bore Her up in their arms, in order that She might rest and recuperate. The sick, afflicted and indigent whom She met on the way, She consoled and assisted by asking her most holy Son to come to their aid in their necessities and adversities. She kept Herself silently aloof from the multitude, preoccupied with the Fruit of her divine pregnancy, which was already evident to all. Such was the return which the Mother of mercy made for the inhospitality of mortals.

461. For the greater reproach of human ingratitude, it happened also that once during these wintry days they reached a stopping-place in the midst of a cold rain and snow storm (for the Lord did not spare them this inconvenience),

and they were obliged to take shelter in the stables of the animals, because the owners would not furnish better accommodation. The irrational beasts showed them the courtesy and kindness which was refused by their human fellow-beings; for they retreated in reverence at the entrance of their Maker and of his Mother, who carried Him in her virginal womb. It is true the Queen of creation could command the winds, the frost and the snow not to inconvenience Her; but She would not give such a command in order not to deprive Herself of suffering in imitation of her most holy Son, even before He came forth into the world. Therefore the inclemencies of the weather affected Her to a certain extent. The faithful saint Joseph, however, did his utmost to shield Her; and still more did the holy angels seek to protect Her, especially the holy prince Michael, who remained at the right side of his Queen without leaving Her even for a moment; several times, when She became tired, He led Her by the arm along the way. Whenever the Lord permitted, he also shielded Her against the weather and performed many other services for the heavenly Queen and the blessed Fruit of her womb, Jesus.

462. Thus variously and wonderfully assisted, our travelers arrived at the town of Bethlehem at four o'clock of the fifth day, a Saturday. As it was at the time of the winter solstice, the sun was already sinking and the night was falling. They entered the town, and wandered through many streets in search of a lodging-house or inn for staying over night. They knocked at the doors of their acquaintances and nearer family relations; but they were admitted nowhere and in many places they met with harsh words and insults. The most modest Queen followed her spouse through the crowds of people, while he went from house to house and from door to door. Although She knew that the hearts and the houses of men were to be closed to them, and although to expose her

state at her age to the public gaze was more painful to her modesty than their failure to procure a night lodging, She nevertheless wished to obey saint Joseph and suffer this indignity and unmerited shame. While wandering through the streets they passed the office of the public registry and they inscribed their names and paid the fiscal tribute in order to comply with the edict and not be obliged to return. They continued their search, betaking themselves to other houses. But having already applied at more than fifty different places, they found themselves rejected and sent away from them all. The heavenly spirits were filled with astonishment at these exalted mysteries of the Most High, which manifested the patience and meekness of his Virgin Mother and the unfeeling hardness of men. At the same time they blessed the Almighty in his works and hidden sacraments, since from that day on He began to exalt and honor poverty and humility among men.

463. It was nine o'clock at night when the most faithful Joseph, full of bitter and heartrending sorrow, returned to his most prudent Spouse and said: "My sweetest Lady, my heart is broken with sorrow at the thought of not only not being able to shelter Thee as Thou deservest and as I desire, but in not being able to offer Thee even any kind of protection from the weather, or a place of rest, a thing rarely or never denied to the most poor and despised in the world. No doubt heaven, in thus allowing the hearts of men to be so unmoved as to refuse us a night-lodging, conceals some mystery. I now remember, Lady, that outside the city walls there is a cave, which serves as a shelter for shepherds and their flocks. Let us seek it out; perhaps it is unoccupied, and we may there expect some assistance from heaven, since we receive none from men on earth." The most prudent Virgin answered: "My spouse and my master, let not thy kindest heart be afflicted because the ardent wishes which the love of

thy Lord excites in thee cannot be fulfilled. Since I bear Him in my womb, let us, I beseech thee, give thanks for having disposed events in this way. The place of which thou speakest shall be most satisfactory to me. Let thy tears of sorrow be turned into tears of joy, and let us lovingly embrace poverty, which is the inestimable and precious treasure of my most holy Son. He came from heaven in order to seek it, let us then afford Him an occasion to practice it in the joy of our souls; certainly I cannot be better delighted than to see thee procure it for me. Let us go gladly wherever the Lord shall guide us." The holy angels accompanied the heavenly pair, brilliantly lighting up the way, and when they arrived at the city gate they saw that the cave was forsaken and unoccupied. Full of heavenly consolation, they thanked the Lord for this favor, and then happened what I shall relate in the following chapter.

Words of the Queen

THE VIRGIN MARY SPEAKS TO SISTER MARY OF AGREDA

464. My dearest daughter, if thou art of a meek and docile heart, these mysteries which thou hast written about and hast understood, will stir within thee sweet sentiments of love and affection toward the Author of such great wonders. I wish that, bearing them in mind, thou from this day on embrace with new and great esteem the contempt and neglect of the world. And tell me, dearest, if, in exchange for this forgetfulness and scorn of the world, God look upon thee with eyes of sweetest love, why shouldst thou not buy so cheaply what is worth an infinite price? What can the world give thee, even when it esteems thee and exalts thee most? And what dost thou lose, if thou despise it? Is its favor not all vanity and deceit (Ps. 4, 3)? Is it not all a fleeting and momentary shadow, which eludes the grasp of those that haste after it?

Hence, if thou hadst all worldly advantage in thy possession, what great feat would it be to despise it as of no value? Consider how little thou dost in rejecting all of it for the love of God, for mine and that of the holy angels. And if the world does not neglect thee as much as thou shouldst desire, do thou on thy own behalf despise it, in order to remain free and unhampered to enjoy to the full extent the highest Good with the plenitude of his most delightful love and intercourse.

465. My most holy Son is such a faithful Lover of souls that He hast set me as the teacher and living example of the love of humility and true contempt of worldly vanity and pride. He ordained also for his own glory as well as for my sake that I, his Servant and Mother, should be left without shelter and be turned away by mortals, in order that afterwards his beloved souls might be so much the more readily induced to offer Him a welcome, thus obliging Him, by an artifice of love, to come and remain with them. He also sought destitution and poverty, not because He had any need of them for bringing the practice of virtues to the highest perfection, but in order to teach mortals the shortest and surest way for reaching the heights of divine love and union with God.

466. Thou knowest well, my dearest, that thou hast been incessantly instructed and exhorted by divine enlightenment to forget the terrestrial and visible and to gird thyself with fortitude (Prov, 31, 17), to raise thyself to the imitation of me, copying in thyself, according to thy capacity, the works and virtues manifested to thee in my life. This is the very first purpose of the knowledge which thou receivest in writing this history; for thou hast in me a perfect model, and by it thou canst arrange the converse and conduct of thy life in the same manner as I arranged mine in imitation of my sweetest Son. The dread with which this command to imitate me has

inspired thee as a being above thy strength, thou must moderate and thou must encourage thyself by the words of my most holy Son in the Gospel of saint Matthew: "Be ye perfect as my heavenly Father is perfect" (Matth. 5, 48). This command of the Most High imposed upon his holy Church is not impossible of fulfillment, and, if his faithful children on their part dispose themselves properly, He will deny to none of them the grace of attaining this resemblance to the heavenly Father. All this my most holy Son has merited for them. But the degrading forgetfulness and neglect of men hinder them from maturing within themselves the fruits of his Redemption.

467. Of thee particularly I expect this perfection, and I invite thee to it by the sweet law of love which accompanies my instruction. Ponder and scrutinize, by the divine light, the obligation under which I place thee, and labor to correspond with it like a faithful and anxious child. Let no difficulty or hardship disturb thee, nor deter thee from any virtuous exercise, no matter how hard it may be. Nor be content with striving after the love of God and salvation of thyself alone; if thou wouldst be perfect in imitating me and fulfilling all that the Gospel teaches, thou must work for the salvation of other souls and the exaltation of the holy name of my Son, making thyself an instrument in his powerful hands for the accomplishment of mighty works to advance his pleasure and glory.

Chapter X

CHRIST OUR SAVIOR IS BORN OF THE VIRGIN MARY IN
BETHLEHEM, JUDA.

468. The palace which the supreme King of kings and the
Lord of lords had chosen for entertaining his eternal and
incarnate Son in this world was a most poor and insignificant
hut or cave, to which most holy Mary and Joseph betook
themselves after they had been denied all hospitality and the
most ordinary kindness by their fellow-men, as I have described in the foregoing chapter. This place was held in such
contempt that though the town of Bethlehem was full of
strangers in want of night shelter, none would demean or
degrade himself so far as to make use of it for a lodging; for
there was none who deemed it suitable or desirable for such a
purpose, except the Teachers of humility and poverty, Christ
our Savior and his purest Mother. On this account the
wisdom of the eternal Father had reserved it for Them,
consecrating it in all its bareness, loneliness and poverty as
the first temple of light (Malachy 4, 2, Ps. Ill, 4) and as the
house of the true Sun of justice, which was to arise for the
upright of heart from the resplendent Aurora Mary, turning
the night of sin into the daylight of grace.

469. Most holy Mary and saint Joseph entered the lodging thus provided for them and by the effulgence of the ten

thousand angels of their guard they could easily ascertain its poverty and loneliness, which they esteemed as favors and welcomed with tears of consolation and joy. Without delay the two holy travelers fell on their knees and praised the Lord, giving Him thanks for his benefit, which they knew had been provided by his wisdom for his own hidden designs. Of this mystery the heavenly Princess Mary had a better insight; for as soon as She sanctified the interior of the cave by her sacred footsteps She felt a fullness of joy which entirely elevated and vivified Her. She besought the Lord to bless with a liberal hand all the inhabitants of the neighboring city, because by rejecting Her they had given occasion to the vast favors, which She awaited in this neglected cavern. It was formed entirely of the bare and coarse rocks, without any natural beauty or artificial adornment; a place intended merely for the shelter of animals; yet the eternal Father had selected it for the shelter and dwelling-place of his own Son.

470. The angelic spirits, who like a celestial militia guarded their Queen and Mistress, formed themselves into cohorts in the manner of court guards in a royal palace. They showed themselves in their visible forms also to saint Joseph; for on this occasion it was befitting that he should enjoy such a favor, on the one hand in order to assuage his sorrow by allowing him to behold this poor lodging thus beautified and adorned by their celestial presence, and on the other, in order to enliven and encourage him for the events which the Lord intended to bring about during that night, and in this forsaken place. The great Queen and Empress, who was already informed of the mystery to be transacted here, set about cleaning with her own hands the cave, which was so soon to serve as a royal throne and sacred mercy seat; for neither did She want to miss this occasion for exercising her humility, nor would She deprive her Onlybegotten Son of the worship

and reverence implied by this preparation and cleansing of his temple.

471. Saint Joseph, mindful of the majesty of his heavenly Spouse (which, it seemed to him, She was forgetting in her ardent longing for humiliation), besought Her not to deprive Him of this work, which he considered as his alone; and he hastened to set about cleaning the floor and the corners of the cave, although the humble Queen continued to assist him therein. As the holy angels were then present in visible forms, they were (according to our mode of speaking) abashed at such eagerness for humiliation, and they speedily emulated with each other to join in this work; or rather, in order to say it more succinctly, in the shortest time possible they had cleansed and set in order that cave, filling it with holy fragrance. Saint Joseph started a fire with the material which he had brought for that purpose. As it was very cold, they sat at the fire in order to get warm. They partook of the food which they had brought, and they ate this, their frugal supper, with incomparable joy of their souls. The Queen of heaven was so absorbed and taken up with the thought of the impending mystery of her divine delivery, that She would not have partaken of food if She had not been urged thereto by obedience to her spouse.

472. After their supper they gave thanks to the Lord as was their custom. Having spent a short time in this prayer and conferring about the mysteries of the incarnate Word, the most prudent Virgin felt the approach of the most blessed Birth. She requested her spouse saint Joseph to betake himself to rest and sleep as the night was already far advanced. The man of God yielded to the request of his Spouse and urged Her to do the same; and for this purpose he arranged and prepared a sort of couch with the articles of wear in their possession, making use of a crib or manger, that had been left by the shepherds for their animals. Leaving

most holy Mary in the portion of the cave thus furnished, saint Joseph retired to a corner of the entrance, where he began to pray. He was immediately visited by the divine Spirit and felt a most sweet and extraordinary influence, by which he was wrapt and elevated into an ecstasy. In it was shown him all that passed during that night in this blessed cave; for he did not return to consciousness until his heavenly Spouse called him. Such was the sleep which saint Joseph enjoyed in that night, more exalted and blessed than that of Adam in paradise (Gen. 21, 2).

473. The Queen of all creatures was called from her resting-place by a loud voice of the Most High, which strongly and sweetly raised Her above all created things and caused Her to feel new effects of divine power; for this was one of the most singular and admirable ecstasies of her most holy life. Immediately also She was filled with new enlightenment and divine influences, such as I have described in other places, until She reached the clear vision of the Divinity. The veil fell and She saw intuitively the Godhead itself in such glory and plenitude of insight, as all the capacity of men and angels could not describe or fully understand. All the knowledge of the Divinity and humanity of her most holy Son, which She had ever received in former visions was renewed and, moreover, other secrets of the inexhaustible archives of the bosom of God were revealed to Her. I have not ideas or words sufficient and adequate for expressing what I have been allowed to see of these sacraments by the divine light; and their abundance and multiplicity convince me of the poverty and want of proper expression in created language.

474. The Most High announced to his Virgin Mother, that the time of his coming into the world had arrived and what would be the manner in which this was now to be fulfilled and executed. The most prudent Lady perceived in

this vision the purpose and exalted scope of these wonderful mysteries and sacraments, as well in so far as related to the Lord himself as also in so far as they concerned creatures, for whose benefit they had been primarily decreed. She prostrated Herself before the throne of his Divinity and gave Him glory, magnificence, thanks and praise for Herself and for all creatures, such as was befitting the ineffable mercy and condescension of his divine love. At the same time She asked of the divine Majesty new light and grace in order to be able worthily to undertake the service and worship and the rearing up of the Word made flesh, whom She was to bear in Her arms and nourish with her virginal milk. This petition the heavenly Mother brought forward with the profoundest humility, as one who understood the greatness of this new sacrament. She held Herself unworthy of the office of rearing up and conversing as a Mother with a God incarnate of which even the highest seraphim are incapable. Prudently and humbly did the Mother of wisdom ponder and weigh this matter. And because She humbled Herself to the dust and acknowledged her nothingness in the presence of the Almighty, therefore his Majesty raised Her up and confirmed anew upon Her the title of Mother of God. He commanded Her to exercise this office and ministry of a legitimate and true Mother of Himself; that She should treat Him as the Son of the eternal Father and at the same time the Son of her womb. All this could be easily entrusted to such a Mother, in whom was contained an excellence that words cannot express.

475. The most holy Mary remained in this ecstasy and beatific vision for over an hour immediately preceding her divine delivery. At the moment when She issued from it and regained the use of her senses She felt and saw that the body of the infant God began to move in her virginal womb; how, releasing and freeing Himself from the place which in the

course of nature He had occupied for nine months, He now prepared to issue forth from that sacred bridal chamber. This movement not only did not cause any pain or hardship, as happens with the other daughters of Adam and Eve in their childbirths; but filled Her with incomparable joy and delight, causing in her soul and in her virginal body such exalted and divine effects that they exceed all thoughts of men. Her body became so spiritualized with the beauty of heaven that She seemed no more a human and earthly creature. Her countenance emitted rays of light, like a sun incarnadined, and shone in indescribable earnestness and majesty, all inflamed with fervent love. She was kneeling in the manger, her eyes raised to heaven, her hands joined and folded at her breast, her soul wrapped in the Divinity and She herself was entirely deified. In this position, and at the end of the heavenly rapture, the most exalted Lady gave to the world the Onlybegotten of the Father and her own, our Savior Jesus, true God and man, at the hour of midnight, on a Sunday, in the year of the creation of the world five thousand one hundred and ninety-nine (5199), which is the date given in the Roman Church, and which date has been manifested to me as the true and certain one.

476. There are other wonderful circumstances and particulars, which all the faithful assume to have miraculously accompanied this most divine Birth; but as the only witnesses were the Queen of heaven and her courtiers, they cannot all be certified, except only those which the Lord himself manifests in his holy Church to all or to some particular souls in diverse ways. As I think there is some divergence of opinion in this matter, which is most sublime and venerable, as soon as I had manifested to my superiors and directors what had been made known to me, they commanded me under obedience to consult anew the divine oracle and ask the Empress of heaven, my Mother and Teacher, and the holy angels that

attend on me, for information on some particulars necessary
for a clearer statement of the most sacred parturition of
Mary, the Mother of Jesus, our Redeemer. In order to comply with this command I returned for a better understanding
of these same happenings and it was then expounded to me
in the following manner:

477. At the end of the beatific rapture and vision of the
Mother ever Virgin, which I have described above (No. 473),
was born the Sun of Justice, the Only begotten of the eternal
Father and of Mary most pure, beautiful, refulgent and
immaculate, leaving Her untouched in her virginal integrity
and purity and making Her more godlike and forever sacred;
for He did not divide, but penetrated the virginal chamber as
the rays of the sun penetrate the crystal shrine, lighting it up
in prismatic beauty. Before I describe the miraculous manner
in which this took place, I wish to say that the divine Child
was born pure and disengaged, without the protecting shield
called secundina, surrounded by which other children are
commonly born, and in which they are enveloped in the
wombs of their mothers. I will not detain myself in explaining the cause and origin of the error, which is contrary to this
statement. It it enough to know and suppose that in the
generation and birth of the incarnate Word the arm of the
Almighty selected and made use of all that substantially and
unavoidably belonged to natural human generation, so that
the Word could truly call Himself conceived and engendered
as a true man and born of the substance of his Mother ever
Virgin. In regard to the other circumstances, which are not
essential but accidental to generation and nativity, we must
disconnect our ideas of Christ our Lord and of the most holy
Mary not only from all that are in any way related or consequent upon any sin, original or actual; but also from many
others which are not necessary for the essential reality of the
generation or birth and which imply some impurity or

superfluity, that could in any way lessen or impair the dignity of Mary as the Queen of heaven and as true Mother of Christ our Lord. For many such imperfections of sin or nature were not necessary either for the true humanity of Christ, or for his office of Redeemer or Teacher; and whatever was not necessary for these three ends, and whatever by its absence would redound to the greater dignity of Christ and his Mother, must be denied of Both. Nor must we be niggardly in presuming wonderful intervention of the Author of nature and grace in favor of Her who was his worthy Mother, prepared, adorned and made increasingly beautiful for this purpose: for the divine right hand enriched Her at all times with gifts and graces and reached the utmost limits of his Omnipotence possible in regard to a mere creature.

478. In accordance with this truth her true motherhood was not impaired by her remaining a Virgin in his conception and birth through operation of the Holy Ghost. Although She could have lost her virginity in a natural manner without incurring any fault, yet in that case the Mother of God would also be without this singular prerogative of virginity. Therefore we must say, in order that She might not be without it, the divine power of her most holy Son preserved it for Her. Likewise the divine Child could have been born with this covering or cuticle in which others are born; yet this was not necessary in order to be born a natural Son of the blessed Mother; hence He could choose not to take it forth with Him from the virginal and maternal womb, just as He chose not to pay to nature other penal tributes of impurity, which other human beings do pay at their coming into the light. It was not just that the incarnate Word should be subject to all the laws of the sons of Adam; but it was consequent upon his miraculous Birth that He be exempt and free from all that could be caused by the corruption or uncleanness of matter. Thus also this covering, or secundina, was not

to fall a prey to corruption outside of the virginal womb, because it had been so closely connected and attached to his most holy body and because it was composed of the blood and substance of his Mother; in like manner it was not advisable to keep and preserve it outside of Her, nor was it becoming to give it the same privileges and importance as to his divine body in coming forth from the body of his most holy Mother, as I will yet explain. The wonder which would have to be wrought to dispose of that sacred covering outside of the womb could be wrought much more appropriately within.

479. The infant God therefore was brought forth from the virginal chamber unencumbered by any corporeal or material substance foreign to Himself. But He came forth glorious and transfigured for the divine and infinite wisdom decreed and ordained that the glory of his most holy soul should in his Birth overflow and communicate itself to his body, participating in the gifts of glory in the same way as happened afterwards in his Transfiguration on mount Tabor in the presence of the Apostles (Matth. 17, 2). This miracle was not necessary in order to penetrate the virginal enclosure and to leave unimpaired the virginal integrity; for without this Transfiguration God could have brought this about by other miracles. Thus say the holy doctors, who see no other miracle in this Birth than that the Child was born without impairing the virginity of the Mother. It was the will of God that the most blessed Virgin should look upon the body of her Son, the Godman, for this first time in a glorified state for two reasons. The one was in order that by this divine vision the most prudent Mother should conceive the highest reverence for the Majesty of Him whom She was to treat as her Son, the true God-man. Although She was already informed of his two-fold nature, the Lord nevertheless ordained that by ocular demonstration She be filled with new

graces, corresponding to the greatness of her most holy Son, which was thus manifested to Her in a visible manner. The second reason was to reward by this wonder the fidelity and holiness of the divine Mother; for her most pure and chaste eyes, that had turned away from all earthly things for love of her most holy Son, were to see Him at his very Birth in this glory and thus be rejoiced and rewarded for her loyalty and beautiful love.

480. The sacred evangelist Luke tells us that the Mother Virgin, having brought forth her firstbegotten Son, wrapped Him in swathing clothes and placed Him in a manger. He does not say that She received Him in her arms from her virginal womb; for this did not pertain to the purpose of his narrative. But the two sovereign princes, saint Michael and saint Gabriel, were the assistants of the Virgin on this occasion. They stood by at proper distance in human corporeal forms at the moment when the incarnate Word, penetrating the virginal chamber by divine power, issued forth to the light, and they received Him in their hands with ineffable reverence. In the same manner as a priest exhibits the sacred host to the people for adoration, so these two celestial ministers presented to the divine Mother her glorious and refulgent Son. All this happened in a short space of time. In the same moment in which the holy angels thus presented the divine Child to his Mother, both Son and Mother looked upon each other, and in this look, She wounded with love the sweet Infant and was at the same time exalted and transformed in Him. From the arms of the holy princes the Prince of all the heavens spoke to his holy Mother: "Mother, become like unto Me, since on this day, for the human existence, which thou hast today given Me, I will give thee another more exalted existence in grace, assimilating thy existence as a mere creature to the likeness of Me, who am God and Man." The most prudent Mother answered: "Trahe me post

Te, curremus in odorem unguentorum tuorum" (Cant. 1, 3). Raise me, elevate me, Lord, and I will run after Thee in the odor of thy ointments. In the same way many of the hidden mysteries of the Canticles were fulfilled; and other sayings which passed between the infant God and the Virgin Mother had been recorded in that book of songs, as for instance: "My Beloved to me, and I to Him, and his desire is toward me" (Cant. 2, 16). "Behold thou art beautiful, my friend, and thy eyes are dove's eyes. Behold, my beloved, for thou art beautiful"; and many other sacramental words which to mention would unduly prolong this chapter.

481. The words, which most holy Mary heard from the mouth of her most holy Son, served to make Her understand at the same time the interior acts of his holiest soul united with the Divinity; in order that by imitating them She might become like unto Him. This was one of the greatest blessings, which the most faithful and fortunate Mother received at the hands of her Son, the true God and man, not only because it was continued from that day on through all her life, but because it furnished Her the means of copying his own divine life as faithfully as was possible to a mere creature. At the same time the heavenly Lady perceived and felt the presence of the most holy Trinity, and She heard the voice of the eternal Father saying: "This is my beloved Son, in whom I am greatly pleased and delighted" (Matth. 17, 5). The most prudent Mother made entirely godlike in the overflow of so many sacraments, answered:

"Eternal Father and exalted God, Lord and Creator of the universe, give me anew thy permission and benediction to receive in my arms the Desired of nations (Agg. 2, 8); and teach me to fulfill as thy unworthy Mother and lowly slave, thy holy will." Immediately She heard a voice, which said: "Receive thy Onlybegotten Son, imitate Him and rear Him; and remember, that thou must sacrifice Him when I shall demand it of thee." The divine Mother answered: "Behold the creature of thy hands, adorn me with thy grace so that thy Son and my God receive me for his slave; and if Thou wilt come to my aid with thy Omnipotence, I shall be faithful in his service; and do Thou count it no presumption in thy insignificant creature, that she bear in her arms and nourish at her breast her own Lord and Creator."

482. After this interchange of words, so full of mysteries, the divine Child suspended the miracle of his transfiguration, or rather He inaugurated the other miracle, that of suspending the effects of glory in his most holy body, confining them solely to his soul; and He now assumed the appearance of one capable of suffering. In this form the most pure Mother now saw Him and, still remaining in a kneeling position and adoring Him with profound humility and reverence, She received Him in her arms from the hands of the holy angels. And when She saw Him in her arms, She spoke to Him and said: "My sweetest Love and light of my eyes and being of my soul, Thou hast arrived in good hour into this world as the Sun of justice (Malach. 4, 2), in order to disperse the darkness of sin and death! True God of the true God, save thy servants and let all flesh see Him, who shall draw upon it salvation (Is. 9, 2). Receive me thy servant as thy slave and supply my deficiency, in order that I may properly serve Thee. Make me, my Son, such as Thou desirest me to be in thy service." Then the most prudent Mother turned toward the eternal Father to offer up to Him his Onlybegotten, saying: "Exalted Creator of all the Universe, here is the altar and the sacrifice acceptable in thy eyes (Malachy 3, 4). From this hour on, O Lord, look upon the human race with mercy; and inasmuch as we have deserved thy anger, it is now time that Thou be appeased in thy Son and mine. Let thy justice now come to rest, and let thy mercy be exalted; for On this account the Word has clothed itself in the semblance of

sinful flesh (Rom. 8, 3), and became a Brother of mortals and sinners (Philip 2, 7). In this title I recognize them as brothers and I intercede for them from my inmost soul. Thou, Lord, hast made me the Mother of thy Onlybegotten without my merit, since this dignity is above all merit of a creature; but I partly owe to men the occasion of this incomparable good fortune; since it is on their account that I am the Mother of the Word made man and Redeemer of them all. I will not deny them my love, or remit my care and watchfulness for their salvation. Receive, eternal God, my wishes and petitions for that which is according to thy pleasure and good will."

483. The Mother of mercy turned also toward all mortals and addressed them, saying: "Be consoled ye afflicted and rejoice ye disconsolate, be raised up ye fallen, come to rest ye uneasy. Let the just be gladdened and the saints be rejoiced; let the heavenly spirits break out in new jubilee, let the Prophets and Patriarchs of limbo draw new hope, and let all the generations praise and magnify the Lord, who renews his wonders. Come, come ye poor; approach ye little ones, without fear, for in my arms I bear the Lion made a lamb, the Almighty, become weak, the Invincible subdued. Come to draw life, hasten to obtain salvation, approach to gain eternal rest, since I have all this for all, and it will be given to you freely and communicated to you without envy. Do not be slow and heavy of heart, ye sons of men; and Thou, O sweetest joy of my soul, give me permission to receive from Thee that kiss desired by all creatures." Therewith the most blessed Mother applied her most chaste and heavenly lips in order to receive the loving caresses of the divine Child, who on his part, as her true Son, had desired them from Her.

484. Holding Him in Her arms She thus served as the altar and the sanctuary, where the ten thousand angels adored in visible human forms their Creator incarnate. And as the most blessed Trinity assisted in an especial manner at the

birth of the Word, heaven was as it were emptied of its inhabitants, for the whole heavenly court had betaken itself to that blessed cave of Bethlehem and was adoring the Creator in his garb and habit of a pilgrim (Phil. 2, 7). And in their concert of praise the holy angels intoned the new canticle: "Gloria in excelsis Deo, et in terra pax hominibus bonae voluntatis" (Luke 2, 14). In sweetest and sonorous harmony they repeated it, transfixed in wonder at the new miracles then being fulfilled and at the unspeakable prudence, grace, humility and beauty of that tender Maiden of fifteen years, who had become the worthy Trustee and Minister of such vast and magnificent sacraments.

485. It was now time to call saint Joseph, the faithful spouse of the most discreet and attentive Lady. As I have said above (No. 472) he was wrapped in ecstasy, in which he was informed by divine revelation of all the mysteries of this sacred Birth during this night. But it was becoming that he should see, and, before all other mortals, should in his corporeal faculties and senses be present and experience, adore and reverence the Word made flesh; for he of all others had been chosen to act as the faithful warden of this great sacrament. At the desire of his heavenly Spouse he issued from his ecstasy and, on being restored to consciousness, the first sight of his eyes was the divine Child in the arms of the Virgin Mother reclining against her sacred countenance and breast. There he adored Him in profoundest humility and in tears of joy. He kissed his feet in great joy and admiration, which no doubt would have taken away and destroyed life in him, if divine power had not preserved it; and he certainly would have lost all the use of his senses, if the occasion had permitted. When saint Joseph had begun to adore the Child, the most prudent Mother asked leave of her Son to arise (for until then She had remained on her knees) and, while saint Joseph handed Her the wrappings and swaddling clothes,

which She had brought, She clothed Him with incomparable reverence, devotion and tenderness. Having thus swathed and clothed Him, his Mother, with heavenly wisdom, laid Him in the crib, as related by saint Luke (Luke 2, 7). For this purpose She had arranged some straw and hay upon a stone in order to prepare for the God-Man his first resting-place upon earth next to that which He had found in her arms. According to divine ordainment an ox from the neighboring fields ran up in great haste and, entering the cave, joined the beast of burden brought by the Queen. The blessed Mother commanded them, with what show of reverence was possible to them to acknowledge and adore their Creator. The humble animals obeyed their Mistress and prostrated themselves before the Child, warming Him with their breath and rendering Him the service refused by men. And thus the God made man was placed between two animals, wrapped in swaddling clothes and wonderfully fulfilling the prophecy, that "the ox knoweth his owner, and the ass his master's crib; but Israel hath not known me, and my people hath not understood."

Words of the Queen

THE VIRGIN MARY SPEAKS TO SISTER MARY OF AGREDA

486. My daughter, if men would keep their heart disengaged and if they would rightly and worthily consider this great sacrament of the kindness of the Most High towards men, it would be a powerful means of conducting them in the pathway of life and subjecting them to the love of their Creator and Redeemer. For as men are capable of reasoning, if they would only make use of their freedom to treat this sacrament with the reverence due to its greatness, who would be so hardened as not to be moved to tenderness at the sight of their God become man, humiliated in poverty, despised,

unknown, entering the world in a cave, lying in a manger surrounded by brute animals, protected only by a poverty-stricken Mother, and cast off by the foolish arrogance of the world? Who will dare to love the vanity and pride, which was openly abhorred and condemned by the Creator of heaven and earth in his conduct? No one can despise the humility, poverty and indigence, which the Lord loved and chose for Himself as the very means of teaching the way of eternal life. Few there are, who stop to consider this truth and example: and on account of this vile ingratitude only the few will reap the fruit of these great sacraments.

487. But if the condescension of my most holy Son was so great as to bestow so liberally upon thee his light and knowledge concerning these vast blessings, ponder well how much thou art bound to co-operate with this light In order that thou mayest correspond to this obligation, I remind and exhort thee to forget all that is of earth and lose it out of thy sight; that thou seek nothing, or engage thyself with nothing except what can help thee to withdraw and detach thee from the world and its inhabitants; so that, with a heart freed from all terrestrial affection, thou dispose thyself to celebrate in it the mysteries of the poverty, humility and divine love of the incarnate God. Learn from my example the reverence, fear and respect, with which thou must treat Him, remembering how I acted, when I held Him in my arms; follow my example, whenever thou receivest Him in thy heart in the venerable sacrament of the holy Eucharist, wherein is contained the same God-Man, who was born of my womb. In this holy Sacrament thou receivest Him and possessest Him just as really, and He remains in thee just as actually, as I possessed Him and conversed with Him, although in another manner.

488. I desire that thou go even to extremes in this holy reverence and fear; and I wish that thou take notice and be convinced, that in entering into thy heart in the holy Sacra-

ment, thy God exhorts thee in the same words, which thou
hast recorded as spoken to me: become like unto Me. His
coming down from heaven onto the earth, his being born in
humility and poverty, his living and dying in it, giving such
rare example of the contempt of the world and its deceits; the
knowledge, which thou hast received concerning his conduct
and which thou hast penetrated so deeply by divine intelligence: all these things should be for thee like living voices,
which thou must heed and inscribe into the interior of thy
heart. These privileges have all been granted to thee in order
that thou discreetly use the common blessings to their fullest
extent, and in order that thou mayest understand, how
thankful thou must be to my most holy Son and Lord, and
how thou shouldst strive to make as great a return for his
goodness, as if He had come from heaven to redeem thee
alone and as if He had instituted all his wonders and doctrines in the holy Church for none else than thee (Gal. 7,
20).

Chapter XI

THE HOLY ANGELS ANNOUNCE THE BIRTH OF OUR LORD IN DIFFERENT PARTS OF THE WORLD, AND THE SHEPHERDS COME TO ADORE HIM.

489. After the courtiers of heaven had thus celebrated the birth of God made man near the portals of Bethlehem, some of them were immediately dispatched to different places, in order to announce the happy news to those, who according to the divine will were properly disposed to hear it. The holy prince Michael betook himself to the holy Patriarchs in limbo and announced to them, how the Onlybegotten of the eternal Father was already born into the world and was resting, humble and meek, as they had prophesied, in a manger between two beasts. He addressed also in a special manner holy Joachim and Anne in the name of the blessed Mother, who had enjoined this upon him; he congratulated them, that their Daughter now held in her arms the Desired of nations and Him, who had been foretold by all the Patriarchs and Prophets (Is. 7, 14; 9, 7, etc.), It was the most consoling and joyful day, which this great gathering of the just and the saints had yet had during their long banishment. All of them acknowledged this new Godman as the true Author of eternal salvation, and they composed and sang new songs of adoration and worship in his praise. Saint Joachim and Anne enjoined the messenger of heaven, saint Michael,

to ask Mary their Daughter to worship in their name the divine Child, the blessed Fruit of her womb; and this the great Queen of the world immediately did for them, listening with great jubilee to all that the holy prince reported concerning the Patriarchs of limbo.

490. Another of the holy angels that attended and guarded the heavenly Mother was sent to saint Elisabeth and her son John. On hearing this news of the birth of the Redeemer, the prudent matron and her son, although he was yet of so tender an age, prostrated themselves upon the earth and adored their God made man in spirit and in truth (John 4, 23). The child which had been consecrated as his Precursor, was renewed interiorly with a spirit more inflamed than that of Elias, causing new admiration and jubilation in the angels themselves. Saint John and his mother requested our Queen through the angels, that She in the name of them both, adore her most holy Son and offer Him their services; all of which the heavenly Queen immediately fulfilled.

491. Having thus been informed of what had happened, saint Elisabeth hastened to send one of her domestics to Bethlehem with presents for the blessed Mother and the infant God. They consisted in some money, some linen and other things for the comfort of the newly born and of his poor Mother and her spouse. The servant betook himself on the way with no other instruction than that he visit the blessed Virgin and saint Joseph and take notice of what comfort or want was theirs, so that he might bring back certain information of their circumstances and well-being. He had no other knowledge of the sacrament, except what he himself could perceive with his own eyes; but renewed and touched by an interior and divine force he came back and in wonderful jubilee described to saint Elisabeth the poverty and the charming grace of her Cousin, of the Child and of saint Joseph, and what feelings were excited in him on be-

holding them. Admirable were the sentiments roused in the godly matron by his ingenuous narration. If it had not been for the will of God, that the secret and privacy of this high sacrament should be preserved, she could not have restrained herself from visiting the Virgin Mother and the newborn God. Of the things sent by her, the Queen appropriated some for relieving their extreme poverty, while She distributed the rest of them to the poor; for She did not wish to be deprived of the company of the poor during the days in which She would have to remain in the portal or cave of the Nativity.

492. Other angels were delegated to bring the news to Zachary, Simeon and Anne, the prophetess, and to some other just and holy people, who were worthy to be trusted with this new mystery of our Redemption; for as the Lord found them prepared to receive this news with gratitude and with benefit to themselves, He considered it a just due to their virtue not to hide from them the blessing conferred upon the human race. Although not all the just upon earth were informed at that time of this sacrament; yet in all of them were wrought certain divine effects in the hour in which the Savior of the world was born. For all the just felt in their hearts a new and supernatural joy, though they were ignorant of its cause. There were not only movements of joy in the angels and in the just, but also wonderful movements in the insensible creatures; for all the influences of the planets were renovated and enlivened. The sun much accelerated its course; the stars shone in greater brightness; and for the Magi kings was formed that wonderful star, which showed them the way to Bethlehem (Matth. 2,2). Many trees began to bloom and others to produce fruit. Some temples of the idols were overthrown; and in others the idols were hurled down and their demons put to flight. These wonders and other happenings in the world on that day men accounted for in

different ways, but far from the truth. Only among the just there were many, who by divine impulse suspected or believed that God had come into the world; yet no one knew it with certainty, except those to whom it was revealed. Among these were the three Magi, to each of whom in their separate Oriental kingdoms angels of the Queen's guard were sent to inform them by interior and intellectual enlightenment that the Redeemer of the human race had been born in poverty and humility. At the same time they were inspired with the sudden desire of seeking Him and adoring Him and immediately they saw the star as a guide to Bethlehem, as I will relate farther on.

493. Amongst all these, the shepherds of that region, who were watching their flocks at the time of the birth of Christ, were especially blessed (Luke 2, 8) ; not only because they accepted the labor and inconvenience of their calling with resignation from the hand of God; but also because, being poor and humble, and despised by the world, they belonged in sincerity and uprightness of heart to those Israelites, who fervently hoped and longed for the coming of the Messias, speaking and discoursing of Him among themselves many times. They resembled the Author of life, as they were removed from the riches, vanity and ostentation of the world and far from its diabolical cunning (John 10, 14). They exhibited in the circumstances of their calling the office, which the good Shepherd had come to fulfill in knowing his Sheep and being known to them. Hence they merited to be called and invited, as the first fruits of the saints by the Savior himself, to be the very first ones, to whom the eternal and incarnate Word manifested Himself and by whom He wished to be praised, served and adored. Hence the archangel Gabriel was sent to them as they watched over the field, appearing to them in human form and with great splendor.

494. The shepherds found themselves suddenly enveloped and bathed in the celestial radiance of the angel, and at his sight, being little versed in such visions, they were filled with great fear. The holy prince reassured them and said: "Ye upright men, be not afraid: for I announce to you tidings of great joy, which is, that for you is born today the Redeemer Christ, our Lord, in the city of David. And as a sign of this truth, I announce to you, that you shall find the Infant wrapped in swaddling-clothes and placed in a manger" (Luke 2, 10, 12). At these words of the angel, suddenly appeared a great multitude of the celestial army, who in voices of sweet harmony sang to the Most High these words: "Glory to God in the highest and on earth peace to men of good will." Rehearsing this divine canticle, so new to the world, the holy angels disappeared. All this happened in the fourth watch of the night. By this angelic vision the humble and fortunate shepherds were filled with divine enlightenment and were unanimously impelled by a fervent longing to make certain of this blessing and to witness with their own eyes the most high mystery of which they had been informed.

495. The signs which the holy angels had indicated to them did not seem appropriate or proportioned for attesting the greatness of the Newborn to eyes of the flesh. For to lie in a manger and to be wrapped in swaddling-clothes, would not have been convincing proof of the majesty of a king, if these shepherds had not been illumined by divine light and been enabled to penetrate the mystery. As they were free from the arrogant wisdom of the world, they were easily made proficient in the divine wisdom. Conferring among themselves the thoughts excited by this message, they resolved to hasten in all speed to Bethlehem and see the wonder made known to them by the Lord. They departed without delay and entering the cave or portal, they found, as saint Luke tells us, Mary and Joseph, and the Infant lying in a

manger. Seeing all this they recognized the truth of what they had heard of the Child. Upon this followed an interior enlightenment consequent upon seeing the Word made flesh; for when the shepherds looked upon Him, He also glanced at them, emitting from his countenance a great effulgence, which wounded with love the sincere heart of each of these poor yet fortunate men; with divine efficiency it changed them and renewed them, constituting them in a new state of grace and holiness and filling them with an exalted knowledge of the divine mysteries of the Incarnation and the Redemption of the human race.

496. Prostrating themselves on the earth they adored the Word made flesh. Not any more as ignorant rustics, but as wise and prudent men they adored Him, acknowledged and magnified Him as true God and man, as Restorer and Redeemer of the human race. The heavenly Lady and Mother of the Child took notice of all that they did interiorly and exteriorly; for She saw into their inmost hearts. In highest wisdom and prudence She preserved the memory of all these happenings and pondered them in her soul, (Luke 2, 19), comparing them with the other mysteries therein contained and with the holy prophecies and sayings of the Scriptures. As She was then the organ of the holy Spirit and the representative of the Infant, She spoke to the shepherds, instructing and exhorting them to persevere in divine love and in the service of the Most High. They also conversed with Her on their part and showed by their answers that they understood many of the mysteries. They remained in the cave from the beginning of dawn until mid-day, when, having given them something to eat, our great Queen sent them off full of heavenly grace and consolation.

497. During the days in which most holy Mary, the Child and saint Joseph remained in the gates of Bethlehem, these holy shepherds returned a few times and brought such pre-

sents as in their poverty they could spare. What saint Luke says about those that wondered at what the shepherds said concerning the holy Family, happened later, after the Queen, the Child and saint Joseph had departed and fled from the neighborhood of Bethlehem; for divine Providence so arranged things, that the shepherds were unable to spread about this news before that time. Not all of those that heard them speaking about this matter believed them, for they held them to be uncultured and ignorant people. These shepherds however were saints and were filled with divine knowledge until they died. Among those who believed them was Herod, although not because of any laudable faith or piety, but on account of his worldly and wicked fear of losing his kingdom. Among the children, who merited to be sacrificed by him, there were also some belonging to these holy men. Their parents consented joyfully to the martyrdom, which the children themselves desired and offering themselves up to the Lord, whom they were made to know beforehand.

Words of the Queen

THE VIRGIN MARY SPEAKS TO SISTER MARY OF AGREDA

498. My daughter, forgetfulness and inattention regarding the works of the Redeemer are as reprehensible as they are common and frequent among mortals. Yet these works are most mysterious, loving, merciful and instructive. Thou hast been called and chosen to receive knowledge and enlightenment for avoiding such dangerous and gross torpidity; therefore I wish, that in the mysteries thou hast just written, thou take notice of and ponder over the burning love of my most holy Son in communicating Himself to men as soon as He was born, in order to make them immediate partakers of the joyful fruit of his coming. Men do not know of this obligation, because few of them penetrate to the significance of this

great blessing, just as there were few who saw the Word at his Birth and thanked Him for his arrival. They are not aware of the cause of their evil state and of their blindness, which neither was nor is to be ascribed to the Lord nor to any fault in his love, but to the sins and the bad dispositions of men. If their own bad dispositions would not impede or make them unworthy of this favor, the same light, which was given to the just, to the shepherds and to the kings, would have been vouchsafed to all or to many. That there should be so few, will make thee understand in what an unhappy condition the world was at the time of the coming of the incarnate Word; and also the unhappiness of the present times, when these mysteries have become so evident and when grateful memory of them is become so scarce.

499. Consider the wicked disposition of mortals in the present age, in which the light of the Gospel has been spread out and confirmed by so many miracles wrought by God in his Church. In spite of all this there are so few, who are perfect and who seek to dispose themselves for greater participation in the fruits and benefits of the Redemption. Although the number of fools is so great and the vices are become so measureless, there are those who think, that also the perfect are numerous, because, forsooth, men do not so openly dare to act in opposition to God: there are fewer than one thinks, and many less than there should be, seeing that God is so much offended by the infidels and continually desires to communicate the treasures of grace in his Church according to the merits of his Onlybegotten made man. Be mindful, dearest, of the obligation imposed upon thee by thy clear knowledge of these truths. Live cautiously, with great attention and watchfulness correspond to his graces, losing no time, occasion or circumstance for acting in the most holy and perfect manner known to thee; for thou canst not fulfill thy duty otherwise. Remember what I tell thee, command

and urge upon thee, that thou receive not such great favor in vain (II Cor. 6, 1); do not allow thy grace and light to be without profit, but make use of them in the perfection of thankfulness.

Chapter XII

WHAT WAS CONCEALED FROM THE DEMON CONCERNING
THE MYSTERY OF THE BIRTH OF THE INCARNATE WORD,
AND OF OTHER HAPPENINGS UNTIL THE CIRCUMCISION.

500. As far as depended upon the Lord the coming of the
eternal Word as man was most fortunate and blessed for all
the mortals; for He came in order to give light and life to all
those that were in darkness and in the shadows of death
(Luke 1, 79). If the foreknown and incredulous stumbled
and hurt themselves on this cornerstone (Rom. 9, 33),
seeking ruin where they could and should have found resurrection to an eternal life, that was not the fault of the stone,
but of those that made of it an occasion of scandal and of
harm to themselves. Only for hell the birth of the infant God
was terrible, since He was the strong and invincible One,
who came to despoil that armed enemy of his tyrannous rule,
founded in lies (Psalm 23, 8), who had held his fortification
in unjust yet peaceful possession for a long time. In order to
depose this prince of the world and of darkness, it was befitting, that the sacrament of the coming of the Word should
be hidden from him. Because of his malice he was not only
unworthy to be informed of the mysteries of the divine
wisdom (Wisd. 2, 21, 24) ; but it was just that by divine
Providence the malice of this enemy should be blinded and
confused; in his malice he had brought into the world the

deceit and blindness of sin and cast down the whole human race by the fall of Adam.

501. Accordingly Lucifer and his ministers were left in ignorance of many things, which they could naturally have known concerning the incarnation of the Word and other events in the course of his most holy life, a fact which it is necessary to take notice of in this history (Nos. 326, Vol. 111,217,226, 284). For if he had known for certain, that Christ was the true God, he evidently would not have procured his death (I Cor. 2, 8), but he would have sought to prevent it, as will be said in its proper place (Vol. III, 494, 540, 613). Concerning the mystery of the Nativity he knew only that most holy Mary had given birth to a Son in poverty and in a forsaken cave, and that She had not found even lodging and shelter; also that the Child was circumcised and otherwise treated as mere man: all of which was calculated rather to mislead his pride than to enlighten it. But he was ignorant of the manner of his Birth, and of the virginity of the blessed Mother before and after the Birth; likewise of the message of the angels to the just, and to the shepherds; of their conversations, and of their adoration of the infant God. Nor did he see the star, nor did he know the purpose of the kings in coming to Bethlehem, although he saw them make the journey and attributed it to some worldly enterprise. The demons were also unable to account for the changes in the elements, the stars and planets; though they well perceived these changes and wonderful effects. They misjudged the words of the Magi in the presence of Herod, their arrival at the stable and the adoration, and the gifts offered. Notwithstanding, that they perceived the fury of Herod against the children and abetted it; yet they did not understand his object and they stirred up his cruelty. Although Lucifer suspected, that Herod was seeking to kill the Messias, he considered him demented and treated him with derision. For

in his pride he obstinately held fast to the opinion, that the
Word, upon entering into the world in order to set up his
dominion, would not come humbly and in a hidden manner,
but with ostentatious power and majesty, while in reality the
infant God chose a far different way, being born of a Mother
poor and despised by men.

502. Thus misled, Lucifer, having noticed some of the
strange events connected with the Nativity, called together
his helpers in hell, and said to them: "I do not find any
occasion for fear in the events, which we have noticed in the
world. It is true, the Woman whom we persecuted so much,
has given birth to a Son, but in such poverty and neglect,
that She could not even procure a lodging-place in order to
be delivered. We know all this to be far from the power and
greatness of God. If He is to advance against us as weak as we
have seen this Child and as we have assured ourselves concerning It, He certainly can make no headway against our
power. We need not fear that He is the Messias, since there is
even a plot to kill Him as being mortal like the rest of men.
This does not seem to point to the salvation of the world,
since He himself seems to stand in need of atoning for his
fault by death. All these signs conflict with the purpose of the
Messias in coming into the world and therefore it seems to
me, that we can rest assured, that He has not yet come." The
ministers of evil approved of the decision of their damned
chief and they were all satisfied, that the Messias had not yet
come, for they were all accomplices in the malice and pride
which blinded him (Wis. 2, 21). It never occurred to satan in
his vanity and indomitable pride, that the majesty and greatness of God should humiliate itself; because he himself
sought after applause, ostentation, reverence and exaltation,
wishing if possible to appropriate all honor to himself. Since
all honor was attainable by God, it never entered his mind,

that He would consent to the contrary and subject Himself to humiliation, so much abhorred by the spirits of evil.

503. O sons of vanity I What examples are not here given to you for your enlightenment! Great is the lesson, which the humility of Christ, our Teacher and our highest Good, teaches and urges upon us: but if this does not move us, let the pride of Lucifer at least deter and frighten us. O vice, O sin, dreadful beyond human imagination! since it confused an angel of such high intellect so much, that he could judge of the infinite bounty by no other standard than that by which he judged himself and of his own malicious disposition! How far then does not man proceed in malice, if to his ignorance he joins guilt and pride? O unhappy and most foolish Lucifer! How far didst thou go astray in judging of so reasonable and commendable a proceeding! What is more beautiful than humility and meekness joined with majesty and power? Why dost thou fail to see, insignificant creature, that not to know how to humiliate thyself is only weakness of mind and comes from a base heart? The magnanimous and truly great do not seek payment in vanity, nor do they seek after what is low, nor can they be satisfied with what is false and apparent. It is evident, O Lucifer, that thou art shut out from truth and but an ignorant guide for the blind (Matth. 15, 14); since thou didst fail to understand, that the greatness of the bounty and love of God (Rom. 5, 8) manifested and magnified itself in humility and obedience even to the death of the Cross (Phil. 2, 8).

504. All these errors and insanities of Lucifer and his ministers were known to the Mother of wisdom and our Mistress; and with a just appreciation of such high mysteries She magnified and blessed the Lord, because He had concealed them from the proud and arrogant and revealed them to the poor and humble, thus beginning to overcome the tyranny of the demons (Matth. 11, 25). The kind Mother offered up

fervent prayers for all the mortals, who on account of their faults were unworthy of seeing the light, which for their salvation had appeared in the world; of all this She reminded her most sweet Son with incomparable compassion and love for sinners. In these affections She spent most of the time of her stay in the cave of the Nativity. But as this place was bare of all comfort and much exposed to the inclemencies of the weather, the great Lady was most solicitous for the shelter of her tender and sweet Child. As a most prudent Mother She had brought along a mantle, with which She covered Him in addition to the ordinary swaddling-clothes. Moreover She held Him continually in the embrace of her sacred arms, except at times, when, in order to make saint Joseph happy, She asked him to hold his incarnate God in his arms and serve him as a father.

505. When for the first time She placed the infant God in his arms, the most holy Mary said to him: My husband and my helper, receive in thy arms the Creator of heaven and earth and enjoy his amiable and sweet company, in order that my Lord and my God may be delighted and recompensed by thy faithful services (Prov. 8, 31). Take to thyself the Treasure of the eternal Father and participate in this blessing of the human race." And speaking interiorly to the divine Infant, She said: "Sweetest Love of my soul and Light of my eyes, rest in the arms of Joseph, my friend and spouse: do thou hold sweet intercourse with him and pardon me my shortcomings. Much do I feel the loss of Thee even for one instant, but I wish to communicate without envy the good I have received, to all that are worthy" (Wis. 7, 13). Her most faithful husband, acknowledging this new blessing, humbled himself to the earth and answered: "Lady and Sovereign of the world, my Spouse, how can I, being so unworthy, presume to hold in my arms God himself, in whose presence tremble the pillars of heaven? (Job 26, 11). How can this vile

wormlet have courage to accept such an exalted favor? I am but dust and ashes, but do Thou, Lady, assist me in my lowliness and ask his Majesty to look upon me with clemency and make me worthy through his grace."

506. His desire of holding the infant God and his reverential fear of Him caused in saint Joseph heroic acts of love, of faith, of humility and profoundest reverence. Trembling with discreet fear He fell on his knees to receive Him from the hands of his most holy Mother, while sweetest tears of joy and delight copiously flowed from his eyes at a happiness so extraordinary. The divine Infant looked at him caressingly and at the same time renewed his inmost soul with such divine efficacy as no words will suffice to explain. He broke out in new canticles of praise at seeing himself thus enriched with such magnificent blessings and favors. After having for some time enjoyed in spirit the sweetest effects of holding in his arms the Lord, who contains heaven and earth (Is. 40, 12), He replaced Him into the arms of his fortunate Mother, both of them being on their knees in receiving and giving Him. Similar reverence the most prudent Mother observed every time She took Him up or relinquished Him, in which also saint Joseph imitated Her, as often as it was his happy lot to hold the incarnate Word. When they approached his Majesty, they also made three genuflections, kissing the earth and exciting heroic acts of humility, worship and reverence. Thus both the great Queen and the blessed Joseph observed all propriety in receiving or giving the Child from and to one another.

507. When the heavenly Mother judged it time to nourish Him at her breast, She reverently asked permission of her Son; for although She knew, that She was to nourish Him as her true and human Child, She nevertheless bore in mind, that He was at the same time the true God and Lord and that a great distance intervened between the infinite Being and a

mere creature such as She was. As this consciousness was
unfailing in the most prudent Virgin, her reverence remained
faultless and undiminished and permitted not the least
forgetfulness in Her. She was always filled with a comprehen-
sive insight and She always reached perfection in all her acts.
Therefore She nourished, served and tended her Child, not
with an uneasy haste, but with unremitting care, reverence
and discretion, causing ever new admiration in the angels,
whose celestial understanding reached not so far as to comprehend such heroic acts of a tender Maiden. As they were
always corporally present during the time which She spent at
the gates of Bethlehem, they administered to Her in all
things demanded by the service of the infant God and of
Her. All these mysteries are so wonderful and admirable, and
so worthy of our attention and remembrance, that we cannot
deny our negligence in forgetting them, and we cannot
acknowledge sufficiently, what harm we are doing ourselves
in ceasing to think of them, nor do we sufficiently understand the divine effect, which the memory of them produces
in the faithful and grateful children of the Church.

508. From what has been revealed to me of the reverence,
with which most holy Mary and the glorious saint Joseph as
well as the angelic hosts treated the Incarnate God, I could
easily extend my discourse on the subject. Though I refrain, I
yet wish to confess the want of reverence, with which I have
until now audaciously behaved toward God, and how many
faults, of which I have been guilty toward Him in this respect, have become known to me. As I said, and will relate
further on, in order to assist the Queen, all the angels of her
guard remained present in visible forms from the time of the
Birth until the flight of the Child into Egypt. The solicitude
of the humble and loving Mother for her divine Infant was
so unremitting, that She would not part with Him to place
Him in the arms of saint Joseph or into those of the holy

princes Michael or Gabriel, except on rare occasions when She was obliged to take some nourishment; for these two archangels had besought Her, to consign the Child to their care during meals or when saint Joseph was at his work. Thus He was placed into the hands of the angels, in admirable fulfillment of the words of David: "In their hands they shall bear Thee up," etc. (Ps. 90, 12). The most watchful Mother would not take any sleep in her solicitude for her most holy Son, except when his Majesty commanded Her to do so. In reward for her diligence He provided for Her a new and more miraculous kind of sleep than that which She had until then enjoyed; for while She slept, her heart was awake, continuing or rather not interrupting the divine intelligence and contemplation of the Divinity (Cant. 5, 2). But from this day on the Lord added still another miracle, namely, during the sleep, which was necessary, She retained in her arms the power of holding and embracing the Child in the same way as if She were awake; and She gazed upon Him with the eyes of her intellect, as if She were looking upon Him with her bodily eyes, understanding all that She herself and her Child did exteriorly in the meanwhile. Thus was miraculously fulfilled, what is said in the Canticles: "I sleep, but my heart is awake."

509. The canticles of praise and exaltation of the Lord, which our celestial Queen composed in honor of the Child, alternately singing them with the holy angels and also with her spouse Joseph, I cannot express by my limited terms of speech. Of them alone there would be much to write, for they were uninterrupted; but the knowledge of them is reserved for the special enjoyment of the elect Among all mortals the most faithful Joseph was privileged and blessed in this respect, for in many of them he himself participated and many of them he understood. Beside this he enjoyed another favor, of singular benefit and consolation to his soul and

procured for him by the most prudent Virgin: namely, many
times, in conversing with him of the Child, She spoke of
Him as of "our Son" (Luke 2, 48); not that He was the
natural Son of saint Joseph, since in the supernatural order
He was the Son of the eternal Father and in the natural
order, the Son of his Virgin Mother; but because in the
opinion of men He was reputed to be the son of Joseph. This
favor and privilege was of inestimable value to the saint and
caused him immeasurable delight; on this account his heavenly Spouse delighted in using this appellation when conversing about her Son.

Words of the Queen

THE VIRGIN MARY SPEAKS TO SISTER MARY OF AGREDA

510. My daughter, I see thee full of devout emulation of the
happiness, which the intercourse with my Son afforded me,
my spouse and the holy angels, since we beheld Him present
to our bodily eyes as thou desirest for thyself, if it were
possible. I wish to console thee and guide thy affections
toward that which thou thyself canst and shouldst do according to thy condition in order to attain the same happiness
which thou covetest in us. For this purpose, beloved, recall
what thou hast already sufficiently understood concerning
the ways of God in raising up those souls, whom He seeks
with paternal love and affection. Thou hast attained this
knowledge by being favored with so many particular calls and
enlightenments of the Lord, wherein He continually waits at
the portals of thy heart, and urges thee onward expecting thy
conversion (Wis. 6, 15). Thou hast seen Him drawing thee
to Himself by repeated favors and by most exalted doctrines,
selecting thee for the narrow bands of his loving intercourse
(Coloss. 3, 14); and the great purity due to this concession.

511. Faith likewise teaches thee, that God is present in all places by his essence and by the power of his Divinity; and that to Him are open all thy thoughts. thy desires and sighs without exception. If thou cooperate with this truth so as to preserve the graces, which thou receivest through the sacraments and other channels divinely instituted, the Lord will remain with thee also by divine and special assistance; and in it He will regale thee with his love as his chosen spouse. Now since thou knowest and understandest all these truths, tell me, what more canst thou envy or desire, when thou already possessest all that thou so anxiously sighest after? What I require of thee, and all that remains for thee to do, is, that thou exert thyself in holy emulation to imitate this intercourse and reproduce in thyself the disposition of the angels, the purity of my husband, and to copy in thyself my life, as far as possible, in order to be a fit dwelling-place of the Most High (I Cor. 3, 17). Thou must direct all those endeavors, all those desires and exertions, with which thou wouldst have wished thyself to be animated if thou hadst seen and adored my most holy Son in his birth and infancy, toward the fulfillment of this doctrine; for if thou imitatest me, thou mayest rest secure, that thou hast me as a Teacher and the Lord for an assured possession of thy soul. In this assurance thou canst speak to Him, embrace Him and delight thyself with Him, as with One who is present; for in order to communicate these delights to the pure and untainted souls He has assumed human flesh and become a Child. But always look upon Him as the great God, though a Child, in order that thy caresses may be guarded by reverence and thy love accompanied by holy fear; for the one is due to Him as God, and the other befits his immense bounty and merciful magnificence.

512. In this manner of intercourse thou must continue without intervals of lukewarmness, lest thou disgust Him.

Thy legitimate and chosen occupation should be none other than the love and the praise of the infinite God. All the rest thou must enter into only sparingly, in such a way as if visible and earthly things scarcely concerned thee and cannot detain thee even for a moment. Thou must maintain thyself in this soaring height, so that thou seem not to have anything earnestly to attend to, except to seek the highest and true God. Me thou shouldst imitate and for God alone thou shouldst live; all the rest should not exist for thee, nor shouldst thou exist for it. But the gifts and blessings, which thou receivest I wish thou dispense and communicate for the good of thy fellowmen, observing the perfect order of holy charity; thus thy gifts will not evaporate, but be still more increased (I Cor. 13, 8). In all this thou must keep the regulations, which befit thy condition and state, as I have already shown and instructed thee in other places at other times.

Chapter XIII

THE MOST HOLY MARY IS INFORMED OF THE WILL OF THE LORD. THAT HIS ONLYBEGOTTEN SON BE CIRCUMCISED. AND SHE CONFERS ABOUT IT WITH SAINT JOSEPH: THE MOST HOLY NAME OF JESUS IS BROUGHT FROM HEAVEN.

513. From the moment the most prudent Virgin found Herself chosen as the Mother of the divine Word, She began to ponder upon the labors and sufferings in store for her sweetest Son. As her knowledge of Scripture was so profound, She understood all the mysteries contained therein and She began to foresee and prepare with incomparable compassion for all that He was to suffer for the Redemption of Man. This sorrow, foreseen and expected with such a full knowledge of details, was a prolonged martyrdom for the most meek Mother of the sacrificial Lamb of God (Jer. 11, 19). But in regard to the Circumcision, which was to take place after the birth of the Child, the heavenly Lady had received no command or intimation of the will of the eternal Father. This uncertainty excited the loving solicitude and sweet plaints of the tender and affectionate Mother. Her prudent foresight enabled Her to conjecture, that, as her most holy Son had come to honor and confirm his law by fulfilling it and as He had moreover come in order to suffer for men, He would be constrained by his burning love and by other motives to undergo the pains of circumcision.

514. On the other hand her maternal love and compassion longed to exempt her sweet Child if possible, from this suffering; moreover She knew, that circumcision was a rite instituted for cleansing the newborn children from original sin, whereas the divine Infant was entirely free from this guilt, not having contracted it in Adam. In this hesitation between love of her divine Son and obedience to the eternal Father, the most prudent Virgin practiced many heroic acts of virtue, unspeakably pleasing to his Majesty. Although She could have easily escaped this uncertainty by directly asking the Lord what was to be done; yet, being as humble as She was prudent, She refrained. Neither would She ask her angels; for with admirable wisdom, She awaited the opportune time and occasion, assigned by divine Providence for all things, and She would not presume curiously to search or pry into his decrees by consulting supernatural sources of information, especially in order to rid Herself of any suffering. When any grave and doubtful affair arose, in which there was danger of offending God, or some urgent undertaking for the good of creatures, in which it would be necessary to know the divine will, She first asked permission to submit her petition for enlightenment regarding the divine pleasure.

515. This does not conflict with what I said in book second, chapter tenth, namely, that the most holy Mary undertook nothing without asking permission and counsel of God, for this consultation concerning the divine pleasure was not coupled with the desire of special revelation. In this as I have said, She was most discreet and diffident, rarely asking for such extraordinary intervention. Without aspiring to new revelation She was in the habit of consulting the habitual and supernatural aid of the Holy Ghost, who governed and guided Her in all her actions. In directing Her faculties by this interior light, She perceived the greater perfection and sanctity open to Her in the affairs and transactions of every-

day life. Although it is true, that the Queen of heaven possessed special claims and rights to be informed of the will of God in different ways; yet, as She was the model of all sanctity and discretion, She would not avail Herself of this supernatural order and direction, except in such cases as were appropriate. As for the rest She guided Herself by fulfilling to the letter the words of David: "As the eyes of the handmaid are on the hands of her mistress, so are our eyes unto the Lord our God, until He have mercy on us" (Ps. 122, 2). But this natural and ordinary light in the Mistress of the world was greater than that of all the mortals together; and in it She sought the fiat of the divine will.

516. The mystery of the Circumcision required a special and particular dispensation; it demanded a separate enlightenment of the Lord, and for this the prudent Mother was waiting. In the meanwhile, addressing in these words the law that required it, She said: "O law, made for all, thou art just and holy; but thou dost afflict my heart by thy hardness, if thou art to wound Him, who is thy life and thy Author I That thou shouldst inflict thy sufferings upon those, who must be cleansed of guilt, is just; but that thou shouldst visit with thy severity the Innocent, who is without fault (Heb. 7,26), seems the excess of rigor unless his own love concedes this right to thee. O would that it might please my Beloved to exempt Himself from this punishment! But how shall He refuse to undergo it, since He came to seek pain, to embrace the Cross, to fulfill and accomplish the law? (Matth. 5, 27). O cruel knife! Would thou couldst direct thy attacks upon my own life, and not upon the Lord, who gave it to me! O my Son, sweet Love and Light of my soul, is it possible, that Thou so soon shalt shed thy blood, which is more precious than heaven and earth? My loving compassion inclines me to hold Thee exempt from the common law, from which Thou art excluded as its Author. But the desire to fulfill it urges me

to comply with it, leaving Thee a prey to its rigor, unless Thou, my sweet Life, art willing to change the decree and punish me instead. The human nature, which Thou hast from Adam, my Lord, I have given Thee, but without its fault or guilt; since in thy Omnipotence Thou hast preserved it among all the rest from original stain. Since Thou art the Son of the eternal Father and the figure of his substance (Heb. 1, 3), and since thy generation is eternal, Thou art infinitely removed from sin. Why then, my Lord, shouldst Thou subject thyself to the remedy provided for sin by the law? Yet am I aware, my Son, that Thou art the Teacher and Redeemer of men and that Thou must confirm thy precepts by the example: Thou wilt not yield the least point in this matter. O eternal Father, let the knife now lose its sharpness and the flesh its sensitiveness! Let pain descend rather upon me, insignificant wormlet; let thy Onlybegotten Son fulfill the law, but let me alone feel the punishment. O inhuman and cruel sin, which so soon profferest the gall to Him, who cannot be guilty of thee! O sons of Adam, abhor and fear sin, which, for a remedy, demands bloody punishment of the Lord and God himself."

517. Such grief the sorrowful Mother mixed with the joy of seeing the Onlybegotten of the Father born of Her and resting in her arms, and thus She passed the days which remained before the Circumcision, being faithfully attended by her most chaste spouse Joseph. To him alone She spoke of the Circumcision; yet only in few words and mixed with the tears of compassion of them both. Before the eight days after the Birth were completed, the most prudent Queen placed Herself on her knees in the presence of the Lord and thus addressed Him: "Highest King, Father of my Lord (Eph, 5, 2), behold here thy slave with the true Sacrifice and Victim in her arms. My sighs and their cause are not unknown to thy wisdom (Ps. 37, 10). I know, my Lord, what according

to the law is thy pleasure and what should be done with thy Son. If by suffering much more rigorous pains I can rescue my Son and God, my heart is prepared. But I am likewise ready to see Him submit to circumcision, if that is thy will."

518. The Most High answered Her, saying: "My Daughter and my Dove, do not let thy heart be afflicted because thy Son is to be subjected to the knife and to the pains of circumcision. I have sent Him into the world as an example, that He put an end to the law of Moses by entirely fulfilling it (Matth. 5, 17). Though it is true that the habitation of his humanity, which thou hast given Him as his natural Mother, is to be violated, and his flesh wounded together with thy soul, yet remember: He is my natural Son by an eternal generation (Ps. 2, 7), the image of my substance (Heb. 1, 3), equal to Me in essence, majesty and glory, and by thus subjecting Himself to the sacramental law freeing from sin (John 10, 3Q), without letting man know that He is exempt therefrom, He suffers also in his honor (II Cor. 2,21). Thou knowest beforehand, my Daughter, that thou must reserve thy Onlybegotten and Mine for this and other greater sufferings. Resign thyself, then, to the shedding of his blood and willingly yield to Me the first fruits of the eternal salvation of men."

519. To this decree of the eternal Father the heavenly Lady, as the Co-operatrix of our salvation, conformed Herself with such a plenitude of all sanctity as is far beyond human understanding. With complete and most loving obedience She offered up her Onlybegotten, saying: "Supreme Lord and God, I offer to Thee this Victim and Host of acceptable sacrifice with all my heart, although I am full of compassion and sorrow that men have offended thy immense Goodness in such a way as to force a God to make amends. Eternally shall I praise Thee for looking with such infinite love upon thy creatures and for preferring to refuse pardon to thy own

Son rather than hinder the salvation of man (Eph, 5,2). I, who by thy condescension am his Mother, must before all other mortals subject myself to thy pleasure and therefore I offer to Thee the most meek Lamb, which is to take away the sins of the world by his innocence (John 1, 29). But if it is possible to mitigate the pains caused by this knife at the expense of suffering in me, thy arm is mighty to effect this exchange."

520. Most holy Mary issued from her prayer and requested saint Joseph to take the necessary steps for the Circumcision of the divine Infant. With rarest prudence She avoided telling Him anything of what She had been told in answer to her prayer. She spoke as if She wished to consult Him or ask his opinion in regard to the Circumcision, saying that the time appointed by law for the Circumcision of the Child had arrived and since they had not received any orders to the contrary, it seemed necessary to comply with it. They themselves, She said, were more bound to please the Most High, to obey more punctually his precepts, and to be more zealous in the love and care of his most holy Son than all the rest of creatures, seeking to fulfill in all things the divine pleasure in return for his incomparable favors. To these words saint Joseph answered with the greatest modesty and discretion, saying, that, as no command to the contrary had been given concerning the Child he wished in all things to conform himself to the divine will manifested in the common law; that, although as God the incarnate Word was not subject to the law, yet He was now clothed with our humanity, and, as a most perfect Teacher and Savior, no doubt wished to conform with other men in its fulfillment. Then he asked his heavenly Spouse how the Circumcision was to take place.

521. The most holy Mary answered, that the Circumcision should be performed substantially in the same way as it was performed on other children: but that She need not hand

Him over or consign Him to any other person, but that She would herself hold Him in her arms. And because the delicacy and tenderness of the Infant would make this ceremony more painful to Him than to other children, they should have at hand the soothing medicine, which was ordinarily applied at circumcision. Moreover, She requested saint Joseph to procure a crystal or glass vessel for preserving the sacred relic of the Circumcision of the divine Infant. In the meanwhile the cautious Mother prepared some linen cloths to catch the sacred blood, which was now for the first time to be shed for our rescue, so that not one drop of it might be lost or fall upon the ground. After these preparations the heavenly Lady asked saint Joseph to inform the priest and request him to come to the cave where, without the necessity of bringing the Child to any other place, he might, as a fit and worthy minister of so hidden and great a sacrament, with his priestly hands perform the rite of the Circumcision.

522. Then most holy Mary and Joseph took counsel concerning the name to be given to the divine Infant in the Circumcision, and the holy spouse said: "My Lady, when the holy angel of the Most High informed me of this great sacrament, he also told me that thy most sacred Son should be called JESUS." The Virgin Mother answered: "This same name was revealed to me when He assumed flesh in my womb; and thus receiving this name from the Most High through the mouth of his holy angels, his ministers, it is befitting that we conform in humble reverence with the hidden and inscrutable judgments of his infinite wisdom in conferring it on my Son and Lord, and that we call Him JESUS. This name we will propose to the priest, for inscription in the register of the other circumcised children."

523. While the great Mistress of heaven and saint Joseph thus conversed with each other, innumerable angels descended in human forms from on high, clothed in shining white

garments, on which were woven red embroideries of wonderful beauty. They had palms in their hands and crowns upon their heads and emitted a greater splendor than many suns. In comparison with the beauty of these holy princes all the loveliness seen in this world appeared repulsive. But preeminent in splendor were the devices or escutcheons on their breasts, on each of which the sweet name of Jesus was engraved or embossed. The effulgence which each of these escutcheons emitted exceeded that of all the angels together, and the variety of the beauty thus exhibited in this great multitude was so rare and exquisite as neither human tongue can express nor human imagination ever compass. The holy angels divided into two choirs in the cave, keeping their gaze fixed upon the King and Lord in the arms of his virginal Mother. The chiefs of these heavenly cohorts were the two princes, saint Michael and saint Gabriel, shining in greater splendor than the rest and bearing in their hands, as a special distinction, the most holy name of JESUS, written in larger letters on something like cards of incomparable beauty and splendor.

524. The two princes presented themselves apart from the rest before their Queen and said: "Lady, this is the name of thy Son (Matth. 1,21), which was written in the mind of God from all eternity and which the blessed Trinity has given to thy Onlybegotten Son and our Lord as the signal of salvation for the whole human race; establishing Him at the same time on the throne of David. He shall reign upon it, chastise his enemies and triumph over them, making them his footstool and passing judgment upon them; He shall raise his friends to the glory of his right hand. But all this is to happen at the cost of suffering and blood; and even now He is to shed it in receiving this name, since it is that of the Savior and Redeemer; it shall be the beginning of his sufferings in obedience to the will of his eternal Father. We all are

come as ministering spirits of the Most High, appointed and sent by the holy Trinity in order to serve the Onlybegotten of the Father and thy own in all the mysteries and sacraments of the law of grace. We are to accompany Him and minister to Him until He shall ascend triumphantly to the celestial Jerusalem and open the portals of heaven; afterwards we shall enjoy an especial accidental glory beyond that of the other blessed, to whom no such commission has been given." All this was witnessed by the most fortunate spouse Joseph conjointly with the Queen of heaven; but his understanding of these happenings was not so deep as hers, for the Mother of wisdom understood and comprehended the highest mysteries of the Redemption. Although saint Joseph understood many more mysteries than other mortals, yet he did not penetrate them in the same way as his heavenly Spouse. Both of them, however, were full of heavenly joy and admiration, and extolled the Lord in new canticles of glory. All that they experienced in these various and wonderful events surpasses human language, and certainly my own powers, and I cannot find adequate words for expressing my conceptions.

Words of the Queen

THE VIRGIN MARY SPEAKS TO SISTER MARY OF AGREDA

525. My daughter, I wish to renovate in thee the enlightened teaching which thou hast received in order that thou mayst treat with thy Spouse in the highest reverence; for humility and reverential fear should increase in the soul in the same measure in which especial and extraordinary favors are conferred upon it. On account of not being mindful of this truth, many souls either make themselves unworthy or incapable of great blessings, or, if they receive them, grow into a dangerous rudeness and torpidity, which offends the Lord very much. The loving sweetness with which the Lord

often treats them engenders in them a certain presumption and disrespectful forwardness, causing them to deal with his infinite Majesty in an irreverent manner, and with a vain desire of searching and inquiring into those hidden ways of God which are far above their comprehension and capacity. They fall into this presumption because they judge of the familiar intercourse with God according to the imperfect insight of mortals, presuming to regulate it after the friendly intercourse of human creatures with one another.

526. But in this way of judging the soul is much deceived, measuring the reverence and respect due to the infinite Majesty by the familiarity and equality caused by the human love of mortals to one another. The rational creatures are by nature equal to each other, although the conditions and circumstances of each may be different; and the familiarity of human love and friendship may disregard the accidental differences in yielding to the human feelings. But the love of God must ever be mindful of the immeasurable excellence of the infinite Being, since its object is as well the infinite goodness as the infinite majesty of God: for just because the goodness and majesty in God are inseparable, therefore also reverence must not be separated from love of God in the creature. The light of divine faith must always go before, manifesting to the one that loves the greatness of the Object loved, awakening and fomenting reverential fear, restraining the exuberance of blind affections, and bridling them by the memory of the excellence and superiority of the Beloved.

527. If the creature is noble-hearted, practiced in and accustomed to holy and reverential fear, it is not in such danger of forgetting the respect due to the Most High, no matter how great the favors it receives; for it does not give itself up unguardedly to the spiritual delights and does not lose, on account of them, the discreet consciousness of the supreme Majesty; but it respects and reverences Him in proportion to

the greatness of his divine love and enlightenment. With such souls the Lord converses as one friend with another (Exod, 33, 11). Let it therefore, my daughter, be to thee an inviolable rule that the closer the embraces, and the greater the delights with which the Most High visits thee, so much the more unremitting shall be the consciousness of his immutable and infinite Majesty, extolling and loving Him at one and the same time. In this wise consciousness thou wilt learn to know and estimate more becomingly the greatness of his favors. Thou wilt avoid the dangerous presumption of those who lightly inquire into the secrets of the Lord at each trivial or even important event, imagining that his most wise Providence should pay attention to or regard the vain curiosity excited by some passion or disorder, or some human and reprehensible affection far removed from holy zeal and love.

528. Take notice of the cautiousness with which I proceeded in my duties; since, as regards finding grace in the eyes of the Lord, a vast difference always remains between the efforts of other creatures and my own. Nevertheless, though I held in my arms God himself as his true Mother, I never presumed to ask Him to explain to me anything whatever by extraordinary revelation, neither for the sake of knowing it or for the sake of ridding myself of suffering, nor for any other merely human reason; for all this would have been human weakness, vain and vicious curiosity, which could find no room in me. Whenever necessity urged it upon me for the glory of his Majesty, or some circumstances made it unavoidable, I asked permission to propose my wishes. Although I always found Him most propitious, ready to answer me with kindness and mercifully urging me to declare my wishes, I nevertheless humiliated myself to the dust and merely asked Him to inform me of what was most pleasing and acceptable in his eyes.

529. Write this doctrine in thy heart, my daughter, and guard thyself against the disorderly and curious desire of searching into or knowing anything above the powers of the human intellect. For besides the fact that the Lord makes no response to such foolish inquiry, because it displeases Him very much, remember that the demon is the real author of this fault in those who are in pursuit of a spiritual life. As he is ordinarily the author of such blameworthy inquiries, astutely promoting them in the soul, he also satisfies its curiosity by answering them himself at the same time assuming the appearance of an angel of light and thus deceiving the imperfect and the unwary (II Cor. 12, 14). When such inquisitiveness arises from one's own natural inclination, one must be equally careful not to follow or attend to it. For in what concerns such high matters as familiar intercourse with the Lord, one's own reason and judgment is not a safe guide, it being hampered by evil inclinations and passions. Our depraved and infected nature has been thrown into great disorder by sin, and is subject to much confusion and excess, making it unfit for guidance and direction in the high things of God. Equally wrong is it for the soul to rely on divine revelations in order to free itself from suffering and labor; for the spouses of Christ and his true servants must not seek his favors for the purpose of avoiding the cross, but in order to seek and bear it with the Lord (Matth. 16, 24), patiently enduring the sufferings which his divine Providence chooses to send. This course of action I desire thee to maintain in humble fear, and rather to go to extremes in this regard so as to avoid so much the more securely the opposite fault. From now on I wish that thou perfect all thy motives and thy undertakings by divine love (Phil. 1, 9), as being the great end of all thy undertakings. In this thou needst not observe degree or measure; on the contrary I wish thee to create in thee an excess of love, accompanied by so much of holy fear

as will suffice to keep thee from transgressing the law of the Most High, and to perform all thy exterior and interior acts in rectitude. Be careful and diligent therein, even if it cost thee much exertion and pain; for I have endured the same in the Circumcision of my most holy Son, and for no other reason than because in his holy law this was manifested and intimated to me as the will of the Lord, whom we must in all things fully obey.

Chapter XIV

THE DIVINE INFANT IS CIRCUMCISED AND RECEIVES HIS
NAME JESUS.

530. Like other towns of Israel, the city of Bethlehem had its
own synagogue, where the people came together to pray
(wherefore it was also called the house of prayer), and to hear
the law of Moses. This was read and explained by a priest
from the pulpit in a loud voice, in order that the people
might understand its precepts. But in these synagogues no
sacrifices were offered; this was reserved for the temple of
Jerusalem, except when the Lord commanded otherwise. It
was not left to the choice of the people, in order to avoid the
danger of idolatry, as is mentioned in Deuteronomy (12, 6).
But the priest, who was the teacher or minister of the law in
those places, was usually also charged with administering the
circumcision; not that this was a binding law, for not only
priests but anyone could perform the circumcision; but
because the pious mothers firmly believed that the infants
would run less danger in being circumcised by the hands of a
priest. Our great Queen, not on account of any apprehension
of danger, but because of the dignity of the Child, also
wished a priest to administer this rite to Him; and therefore
She sent her most fortunate spouse to Bethlehem to call the
priest of that town.

531. The priest came to the gates or cave of the Nativity, where the incarnate Word, resting in the arms of his Virgin Mother, awaited him. With the priest came also two other officials, who were to render such assistance as was customary at the performance of the rite. The rudeness of the dwelling at first astonished and somewhat disconcerted the priest. But the most prudent Queen spoke to him and welcomed him with such modesty and grace that his constraint soon changed into devotion and into admiration at the composure and noblest majesty of the Mother; and without knowing the cause he was moved to reverence and esteem for such an unusual personage. When the priest looked upon the face of Mary and of the Child in her arms he was filled with great devotion and tenderness, wondering at the contrast exhibited amid such poverty and in a place so lowly and despised. And when he proceeded to touch the divine flesh of the Infant, he was renovated by a secret influence which sanctified and perfected him; it gave him a new existence in grace, and raised him up to a state of holiness very pleasing to the most high Lord.

532. In order to show as much exterior reverence for the sacred rite of circumcision as was possible in that place, saint Joseph lighted two wax candles. The priest requested the Virgin Mother to consign the Child to the arms of the two assistants and withdraw for a little while in order not to be obliged to witness the sacrifice. This command caused some hesitation in the great Lady; for her humility and spirit of obedience inclined Her to obey the priest, while on the other hand She was withheld by the love and reverence for her Onlybegotten. In order not to fail against either of these virtues, She humbly requested to be allowed to remain, saying that She desired to be present at the performance of this rite, since She held it in great esteem, and that She would have courage to hold her Son in her arms, as She

wished not to leave Him alone on such an occasion. All that She would ask would be that the circumcision be performed with as much tenderness as possible on account of the delicacy of the Child. The priest promised to fulfill her request, and permitted the Child to be held in the arms of his Mother for fulfilling the mystery. Thus She became the sacred altar on which the truths typified in the ancient sacrifice became a reality (Heb. 9, 6) ; and She herself offered up this new morning's sacrifice on her own arms in order that it might be acceptable to the eternal Father in all particulars.

533. The divine Mother then unwound the swaddling clothes in which her most holy Son was wrapped and drew from her bosom a towel or linen cloth, which She had previously placed there for the purpose of warming it; for the weather was very cold on that day. While holding the Child in her hands She so placed this towel that the relics and the blood of the Circumcision would fall upon it. The priest thereupon proceeded to his duty and circumcised the Child, the true God and man. At the same time the Son of God, with immeasurable love, offered up to the eternal Father three sacrifices of so great value that each one would have been sufficient for the Redemption of a thousand worlds. The first was that He, being innocent and the Son of the true God, assumed the condition of a sinner (Phil. 2, 7) by subjecting Himself to a rite instituted as a remedy for original sin, and to a law not binding on Him (II Cor. 5, 21). The second was his willingness to suffer the pains of circumcision, which He felt as a true and perfect man. The third was the most ardent love with which He began to shed his blood for the human race, giving thanks to the eternal Father for having given Him a human nature capable of suffering for his exaltation and glory.

534. This prayerful sacrifice of JESUS our Savior the Father accepted, and, according to our way of speaking, He

began to declare Himself satisfied and paid for the indebtedness of humanity. The incarnate Word offered these first fruits of his blood as pledges that He would give it all in order to consummate the Redemption and extinguish the debt of the sons of Adam. All these interior acts and movements of the Onlybegotten his most holy Mother perceived, and in her heavenly wisdom She penetrated the mystery of this sacrament, acting as his Mother and in concert with Her Son and Lord in all that He was doing and suffering. True to his human nature, the divine Infant shed tears as other children. Although the pains caused by the wounding were most severe, as well on account of the delicacy of his body as on account of the coarseness of the knife, which was made of flint, yet his tears were caused not so much by the sensible pain as by the supernatural sorrow caused by his knowledge of the hard-heartedness of mortals. For this was more rude and unyielding than the flint, resisting his sweetest love and the divine fire He had come to enkindle in the world and in the hearts of the faithful (Luke 12,49). Also the tender and affectionate Mother wept, like the guileless sheep, which raises its voice in unison with the innocent lamb. In reciprocal love and compassion the Child clung to his Mother, while She sweetly caressed Him at her virginal breast and caught the sacred relics and the falling blood in the towel. These She entrusted to saint Joseph, in order to tend to the divine Infant and wrap Him once more in the swaddling-clothes. The priest was somewhat surprised at the tears of the Mother; yet, not understanding the mystery, he conjectured that the beauty of the Child might well cause such deep and loving sorrow in Her who had given Him birth.

535. In all these proceedings the Queen of heaven was so prudent, circumspect and magnanimous, that She caused admiration in the angelic choirs and highest delight to her Creator. She gave forth the effulgence of the divine wisdom,

which filled Her, performing each of her actions as perfectly as if She had that alone to perform. She was unyielding in her desire of holding the Child in her arms during the Circumcision, most careful in preserving the relics, most compassionate in her affliction and tears, feeling Herself his pains, most loving in her caresses, most diligent in procuring his comfort, fervent in imitating Him in his works, always careful to treat Him with the highest reverence, without ever failing or intermitting her acts of virtue, and without ever letting the perfection of one disturb that of the other. Wonderful spectacle exhibited by a Maiden of fifteen years, and affording even the angels a sort of new lesson and cause of admiration! In the meanwhile the priest asked the parents what name they wished to give to the Child in Circumcision; the great Lady, always attentive to honor her spouse, asked saint Joseph to mention the name. Saint Joseph turned toward Her in like reverence and gave Her to understand that He thought it proper this sweet name should first flow from her mouth. Therefore, by divine interference, both Mary and Joseph said at the same time: "JESUS is his name." The priest answered: "The parents are unanimously agreed, and great is the name which they give to the Child"; and thereupon he inscribed it in the tablet or register of names of the rest of the children. While writing it the priest felt great interior movements, so that he shed copious tears; and wondering at what he felt yet not being able to account for, he said: "I am convinced that this Child is to be a great Prophet of the Lord. Have great care in raising Him, and tell me in what I can relieve your needs." Most holy Mary and Joseph answered the priest with humble gratitude and dismissed him after offering him the gift of some candles and other articles.

536. Being again left alone with the Child, most holy Mary and Joseph celebrated anew the mystery of the Cir-

cumcision, commenting on the holy name of JESUS amid
sweet canticles and tears of joy, the fuller knowledge of which
(as also of other mysteries which I have mentioned) is reserved as an additional accidental glory to the saints in heav-
en. The most prudent Mother applied to the wound caused
by the knife such medicines as were wont to be used on such
occasions for other children, and during the time while the
pain and the healing lasted She would not for a moment part
with Him, holding Him in her arms day and night. The
tender love of the heavenly Mother is beyond all comprehension or understanding of man; for her natural love was
greater than any other mother was capable of, and her supernatural love exceeded that of all the angels and saints together. Her reverence and worship cannot be compared with that
of any other created being. These were the delights of the
incarnate Word (Prov. 8, 31), which He desired and longed
for among the children of men; and this was the recompense,
which his loving heart drew from the exceeding sanctity of
the Virgin Mother for the sorrows occasioned Him by their
behavior. Although He pleased Himself in Her alone above
all the mortals and in Her found full satisfaction of his love,
yet the humble Queen sought to alleviate his bodily pains by
all the means within her power. Therefore She besought the
holy angels to assist Her and produce sweet harmony for
their incarnate God, and her suffering Child. The ministers
of the Most High obeyed their Queen and Lady and in
audible voices they rehearsed the canticles which She herself
had composed with her spouse in praise of the new and sweet
name of JESUS.

537. With this music, so sweet that in comparison to it all
human music seemed but irksome discord, the heavenly Lady
entertained her most holy Son; and sweeter yet was the
harmony of her heroic virtues, which in her soul formed
"choirs as of serried armies," as the Lord and Spouse himself

says in the Canticles. Hard are human hearts, and more than slow and dull in recognizing and thankfully acknowledging such venerable sacraments, instituted for their eternal salvation by the immense love of the Creator and Redeemer. O sweetest Good of my soul and of my life! What wicked return do we make for the exquisite artifices of thy eternal love! O measureless charity, which is not extinguished by the overwhelming waters of our gross and faithless ingratitude! Truly the essential Bounty and Holiness could not go to a greater length of condescension for love of us, nor exercise more exquisite love than to assume the form of a sinner (Phil. 2, 7), drawing upon his own innocence the punishment of the sin, which otherwise could never approach Him. If men despise such an example and forget such a benefit, how can they be said to retain the use of their reason? How can they presume upon and glory in their wisdom, prudence or judgment? It would be prudence, ungrateful man, if thou wouldst afflict thyself and weep over thy notorious dullness and darkness of mind in not being moved by such great works of thy God; since not even the divine love can melt the iciness of thy heart.

538. My daughter, I wish thee to consider attentively the blessed favor conferred upon thee by being informed of the solicitous care and attention which I lavished upon my most holy and sweetest Son in the mysteries just now described. The Most High does not give thee this special light in order only to be regaled by the knowledge of these mysteries; but in order to imitate me in all these things as a faithful handmaid and in order to distinguish thyself in rendering thanks for his works in the same measure as thou art distinguished in knowing them more fully. Ponder, then, dearest, upon the small return given for the love of my Son and Lord by mortals, and how forgetful of thanks even his faithful continue to be. Assume it as thy task, as far as thy weak powers allow, to

render satisfaction for this grievous offense: loving Him, thanking Him and serving Him with all thy powers, for all the other men who fail to do so. Therefore thou must be an angel in promptitude, most fervent and punctual on all occasions; thou must die to all earthly things, eliminating and crushing all human inclinations and rising upon the wings of love to the heights of love designed for thee by the Lord.

539. Thou art not ignorant of the sweet efficacy contained in the memory of the works performed by my most holy Son: and although thou canst so copiously avail thyself of the light given thee to be thankful: yet, in order that thou mayest fear so much the more the danger of forgetfulness, I particularly inform thee that the saints in heaven, comprehending by the divine light these mysteries, are astonished at themselves for not having paid more attention to them during their life. And if they were capable of pain, they would be deeply grieved for their tardiness and carelessness in not having set proper value upon the works for the Redemption, and for failing in the imitation of Christ. All the angels and saints, by an insight hidden to mortals, wonder at the cruelty of human hearts against themselves and against Christ their Redeemer. Men have compassion neither for the sufferings of the lord, nor for the sufferings they themselves stand in danger of incurring. When the foreknown, in unending bitterness shall recognize their dreadful forgetfulness and their indifference to the works of Christ their Savior, their confusion and despair will be an intolerable punishment, and it alone will be a chastisement beyond all imagination; for they will then see the copiousness of the Redemption, which they have despised (Ps. 44, 11). Hear me, my daughter, and bend thy ears to these counsels and doctrines of eternal life. Cast out from thy faculties every image and affection toward human creatures and turn all the powers of thy heart and

soul toward the mysteries and blessings of the Redemption. Occupy thyself wholly with them, ponder and weigh them, give thanks for them as if thou alone wert in existence, as if they had been wrought solely for thee, and singly for each human being in particular (Gal. 2, 20). Thus thou wilt find life and the way of life, proceeding thus thou canst not err; but thou shalt find therein the light of thy eyes and true peace.

Chapter XV

THE MOST HOLY MARY REMAINS IN THE PORTAL OF THE NATIVITY UNTIL THE COMING OF THE MAGI KINGS.

540. By the infused knowledge of holy Scriptures and her high supernatural enlightenment, our great Queen knew that the Magi Kings of the Orient would come to acknowledge and adore her most holy Son as their true God. She was aware of it also more particularly because an angel had been sent to them to announce the birth of the incarnate Word, as mentioned in chapter second (No. 492), and the Virgin Mother was not ignorant of this message. Saint Joseph had no foreknowledge of these mysteries; because they had not been revealed to him, nor had his most prudent Spouse informed him of this secret. In all things She was most wise and discreet, awaiting the sweet and timely dispositions of the divine Providence (Wis. 8, 1). After the Circumcision, the holy spouse suggested to the Mistress of heaven that they leave their poor and forsaken habitation on account of the insufficient shelter which it afforded the divine Infant and to Her; for it would now be possible to find a lodging in Bethlehem, where they could remain until after presenting the Child in the temple of Jerusalem. This proposal of the most faithful spouse arose from his solicitude and anxiety lest the Child and the Mother should want even that comfort and

convenience which it was possible for their poverty to procure; but he left it all to the disposition of his heavenly
Spouse.

541. Without revealing the mystery, the humble Queen
answered: "My spouse and master, I resign myself to thy will,
and wherever thou wishest to go I will follow with great
pleasure: arrange it as thou pleasest," The heavenly Lady had
an affection for the cave on account of its humbleness and
poverty, and because the incarnate Word had consecrated it
by the mysteries of his Nativity and Circumcision, and was
to hallow it by the mystery of the Magi's visit, although She
did not know at what time that would happen. This was a
most pious affection, full of devotion and reverence; yet She
preferred to give an example of the highest perfection in all
things. She considered it more important to resign and
submit to saint Joseph, letting her spouse decide what was to
be done. While they were thus conferring with each other,
the Lord himself informed them through the two celestial
princes Michael and Gabriel, who were attending in corporeal forms to the service of their Lord and God and of their
great Queen. They spoke to Mary and Joseph, saying: "Divine Providence has ordained that three kings of the earth,
coming from the Orient in search of the King of heaven,
should adore the divine Word in this very place (Ps. 71, 6).
They are already ten days on the way; for at the hour of the
birth of Jesus they were informed of it, and they immediately
set out on their journey. Therefore they will shortly arrive,
fulfilling all that the Prophets had from very ancient times
foreknown and foretold."

542. By this announcement saint Joseph was instructed
on his part concerning the will of the Lord, and Mary his
most holy Spouse said to him: "My master, this place, chosen
by the Most High for such magnificent mysteries, although it
is poor and ill-furnished in the eyes of the world, in the sight

of eternal Wisdom is rich, precious, the most estimable and preferable on this earth, since the Lord of heaven is satisfied with it and has consecrated it by his presence. He who is the true land of promise can favor us with his vision in this place. And if it is his pleasure, He will afford us some protection and shelter against the inclemencies of the weather during the few days in which we are to stay here." Saint Joseph was much consoled and encouraged by these words of the most prudent Queen. He answered Her, that, since the divine Child was to fulfill the law, which required Him to be presented in the temple, just as He had subjected Himself to the law of Circumcision, they could remain in this sacred place until that day should arrive, without first undertaking the distant and wearisome journey to Nazareth during the inclement weather. If, perhaps, the severity of the season would compel them to seek shelter in the city, they could easily do so; since from Bethlehem to Jerusalem there was only a distance of two hours.

543. In all these matters the most holy Mary conformed Herself to the will of her watchful spouse; for She knew his solicitude for the sacred tabernacle which was confided to his care, and which was more holy and venerable than the Holy of Holies in the temple. Awaiting the time when her Only-begotten should be presented in the temple, She was unremitting in her care of Him, lest She forget anything necessary to protect Him against the cold and the roughness of the weather. She also prepared the cave for the arrival of the Kings, cleaning it once more and arranging it anew as far as the rudeness and destitution of the place allowed. But her greatest attention and care was always reserved for the Child itself, bearing It in her arms continually unless absolute necessity demanded otherwise. Besides all this She made use of her power as Queen of all creation whenever the rigors of winter rose to excess; for She commanded the frost and the

winds, the snow and the ice not to incommode their Creator, and to spend their elemental fury and asperity upon her person alone. The heavenly Queen gave her commands as follows: "Restrain your wrath before your Creator, Author, Lord and Preserver, who has called you into existence and given you strength and activity. Be mindful, creatures of my Beloved, that you are furnished with rigor on account of sin for the chastisement of the disobedience of the first Adam and his progeny. But with the second Adam, who comes to repair this fall and cannot have any part therein, you must be courteous, reverencing and not offending Him, to whom you owe worship and subjection. And therefore I command you in his name to cause no inconvenience or displeasure to Him."

544. It is worthy of our admiration and imitation to notice the ready obedience of the irrational creatures to the divine will, intimated to them by the Mother of God : for upon her command, the snow and rain approached no nearer than ten yards, the winds stopped short and the surrounding air retained a mild temperature. To this miracle was added another one: at the same time in which the divine Infant in her arms received this homage of the elements and was protected from their asperity, the Virgin Mother felt and suffered the cold and inclemency of the weather as if it were exerting all its natural influences in that place. In this they obeyed the loving Mother and sovereign Mistress of creatures to the letter, as She wished not to exempt Herself from their asperity while She prevented her tender Child and her God from suffering under it. Saint Joseph enjoyed the same privilege as the sweet Infant; he noticed the favorable change of the temperature, without knowing that it was due to the commands of his heavenly Spouse and an effect of her power; for She had not manifested to him this privilege, because She had no command to that effect from the Most High.

545. As to the order and manner in which the great Queen nourished her Child JESUS, it is to be remarked that She offered Him her virginal milk three times a day, and always with such reverence that She asked his permission beforehand and his pardon for the indignity, considering Herself and acknowledging Herself unworthy of such a privilege. Many times, while holding Him in her arms, She was on her knees adoring Him; and if at any time it was necessary to seat Herself She always asked his permission. With the same tokens of reverence She handed Him to saint Joseph and received Him from his arms, as I have said above. Many times She kissed his feet, and when She wished to kiss his face She interiorly asked his benevolent consent. The sweetest Child returned these caresses of his Mother not only by the expression of pleasure in his countenance, which was at the same time full of majesty, but also by other actions usual in children. In Him, however, they were accompanied by a serene deliberation. The most ordinary token of his love was to recline sweetly upon the breast of the most pure Mother, or upon her shoulder, encircling her neck with his divine arms. These caresses the Empress Mary met with so much attention and discretion that She neither petulantly sought them as other mothers, nor too timidly withdrew from them. In all these things She behaved most perfectly and prudently, without defect or excess of any kind: the more openly and affectionately her most holy Son manifested his love toward Her, so much the more deeply did She humiliate Herself, and so much the greater was her reverence; in the same manner She gaged also the tokens of her affection and lent new glory to her magnanimity.

546. There was an interchange of caresses of another kind between the Infant and his Mother: for besides understanding by divine enlightenment all the interior acts of the most holy soul of her Onlybegotten, as I have already stated (481,

534), it often happened that, holding Him in her arms, She was privileged to see through his humanity as through a crystal casement, thus perceiving the hypostatic union of the Son of God with his human nature, and witnessing the activity of his soul in interceding with the eternal Father for the human race. These operations and intercessions the heavenly Lady faithfully imitated, being entirely absorbed and transformed in her divine Son. His Majesty on his part looked upon Her with new accidental joy and delight, regaling Himself in the purity of this Creature, rejoicing that He had created Her, and that his becoming man had resulted in such a living image of his Divinity and humanity. In regard to this mystery the words of the soldiers of Holofernes when they beheld the beauty of Judith in the camp of Bethulia, occurred to me: "Who can despise the people of the Hebrews, who have such beautiful women? Shall we not think it worth our while for their sakes to fight against them?" This saying seemed to be mysteriously realized in the incarnate Word, since He, with greater cause, could address them to his eternal Father and to all the rest of the creatures:

"Who shall fail to see, that my coming from heaven and assuming flesh is fully justified, since by coming upon the earth and dethroning the demon, the world and the flesh, and by conquering and vanquishing them, such a Woman is called into existence as is my Mother among the children of Adam?" O sweetest love, essence of my virtue, life of my soul, most loving Jesus, behold and see that most holy Mary by Herself possesses such immense beauty as exceeds that of all the human race! She is the only and chosen One (Cant. 6, 8), so perfectly pleasing to Thee, my Lord and my God, that She not only equals but far surpasses all the rest of thy people; and that She alone compensates God for all the wickedness of the race of Adam.

547. So powerful were the effects of this delightful intercourse with her Son and true God, that She was more and more spiritualized and made Godlike. Many times in these flights of her soul the force of her burning love would have torn asunder the ligaments of her members and destroyed the union of her soul and body, if She had not been miraculously comforted and preserved. She spoke to her most holy Son secret words so exalted and full of weight that they cannot come within the range of our expression. All that I can reproduce can never be anything more than a mere shadow of that which was manifested to me. She said to Him: "0 my Love, sweet Life of my soul, who art Thou, and who am I? What dost Thou wish to make of me by thus becoming man of man, lowering thy greatness and magnificence in favor of such useless dust? O what shall thy slave do to pay the debt of love which she owes to Thee? What return shall I make for the great things which thou hast done to me (Ps. 115, 12)? My being, my life, my faculties, my feelings, my desires and longings, all is for Thee. Comfort thy servant and thy Mother, in order that She may not fail in thy service at the sight of her own insignificance, and in order that she may not die for love of Thee. O how limited is the power of man! How circumscribed his capacity! How insufficient is human affection, as it cannot sufficiently render a just return for thy love! But the victory of mercy and magnificence must always be thine, and to Thee belong the triumphal songs of love; while we must on the contrary always consider ourselves overcome and vanquished by thy power. Let us be humiliated and let us grovel in the dust, while thy greatness is magnified and exalted in all the eternities." The heavenly Lady, partaking of the science of her most holy Son, sometimes beheld the souls which in the course of the new law of grace were to distinguish themselves in divine love, the works which they were to perform, the martyrdom which they were to suffer in imita-

tion of the Lord; in this knowledge She became so inflamed with love that her longings of love caused in Her a greater martyrdom than those actually suffered by the saints. To her happened what the Spouse in the Canticles mentions (Cant. 8, 6), that the emulations of love are strong as death and hard as hell. To these agonies of the loving Mother, caused by the mortal wounds of divine affection, her most holy Son answered in the words there used: "Place Me as a sign or seal in thy heart and upon thy arm," causing in Her at the same time the full understanding of these words as well as their actual fulfillment. By this divine suffering most holy Mary was a Martyr above all other martyrs. Among such beds of lilies the meekest Lamb, Jesus, wandered, while the day of grace began to break and the shades of the ancient Law receded.

548. The divine Child ate nothing during the time in which He was nourished at the virginal breast of his most holy Mother, for this milk was his only sustenance. This was most sweet and substantial, since it originated in a body so pure, perfect and refined, and one built up in exquisite harmony without any disorder or inequality. No other body was equal to it in healthfulness; and the sacred milk, even if it would have been preserved a long time, would have remained free from corruption; by an especial privilege it never changed or soured, though the milk of other women immediately degenerates and becomes corrupt, as experience teaches.

549. The most fortunate Joseph not only witnessed the favors and caresses which passed between the Child and its Mother; but he himself shared in others, which Jesus deigned to confer upon him. Many times his heavenly Spouse placed him in his arms. This happened whenever She had to do some work during which She could not hold Him herself; as for instance, when She prepared the meals, or arranged the

clothes of the Infant or cleaned the house. On these occasions saint Joseph held Him in his arms and he always felt
divine effects in his soul. The Child Jesus showed exterior
signs of affection by his pleased looks, by reclining upon his
breast, and by other tokens of affection usual with children in
regard to their fathers, but in Him these tokens were always
tempered with kingly majesty. Yet all this was not so frequent
in his dealings with saint Joseph, nor with such endearment,
as with his true Virgin Mother. Whenever She left Jesus in
his care, She received from saint Joseph the relic of the
Circumcision, which the latter ordinarily bore about with
him for his consolation. Thus both the two Spouses were
continually enriched: She by holding her most holy Son, he
by his sacred blood and deified flesh. They preserved it in a
crystal vase, which saint Joseph had purchased with the
money sent to them by saint Elisabeth. In this they had
enclosed the particle of flesh and the sacred blood shed at the
Circumcision, which had been caught up in pieces of linen.
The opening of the vase was encased in silver, which the
mighty Queen, in order to preserve the sacred relics more
securely, had sealed by her mere command. Thus the silver
opening was more firmly sealed than if it had been soldered
by the artisan, who had made the vessel. In this vase the
prudent Mother treasured the relics during her whole life and
afterwards She entrusted it to the Apostles, leaving it as an
inheritance to the holy Church. In this immense sea of
mysteries I find myself so annihilated and dumbfounded by
my ignorance as a woman, and so narrowed in my powers of
expression, that I must leave much of it to be fathomed by
the faith and piety of the Christians.

Words of the Queen

THE VIRGIN MARY SPEAKS TO SISTER MARY OF AGREDA

550. My daughter, in the foregoing chapter, thou hast been instructed not to seek information from the Lord by supernatural means, neither in order to relieve any suffering, nor in order to satisfy a natural hankering of curiosity. Now I exhort thee likewise not to yield, for any of these reasons, to the desire of performing any exterior action according to the promptings of nature. For in all the activity of thy exterior faculties and senses thou must seek to moderate and subject thy inclinations, not yielding to them in their demands, although they may have the color of virtue or piety. I was in no danger of going to excess in these affections on account of my sinlessness; nor was there a want of piety in my desire of remaining in the cave, where my most holy Son had been born and had been circumcised. Yet I did not wish to express my desire, even when asked about it by my spouse; for I preferred obedience to this pious inclination, and I knew that it is more secure for the souls and more according to the pleasure of the Lord to seek his will in the counsel and decision coming from other, rather than in their own inclination. In me this course of action was advisable only on account of the greater perfection contained therein, but in thee and in other souls, who are subject to error in their judgment, this rule must be observed most rigorously, so as to prevent and avoid mistakes diligently and discreetly. For in their ignorance and pusillanimity men are easily carried away by their feelings and inclinations toward insignificant things, and very often they occupy themselves with trifles as if they were important matters, and with vanities, as if they were realities. All such activity weakens the soul and deprives it of great spiritual blessings, of grace, enlightenment and merit.

551. This doctrine shalt thou write in thy heart together with all the others which I am to give thee. Seek to use it as a reminder of all that I did, so that as thou hast come to know it thou mayest also understand and execute it in thy life. Take notice of the reverence, love and solicitude, the holy and discreet fear, with which I conversed with my most holy Son. I always lived in this kind of watchfulness; and even after I had conceived Him in my womb, I never lost it out of sight, nor did the great love which He showed me diminish it in me. In this ardent desire to please Him my heart found no rest until it was entirely united and absorbed in the enjoyment of this my highest Good and ultimate End. Excepting at certain times, during which I rested in his love as in my sole joy, I invariably carried about with me this continual solicitude, like one who restlessly pursues his way, and who permits himself not to be delayed by anything that is useless or hinders the attainment of his desired object. So far was my heart from attaching itself to any earthly thing, or from following the inclination of the senses, that I lived as if I had not been composed of earthly substance. If other creatures are not free from passions, or do not overcome them as much as possible, let them not blame nature, but their own will: on the contrary, they justly incur the reproaches of weak nature; because, instead of governing and directing nature by the sovereign power of the will, they make no use of that power. They allow the natural inclinations to involve them in disorders, abetting it by the free will and using their understanding to find still more dangerous occupations and occasions of ruin. On account of these pitfalls presenting themselves in mortal life, I warn thee, my dearest, not to hanker after or seek any of the visible things, although they may appear to thee necessary and most appropriate for the circumstances. Use all things, thy cell, thy garments, thy sustenance, and whatever else of this life, only in obedience and with the full

consent of thy superiors; because the Lord requires this of thee; and it is also my pleasure to see thee apply all things for the service of the Omnipotent. According to these great rules which I have given thee thou must regulate all thy activity.

Chapter XVI

THE THREE KINGS OF' THE ORIENT COME TO ADORE THE
WORD MADE MAN IN BETHLEHEM.

552. The three Magi Kings, who came to find the divine
Infant after his birth, were natives of Persia, Arabia and
Sabba (Ps. 71, 10), countries to the east of Palestine. Their
coming was prophesied especially by David, and before him,
by Balaam, who, having been hired by Balaac, king of the
Moabites, to curse the Israelites, blessed them instead
(Numb. 24, 17). In this blessing Balaam said, that he would
see the King Christ, although not at once, and that he would
behold Him, although not be present; for he did not see Him
with his own eyes, but through the Magi, his descendants
many centuries after. He said, also, that a star would arise
unto Jacob, which was Christ, who arose to reign forever in
the house of Jacob (Luke 1, 32).

553. These three Kings were well versed in the natural
sciences, and well read in the Scriptures of the people of
God; and on account of their learning they were called Magi.
By their knowledge of Scripture, and by conferring with
some of the Jews, they were imbued with a belief in the
coming of the Messias expected by that people. They were,
moreover, upright men, truthful and very just in the government of their countries. Since their dominions were not

so extended as those of our times, they governed them easily, and personally administered justice as wise and prudent sovereigns. This is the true office of kings, and therefore the Holy Ghost says, that He holds their hearts in his hands in order to direct them like irrigated waters to the fulfillment of his holy will (Prov, 21, 1). They were also of noble and magnanimous disposition, free from avarice and covetousness, which so oppresses, degrades and belittles the spirits of princes. Because these Magi governed adjoining countries and lived not far from each other, they were mutual friends and shared with each other the virtues and the knowledge which they had acquired, consulting each other in the more important events of their reigns. In all things they communicated with each other as most faithful friends.

554. I have already mentioned in the eleventh chapter (No. 492) that in the same night in which the incarnate Word was born, they were informed of his Birth by the ministry of the holy angels. It happened in the following manner: one of the guardian angels of our Queen, of a higher order than that of the guardian angels of the three kings, was sent from the cave of the Nativity. By his superior faculties he enlightened the three guardian angels of the Kings informing them at the same time of the will and command of the Lord, that each of them should manifest to his charge the mystery of the Incarnation and of the birth of Christ our Redeemer. Immediately and in the same hour each of the three angels spoke in dreams to the wise man under his care. This is the usual course of angelic revelations when the Lord communicates with souls through the angels. This enlightenment of the Kings concerning the mysteries of the Incarnation was very copious and clear. They were informed that the King of the Jews was born as true God and man; that He was the Messias and Savior who was expected; that it was the One who was promised in the Scriptures and prophecies

(Gen. 3, 10); and that they themselves, the three Kings, were singled out by the Lord to seek the star, which Balaam had foretold. Each one of the three Kings also was made aware that the same revelation was being made to the other two in the same way; and that it was not a favor or miracle which should remain unused, but that they were expected to co-operate with the divine light and execute what it pointed out. They were inspired and inflamed with a great love and with a desire to know the God made man, to adore Him as their Creator and Redeemer, and serve Him with most perfect devotion. In all this they were greatly assisted by their distinguished moral virtues, which they had acquired; for on account of them they were excellently disposed for the operation of the divine enlightenment.

555. After receiving these heavenly revelations in their sleep, the three Kings awoke at the same hour of the night, and prostrating themselves on the ground and humiliating themselves to the dust, they adored in spirit the immutable being of God. They exalted his infinite mercy and goodness for having sent the divine Word to assume flesh of a Virgin (Is. 7, 14) in order to redeem the world and give eternal salvation to men. Then all three of them, governed by an impulse of the same Spirit, resolved to depart without delay for Judea in search of the divine Child in order to adore Him. The three Kings prepared gifts of gold, incense and myrrh in equal quantities, being guided by the same mysterious impulse; and without having conferred with each other concerning their undertaking, the three of them arrived at the same resolve and the same plan of executing it. In order to set out immediately, they procured on the same day the necessary camels and provisions together with a number of servants for the journey. Without heeding the commotion caused among their people, or considering that they were to travel in foreign regions, or caring for any outward show of

authority, without ascertaining particulars of the place whither they were to go, or gathering information for identifying the Child, they at once resolved with fervent zeal and ardent love to depart in order to seek the newborn King.

556. At the same time the holy angel, who had brought the news from Bethlehem to the kings, formed of the material air a most resplendent star, although not so large as those of the firmament; for it was not to ascend higher than was necessary for the purpose of its formation. It took its course through the atmospheric regions in order to guide and direct the holy Kings to the cave, where the Child awaited them. Its splendor was of a different kind from that of the sun and the other stars; with its most beautiful light it illumined the night like a brilliant torch, and it mingled its own most active brilliancy with that of the sun by day. On coming out of their palaces each one of the kings saw this new star (Matth. 2, 2) although each from a different standpoint, because it was only one star and it was placed in such distance and height that it could be seen by each one at the same time. As the three of them followed the guidance of this miraculous star, they soon met. Thereupon it immediately approached them much more closely, descending through many shifts of the aerial space and rejoicing them by shedding its refulgence over them at closer range. They began to confer among themselves about the revelation they had received and about their plans, finding that they were identical. They were more and more inflamed with devotion and with the pious desire of adoring the newborn God, and broke out in praise and admiration at the inscrutable works and mysteries of the Almighty.

557. The Magi pursued their journey under the guidance of the star without losing sight of it until they arrived at Jerusalem. As well on this account as also because this city was the capital and metropolis of the Jews, they suspected

that this was the birthplace of their legitimate and true King. They entered into the city and openly inquired after Him, saying (Matth. 2, 8) :

Where is the king of the Jews, who is born? For we have seen his star in the East, announcing to us his Birth and we have come to see Him and adore Him. Their inquiry came to the ears of Herod, who at that time unjustly reigned in Judea and lived in Jerusalem. The wicked king, panic-stricken at the thought that a more legitimate claimant to the throne should have been born, felt much disturbed and outraged by this report. With him the whole city was aroused, some of the people, out of flattery to the king, others on account of the fear of disturbance. Immediately, as saint Matthew relates, Herod called together a meeting of the principal priests and scribes in order to ask them where Christ was to be born according to the prophecies and holy Scriptures. They answered that, according to the words Of one of the Prophets, Micheas (Mich. 5, 2), He was to be born in Bethlehem; since it was written by him that thence the Ruler of Israel was to arise.

558. Thus informed of the birthplace of the new King of Israel, and insidiously plotting from that very moment to destroy Him, Herod dismissed the priests. Then he secretly called the Magi in order to learn of them at what time they had seen the star as harbinger of his Birth (Matth. 2, 7). They ingenuously informed him, and he sent them away to Bethlehem, saying to them in covert malice: "Go and inquire after the Infant, and when you have found Him, announce it to me, in order that I, too, may go to recognize and adore Him." The Magi departed, leaving the hypocritical king ill at ease and in great consternation at such indisputable signs of the coming of the legitimate King of Israel into the world. Although he could have eased his mind in regard to his sovereignty by the thought that a recently born infant could

not be enthroned so very soon, yet human prosperity is so unstable and deceitful that it can be overthrown even by an infant, or by the mere threat of faroff danger. Thus can even an imagined uncertainty destroy all the enjoyment and happiness so deceitfully offered to its possessors.

559. On leaving Jerusalem the Magi again found the star, which at their entrance they had lost from view. By its light they were conducted to Bethlehem and to the cave of the Nativity. Diminishing in size it hovered over the head of the infant Jesus and bathed Him in its light; whereupon the matter of which it had been composed dissolved and disappeared. Our great Queen had already been prepared by the Lord for the coming of the Kings, and when She understood that they were approaching the cave, She requested saint Joseph not to leave it, but to stay at her side. This he did, although the sacred text does not mention it. Like many other things passed over in the Gospels, this was not necessary for establishing the truth of the mystery. Nevertheless it is certain that saint Joseph was present when the Kings adored the infant Jesus. The precaution of sending him away was not necessary; for the Magi had already been instructed that the Mother of the Newborn was a Virgin, and that He was the true God and not a son of saint Joseph. Nor would God have permitted them to be led to the cave ignorant of such an important circumstance as his origin, allowing them to adore the Child as the son of Joseph and of a Mother not a Virgin. They were fully instructed as to all these things, and they were deeply impressed by the sacramental character of all these exalted and complicated mysteries.

560. The heavenly Mother awaited the pious and devout kings, standing with the Child in her arms. Amid the humble and poor surroundings of the cave, in incomparable modesty and beauty, she exhibited at the same time a majesty more than human, the light-of heaven shining in her countenance.

Still more visible was this light in the Child, shedding through the cavern effulgent splendor, which made it like a heaven. The three kings of the East entered and at the first sight of the Son and Mother they were for a considerable space of time overwhelmed with wonder. They prostrated themselves upon the earth, and in this position they worshiped and adored the Infant, acknowledging Him as the true God and man, and as the Savior of the human race. By the divine power, which the sight of Him and his presence exerted in their souls, they were filled with new enlightenment. They perceived the multitude of angelic spirits, who as servants and ministers of the King of kings and Lord of lords attended upon Him in reverential fear (Heb. 1, 4). Arising, they congratulated their and our Queen as Mother of the Son of the eternal Father; and they approached to reverence Her on their knees. They sought her hand in order to kiss it, as they were accustomed to do to their queens in their countries. But the most prudent Lady withdrew her hand, and offered instead that of the Redeemer of the world, saying: "My spirit rejoices in the Lord and my soul blesses and extols Him; because among all the nations He has called and selected you to look upon and behold that which many kings and prophets have in vain desired to see, namely, Him who is the eternal Word incarnate (Luke 10, 24). Let us extol and praise his name on account of the sacraments and mysteries wrought among his people; let us kiss the earth which He sanctifies by his real presence."

561. At these words of most holy Mary the three kings humiliated themselves anew, adoring the infant Jesus; they acknowledged the great blessings of living in the time when the Sun of justice was arising in order to illumine the darkness (Malachy 4, 2). Thereupon they spoke to saint Joseph, congratulating him and extolling his good fortune in being chosen as the spouse of the Mother of God; and they ex-

pressed wonder and compassion at the great poverty, beneath which were hidden the greatest mysteries of heaven and earth. In this intercourse they consumed three hours, and then the kings asked permission of most holy Mary to go to the city in order to seek a lodging, as they could find no room for themselves in the cave. Some people had accompanied them; but the Magi alone participated in the light and the grace of this visit. The others took notice merely of what passed exteriorly, and witnessed only the destitute and neglected condition of the Mother and her husband. Though wondering at the strange event, they perceived nothing of its mystery. The Magi took leave and departed, while most holy Mary and Joseph, being again alone with their Child, glorified his Majesty with new songs of praise, because his name was beginning to be known and adored among the Gentiles (Ps. 85, 9). What else the three wise men did will be related in the following chapter.

Words of the Queen

THE VIRGIN MARY SPEAKS TO SISTER MARY OF AGREDA

562. My daughter, the events recorded in this chapter contain much for the instruction of kings and princes and for the other faithful; as for instance, the prompt obedience and humility of the Magi, which men should imitate, and the obdurate wickedness of Herod, which they are to fear and abhor; for each reaped the fruit of his actions. The kings reaped the fruit of justice and other virtues, which they practiced; while Herod reaped those of ambition and pride by which he had usurped the government, and of other vices into which he cast himself without restriction or moderation. But let this remark, together with the other teachings of the holy church, suffice for those that live in the world. To thyself must thou apply the doctrine contained in what thou

hast written; always remembering that all the perfection of a Christian life must be founded upon the Catholic truths, and in the constant and firm acknowledgment of them, as they are taught by holy faith. In order to impress them upon thy heart, thou must profit of all that thou readest or hearest of the divine Writings, and of what is contained in the other devout and instructive books concerning the virtues. Thy faith thou must accompany by the practice and abundance of all good works, hoping ever in the visitation and coming of the Most High (Tit. 2, 13).

563. By such a disposition thy soul will be prepared in the manner I require of thee. For I desire that the Almighty find in thee the sweet readiness to adopt whatever is manifested to thee, and to put in practice whatever may be enjoined without any human respect. I promise, that if thou follow my counsel as thou shouldst, I will be thy star and guide on the ways of the Lord, so that thou wilt quickly arrive at the vision and enjoyment of thy God and of thy highest good in Sion (Ps. 83,8). In this doctrine, and in what happened to the devout kings of the Orient, there is contained a most effective means for the salvation of souls; yet this is known to few and heeded by a still smaller number of men. It is this: that the inspirations and enlightenments are usually sent by God to creatures in a certain order. At first some are sent to incite the soul to practice some of the virtues; if the soul corresponds, the Most High sends other and greater ones in order to move the soul to greater perfection in virtue; and thus, profiting from previous graces, the soul is disposed for still others, receiving ever greater helps and securing an increase of the favors of the Lord according as it corresponds to them. Thou wilt therefore understand two things: first, how great a damage it is to neglect the exercise of any virtue and not to practice perfection according to the dictates of the divine inspirations; secondly, how often God would give great

assistance to the souls, if they would begin to correspond to the smaller ones; since He is as it were in expectation and hope that they will prepare for his greater ones (Apoc. 6, 20). For He wishes to deal with the soul according to his just judgments. But because they overlook this orderly manner of proceeding in his invitations, He suspends the flow of his divine gifts and He refuses to the souls, what was intended for them if they had not placed an obstacle, allowing them to fall from one abyss to the other (Ps. 41, 8).

564. The Magi and Herod pursued opposite courses: the Magi met the first inspirations and graces by the practice of the good works; thus they disposed themselves by many virtues for being called and drawn by divine revelation to the knowledge of the mysteries of the Incarnation, the birth of the divine Word and the Redemption of the human race; and through this to the happiness and perfection of the way of life. But Herod, on the other hand, by his hard-heartedness and neglect of the helps, which God offered him for the practice of virtue, was drawn into the abyss of his measureless pride and ambition. These vices hurled him into such vast precipices of cruelty as to be the first one among men to seek the life of the Redeemer of the world under the cloak of simulated devotion and piety. In giving vent to his furious rage, he took away the life of the innocent children and attempted by so foul a measure to advance his damned and perverse undertaking.

Chapter XVII

THE MAGI KINGS RETURN ONCE MORE TO SEE AND ADORE
THE INFANT JESUS: THEY OFFER THEIR GIFTS ON TAKING
LEAVE, AND RETURN BY A DIFFERENT ROUTS TO THEIR
HOMES.

565. From the grotto of the Nativity, into which the three
Kings had entered directly on their way to Jerusalem, they
betook themselves to a lodging inside of the town of Bethlehem. They retired to a room where, in an abundance of
affectionate tears and aspirations, they spent the greater part
of the night, speaking of what they had seen, of the feelings
and affections aroused in each, and of what each had noticed
for himself in the divine Child and his Mother. During this
conference they were more and more inflamed with divine
love, amazed at the majesty and divine effulgence of the
Infant Jesus; at the prudence; modesty and reserve of his
Mother; at the holiness of her spouse Joseph, and the poverty
of all three; at the humbleness of the place, where the Lord of
heaven and earth had wished to be born. The devout kings
felt a divine fire, which flamed up in their hearts, and, not
being able to restrain themselves, they broke out into exclamations of sweet affection and acts of great reverence and
love. "What is this that we feel?" they said. "What influence
of this great King is it that moves us to such desires and
affections? After this, how shall we converse with men? What

can we do, who have been instructed in such new, hidden and supernatural mysteries? O greatness of his Omnipotence unknown to men and concealed beneath so much poverty! O humility unimaginable for mortals! Would that all be drawn to it, in order that they may not be deprived of such happiness!"

566. During these divine colloquies the Magi remembered the dire destitution of Jesus, Mary and Joseph in their cave, and they resolved immediately to send them some gifts in order to show their affection and to satisfy their desire of serving them, since they could not do anything else for them. They sent through their servants many of the presents, which they had already set aside for them, and others which they could procure. Most holy Mary and Joseph received these gifts with humble acknowledgment and they made a return not of emptyworded thanks, as other men are apt to make, but many efficacious blessings for the spiritual consolation of the three Kings. These gifts enabled our great Queen to prepare for her ordinary guests, the poor, an abundant repast; for the needy ones were accustomed to receive alms from Her, and, attracted still more by her sweet words, were wont to come and visit Her. The Kings went to rest full of incomparable joy in the Lord; and in their sleep the angels advised them as to their journey homeward.

567. On the following day at dawn they returned to the cave of the Nativity in order to offer to the heavenly King the special gifts which they had provided. Arriving they prostrated themselves anew in profound humility; and opening their treasures, as Scripture relates, they offered Him gold, incense and myrrh (Matth. 2, 11). They consulted the heavenly Mother in regard to many mysteries and practices of faith, and concerning matters pertaining to their consciences and to the government of their countries; for they wished to return well instructed and capable of directing themselves to

holiness and perfection in their daily life. The great Lady heard them with exceeding pleasure and She conferred interiorly with the divine Infant concerning all that they had asked, in order to answer and properly to instruct these sons of the new Law. As a Teacher and an instrument of divine wisdom She answered all their questions, giving them such high precepts of sanctity that they could scarcely part from Her on account of the sweetness and attraction of her words. However, an angel of the Lord appeared to them, reminding them of the necessity and of the will of the Lord that they should return to their country. No wonder that her words should so deeply affect these Kings; for all her words were inspired by the holy Spirit and full of infused science regarding all that they had inquired and many other matters.

568. The heavenly Mother received the gifts of the Kings and in their name offered them to the Infant Jesus. His Majesty showed by signs of highest pleasure, that He accepted their gifts: they themselves became aware of the exalted and heavenly blessings with which He repaid them more than a hundredfold (Matth. 19, 29). According to the custom of their country they also offered to the heavenly Princess some gems of great value; but because these gifts had no mysterious signification and referred not to Jesus, She returned them to the Kings, reserving only the gifts of gold, incense and myrrh. In order to send them away more rejoiced, She gave them some of the clothes in which She had wrapped the infant God; for She neither had nor could have had any greater visible pledges of esteem with which to enrich them at their departure. The three Kings received these relics with such reverence and esteem that they encased them in gold and precious stones in order to keep them ever after. As a proof of their value these relics spread about such a copious fragrance that they revealed their presence a league in circumference. However, only those who believed in the

coming of God into the world were able to perceive it; while the incredulous perceived none of the fragrance emitted by the relics. In their own countries the Magi performed great miracles with these relics.

569. The holy Kings also offered their property and possession to the Mother of the sweetest Jesus, or, if She did not wish to accept of them and preferred to live in this place, where her most holy Son had been born, they would build Her a house, wherein She could live more comfortably. The most prudent Mother thanked them for their offers without accepting them. On taking leave of Her, the three Kings besought Her from their inmost hearts not to forget them, which She promised and fulfilled; in the same way they spoke to saint Joseph. With the blessing of Jesus, Mary and Joseph, they departed, so moved by tenderest affection that it seemed to them they had left their hearts all melted into sighs and tears in that place. They chose another way for their return journey, in order not to meet Herod in Jerusalem; for thus they had been instructed by the angel on the preceding night. On their departure from Bethlehem the same or a similar star appeared in order to guide them home, conducting them on their new route to the place where they had first met, whence each one separated to reach his own country.

570. For the rest of their lives these most fortunate Kings lived up to their divine vocation as true disciples of the Mistress of holiness, governing both their souls and the people of their states according to her teaching. By the example of their lives and the knowledge of the Messias, which they spread about, they converted a great number of souls to the belief in the true God and to the way of salvation. Finally, full of days and merits, they closed their careers in sanctity and justice, having been favored both in life and in death by the Mother of mercy. After dismissing the Kings, the heavenly Queen and saint Joseph spent their time in new

canticles of praise of the wonders of the Most High, conferring them with the sayings of the Scriptures and the prophecies of the Patriarchs, which they saw fulfilled one after another in the Infant Jesus. But the most prudent Mother, who profoundly penetrated into the deepest meaning of these high sacraments, remembered them all and treasured them up in her bosom (Luke 2, 19). The holy angels, who were witnesses of these holy mysteries, congratulated their Queen, that her most holy Son had been manifested and that his Majesty had been adored by men; and they sang to Him new canticles, magnifying his mercies wrought upon mankind.

Words of the Queen

THE VIRGIN MARY SPEAKS TO SISTER MARY OF AGREDA

571. My daughter, great were the gifts which the Kings offered to my most holy Son; but greater still was the affection with which they offered them and the mystery concealed beneath them. On account of all this they were most acceptable to his Majesty. I wish that thou also offer up similar gifts, thanking Him for having made thee poor in condition and profession. For I assure thee, my dearest, there is no more acceptable gift to the Most High than voluntary poverty. There are very few in the world in our days who use well the temporal riches and offer them to their God and Lord with the generosity and love of these holy Kings. The poor of the Lord, so numerous in our day, experience and give witness how cruel and avaricious human nature has become; since in their great necessities they are so little succored by the rich. This gross uncharitableness of men offends the holy angels and grieves the Holy Ghost, since they are bound to witness the nobility of the souls so degraded and abased in the service of vile greed of gold with all its evil powers (Eccles. 10, 20). As if all things had been created

for the individual use of the rich, they appropriate them to themselves and deprive the poor, their brothers springing from the same nature and flesh; and denying them even to God, who created and preserves all things, and who can give or take at will. It is most lamentable that while the rich might purchase eternal life with their possessions, they abuse them to draw upon themselves damnation as senseless and foolish creatures (Luke 16, 9).

572. This evil is common among the children of Adam; and therefore voluntary poverty is so excellent and safe a remedy. By it, making man willing to part joyfully with his possessions for the sake of the poor, a great sacrifice is offered to the Lord. Thou also canst make such an offering of the things necessary for sustenance, giving a part of it to the poor and desiring, if it were possible by thy labor and sweat, to help all of them. Thy ceaseless offer, however, must be love, which is the gold; continual prayer, which is the incense; and the patient acceptance of labors and true mortifications, which is the myrrh. All that thou dost for the Lord, thou should offer up to Him with fervent affection and promptitude, without negligence or fear; for negligent works, and those not enlivened by love, are not an acceptable sacrifice in the eyes of his Majesty. In order to make those incessant offerings, it is necessary that divine faith and light continually inflame thy heart, having before thy eyes the great object of thy praise and exaltation, and the stimulus of love, by which thou art bound to the right hand of the Most High. Thus shouldst thou continue incessantly in this sweet exercise of love, so proper to the spouses of his Majesty; for their name implies such a continual payment of the debt of love and affection.

Chapter XVIII

MOST HOLY MARY AND JOSEPH DISTRIBUTE THE GIFTS RECEIVED FROM THE MAGI; AND THEY REMAIN IN BETH-LEHEM UNTIL THEIR DEPARTURE FOR THE PRESENTATION OF THE INFANT JESUS IN THE TEMPLE.

573. After the departure of the three Kings and after the due celebration of the great mystery of the adoration of the Infant Jesus, there was really nothing to wait for in that poor yet sacred place, and they were free to leave it. The most prudent Mother then said to saint Joseph: "My master and spouse, the offerings which the Kings have made to our God and Child must not remain here idle; but they must be applied in the service of his Majesty and should be used according to his will and pleasure. I deserve nothing, even of temporal goods; dispose of all these gifts as belonging to my Son and to thee." The most faithful of husbands answered, with his accustomed humility and courtesy, that he would leave all to Her and would be pleased to see Her dispose of them. But her Majesty insisted anew and said:

"Since thou makest an excuse of humility, my master, do it then for love of the poor, who are waiting for their share; they have a right to the things which their heavenly Father has created for their sustenance." They therefore immediately concluded to divide the gifts into three parts: one destined for the temple of Jerusalem, namely the incense and myrrh, as well as part of the gold; another part as offering to the priest, who had circumcised the Child, in order that he might use it for himself and for the synagogue or oratory in Bethlehem, and the third part for distribution among the poor. This resolve they executed with generous and fervent affection.

574. The Almighty made use of a poor but honorable and pious woman to be the occasion of their leaving the cave. She had come a few times to visit our Queen; for the house in which She lived was built up against the wall of the city, not far from the cave. Some time later this devout woman, not being aware of what had happened, but having heard the rumor of the Kings' coming, held a conversation with most holy Mary and asked Her whether She had heard that some wise men, who were said to be kings, had come from far seeking the Messias? The heavenly Princess, aware of the good disposition of this woman, took occasion to instruct her and catechize her in the common belief, without revealing to her the hidden sacrament connected with Herself and the sweetest Child whom She held in her arms (Tob. 12, 7). In order to relieve her poverty She gave her some of the gold destined for the poor. Thereby the condition of this fortunate woman was much improved and she became attached with heart and soul to her Teacher and Benefactress. She invited the holy Family to live in her house; and as it was a poor one, it was so much the more accommodated to the Founders and Builders of holy poverty. The poor woman pleaded with great persistence, as she saw the great inconvenience to which the most holy Mary and Joseph with the Child were subject in the cave. The Queen did not refuse her offer and answered, that She would let her know of her decision. Mary and saint Joseph conferred with each other and they resolved to leave the cave and lodge in the house of this woman, awaiting there the time of the purification and

the presentation in the temple. They did it so much the more willingly as it afforded them a chance to remain near the cave of the Nativity; and also because many people began to frequent the cave on account of the rumor of the visit of the Kings, which had been spread about.

575. On account of these and other considerations most holy Mary, with saint Joseph and the sacred Child took leave of the cave although with tenderest regret. They accepted the hospitality of that fortunate woman, who received them with the greatest charity and assigned to them the larger portion of her dwelling. The holy angels and ministers of the Most High accompanied them in human forms, which they had always retained. Whenever the heavenly Mother and saint Joseph her spouse piously revisited the memorable spots of this sanctuary, they came and went with them as numerous courtiers delegated to their service. Moreover, when the Child and his Mother took leave of the cave, God appointed an angel as its keeper and watcher, as He had done with the garden of Paradise (Gen. 3, 24). And this guard remained and does remain to this day sword in hand at the opening of the cave; and never since then has an animal entered there. That this holy angel does not hinder the entrance of hostile infidels, in whose possession this and the other holy places are, is because of the judgments of the Most High, who allows men to execute the designs of his wisdom and justice. This permission would not be necessary, if Christian princes were filled with fervent zeal for the honor and glory of Christ and would seek the restoration of these holy places, conse-crated by the blood and the labors of the Lord and of his most holy Mother, and by the works of our Redemption. And even if this would not be possible, there is no excuse for not attending with faithful diligence to the decent keeping of the mysterious places; since nothing is impossible to the believer, who can overcome the mountains (Matth. 17, 19). I

was given to understand, that the pious devotion and veneration for the Holy Land is one of the most powerful and
efficacious means for establishing and confirming Catholic
monarchies; and no one can deny, that many of their excessive and unnecessary expenses could be avoided by employ-
ing their resources in such a pious enterprise, which would be
pleasing both to God and to men; for in making such an
honest use of their incomes there is no need of outward
justification.

576. The most pure Mary and her spouse, having with
her divine Child moved to the dwelling in the vicinity of the
cave, remained there until, according to the requirements of
the law, She was to be present Herself with her First-born for
purification in the temple. For this mystery the most holy of
creatures resolved to dispose Herself worthily by a fervent
desire of carrying the infant Jesus as an offering to the eternal
Father in his temple; by imitating her Son and by seeking the
adornment and beauty of great virtues as a worthy offering
and victim for the Most High. With this intention the
heavenly Lady, during the days which still remained until her
purification, performed such heroic acts of love and of all
other virtues, that neither the tongue of angels nor of men
can explain them. How much lese can this then be done by a
useless and entirely ignorant woman? By sincere piety and
devotion, the Christians who dispose themselves by reverent
contemplation, will merit to feel these mysteries. Judging of
the more intelligible favors received by the Virgin Mother,
they can surmise and imagine the others, which do not fall
within the scope of human words.

577. From his very Birth the infant Jesus spoke to his
sweetest Mother in audible words; for immediately after his
Birth (as mentioned in chapter the tenth), He said to Her:
"Imitate Me, my Spouse, make thyself like unto Me." This
was when They were alone, and although He always spoke to

Her most plainly, saint Joseph never heard his words until the Child was one year of age, when He also spoke to him. Nor did the heavenly Lady reveal this secret, for She understood, that it was only for Her. The conversations of the infant God were such as were worthy of the greatness of his majesty and his infinite power; such as were befitting the most pure and holy, the most wise and prudent of all creatures next to Himself, and One who was his true Mother. Sometimes He said: "My Dove, my chosen One, my dearest Mother." (Cant. 2, 10). In such caressing words as were contained in the Canticles and other continual interior intercourse the most holy Son and Mother passed their time; and in these the heavenly Princess received favors, and was delighted by caresses so sweet and loving, as exceed those of the Canticles of Solomon; and greater ones than all the just and holy souls enjoyed from the beginning to the end of the world. Many times, during these mysteries of his love, the Infant Jesus repeated these words already mentioned:

"Make thyself like unto Me, my Mother and my Dove." As they were words of life and infinite power, and as most holy Mary at the same time was furnished with the infused knowledge of all the interior operations of the soul of her Onlybegotten, no tongue can declare nor thought can comprehend the effects wrought in the most candid and inflamed heart of this Mother of the Godman.

578. Among the more rare and excellent privileges of most pure Mary, the chief one is, that She is Mother of God, which is the foundation of all the rest. The second is, that She was conceived without sin. The third, that She enjoyed many times the beatific vision in this mortal life, and the fourth is that She continually saw clearly the most holy soul of her Son and all its operations for her imitation. She had it present to her eyes, as a most clear and pure mirror, in which She could behold Herself again and again in order to adorn

Herself with most precious gems of virtue, made in imitation of those seen in that most holy Soul. There She saw it united with the divine Word and She exercised her humility in seeing how much her own human nature was inferior to that of Christ. She perceived with the clearest insight the acts of gratitude and praise, with which the soul of Christ praised the Almighty for having been created out of nothing as the rest of the souls, and for the graces and gifts, with which it was endowed above others as a creature; and especially, for having been elevated and made godlike by the union of the human nature with the Divinity. She pondered over his petitions, prayers and supplications to his eternal Father for the human race; and how in all his other activity He prepared Himself for its Redemption and instruction, as the sole Redeemer and Teacher of man for eternal life.

579. All these works of the most holy humanity of Christ, our supreme Good, his most pure Mother continually sought to imitate. There is much to say concerning this great mystery of her imitation in this history; for She had this example and model incessantly before her eyes, and according to it She regulated her own activity and behavior during the Incarnation and Nativity of her Son. Like a busy bee She continually built up the sweetest honeycomb of delights for the incarnate Word. His Majesty, having come from heaven as our Redeemer and Teacher, wished that his most holy Mother, of whom He had formed his human existence, should participate in a most exalted and singular manner in the fruits of the common Redemption and that She should be the chosen and selected Disciple, in whom his teaching should be vividly stamped and whom He wished to make as similar to Himself as possible. In the light of these intentions and blessed purposes of the incarnate Word we must judge of the greatness of Mary's deeds, and of the delights, which He enjoyed while resting upon her arms and reclining upon her

breast; for it was indeed the bridal-chamber and the couch of this the true Spouse (Cant. 1, 15).

580. During the days in which the most holy Queen tarried near Bethlehem before the purification, some of the people came to see and speak with Her; but almost all of them were of the poorest class. Some of them came because of the alms which She distributed, others, because they had heard of the Kings, who had visited the cave. All of them spoke of this visit and of the coming of the Redeemer; for in those days, (not without divine predisposal), the belief, that the birth of the Messias was at hand, was very widespread among the Jews, and the talk about it was very frequent. This gave the most prudent Mother repeated occasion to exercise Herself in magnanimous works, not only by guarding the secret of her bosom and by conferring within Herself about all that She saw and heard, but also by directing many souls toward the knowledge of God, by confirming them in the faith, instructing them in the practice of virtues, enlightening them in the mysteries of the Messias whom they were expecting, and dispelling the ignorance, in which they were cast as a low-minded people, little versed in the things of God. Sometimes their talk about these matters was so full of error and womanish prattle, that the simple saint Joseph smiled in secret. He wondered at the heavenly wisdom and force of the answers, with which the great Lady met their gossip and instructed them; at her patience and gentleness in leading them to the truth and to the perception of the light; at her profound humility and yet patient reserve, with which She knew how to dismiss all of them consoled, rejoiced and furnished with all that was good for them to know. She spoke to them words of eternal life, which penetrated, inflamed and strengthened their hearts (John 6, 69).

Words of the Queen

THE VIRGIN MARY SPEAKS TO SISTER MARY OF AGREDA

581. My daughter, by the divine light I knew, better than all other creatures, at what a low value the Most High esteems earthly blessings and riches. Therefore, in my holy liberty of spirit, I felt myself troubled and inconvenienced by the possession of the treasures of the Kings offered to my most holy Son. As in all my deeds I was to shine in humility and obedience, I did not wish to appropriate them to myself, nor dispose of them according to my own will, but according to the wishes of my spouse Joseph. In this resignation I managed to act as if I were his handmaid and as if none of these gifts concerned me in any way; for it is debasing, and for you weak creatures, very dangerous to appropriate or attribute any of the goods of the earth, be they of material possessions or goods of honor; for all this cannot be done without covetousness, ambition and vain ostentation.

582. I wished to tell thee all this, my dearest, in order that thou mayest know how to refuse riches or honor as due to thee, and not appropriate to thyself any of them; especially not if thou receive them from persons of influence and exalted station. Preserve thy interior liberty and make no show of a thing which is worth nothing and which cannot justify thee before God. If anything is brought to thee, never say: "This is given to me, or is presented to me;" but "This the Lord sends to our convent; pray to God for those, whom his Majesty has sent as the instruments of his mercies." And mention the name of the giver, in order that they may pray particularly for him and that he may not be disappointed in the purpose of his gift. Also do not receive it personally, lest you raise a suspicion of covetousness, but let those appointed for this duty receive it. And, if in thy office as superior, thou must make distribution of things within the convent, let it be

with detachment and without any show of personal rights of possession in them; yet at the same time, as one who knows that she does not deserve any favors, do not forget to thank the Most High and the giver. That which is brought to the other religious thou must acknowledge thankfully as the superior and immediately see that thou apply it for the community, without reserving any part of it for thy own use. Do not inquire curiously about the incomes of the convent, in order that thou mayest not take a sensible pleasure therein and that thou mayest not seek delight in the reception of such favors; for frail and passionate nature incurs many defects in such a transaction and of few of the defects does it render much account to itself. Nothing can be trusted to infected human nature; for it always seeks after more than it possesses, and it never says enough, and the more it receives the greater thirst it has for more.

583. But it is to the intimate and frequent intercourse with the Lord by unceasing love, praise and reverence, that I wish thee to attend most of all. In this I wish, my daughter, that thou work with all thy strength, and that thou apply thy faculties and powers incessantly with great watchfulness and care; for without this the inferior parts will inevitably weigh down thy soul, derange and upset it, divert and cast it down, causing it to lose the vision of the highest Good (Wis. 9, 15). This loving intercourse of the Lord is so delicate, that even by listening or attending to the deceits of the enemy, the soul loses it. On this account the enemy makes great efforts to draw thy attention toward himself, knowing that the punishment of listening to him will be the concealment of the object of its love from the soul (Cant. 5, 6). As soon as it carelessly ignores the beauty of the Lord, it enters upon the byways of neglect and is deprived of the divine sweetness (Cant. 1,7). When afterwards the soul, having with sorrow experienced the evils of such inadvertence wishes to return to

seek Him, it does not always find or recover Him (Cant. 3, 1, 2). As the demon, who deceived it, then presents other delights so vile and unlike those to which the soul has been accustomed interiorly, new cause of sadness, disturbance, dejection, lukewarmness and dissatisfaction arises and its whole interior is filled with dangerous confusion.

584. Of this truth, my dearest, thou thyself hast some experience, wherein thou couldst notice the effects of neglect and tardiness in believing the favors of the Lord. It is time that thou be prudent in thy sincerity and constant in keeping up the fire of the sanctuary (Lev. 6, 12), without ever losing sight for a moment of that same object. which I attended to with all the powers of my soul and all my faculties. Although the distance between thy conduct, that of a mere wormlet, and that which I propose for thy imitation is great, and although thou canst not enjoy the supreme Good so unreservedly as I, nor live in the same condition as I; yet, since I instruct thee and show thee what I did to assimilate myself to my most holy Son, thou canst imitate me according to thy strength using my doings as a mirror. I saw Him in the mirror of his humanity, thou in my soul and person. If the Almighty calls and invites all men to the highest perfection by following Him, consider what thou art obliged to do, since thou hast been drawn toward the Most High by such a generous and powerful influence of his right hand (Matth. 11, 28; Cant. I, 3).

Chapter XIX

MOST HOLY MARY AND JOSEPH DEPART WITH THE INFANT JESUS, IN ORDER TO FULFILL THE LAW, BY PRESENTING HIM IN THE TEMPLE OF JERUSALEM.

585. Already the forty days after the birth of a son, during which a woman, according to the law, was considered unclean and during which she was obliged to continue her purification for her re-admittance into the temple, were coming to a close (Lev. 22, 4). In order to comply with this law and satisfy another obligation contained in Exodus, chapter thirteenth, which demanded the sanctification and presentation to the Lord of all the firstborn sons, the Mother of all purity prepared to go to Jerusalem, where She was to appear in the temple with her Son as the Onlybegotten of the eternal Father and purify Herself according to the custom of other women. She had no doubts about complying with that part of the law, which applied to Herself in common with other mothers. Not that She was ignorant of her innocence and purity; for, ever since the incarnation of the Word, She knew of her exemption from actual sin and from the stain of original sin. Nor was She ignorant of the fact that She had conceived by the Holy Ghost, and brought forth without labor, remaining a virgin more pure than the sun (Luke 1, 15). Yet She hesitated not to subject Herself to the common law; on the contrary, in the ardent longing of her heart after

humiliation and annihilation to the dust, She desired to do this of her own free will.

586. In regard to the presentation of her most holy Son there was some occasion for the same doubt as in regard to the Circumcision, for She knew Him to be the true God, superior to the laws, which He himself had made. But She was informed of the will of the Lord by divine light and by the interior acts of the most holy soul of the incarnate Word; for She saw his desire of sacrificing Himself and offering Himself as a living Victim (Eph. 5, 2) to the eternal Father, in thanksgiving for having formed his most pure body and created his most holy soul; for having destined Him as an acceptable sacrifice for the human race and for the welfare of mortals. These acts of the most sacred humanity of the Word were continual, conforming Himself to the divine will not only in so far as He was already beatified, but also in so far as He was still a wayfarer upon earth and our Redeemer. Yet, in addition to these interior acts and in obedience to the law, He wished to be offered to the eternal Father in the temple where all adored and magnified Him, as in a house of prayer, expiation and sacrifice (Deut. 12, 5).

587. The great Lady conferred about the journey with her husband, and, having resolved to be in Jerusalem on the very day appointed by the law and having made the necessary preparations, they took leave of the good woman, who had so devotedly entertained them. Although this woman was left in ignorance of the divine mysteries connected with her Guests, she was filled with the blessings of heaven, which brought her abundant fruit. Mary and Joseph betook themselves to the cave of the Nativity, not wishing to begin their journey without once more venerating that sanctuary so humble and yet so rich in happiness, though at that time this was yet unknown to the world. The Mother handed the Child Jesus to saint Joseph in order to prostrate Herself and worship the

earth which had been witness to such venerable mysteries. Having done this with incomparable devotion and tenderness, She said to her husband: "My master, give me thy benediction for this journey, as thou art wont to do at departing from home. I beseech thee also to allow me to perform this journey on foot and unshod; since I am to bear in my arms the Victim, which is to be offered to the eternal Father. This is a mysterious work and as far as it is possible, I should wish to perform it with due reverence and ceremony." Our Queen was accustomed, for the sake of modesty, to wear shoes, which covered her feet and served as a sort of stocking. They were made of a certain plant used by the poor and something like hemp or mallow, dried and woven into a coarse and strong texture, which, though poor, was yet cleanly and appropriate.

588. Saint Joseph told Her to arise, for She was kneeling before him, and said: "May the Most High Son of the eternal Father, whom I hold in my arms, give Thee his blessing. As for the rest it is well and good, that Thou journey afoot in bringing Him to Jerusalem. But Thou must not go barefoot, because the weather does not permit it; and thy desire will be accepted by the Lord instead of the deed." Thus saint Joseph, in order not to deprive most holy Mary of the joy of humiliation and obedience, made use of his authority as husband, although with great reverence. And as saint Joseph only obeyed Her and humiliated and mortified himself in commanding Her, it happened that both of them exercised humility and obedience reciprocally. That he refused Her permission to go barefoot to Jerusalem was occasioned by his apprehensions, lest the cold should injure her health; for he did not know the wonderful qualities and composition of her virginal and perfect body, nor the other privileges, conferred upon Her by the divine right hand. The obedient Queen made no reply to the orders of her husband and obeyed his

wish not to go unshod. In order to again receive in her arms the Infant Jesus She prostrated Herself on the earth, thanking Him and adoring Him for the blessings, which He had wrought for them and for the whole human race in that cave. She besought his Majesty, that this sanctuary be held in esteem and reverence by the Catholics and that it remain in their possession; and She again placed it in charge of the holy angel, who had been set as its guardian. She covered Herself with a cloak for the journey and, receiving in Her arms Jesus, the Treasure of heaven, She pressed Him to her breast, tenderly shielding Him from the inclemency of the wintry weather.

589. They departed from the cave, asking the blessing of the infant God, which his Majesty gave them in a visible manner. Saint Joseph placed upon the ass the chest containing the clothes of the Infant and the gifts of the Kings destined for their temple-offering. Thus began the most solemn procession, which was ever held from Bethlehem to the temple in Jerusalem; for in company with the Prince of the eternities, Jesus, the Queen, his Mother, and saint Joseph, her spouse, journeyed the ten thousand angels, that had assisted at these mysteries, and the other legions, that had brought from heaven the sweet and holy name of Jesus at the Circumcision (No. 523). All these heavenly courtiers passed along in visible human forms, so beautiful and shining, that in comparison with them, all that is delightful or precious in the world, is less than dirt or mud compared to the finest and purest gold; and in their splendor they obliterated the sun in its brightest light and would have turned night into the brightest day. The heavenly Queen and saint Joseph rejoiced in their effulgence, while all of them together exalted these mysteries by new canticles of praise in honor of the divine Child about to be presented in the temple. In this fashion they journeyed the two leagues from Bethlehem to Jerusalem.

590. On this occasion, not without divine dispensation, the weather was unusually severe, so that, without regard for the tender Child, its Creator, the cold and sleety blasts pierced to his shivering limbs and caused the divine Infant to weep as it rested in the arms of his loving Mother, being however moved thereto more by his compassion and love for men than by the effects of the inclemency of the weather upon his body. The mighty Empress turned to the winds and elements and as Mistress of creation reprehended them with indignation, that they should thus persecute their Maker. She commanded them to moderate their rigor toward the Child but not toward Her. The elements obeyed the commands of their true and rightful Mistress: the cold blasts were changed into a soft and balmy air for the Infant, without diminishing their inclemency toward the Mother; thus She herself felt it, but not her Infant, as on other occasions already mentioned and yet to be mentioned. She addressed also sin, which She had not contracted, and said: "0 sin, how most disorderly and inhuman art thou, since, in order to satisfy for thee, the Creator of all things is afflicted by the very creatures, which He has made and preserves in being! Thou art a terrible and horrible monster, offensive to God and destructive of creatures; thou turnest them into abominations and deprivest them of their greatest happiness, that of being friends of God. O children of men, how long will you be so heavy-hearted as to love vanity and deceit? Be not so ungrateful toward the Most High and so cruel to yourselves. Open your eyes and recognize your dangers. Do not despise the precepts of your eternal Father, and do not forget the teachings of your Mother, who has brought you forth by charity; for since the Onlybegotten of the Father has assumed flesh in my womb, He has made me the Mother of all creation. As such I love you and if it were possible and according to the will of the Most High, that I suffer all the punishments visited upon

you from the time of Adam until now, I would accept them with pleasure."

591. During the journey of our Lady with the infant God, it happened in Jerusalem that Simeon, the highpriest, was enlightened by the Holy Ghost concerning the coming of the incarnate Word and his presentation in the temple on the arms of his Mother. The same revelation was given to the holy widow Anne, and she was also informed of the poverty and suffering of saint Joseph and the most pure Lady on their way to Jerusalem. These two holy persons, immediately conferring with each other about their revelations and enlightenments, called the chief procurator of the temporal affairs of the temple, and, describing to him the signs, whereby he should recognize the holy Travelers, they ordered him to proceed to the gate leading out to Bethlehem and receive them into his house with all benevolence and hospitality. This the procurator did and thus the Queen and her spouse were much relieved, since they had been anxious about finding a proper lodging for the divine Infant. Leaving Them well provided in his house, the fortunate host returned in order to report to the high priest.

592. On that evening, before they retired, most holy Mary and Joseph conferred with each other about what they were to do. The most prudent Lady reminded him that it was better to bring the gifts of the Kings on that same evening to the temple in order to be able to make the offering in silence and without noisy demonstration, as was proper with all donations and sacrifices, and that on the way he might procure the two turtledoves, which on the next day were to be the public offering for the Infant Jesus. Saint Joseph complied with her request. As a stranger and one little known he gave the myrrh, incense and gold to the one who usually received such gifts for the temple, but saint Joseph took care not to reveal himself to anyone as the donor of

these great presents. Although he could have bought the lamb, which the rich usually offered for their first-born, he chose not to do so; because the humble and poor apparel of the Mother and the Child as well as of the husband, would not have agreed with a public offering as valuable as that of the rich (Matth. 8, 20). In no particular did the Mother of wisdom deem it befitting to depart from poverty and humility, even under the cover of a pious and honorable intention. For in all things was She the Teacher of perfection, and her most holy Son, that of holy poverty, in which He was born, lived and died.

593. Simeon, as saint Luke tells us, was a just and god-fearing man and was hoping in the consolation of Israel (Luke 2, 24) ; the Holy Ghost, who dwelt in him, had revealed to him, that he should not taste death until he had seen the Christ, the Lord. Moved by the holy Spirit he came to the temple; for in that night, besides the revelations he had already received, he was again divinely enlightened and made to understand more clearly the mysteries of the Incarnation and Redemption of man, the fulfillment of the prophecies of Isaias, that a Virgin should conceive and bear a Son and that from the root of Jesse a flower should blossom, namely Christ (Is. 7, 14); likewise all the rest contained in these and other prophecies. He received a clear understanding of the hypostatic union of the two natures in the person of the Word, and of the mysteries of the passion and death of the Redeemer. Thus instructed in these two high things, saint Simeon was lifted up and inflamed with the desire of seeing the Redeemer of the world. On the following day then, as soon as he had received notice that Christ was coming to present Himself in the temple to the Father, he was carried in spirit to the temple, for so great is the force of divine enlightenment. Whereupon succeeded that, which I shall relate in the following chapter. Also the holy matron Anne was fa-

vored with a revelation during the same night concerning many of these mysteries and great was the joy of her spirit on that account; for, as I have said in the first part of this history, she had been the teacher of our Queen, during her stay in the temple. The Evangelist tells us that She never left the temple-grounds serving in it day and night in prayer and fasting (Luke I, 27); that she was a prophetess, daughter of Samuel, of the tribe of Aser. She had lived seven years with her husband and was now eighty years old. As will be seen, she spoke prophetically of the Child's future.

Words of the Queen

THE VIRGIN MARY SPEAKS TO SISTER MARY OF AGREDA

594. My daughter, one of the misfortunes, which deprive souls of happiness, or at least diminish it, is that they content themselves with performing good works negligently or without fervor, as if they were engaged in things unimportant or merely accidental. On account of this ignorance and meanness of heart few of them arrive at an intimate friendship of God, which they can attain only by fervent love. This is called fervent precisely because of its similarity to boiling water. For just as water is made to boil and foam by the fire, so the soul, by the sweet violence of the divine conflagration of love, is raised above itself and above all created things as well as above its own doings. In loving, it is more and more inflamed, and from this very love springs an unquenchable affection, which makes the soul despise and forget all earthly things while at the same time it becomes dissatisfied with all temporal goodness. And as the human heart, when it does not attain what it dearly loves (if that attainment is possible) is inflamed with ever greater desire of reaching it by other means; therefore, the loving soul, finds ever new things to strive after for the sake of the Beloved and all service will

seem to it but little. Thus it will pass from good will to a perfect will, and from this to what will please the Lord still more, until it arrives at the most intimate union with Him and at a perfect conformation with the will of God.

595. Hence thou wilt understand, my dearest, why I desired to go barefooted to the temple, carrying at the same time my most holy Son in order to present Him there; and why I also wished to comply with the law of the purification; for, urged on by my love, which incessantly demanded what was most perfect and agreeable to the Lord, I sought the fullness of perfection in all my doings and it was precisely this anxiety, which created in me such a desire of excellence in all my works. Labor to imitate me with all diligence in all that I did; for I assure thee, my dear, that it is this exercise of thy love, which the Most High is desiring and expecting of thee, and, as is mentioned by the spouse in the Canticles (Cant. 2, 9), He is watching thee so close at hand, that not more than a slight screen intervenes between the soul and its vision of the Lord. Enamoured and drawn onward He approaches closely to those souls, who thus love and serve Him in all things, while He withdraws from the lukewarm and negligent ones, or deals with them only according to the general rules of his divine Providence. Do thou aspire continually to the most pure and perfect in the practice of virtues and study and invent new schemes and projects of love; so that all the forces of thy interior and exterior faculties continue to be zealously occupied in what is most exalted and excellent in the service of the Lord. At the same time mention all these affections to thy spiritual father and subject them to the obedience and advice of thy counselor, following his instructions: for this will always be the most preferable and secure way.

Chapter XX

THE PRESENTATION OF THE INFANT JESUS IN THE TEMPLE
AND WHAT HAPPENED ON THAT OCCASION.

596. The sacred humanity of Christ belonged to the eternal
Father not only because it was created like other beings, but
it was his special property by virtue of the hypostatic union
with the person of the Word, for this person of the Word,
being his Onlybegotten Son, was engendered of his substance, true God of true God. Nevertheless the eternal Father
had decreed, that his Son should be presented to Him in the
temple in mysterious compliance with the law, of which
Christ our Lord was the end (Rom. 10, 4). It was established
for no other purpose than that the just men of the old Testament should perpetually sanctify and offer to the Lord their
first-born sons, in the hope that one thus presented might
prove to be the Son of God and a Child of the Mother of the
expected Messias (Exod. 13, 2). According to our way of
thinking his Majesty acted like men, who are apt to repeat
and enjoy over and over again a thing which has caused them
enjoyment. For although the Father understood and knew all
things in his infinite wisdom, He sought pleasure in the
offering of the incarnate Word, which by so many titles
already belonged to Him.

597. This will of the eternal Father, which was conformable to that of his Son in so far as He was God, was known to the Mother of life and of the human nature of the Word; for She saw that all his interior actions were in unison with the will of his eternal Father. Full of this holy science the great Princess passed the night before his presentation in the temple in divine colloquies. Speaking to the Father She said: "My Lord and God most high, Father of my Lord, a festive day for heaven and earth will be that, in which I shall bring and offer to Thee in thy holy temple the living Host, which is at the same time the Treasure of thy Divinity. Rich, O my Lord and God, is this oblation; and Thou canst well pour forth, in return for it, thy mercies upon the human race: pardoning the sinners, that have turned from the straight path, consoling the afflicted, helping the needy, enriching the poor, succoring the weak, enlightening the blind, and meeting those who have strayed away. This is, my Lord, what I ask of thee in offering to Thee thy Onlybegotten, who, by thy merciful condescension is also my Son. If Thou hast given Him to me as a God, I return Him to Thee as God and man; his value is infinite, and what I ask of Thee is much less. In opulence do I return to thy holy temple, from which I departed poor; and my soul shall magnify Thee forever, because thy divine right hand has shown itself toward me so liberal and powerful."

598. On the next morning, the Sun of heaven being now ready to issue from its purest dawning, the Virgin Mary, on whose arms He reclined, and being about to rise up in full view of the world, the heavenly Lady, having provided the turtle-dove and two candles, wrapped Him in swaddling-clothes and betook Herself with saint Joseph from their lodging to the temple. The holy angels, who had come with them from Bethlehem, again formed in procession in corporeal and most beautiful forms, just as has been said concern-

ing the journey of the preceding day. On this occasion however the holy spirits added many other hymns of the sweetest and most entrancing harmony in honor of the infant God, which were heard only by the most pure Mary. Besides the ten thousand, who had formed the procession on the previous day, innumerable others descended from heaven, who, accompanied by those that bore the shields of the holy name of Jesus, formed the guard of honor of the incarnate Word on the occasion of his presentation. These however were not in corporeal shapes and only the heavenly Princess perceived their presence. Having arrived at the temple-gate, the most blessed Mother was filled with new and exalted sentiments of devotion. Joining the other women, She bowed and knelt to adore the Lord in spirit and in truth in his holy temple and She presented Herself before the exalted Majesty of God with his Son upon her arms (John 4, 23). Immediately She was immersed in an intellectual vision of the most holy Trinity and She heard a voice issuing from the eternal Father, saying: "This is my beloved Son, in whom I am well pleased" (Matth. 27, 20). Saint Joseph, the most fortunate of men, felt at the same time a new sweetness of the Holy Ghost, which filled him with joy and divine light.

599. The holy high-priest Simeon, moved by the Holy Ghost as explained in the preceding chapter, also entered the temple at that time (Luke 2, 27). Approaching the place where the Queen stood with the Infant Jesus in her arms, he saw both Mother and Child enveloped in splendor and glory. The prophetess Anne, who, as the Evangelist says, had come at the same hour, also saw Mary and her Infant surrounded by this wonderful light. In the joy of their spirit both of them approached the Queen of heaven, and the priest received the Infant Jesus from her arms upon his hands. Raising up his eyes to heaven he offered Him up to the eternal Father, pronouncing at the same time these words so full of myster-

ies: "Now dost thou dismiss thy servant, O Lord, according to thy Word in peace. Because my eyes have seen thy salvation, which thou hast prepared before the face of all peoples: a light for the revelation of the gentiles, and the glory of thy people Israel" (Luke 2, 29). It was as if He had said: "Now, Lord, thou wilt release me from the bondage of this mortal body and let me go free and in peace; for until now have I been detained in it by the hope of seeing thy promises fulfilled and by the desire of seeing thy Onlybegotten made man. Now that my eyes have seen thy salvation, the Onlybegotten made man, joined to our nature in order to give it eternal welfare according to the intention and eternal decree of thy infinite wisdom and mercy, I shall enjoy true and secure peace. Now, O Lord, Thou hast prepared and placed before all mortals thy divine light that it may shine upon the world and that all who wish may enjoy it throughout the universe and derive therefrom guidance and salvation. For this is the light which is revealed to the gentiles for the glory of thy chosen people of Israel" (John I, 9, 32).

600. Most holy Mary and saint Joseph heard this canticle of Simeon, wondering at the exalted revelation it contained. The Evangelist calls them in this place the parents of the divine Infant, for such they were in the estimation of the people who were present at this event. Simeon, addressing himself to the most holy Mother of the Infant Jesus, then added: "Behold this Child is set for the fall and for the resurrection of many in Israel, and for a sign which shall be contradicted. And thy own soul a sword shall pierce, that out of many hearts thoughts may be revealed." Thus saint Simeon; and being a priest he gave his blessing to the happy parents of the Child. Then also the prophetess Anne acknowledged the incarnate Word, and full of the Holy Ghost, she spoke of the mysteries of the Messias to many, who were expecting the redemption of Israel. By these two

holy old people public testimony of the coming of the Redeemer was given to the world.

601. At the moment when the priest Simeon mentioned the sword and the sign of contradiction, which were prophetical of the passion and death of the Lord, the Child bowed its head. Thereby, and by many interior acts of obedience, Jesus ratified the prophecy of the priest and accepted it as the sentence of the eternal Father pronounced by his minister. All this the loving Mother noticed and understood; She presently began to feel the sorrow predicted by Simeon and thus in advance was She wounded by the sword, of which She had thus been warned. As in a mirror her spirit was made to see all the mysteries included in this prophecy; how her most holy Son was to be the stone of stumbling, the perdition of the unbelievers, and the salvation of the faithful; the fall of the synagogue and the establishment of the Church among the heathens; She foresaw the triumph to be gained over the devils and over death, but also that a great price was to be paid for it, namely the frightful agony and death of the Cross (Colos, 2, 15). She foresaw the boundless opposition and contradiction, which the Lord Jesus was to sustain both personally and in his Church (John 15, 20). At the same time She also saw the glory and excellence of the predestined souls. Most holy Mary knew it all and in the joy and sorrow of her most pure soul, excited by the prophecies of Simeon and these hidden mysteries, She performed heroic acts of virtue. All these sayings and happenings were indelibly impressed upon her memory and of all that She understood and experienced. She forgot not the least iota. At all times She looked upon her most holy Son with such a living sorrow, as we, mere human creatures with hearts so full of ingratitude, shall never be able to feel. The holy spouse saint Joseph was by these prophecies also made to see many of the mysteries of the Redemption and of the labors and sufferings of Jesus. But

the Lord did not reveal them to him so copiously and openly as they were perceived and understood by his heavenly spouse; for in him these revelations were to serve a different purpose, and besides, saint Joseph was not to be an eyewitness of them during his mortal life.

602. The ceremony of the presentation thus being over, the great Lady kissed the hand of the priest and again asked his blessing. The same She did also to Anne, her former teacher; for her dignity as Mother of God, the highest possible to angels or men, did not prevent Her from these acts of deepest humility. Then, in the company of saint Joseph, her spouse, and of the fourteen thousand angels in procession, She returned with the divine Infant to her lodging. They remained, as I shall relate farther on, for some days in Jerusalem, in order to satisfy their devotion and during that time She spoke a few times with the priest about the mysteries of the Redemption and of the prophecies above mentioned. Although the words of the most prudent Virgin Mother were few, measured and reserved, they were also so weighty and full of wisdom, that they filled the priest with wonder and excited in him the most exalted and the sweetest sentiments of joy in his soul. The same happened also to the prophetess Anne. Both of them died in the Lord shortly afterwards. The holy Family lodged at the expense of Simeon. During these days the Queen frequented the temple and in it She was visited with many favors and consolations in recompense for the sorrow caused by the prophecies of the priest. In order to heighten their sweetness her most holy Son spoke to Her on one of these days saying: "My dearest Mother and my Dove, dry up thy tears and let thy purest heart be expanded; since it is the will of my Father, that I accept the death of the Cross. I desire that Thou be my companion in my labors and sufferings; I long to undergo them for the souls, who are the works of my hands (Ephes, 2, 10), made according to my

image and likeness, in order to make them partakers of my reign and of eternal life in triumph over my enemies (Coloss. 2, 15). This is what Thou thyself dost wish in union with Me." The Mother answered: "O my sweetest Love and Son of my womb, if my accompanying Thee shall include not only the privilege of witnessing and pitying thy sufferings, but also of dying with Thee, so much the greater will be my relief; for it will be a greater suffering for me to live, while seeing Thee die." In these exercises of love and compassion She passed some days, until saint Joseph was advised to flee into Egypt, as I shall relate in the following chapter.

Words of the Queen

THE VIRGIN MARY SPEAKS TO SISTER MARY OF AGREDA

603. My daughter, the doctrine and example contained in the foregoing chapter will teach thee to strive after the constancy and expansion of heart, by which thou mayest prepare thyself to accept blessings and adversity, the sweet and the bitter with equanimity. O dearest soul! How narrow and unwilling is the human heart toward that which is contrary and distasteful to its earthly inclinations! How it chafes in labors! How impatiently it meets them! How insufferable it deems all that is contrary to its desires! How persistently it forgets, that its Teacher and Master has first accepted sufferings, and has honored and sanctified them in his own Person! It is a great shame, yea a great boldness, on the part of the faithful, that they should abhor suffering, even after my most holy Son did suffer for them and when so many of the just before his Death were led to embrace the cross solely by the hope that Christ would once suffer upon it, although they would never live to see it. And if this want of correspondence is so base in others, consider well, my dearest, how vile it would be in thee, who art so anxious to obtain the grace and

the friendship of the Most High; who desirest to merit the name of a spouse and friend of God, who wishest to belong entirely to Him and that He belong entirely to thee, who wishest to be my disciple and that I be thy Teacher, who aspirest to follow and imitate me, as a faithful daughter her mother (Matth. 7, 21). All this must not result in mere sentiment and in empty words, or oft-repeated exclamations of: Lord, Lord; and, when the occasion of tasting the chalice and the cross of suffering is at hand, thou must not turn away in sorrow and affliction from the sufferings, by which the sincerity of a loving and affectionate heart is to be tried.

604. All this would be denying in your actions, what you profess in your words, and it would be a swerving from the path of eternal life: for thou canst not follow Christ, if thou refusest to embrace the cross and rejoice in it, nor shalt thou find me by any other way (Matth. 8, 34). If creatures fail thee, if temptation or trouble assail thee, if the sorrows of death encompass thee (Ps. 17, 5), thou must in no wise be disturbed or disheartened; since nothing displeases my most holy Son or me more than placing a hindrance or misapplying the grace given by Him for thy defense. By misusing it and receiving it in vain, thou yieldest great victory to the demon, who glories much in having disturbed or subjected any soul that calls itself a disciple of Christ and of me; and having once brought thee to default in small things, he will soon oppress thee in greater ones. Confide then in the protection of the Most High and press onward trusting in me. Full of this trust, whenever tribulation comes over thee, fervently exclaim: "The Lord is my light and my salvation, whom shall I fear? (Psalm 26, 1). He is my Helper, why should I hesitate? I have a Mother, a Queen and Mistress, who will assist me and take care of me in my affliction."

605. In this security seek to preserve interior peace and keep forever in thy view my works and my footsteps for thy

imitation. Remember the sorrow, which pierced my heart at the prophecies of Simeon, and how I remained in peace and tranquillity, without any sign of disturbance, although my heart and soul were transfixed by a sword of pain. In every event I sought motives for glorifying and adoring his admirable wisdom. If the transitory labors and sufferings are accepted with joy and with serenity of heart, they spiritualize the creature, they elevate it and furnish it with a divine insight; by which the soul begins to esteem affliction at its proper value and soon finds consolation and the blessings of mortification and of freedom from disorderly passions. This is the teaching of the school of the Redeemer, hidden from those living in Babylon and from those who love vanity (Matth. 11,25). I wish also that thou imitate me in respecting the priests and ministers of the Lord, who in the new law hold a much higher dignity than in the old, since the divine Word has now united Itself with human nature and become the eternal High-Priest according to the order of Melchisedech (Ps. 109,4). Listen to their words and instructions, as God requires, whose place they take. Consider the power and authority given them in the Gospels, where it is said: "Who hears you, hears Me; who obeys you obeys Me" (Luke 10, 16). Strive after the perfection they teach thee. Ponder and meditate without intermission upon that, which my most holy Son suffered, so that thy soul be a participant in his sorrows. Let the pious memory of his sufferings engender in thee such a disgust and abhorrence of all earthly pleasures that thou despise and forget all that is visible, and instead, follow the Author of eternal life.

Chapter XXI

THE LORD PREPARES THE MOST HOLY MARY FOR THE PLIGHT INTO EGYPT; THE ANGEL SPEAKS TO SAINT JOSEPH; AND OTHER MATTERS CONNECTED THEREWITH.

606. When the most holy Mary and glorious saint Joseph returned from the presentation of the Infant Jesus in the temple, they concluded to stay in Jerusalem for nine days in order to be able each day to visit the temple and repeat the offering of the sacred Victim, their divine Son, thus rendering fitting thanks for the immense blessing for which they had been singled out from among all men. The heavenly Lady had a special veneration for this number in memory of the nine days, during which She had been prepared and adorned by God for the incarnation of the Word, as I have related in the first ten chapters of this second part; also in memory of the nine months, during which She had borne Jesus in her virginal womb. In honor of these events She wished to make this novena with her divine Child, presenting Him that many times to the eternal Father as an acceptable offering for her lofty purposes. They began the devotions of the novena every day before the third hour, praying in the temple until nightfall. They chose the most obscure and retired place, meriting thereby the invitation of the master of the banquet in the Gospel: "Friend, go up higher" (Luke 14, 10). This invitation was given to Her, on one of those days,

when She was pouring out her spirit in the presence of the eternal Father in the following words:

607. "Highest King, Lord and Creator of all that has being, here in thy presence lies the useless dust and ashes, which thy ineffable condescension has favored with grace such as it neither knew, nor ever could know, how to merit I find myself, O Lord, forced onward by the impetuous flood of thy blessings to give Thee thanks. But what return can she offer, who, being nothing, has received her existence and her life from Thee, and who over and above was overwhelmed by such incomparable mercies and blessings of thy Divinity? What thanks can she render in acknowledgment of thy immense bounty? What reverence worthy of thy Majesty? What gift to thy infinite Deity, since She is only a creature? My soul, my being, and my faculties, all have I received and continue to receive from thy hands. A thousand times do I offer it in sacrifice to thy glory. I acknowledge my indebtedness, not only for having given me all this. but for the love with which Thou hast given it, and because among all creatures, thy infinite bounty has preserved me from the contagion of sin and has chosen me to give human form to thy Onlybegotten Son, to bear Him in my womb and at my breast, though I am only a daughter of Adam and made of lowly and earthly matter. I perceive thy ineffable condescension toward me, O Lord, and in gratitude for it my heart fails and my life is spent in affections of divine love, having nothing else to repay all the favors of thy right hand conferred upon thy handmaid. But now my heart is revived and rejoices in possessing a gift worthy of thy greatness, since I can offer Thee Him, who is one in substance with Thee, equal in majesty, and perfection of attributes, the Onlybegotten of thy intellect, the image of thy being, the fullness of thy own pleasure, thy only and most beloved Son. This, eternal Father and Most High God, is the gift, which I offer, the

Victim which I bring Thee, and this I am sure Thou wilt receive. Having received Him as God, I return Him to Thee God and man. Neither I nor any other creature, O Lord, can ever offer Thee a greater gift, nor can thy Majesty ever demand one more precious. It is so valuable, that it will suffice to repay Thee for what I have received. In his name and in mine I offer and present Him to Thee. I am the Mother of thy Onlybegotten, having given Him human flesh, I have made Him the Brother of mortals, and as He wishes to be their Redeemer and Teacher, it behooves me to be their advocate, to assume their cause and claim assistance for them. Therefore, Father of my Onlybegotten, God of mercies, I offer Him to Thee from all my heart; with Him and because of Him I beg Thee to pardon sinners, to pour out upon the human race thy mercies of old and to open new fountains for the renewal of thy wonders (Eccli, 38, 6). This is the Lion of Juda become a Lamb, which takes away the sins of the world (Apoc. 5, 5). He is the treasure of thy Divinity."

608. Such prayers and petitions the Mother of piety offered up in the first days of her novena in the temple. To all of them the eternal Father responded, accepting the offering of his Onlybegotten as a pleasing sacrifice, being more and more enamored with the purity of his only and chosen Daughter and looking upon her sanctity with benign pleasure. As an answer to her petitions He conceded to Her new and great privileges, among which was also this one, that, as long as the world should last. She should obtain all that She would ever ask for her clients; that the greatest sinners, if they availed themselves of her intercession, should find salvation; that in the new Church and law of the Gospel She should be the CoOperatrix and Teacher of salvation with Christ her most holy Son. This was to be her privilege especially after his Ascension into heaven, when She should remain, as Queen of the universe, as the representative and instrument

of the divine power on earth. This I will show more particularly in the third part of this history. Many other favors and mysteries the Most High confirmed upon the heavenly Mother in answer to her prayers. They, however, are beyond the reach of spoken language, and cannot be described by my short and limited terms.

609. In the course of these manifestations, on the fifth day of the novena after the presentation and purification, while the heavenly Lady was in the temple with the Infant on her arms, the Deity revealed Itself to Her, although not intuitively, and She was wholly raised and filled by the Spirit. It is true, that this had been done to Her before; but as God's power and treasures are infinite, He never gives so much as not to be able to give still more to the creatures. In this abstractive vision the Most High visited anew his only Spouse, wishing to prepare Her for the labors, that were awaiting Her. Speaking to Her, He comforted Her saying: "My Spouse and my Dove, thy wishes and intentions are pleasing in my eyes and I delight in them always. But Thou canst not finish the nine days' devotion, which Thou hast begun, for I have in store for Thee other exercises of Thy love. In order to save the life of thy Son and raise Him up, Thou must leave thy home and thy country, flee with Him and thy spouse Joseph into Egypt, where Thou art to remain until I shall ordain otherwise: for Herod is seeking the life of the Child. The journey is long, most laborious and most fatiguing; do thou suffer it all for my sake; for I am, and always will be, with Thee,"

610. Any other faith and virtue might have been disturbed (as the incredulous really have been) to see the powerful God fleeing from a miserable earthly being, and that He should do so in order to save his life, as if He, being both God and man, could be affected by the fear of death. But the most prudent and obedient Mother advanced no objection or

doubt: She was not in the least disturbed or moved by this unlooked for order. Answering, She said: "My Lord and Master, behold thy servant with a heart prepared to die for thy love if necessary. Dispose of me according to thy will. This only do I ask of thy immense goodness, that, overlooking my want of merit and gratitude, Thou permit not my Son and Lord to suffer, and that Thou turn all pains and labor upon me, who am obliged to suffer them." The Lord referred Her to saint Joseph, bidding Her to follow his directions in all things concerning the journey. Therewith She issued from her vision, which She had enjoyed without losing the use of her exterior senses and while holding in her arms the Infant Jesus. She had been raised up in this vision only as to the superior part of her soul; but from it flowed other gifts, which spiritualized her senses and testified to Her that her soul was living more in its love than in the earthly habitation of her body.

611. On account of the incomparable love, which the Queen bore toward her most holy Son, her maternal and compassionate heart was somewhat harrowed at the thought of the labors which She foresaw in the vision impending upon the infant God. Shedding many tears, She left the temple to go to her lodging-place, without manifesting to her spouse the cause of her sorrow. Saint Joseph therefore thought that She grieved on account of the prophecy of Simeon. As the most faithful Joseph loved Her so much, and as he was of a kind and solicitous disposition, he was troubled to see his Spouse so tearful and afflicted, and that She should not manifest to him the cause of this new affliction, This disturbance of his soul was one of the reasons why the holy angels spoke to him in sleep, as I have related above, when speaking of the pregnancy of the Queen. For in the same night, while saint Joseph was asleep, the angel of the Lord appeared to him, and spoke to him as recorded by saint

Matthew: "Arise, take the Child and its Mother and flee into Egypt; there shalt thou remain until I shall return to give thee other advice; for Herod is seeking after the Child in order to take away its life." Immediately the holy spouse arose full of solicitude and sorrow, foreseeing also that of his most loving Spouse. Entering upon her retirement, he said: "My Lady, God wills that we should be afflicted; for his holy angel has announced to me the pleasure and the decree of the Almighty, that we arise and flee with the Child into Egypt, because Herod is seeking to take away its life. Encourage thyself, my Lady, to bear the labors of this journey and tell me what I can do for thy comfort, since I hold my life and being at the service of thy Child and of Thee."

612. "My husband and my master," answered the Queen, "if we have received from the hands of the Most High such great blessings of grace, it is meet that we joyfully accept temporal afflictions (Job 2, 13). We bear with us the Creator of heaven and earth; if He has placed us so near to Him, what arms shall be able to harm us, even if it be the arm of Herod? Wherever we carry with us all our Good, the highest treasure of heaven, our Lord, our guide and true light, there can be no desert; but He is our rest, our portion, and our country. All these goods we possess in having his company; let us proceed to fulfill his will." Then most holy Mary and Joseph approached the crib where the Infant Jesus lay; and where He, not by chance, slept at that time. The heavenly Mother uncovered Him without awakening Him; for He awaited those tender and sorrowful words of his Beloved: "Flyaway, O my Beloved, and be like the roe and the young hart upon the mountains of aromatical spices. Come, my beloved, let us go forth into the field, let us ride in the villages" (Cant. 8, 14; 7, 11). And the tender Mother added: "Sweetest Love, meekest Lamb, thy power is not limited by that of earthly kings; but Thou wishest, in thy exalted wis-

dom, to hide it for love of men. Who among mortals can think of taking away thy life, O my God? Is it not in thy power to annihilate all life? Since Thou givest life to all, why should men take away thine? (John 10, 10). Since Thou visited them in order to give them eternal life, why should they wish to give Thee death? But who shall comprehend the secrets of thy Providence? (Rom. 11, 34). Allow me, then, O Lord and light of my soul, to awaken Thee; for when thou sleepest thy heart is awake."

613. Some such sentiments were also expressed by saint Joseph. Then the heavenly Mother, falling upon her knees, awakened the sweetest Infant, and took Him in her arms, Jesus, in order to move Her to greater tenderness and in order to show Himself as true man, wept a little. O wonders of the Most High in things according to our judgments so small! Yet He was soon again quieted; and when the most holy Mother and saint Joseph asked his blessing He gave it them in visible manner. Gathering their poor clothing into the casket and loading it on the beast of burden which they had brought from Nazareth, they departed shortly after midnight, and hastened without delay on their journey to Egypt, as I will relate in the following chapter.

614. I will here add what I have been made to understand as to the concordance of the two Gospels of saint Matthew and saint Luke in regard to this event For, since all of them wrote under guidance and light of the Holy Ghost, each of them knew what the other three had written, and what they had omitted to say in their Gospels. Hence it happened that according to divine predisposition some of the happenings of the life of Christ and of the Gospel were described by all four of the Evangelists, while again some other things mentioned by one were omitted by the others. Saint Matthew describes the adoration of the Kings and the flight into Egypt, while these events were not mentioned by saint Luke. He again

describes the Circumcision, Presentation and Purification, which are omitted by saint Matthew. Thus saint Matthew, after referring to the departure of the Magi, immediately, without speaking of the Presentation, relates that the angel appeared to saint Joseph commanding him to flee into Egypt; but it does not follow therefrom that the Child had not been presented before that time in the temple, for it is certain that this was done after the departure of the Kings and before the flight into Egypt, as is narrated by saint Luke. Thus, likewise, although saint Luke, after describing the Presentation and Purification, immediately mentions that the holy Family lived in Nazareth, we must not conclude that they had not before that time lived in Egypt he writes nothing of this flight into Egypt either before or after, because it had already been recorded by saint Matthew. And this flight took place immediately after the Presentation before most holy Mary and Joseph returned to Nazareth. As saint Luke had received no commission to write about this journey it was natural that, in continuing his history, he should mention the return to Nazareth immediately after the Presentation. To say that, having fulfilled what the law commanded, they returned to Galilee, was not to deny the flight into Egypt, but it was merely continuing the narrative without mentioning the flight from Herod. Even the very text of saint Luke intimates that the return to Nazareth happened after their sojourn in Egypt; for he says that the Child grew and increased in wisdom, and that grace was manifested in Him; which could not have been before He had passed the years of infancy. Hence it must have been after his return from Egypt, and at an age when the use of reason usually begins to show itself in children.

615. I was also given to understand how foolish it is in the infidels or incredulous to stumble against this cornerstone of Christ even in his infancy and to take offense at seeing

Him flee to Egypt in order to defend Himself against Herod; as if this were on account of his weakness and not a mystery, and as if it had happened for no higher purpose than to defend his life against the cruelty of a wicked man. For the well-disposed souls the words of the Evangelist are amply sufficient: since he says it happened in order that the prophecy of Osea might be fulfilled, who prophesies in the name of the eternal Father: "And I called my Son out of Egypt" (Osee 11, 1). The ends which He had in view in sending Him there and in calling Him thence are most exalted and mysterious: of these I will say something anon. If not all of the doings of the incarnate Word are equally admirable and sacramental, yet no one with sane judgment can dispute or ignore the sweet providence of God in directing the secondary causes, while allowing full liberty to the human will (Eccli. 15, 14). For this reason, and not for want of power, He permits so many idolatries, heresies and other sins, which are not any smaller than that of Herod; for this reason He permitted the crime of Judas and all those which followed in the sufferings and crucifixion of Christ. Certainly He could have prevented all these sins and yet would not; not only because He wished to work our Redemption, but also in order that He might secure to man freedom of his will in all his actions. He was ready to give to men the helps and graces according to his divine Providence, whereby they could accomplish the good, if they would only use their free will to attain it in the same degree as they were using it to follow evil.

616. In this sweetness of his Providence He gives sinners time, hoping for their conversions, as in the case of Herod. If He would use his absolute power and perform great miracles for preventing the course of secondary causes, the order of nature would be confounded, and to a certain extent He would contradict Himself in his double role as Author of grace and as Author of nature. Therefore, miracles must

happen but rarely, and on special occasions for particular reasons, or when some end is to be served. Therefore, God reserves them for the manifestations of his power at certain times. He makes Himself known as the Author of his works by bringing them into existence and preserving them independently of creatures. Neither must we wonder that He should consent to the death of the innocent children which Herod murdered; for it would not have been to their benefit to save them through a miracle, since by their death they were to gain eternal life together with an abundant reward, which vastly recompensed them for the loss of their temporal life. If they had been allowed to escape the sword and die a natural death, all would eventually not have been saved. The works of the Lord are just and holy in all particulars, although we do not always see the reasons why they are so; but we shall come to know them in the Lord when we shall see him face to face.

Words of the Queen

THE VIRGIN MARY SPEAKS TO SISTER MARY OF AGREDA

617. My daughter, what thou must especially learn from this chapter is, that thou accustom thyself to humble thanksgiving for the benefits which thou receivest, since thou, among many generations, art so specially signalized by the riches of grace with which my Son and I visit thee without any merit of thine. I was wont to repeat many times this verse of David: "What shall I render to the Lord for all the things that he hath rendered to me?" (Ps. 115, 12). In such sentiments I humiliated myself to the dust, esteeming myself altogether useless among creatures. Therefore, if thou knowest what I did as Mother of God, consider what then is thy obligation, since thou must with so much truth confess thyself unworthy and undeserving of all thou receivest, and so poorly furnished

for giving thanks and for making payment. Thou must supply thy insufficiency and thy misery by offering up to the eternal Father the living host of his onlybegotten Son, especially when thou receivest Him in the holy Sacrament and possessest Him within thee: for in this thou shouldst also imitate David, who, after asking the Lord what return he should make for all his benefits, answers: "I will take the chalice of salvation; and I will call upon the name of the Lord" (Ps, 115, 13). Thou must accept the salvation offered to thee and bring forth its fruits by the perfection of thy works, calling upon the name of the Lord, offering up his Onlybegotten. For He it is who gave the virtue of salvation, who merited it, who alone can be an adequate return for the blessings conferred upon the human race and upon thee especially. I have given Him human form in order that He might converse with men and become the property of each one. He conceals Himself under the appearances of bread and wine in order to accommodate Himself to the needs of each one, and that each one might consider Him as his personal property fit to offer to the eternal Father. In this way He furnishes to each one an oblation which no one could otherwise offer, and the Most High rests satisfied with it, since there is not anything more acceptable nor anything more precious in the possession of creatures.

618. In addition to this offering is the resignation with which souls embrace and bear with equanimity and patience the labors and difficulties of mortal life. My most holy Son and I were eminent Masters in the practice of this doctrine. My Son began to teach it from the moment in which He was conceived in my womb. For already then He began to suffer, and as soon as He was born into the world He and I were banished by Herod into a desert, and his sufferings continued until He died on the Cross. I also labored to the end of my life, as thou wilt be informed more and more in the writing

of this history. Since, therefore, We suffered so much for creatures and for their salvation, I desire thee to imitate Us in this conformity to the divine will as being his spouse and my daughter. Suffer with a magnanimous heart, and labor to increase the possessions of thy Lord and Master, namely, souls, which are so precious in his sight and which He has purchased with his life-blood. Never shouldst thou fly from labors, difficulties, bitterness and sorrows, if by any of them thou canst gain a soul for the Lord, or if thou canst thereby induce it to leave the path of sin and enter the path of life. Let not the thought that thou art so useless and poor, or that thy desires and labor avail but little, discourage thee; since thou canst not know how the Lord will accept of them and in how far He shall consider Himself served thereby, At least thou shouldst wish to labor assiduously and eat no unearned bread in his house (Prov. 31, 27).

Chapter XXII

JESUS, MARY AND JOSEPH BEGIN THEIR JOURNEY TO EGYPT; ACCOMPANIED BY THE ANGELIC SPIRITS, THEY ARRIVE AT THE CITY OF GAZA.

619. Our heavenly Pilgrims left Jerusalem and entered upon their banishment while yet the silence and obscurity of night held sway. They were full of solicitude for the Pledge of heaven, which they carried with them into a strange and unknown land. Although faith and hope strengthened them (for in no other beings could these virtues be more firmly and securely established than in our Queen and her most faithful spouse), nevertheless the Lord afforded them occasion for anxiety. Their love for the Infant Jesus would naturally excite in them anxiety and suffering on an occasion like this. They knew not what would happen during such a long journey, nor when it should end, nor how they would fare in Egypt, where they would be entire strangers, nor what comfort or convenience they would find there for raising the Child, nor even how they would be able to ward off great sufferings from Him on the way to Egypt. Therefore the hearts of these holy Parents were filled with many misgivings and anxious thoughts when they parted with so much haste from their lodging-place; but their sorrow was much relieved when the ten thousand heavenly courtiers above mentioned again appeared to them in human forms and in their former

splendor and beauty, and when they again changed the night into the brightest day for the holy Pilgrims. As they set forth from the portals of the city the holy angels humiliated themselves and adored the incarnate Word in the arms of the Virgin Mother. They also encouraged Her by again offering their homage and service, stating that it was the will of the Lord that they guide and accompany Her on the journey.

620. To the afflicted heart the least consolation seems precious; hence this one, being in itself a great relief, comforted our Queen and her spouse Joseph very much. They therefore entered upon their journey with good heart, choosing the way which led through the city gate in the direction of Nazareth. The heavenly Mother longed to visit again the place of the Nativity, in order to venerate the sacred cave and the crib, which had offered shelter and hospitality to her most holy Son at his entrance into the world. But the holy angels, knowing of her unspoken desires, said to Her: "Our Queen and Lady, Mother of our Creator, it behooves us to hasten on our journey without any delay; for on account of the escape of the magi Kings and their failure to return to Jerusalem, and on account of the words spoken by the priest Simeon, and by Anne, the people have been roused to attention. Some of them have begun to say that Thou art the Mother of the Messias; others that Thou knowest of Him; and others say that thy Son is a Prophet. Various rumors are also spread about concerning the visit of the Kings in Bethlehem, and of all these things Herod is informed. He has commanded that You be sought after very carefully and consequently a most diligent search is being made to find You. On this account the Most High has commanded You to fly at night and with so much haste."

621. The Queen of heaven yielded to the will of the Almighty thus made known to Her by the holy angels. She therefore reverenced from afar the sacred place of the birth of

her Onlybegotten, renewing the memory of the mysteries there wrought and the favors there received. The holy angel who stood as guard of the sacred cave approached Them on their way in visible form and adored the incarnate Word in the arms of his Mother. As She was thus allowed to see this angel and speak to him, the heavenly Lady was rejoiced and comforted still more. She would have also preferred to travel by way of Hebron; since it was only a short distance from the one they were now traveling, and Elisabeth was just at that time in that city with her son John, But the anxiety of saint Joseph, who was more timid, prevented also this diversion and delay; for he said to his heavenly Spouse:

"My Lady, I think it is extremely important that we do not delay our journey even for one instant; and that we hasten as much as possible to flee from the place of danger. Therefore it will not be prudent to go to Hebron, where they will find us more easily than in any other parts of the country." "Let it be according to thy pleasure," answered the humble Queen, "yet I wish thou give me permission to send one of these celestial spirits to Elisabeth, in order to inform my cousin of the cause of our flight, so that she herself may protect her son; for the wrath of Herod is so roused that it will extend to them."

622. The Queen of heaven knew of the design to murder the children; but She did not tell saint Joseph of it at that time. Here I must marvel at the obedience and humility of most holy Mary, which was so exquisite and rare: for She obeyed saint Joseph not only in that which he commanded, but also in that which concerned Herself alone, namely in the matter of sending an angel to saint Elisabeth. Although She could have sent the angel by a mere wish, without even expressing it in words, She nevertheless preferred not to do so without permission and in obedience to her spouse. I must confess my shame and my negligence; since having before my

eyes the most pure fountain of waters, I do not satiate my
thirst, nor profit by the light and the example before me,
though it is so vivid, so sweet, so powerful and so attractive
in teaching us all to abjure our own reprehensible wills. With
the permission of saint Joseph, then most holy Mary dispatched one of the principal angels of her guard, in order to
notify saint Elisabeth of what was passing. As the Sovereign
of the angelic spirits She instructed her messenger on this
occasion what he was to say to the holy matron and to the
child John.

623. The angel, according to the order and pleasure of the
Queen, proceeded to inform the fortunate and blessed Elisabeth of all these events as far as was proper. He told her that
the Mother of God was fleeing before the wrath of Herod
into Egypt, as this tyrant was now searching for the Child in
order to kill It. He warned her to see to the safety of saint
John by hiding him in some place of refuge. He also manifested to her other mysteries of the incarnate Word according
to the command of the heavenly Mother. The holy Elisabeth
was filled with joy and wonder at this message, and she
expressed her desire to meet and adore the Infant Jesus, and
to see his Mother; asking him whether they could be reached.
The holy angel answered that his King and Lord was passing
with his Mother at a distance from Hebron and could not
wait for her visit; saint Elisabeth therefore gave up her pro-
ject. Overflowing with tender and tearful affection, she asked
the angel to bring affectionate greetings to the Son and
Mother. The angel then returned with his message to the
Queen. Saint Elisabeth immediately dispatched a servant
with some gifts consisting in provisions, money and material
for clothing the Infant. She foresaw their needs in a strange
country and instructed the servant to overtake them with all
haste. He met them in Gaza, which lies a little less than
twenty hours from Jerusalem, on the river Besor, and on the

road from Palestine to Egypt, not far from the Mediterranean sea.

624. In this town they remained two days, for saint Joseph and the beast of burden which carried the Queen were worn out by the fatigue of the journey. From that place they sent back the servant of saint Elisabeth, taking care to caution him not to tell anyone of their whereabouts. But God provided still more effectually against this danger; for He took away from this man all remembrance of what saint Joseph had charged him to conceal, so that he retained only his message to saint Elisabeth. Most holy Mary expended the presents sent by Elisabeth in entertaining the poor; for She, who was Mother of the poor, could not bear to pass them by unassisted. Of the clothes sent to Her She made a cloak for the divine Infant, and one for saint Joseph, to shelter Them from the discomforts of the season and of the journey. She also used other things in their possession for the comfort of her Child and of saint Joseph. The most prudent Virgin would not rely on miraculous assistance whenever She could provide for the daily needs by her own diligence and labor; for in these matters She desired to subject Herself to the natural order and depend upon her own efforts. During the two days which they spent in that city the most pure Mary, in order to enrich it with great blessings, performed some wonderful deeds. She freed two sick persons from the danger of death and cured their ailments. She restored to another person, a crippled woman, the use of her limbs. In the souls of many, who met Her and conversed with Her, She caused divine effects of the knowledge of God and of a change of life. All of them felt themselves moved to praise their Creator. But neither Mary nor Joseph spoke a word about their native country, nor of the destination or object of their journey; for if this information had been added to the public notice caused by their wonderful actions, the attention of

Herod's agents might have been drawn toward them, and they might have found sufficient inducement to follow them after their departure.

625. Words fail me to describe what I have been made to understand concerning the happenings during this journey of Jesus and Mary; moreover, I fall short of the sentiments of reverence and piety which such admirable mysteries would require. The arms of the most pure Mary continually served as a delightful couch for the new and real King Solomon (Cant. 3, 7). As She penetrated in spirit into the secret of the most holy humanity of Christ, it happened sometimes that the Son and Mother interchanged sweet colloquies and canticles of praise in honor especially of the infinite essence of God and of all his attributes and perfections. On these occasions the Son of God favored his sovereign Mother with new visions of intellectual clearness, in which She perceived the unity of Essence in the three persons of God, the operations ad intra, in the generation of the Word, and in the procession of the Holy Spirit. She perceived how the Three are from eternity, and how the Word is generated by the operation of the eternal Intellect, and the Holy Ghost is breathed forth in the operation of the Will; how there is no need of any succession of before or after, but how all is from eternity; and how it happens that we conceive these operations with the idea of duration or succession of time. She also perceived how these three Persons comprehend each other by one and the same act of understanding, and how this comprehension includes the Divinity of the incarnate Word united to the humanity, forming one Person, and what effects this union produces in the humanity.

626. Filled with this exalted knowledge, the great Lady allowed her thoughts to descend from the Divinity to the humanity and composed new canticles of praise and thanksgiving for the creation of this sacred humanity, most perfect

in soul and body: the soul, in its plenitude and all possible abundance of wisdom, gifts and graces of the Holy Ghost; the body, most pure, and in the highest possible degree well composed and complexioned. Then again She contemplated the exalted and heroic activity of all his faculties, and, having in her soul imitated Him therein, She passed on to bless and give Him thanks for having made Her his Mother, caused Her to be conceived without sin, chosen Her out of thousands, enriched Her with all the favors and gifts of his powerful right hand as far as was possible in a mere creature. In the exaltation and glory of these and other mysteries, the Child spoke to his Mother and She responded in words which are beyond the tongue of angels and beyond the conception of any other created being. To all this the heavenly Lady attended without neglecting the care and comfort of her Child, giving Him nourishment at her breast three times a day, tenderly caressing Him as a Mother more attentive and loving than all other Mothers combined could be toward their children.

627. At other times She said to Him: "My sweetest and most beloved Son, permit me to speak to Thee and to manifest to Thee my desires, although Thou, my Lord, already knowest them; permit me to be delighted in the sound of thy voice. Tell me, life of my soul and light of my eyes, whether the labors of this journey are fatiguing Thee, whether the rigors of the season and of the weather cause Thee affliction, and what I can do for thy service and for thy relief." And the divine Infant answered: "All the labors, O Mother, and all fatigue are most light and sweet to Me, since I undergo them for the honor of my eternal Father and for the instruction and Redemption of men, especially in thy company." The Child wept a few times, yet in great serenity and in the manner of a grown-up and perfect man; and immediately the loving Mother sought the interior cause of these tears, find-

ing it in his soul. She understood that they were tears of love
and compassion for the salvation of men and caused by their
ingratitude; in this sorrow and weeping the sweetest Mother
imitated Him. She was wont to answer his tearful plaints like
a compassionate turtledove lovingly caressing and soothing
Him as his affectionate Mother, and kissing Him with
matchless reverence. The fortunate Joseph often witnessed
these divine mysteries; and shared in some of the enlightenments, thus consoling himself for the hardships of the journey. At other times he would converse with his Spouse as
they journeyed along, asking Her frequently whether She
desired any service for Herself or for the Child; or he would
approach and adore the Infant, kissing his feet and asking his
blessing, and sometimes taking Him in his arms. By these
little offices of kindness the great Patriarch sweetened his
labors, being at the same time consoled and encouraged by
his heavenly Spouse. To all things She attended with a
magnanimous heart, being hindered neither by her interior
prayer, nor by her exalted and fervent contemplation, from
attending to the corporal affairs; for in all things She was
most perfect.

Words of the Queen

THE VIRGIN MARY SPEAKS TO SISTER MARY OF AGREDA

628. My dearest daughter, for thy instruction and imitation I
wish, in what thou hast written, that thou take as an example
the affectionate wonder which the divine light caused in my
soul at seeing my most holy Son subject Himself to the
inhuman fury of wicked men, such as was shown by Herod
in this occasion of our flight from his wrath and afterwards
by the perverse servants of the high priests and magistrates.
In all the works of the Most High his greatness, goodness
and infinite wisdom shine forth. But, since my understand-

ing, by means of the most exalted inspiration, penetrated so deeply into the very essence of God in the person of the Word united to the Divinity, and since I knew that my most holy Son was the eternal, all-powerful, infinite Creator and Preserver of all things, and that this iniquitous king depended for his life and existence entirely upon this very beneficence, I was particularly struck with wonder to see the most sacred humanity pray and beseech his eternal Father to confer upon Herod, at this very time, enlightenment, help and blessing; to see my Son, who had it so much in his power to punish him, by his prayers prevent the full measure of chastisement which he deserved. Although Herod's purpose was frustrated, yet this obstinate reprobate was visited with less chastisement than would have been given to him if my holy Son had not prayed for him. All this, and whatever else is contained in this matchless mercy and kindness of Jesus, I sought to imitate; for as a Teacher He taught me thus early what He afterwards inculcated by his actions, words and example concerning the love of enemies (Matth. 5, 44). When I perceive how he concealed and disguised his infinite power, and how, being the invincible Lion, He became a meek and humble Lamb (Is. 5, 29), amidst the fury of ravenous wolves, my heart was overwhelmed and my faculties failed me in the ardent desire of loving Him, imitating and following Him in his love, charity, patience and meekness.

629. This example I place before thee for thy constant imitation, so that thou mayest understand to what extremes thou must be willing to bear and suffer, forgive and love all who offend thee; for neither thou nor other creatures are innocent and without fault, and many are burdened with numerous and oft-repeated sins, by which they have merited all offenses and insults. Now, if persecutions afford thee the advantage of imitating Him, why shouldst thou not esteem them as a great blessing? Why shouldst thou not love those

who give thee occasion to practice this highest perfection, why not thank them for this benefit, and hold them not as enemies but as benefactors, who afford thee a chance to obtain what is of so much importance for thy welfare? On account of the object-lesson contained in this history, thou wilt not be without guilt if thou fall short in this matter; for the divine light, and all that thou perceivest and understandest through it, is as it were before thy eyes, as in a living example.

Chapter XXIII

JESUS, MARY AND JOSEPH PURSUE THEIR JOURNEY FROM
THE CITY OF GAZA TO HELIOPOLIS IN EGYPT.

630. On the third day after our Pilgrims had touched Gaza,
they departed from that city for Egypt. Soon leaving the
inhabited parts of Palestine, they entered the sandy deserts of
Bersabe, which they were obliged to traverse for sixty leagues
in order to arrive and take their abode in Heliopolis, the
present Cairo in Egypt. This journey through the desert
consumed a number of days, for the distance they could
travel each day was but short, not only on account of the
laborious progress over the deep sand, but also on account of
the hardships occasioned by the want of shelter. There were
many incidents on their way through this solitude; I will
mention some of them, from which others can be conjectured; for it is not necessary to relate all of them. In order to
understand how much Mary and Joseph and also the Infant
Jesus suffered on their pilgrimage, it must be remembered
that the Almighty permitted his Onlybegotten, with his most
holy Mother and saint Joseph, to suffer the inconveniences
and hardships naturally connected with travel through this
desert. And although the heavenly Lady made no complaints,
yet She was much afflicted, which was also true of her most
faithful husband. For both of them suffered many personal

inconveniences and discomforts, while the Mother, in addition thereto, was afflicted still more on account of the sufferings of her Son and of saint Joseph; and the latter was deeply
grieved not to be able by his diligence and care to ease the
hardships of the Child and his Spouse.

631. During all this journey of sixty leagues through the
desert they had no other night-shelter than the sky and open
air; moreover, it was in the time of winter, for this journey
took place in the month of February, only six days after the
Purification, as was indicated in the last chapter. In the first
night on these sandy plains they rested at the foot of a small
hill, this being the only protection they could find. The
Queen of heaven with the Child in her arms seated Herself
on the earth, and with her husband She ate of the victuals
brought with them from Gaza. The Empress of heaven also
nursed the Infant Jesus at her breast and He on his part
rejoiced his Mother and her husband by his contentment. In
order to furnish them with some kind of shelter against the
open air, however narrow and humble it might be, saint
Joseph formed a sort of tent for the divine Word and most
holy Mary by means of his cloak and some sticks. During
that night the ten thousand angels who, full of marvel,
assisted these earthly Pilgrims in visible human shapes,
formed a guard around their King and Queen. The great
Lady perceived that her divine Son offered up to the eternal
Father the hardships and labors both of Himself and of Mary
and Joseph. In these prayers and in the other acts of his
deified Soul, the Queen joined him for the greater part of the
night. The divine Infant slept for a short time in her arms,
while She continued wakeful and engaged in heavenly colloquies with the Most High and his angels. Saint Joseph slept
upon the ground, resting his head upon the chest, which
contained the clothing and other articles of their baggage.

632. On the next day they pursued their journey and their little store of fruit and bread was soon exhausted, so that they began to suffer great want and to feel the hunger. Although Joseph was more deeply concerned, yet both of them felt this privation very much. On one of the first days of their journey they partook of no sustenance until nine o'clock at night, not having any more even of the coarse and poor food which until then had sustained them in their hardships and labor. As nature demanded some refreshment after the exertion and weariness of travel, and as there was no way of supplying their want by natural means, the heavenly Lady addressed Herself to the Most High in these words: "Eternal, great and powerful God, I give Thee thanks and bless Thee for thy magnificent bounty; and also that, without my merits, only on account of thy merciful condescension, Thou gavest me life and being and preservest me in it, though I am but dust and a useless creature. I have not made a proper return for all these benefits; therefore how can I ask for myself what I cannot repay? But, my Lord and Father, look upon thy Onlybegotten and grant me what is necessary to sustain my natural life and also that of my spouse, so that I may serve thy Majesty and thy Word made flesh for the salvation of men."

633. In order that the clamors of the sweetest Mother might proceed from yet greater tribulation, the Most High permitted the elements to afflict them more than at other times and in addition to the sufferings caused by their fatigue, destitution and hunger. For there arose a storm of wind and rain, which harassed and blinded them by its fury. This hardship grieved still more the tender-hearted and loving Mother on account of the delicate Child, which was not yet fifty days old. Although She tried to cover and protect Him as much as possible, yet She could not prevent Him from feeling the inclemency of the weather, so that He shed

tears and shivered from the cold in the same manner as other children are wont to do. Then the anxious Mother, making use of her power as Queen and Mistress of creatures, commanded the elements not to afflict their Creator, but to afford Him shelter and refreshment, and wreak their vengeance upon Her alone. And, as related once before, at the occasion of the birth of Christ and of the journey to Jerusalem, again the wind immediately moderated and the storm abated, not daring to approach the Mother and Child. In return for this loving forethought, the Infant Jesus commanded his angels to assist his kindest Mother and to serve Her as a shield against the inclemency of the weather. They immediately complied and constructed a resplendent and beautiful globe round about and over their incarnate God, his Mother and her spouse. In this they were protected and defended more effectually than all the wealthy and powerful of the world in their palaces and rich garments. The same they did several times during the journey through the desert.

634. Nevertheless, they were in want of food, and they were destitute of other things unprovidable by their own mere human effort; But the Lord allowed them to fall into this need in order that, listening to the acceptable prayers of his Spouse, He might make provision also for this by the hands of the angels. They brought them delicious bread and well-seasoned fruits, and moreover a most delicious drink; all of which they administered and served with their own hands. Then all of them together sang hymns of praise and thanksgiving to the Lord, who gives food to all creatures at opportune times, in order that the poor may eat and be filled (Ps. 135,25) whose eyes and hopes are fixed upon his kingly providence and bounty. Of such a kind was the delicate feast, with which the Lord regaled his three exiled Wanderers in the desert of Bersabe (III Kings 19, 3), for it was the same desert in which Elias, fleeing from Jezebel, was comforted by

the hearth cake, brought to him by the angel in order that he might travel to Horeb mount. Yet neither this bread, nor the bread and meat, which once before the ravens had miraculously brought him every morning and evening at the torrent of Carith, nor the manna which fell from heaven for the Israelites, although it was called the bread of angels and dropped from heaven, nor the quails, which were carried to them by the African winds; nor the cloud-tent, which overshadowed them; none of all these could be compared to the succor and relief which the Lord afforded to his Onlybegotten and to his Mother and saint Joseph. For these favors were not to be conferred upon a prophet, or upon an ungrateful and unthinking people; but they were intended for the nourishment and protection of a God incarnate, for his true Mother: they were intended for the preservation of the natural life of Christ, on which depended the eternal life of the whole human race. But if this food was worthy of the excellence of those who were invited, so was also the thanksgiving and gratitude worthy of the blessings conferred. In order that all this might be so much the more opportune, the Lord permitted the necessity to become extreme and thus naturally call into play the assistance of heaven.

635. Let the poor rejoice in this example, let the hungry confide, let the destitute take new courage, let none complain of divine Providence, no matter how afflicted and needy they may find themselves to be. When has the Lord ever failed him who hoped in his assistance? (Ps. 17,31). When has He ever turned away his countenance from his afflicted and needy children? We are brothers of his only Son incarnate, children and heirs of his blessings, and also children of his kindest Mother. Why, then, ye children of God and of this most holy Mother, do you continue to distrust such Parents in your poverty? Why do you deprive them of this honor, and yourselves of the privilege of being assisted and sustained

by Them? Come, come to Them with humble confidence, so
that They may look upon you with the eyes of Parents and
listen to your crying needs. The arms of this Lady are
stretched out toward the poor and her hands opened for the
needy. And you, ye rich of this world, why will you confide
so much in your uncertain riches, at the imminent danger of
losing your faith, of piling up for yourselves heaviest cares
and sorrows as mentioned by the Apostle? By your avarice
you fail to conduct yourselves as children of God or of his
Mother; by your actions you make of yourselves spurious
offspring; for legitimate children confide in the care and love
of their parents, and abhor trusting in others, who are not
only strangers but enemies. These truths are manifest to me
by the divine light and charity compels me thus to speak.

636. The most high Father not only provided nourishment for our Pilgrims, but also visible relief against the
tediousness of this journey and continued solitude. It happened a few times, when the heavenly Lady rested on the
ground from her fatigue, that, as on other occasions, a great
multitude of birds came flying towards Her from the mountains. By the sweetness of their warbling and the variety of
their plumage they sought to entertain and delight Her,
perching on her shoulders and hands with signs of great joy.
The most prudent Queen gently received them and invited
them to acknowledge their Creator by their songs and to be
thankful for his having created them so beautiful and arrayed
them in their gorgeous plumage, given them the air and the
earth for their enjoyment, and provided them with daily food
and sustenance. The birds responded to her exhortations
with joyous movements and sweet warblings, while the
loving Mother joined them with still more sweet and melo-
dious songs for the Infant Jesus, extolling and blessing Him,
and acknowledging Him as her God and her Son, and as the
Author of all these wonders. Also the holy angels took part in

these colloquies so full of sweetness, and alternated their offerings of praise with that of the great Lady and of these simple birds. All this produced a harmony more perceptible by the spirit than by the senses, and of admirable concord for the rational soul.

637. At other times the heavenly Princess conversed with the Child and said: "My love and light of my soul, how can I diminish thy labor? How can I relieve Thee of thy hardships? What can I do to lighten the sufferings of this journey? O would that I could carry Thee, not in my arms, but in my bosom and make for Thee a soft couch in my heart, in order that Thou mayest rest there without fatigue!" And the sweetest Jesus replied: "My beloved Mother, very easily do I rest in thy arms while making this journey, and reclining on thy breast, I am delighted by thy affection, and entertained by thy words." Sometimes the Son and Mother conversed with each other interiorly; and these conversations were so exalted and divine that our words cannot express them. Saint Joseph shared in many of these mysteries and consolations; and thus he eased his journey, forgot his hardships, feeling within himself the delight and sweetness of such companionship. Yet he did not hear or perceive what the Child said audibly to his Mother; for at that time of the life of Jesus this favor was reserved for Her alone, as I have already remarked above. In this manner our Exiles proceeded on their way to Egypt.

Words of the Queen

THE VIRGIN MARY SPEAKS TO SISTER MARY OF AGREDA

638. My daughter, just as those who know the Lord also know how to trust in Him, so those who do not hope in his goodness and immense love have no perfect knowledge of the Majesty of God. On account of the want of faith and hope, this love also is deficient; for we readily place our love in

whom we have confidence and whom we esteem. In this error lies the source of all the damage done to mortals; for they have such a low conception of the infinite bounty, which gave them being and which preserves them, that they fail to place full confidence in their God. Failing in this, they also fail in the love due to Him and they divert it toward the creatures. They esteem in them what they are seeking, namely power, riches, vain honor and ostentation. Although the faithful can remedy these injurious influences by faith and hope, yet they allow these virtues to remain dead, and unused, and debase themselves to the level of worthless creatures. Those who have riches, trust in them, and those who have none, greedily haste after them; some procure them by very reprehensible ways and means; some confide in influential persons, praising and flattering them. And thus it happens that very few seek the Lord in such a way as to deserve his providential care; very few trust in God and acknowledge Him as their Father, who is willing to provide for his children, who will nourish and sustain them without fail in all necessities.

639. This deceitful error has filled the earth with lovers of the world; has filled it with avarice and concupiscence against the law of the Creator; has made men insane in their desires; for all of them commonly strive after riches and earthly possessions; claiming thereby merely to satisfy their needs, which is only a pretext for hiding their want of interest in higher things. In reality they lie to themselves abominously, since they are seeking the superfluous; not what is really necessary, but what ministers to worldly pride. If men would confine their desires to what is really necessary, it would be unreasonable to put any confidence in creatures instead of placing it in God alone, who ineffably provides even for the young ravens with no less solicitude than if their crowings were prayers sent up to their Creator for help (Prov. 28, 8).

Secure in this confidence, I was not alarmed in my exile and prolonged journey. Since I trusted in the Lord, He provided for me in the time of my need. Thou also, my daughter, who art aware of this exalted Providence, shouldst not afflict thyself in the time of need, nor neglect thy duties in order to make provision for them, nor confide in human efforts, nor in creatures. After having done what is required of thee, the most efficacious means is to confide in the Lord, without being disturbed or confused; hope patiently, even when help is somewhat delayed. It will always be at hand at a time when it will do most good, and when the paternal love of the Lord can manifest itself most conveniently and openly. Thus it happened with me and my spouse in the time of our destitution and necessity.

640. Those that do not bear with adversity and do not put up with privations, who turn toward dried up cisterns (Jer. 2, 5), trusting in deceit and in the powerful of this world; those that are not moderate in their desires and greedily covet what is unnecessary for the sustenance of life; those that anxiously cling to what they possess, fearing that it may be diminished and withholding the alms due to the poor; all of them have reasons to dread lest divine Providence, showing Itself just as niggardly in caring for them as they are in their confidence and in their charities to the poor, deprive them of what they could otherwise easily expect to receive at its hands. But the Father in heaven, who lets the sun rise over the just and the unjust (Matth. 5, 45), and lets the rain fall on the good and the bad, nevertheless helps all, giving them life and nourishment. However, just as his blessings are distributed to the good and to the bad, so also it cannot be a rule with God to give greater temporal goods to the good and less to the bad. On the contrary He prefers that the chosen and predestined ones be poor (James 2, 5), both because they thus gain more merit and reward, and because

there are few who know how to use wealth properly and who can retain it without inordinate greed. Although my most holy Son and I had nothing to fear from this danger, yet He wished to furnish this example to men and to teach them this science, through which eternal life comes to them.

Chapter XXIV

THE HOLY TRAVELERS, JESUS, MARY AND JOSEPH, ARRIVE IN EGYPT, AND AFTER SOME WANDERINGS THEY COME TO HELIOPOLIS, WHERE GREAT MIRACLES ARE WROUGHT.

641. I have already mentioned that the flight of the incarnate Word contained other mysteries and aimed at more exalted ends than to evade Herod and his persecution. The flight into Egypt was to afford the infant Savior an occasion of visiting that country and performing the miracles spoken of by the ancient Prophets. Isaias more expressly prophesies of them, when he says: that the Lord shall ascend upon a swift cloud and enter into Egypt; that the idols of Egypt shall be moved at his presence and that the heart of the Egyptians shall melt in the midst thereof (Is. 19, 1). These and other things contained in this prophecy happened at the time of the birth of Christ our Lord. Yet, passing over what does not pertain to my purpose, I wish to say that, continuing their pilgrimage in the manner already described, Jesus, Mary and Joseph arrived in the populated districts of Egypt. Before They came to the place of their abode in Heliopolis, They were conducted by the angels, according to the ordainment of the Most High, in a roundabout way, so that They might pass through many places, where God wished his miracles and blessings to be wrought for the good of the Egyptians. Thus it came that They consumed in this journey more than

fifty days; and the distance of their journey from Bethlehem or Jerusalem amounted to more than two hundred leagues, while by a direct route such long-protracted travel would not have been necessary.

642. Egypt was much given to idolatry and its concomitant superstition. Even the small villages of this country were full of idols. In many of these places temples had been built, where the demons dwelt; and the inhabitants, instructed by these devils, gathered in them to offer services and sacrifices in their honor, while the demons answered their prayers by oracles, thus obtaining full control of this foolish and superstitious nation. Steeped in these deceits, they lived on in such error and subjection to the demons, that only the strong arm of the Lord (which is the incarnate Word) could rescue these forsaken people and deliver them from the oppression of Lucifer. It was a harder and more dangerous slavery than that in which the Egyptians had held the people of Israel (Exod. 1, 11). In order to obtain this deliverance and enlighten those that were living in the region and the shadows of death (Luke 1, 79), and in order that they might see the great light spoken of by Isaias (Is. 9, 2), the Most High ordained that the Son of justice, Christ (Mal. 4, 2), shortly after his birth, should appear in Egypt in the arms of his most fortunate Mother, and that He should journey and pass through this country, illumining it everywhere by the power of his divine light.

643. So then the Infant Jesus, with his Mother and saint Joseph, reached the inhabited country of Egypt. On entering the towns the divine Infant, in the arms of his Mother, raised his eyes and his hands to the Father asking for the salvation of these inhabitants held captive by satan. And immediately He made use of his sovereign and divine power and drove the demons from the idols and hurled them to the infernal abyss. Like lightning flashed from the clouds they darted forth and

descended to the lowermost caverns of hell and darkness
(Luke 10, 4). At the same instant the idols crashed to the
ground, the altars fell to pieces, and the temples crumbled to
ruins. The cause of these marvelous effects were known to
the heavenly Lady, for She united her prayers with those of
her most holy Son as Cooperatrix of his salvation. Saint
Joseph also knew this to be the work of the incarnate Word;
and He praised and extolled Him in holy admiration. But
the demons, although they felt the divine power, knew not
whence this power proceeded.

644. The Egyptian people were astounded at these inex-
plicable happenings; although among the more learned, ever
since the sojourn of Jeremias in Egypt, an ancient tradition
was current that a King of the Jews would come and that the
temples of the idols would be destroyed. Yet of this prophecy
the common people had no knowledge, nor did the learned
know how it was to be fulfilled: and therefore the terror and
confusion was spread among all of them, as was prophesied
by Isaias (Is. 9, 1). In this disturbance and fear, some, reflect-
ing on these events, came to our great Lady and saint Joseph;
and, in their curiosity at seeing these strangers in their midst,
they also spoke to them about the ruin of their temples and
their idols. Making use of this occasion the Mother of wisdom began to undeceive these people, speaking to them of
the true God and teaching them that He is the one and only
Creator of heaven and earth, who is alone to be adored, and
acknowledged as God; that all others are but false and deceitful gods, nothing more than the wood, or clay, or metal of
which they are made, having neither eyes, nor ears, nor any
power; that the same artisans that made them, and any other
man, could destroy them at pleasure; since any man is more
noble and powerful than they; that the oracles which they
gave forth were answers of the lying and deceitful demons

within them; and that the latter had no power, since there is but one true God.

645. The heavenly Lady was so sweet and kind in her words, and at the same time so full of life and force; her appearance was so charming, and all her intercourse was accompanied by such salutary effects, that the rumor of the arrival of these strange Pilgrims quickly spread about in the different towns, and many people gathered to see and hear Them. Moreover, the powerful prayers of the incarnate Word wrought a change of hearts, and the crumbling of the idols caused an incredible commotion among these people, instilling into their minds knowledge of the true God and sorrow for their sins without their knowing whence or through whom these blessings came to them. Jesus, Mary and Joseph pursued their way through many towns of Egypt, performing these and many other miracles, driving out the demons not only from the idols, but out of many bodies possessed by them, curing many that were grievously and dangerously ill, enlightening the hearts by the doctrines of truth and eternal life. By these temporal benefits and others, so effectual in moving the ignorant, earthly-minded people, many were drawn to listen to the instructions of Mary and Joseph concerning a good and salutary life.

646. They arrived at Hermopolis, which lies in the direction of the Thebaid, and is called by some the city of Mercury. In it there were many idols infested by powerful demons. One of them dwelt in a tree at the entrance of the city; for the neighboring inhabitants had begun to venerate this tree on account of its size and beauty, whence the demon had taken occasion to erect his seat in it. When the incarnate Word came within sight of this tree, not only was the demon hurled from his seat and cast into hell, but the tree bowed down to the ground, as if rejoiced by its good fortune; for even the senseless creatures testified how tyrannical is the

dominion of the devil. This miraculous reverence of the trees happened at other times during this journey of Christ, although these incidents are not all recorded. But the memory of this event remained for centuries, for the leaves and fruits of this tree cured many sicknesses. Of this miracle some authors make mention, as well as of others in other cities visited by the incarnate Word and his Mother (Nicephor 1, 10, c. 31; Sozomen 1, 5, c. 20; Brocard II, Co 4). There is to this day a traditional fountain near Cairo from which the heavenly Lady drew water for Herself and the Child, and for washing his clothes; all this rests on truth and the veneration for these wonders and these places still lives, not only among the faithful who visit the holy places, but also among the infidels, who there occasionally obtain temporal benefits from the hands of the Lord. For also the infidels sometimes obtain certain favors, in order that the Lord may be justified before them, or in order that the memory of his wonders may be preserved. But it is not necessary to speak of them especially just now; since the principal wonders during the stay of our Lord in Egypt were wrought in Heliopolis, which, not without mysterious import, was called city of the sun, and is now called Cairo, the grand.

647. In writing of these wonders, I asked the great Queen in astonishment how She could have traveled with the Child through so many strange provinces and cities? For it appeared to me that She thereby prolonged exceedingly the labors and hardships of their journey. And our Lady replied: "Do not wonder that my most holy Son and I journeyed so far in order to gain souls. For the sake of even one soul, if possible, and if there would be no other way, We would willingly traverse the whole world." If what Jesus and Mary did for the salvation of us men does seem great to us, it is because we do not understand the immensity of their love,

and because we understand just as little how to make a proper return for such love.

648. On account of these strange happenings when so many of the demons were driven by a new and unwonted power to populate hell, Lucifer was highly disturbed. Furiously enraged, He issued forth into the world in order to investigate the cause of such unlooked for events. He roamed about through all Egypt, where so many temples and altars of his idols had been overthrown; and reaching Heliopolis, the largest of the cities and the scene of the greatest destruction in his dominions, he sought to ascertain with the utmost anxiety what kind of people dwelt therein. He found nothing new, except that most holy Mary had arrived in the city. Of the Infant Jesus he made no account, deeming Him a child just like all the rest of that age, for he knew nothing particular about Him. But as he had been so often vanquished by the virtues and holiness of the Virgin Mother, he was seized with new consternation; although he considered a woman far too insignificant for such great works, yet he resolved anew to persecute Her and to stir up against Her his associates in wickedness.

649. He therefore returned immediately to hell and, calling a meeting of the princes of darkness, told them of the destruction of the temples and idols in Egypt. For these demons had been hurled by the divine power from their habitations with such suddenness, confusion and torment that at their departure they were unable to ascertain the fate of the idols and temples which they were forced to leave. Lucifer, informing them of all that had happened, and that he feared the destruction of his reign in Egypt, told them that he could not ascertain or understand what was the cause of this ruin, since he had found there only that Woman, his enemy (for so the dragon called most holy Mary) ; and though he knew that her power was extraordinary, yet he did

not presume it to be so great as to account for such portents. Nevertheless, he wished them to begin a new war against Her, and that all should prepare themselves for it. The satellites of Lucifer proclaimed their readiness to obey, trying to console him in his desperate fury and promising him victory, as if their forces were as great as their arrogance (Is. 16, 6).

650. Many legions of devils accordingly sallied forth from hell and betook themselves to the place where the Queen of heaven was at that time. As they suspected that God had used the most holy Mary as his instrument in causing all their losses in that unfortunate country, they thought they could make up for their defeat and restore their dominion if they succeeded in overcoming Her. But they were astonished to find that when they attempted to approach Her in order to begin their diabolical temptations, they could not come nearer to Her than a distance of two thousand paces; for they were restrained by the divine power, which they perceived issuing forth from the heavenly Lady herself. Although Lucifer and the hostile bands struggled violently, they were paralyzed and as if bound in strong and tormenting shackles, without being able to reach the most unconquerable Queen; while She witnessed their struggles, holding in her arms the omnipotence of God himself. As Lucifer persevered in his attempts, he was suddenly hurled into the abyss of hell with all his squadrons and wicked spirits. This defeat and ruin filled the dragon with vast torment and anxiety, and as the like had overtaken him repeatedly since the Incarnation, he began to have new misgivings, whether the Messias had not come into the world. But since he knew nothing of the mystery, and expected the Messias to come in great splendor and renown, he remained in uncertainty and doubt, full of tormenting fury and wrath. He was consumed with the desire to find out the cause of his sufferings, and the more he

inquired the more was he involved in darkness and so much
the less did he ascertain of the true cause.

Words of the Queen

THE VIRGIN MARY SPEAKS TO SISTER MARY OF AGREDA

651. My daughter, great and above all else to be esteemed, is
the consolation of the faithful friends of my most holy Son,
when they with lively faith and assurance are permitted to
serve the Lord of lords and the God of gods, who alone holds
power and dominion over all creation and who triumphs and
reigns over his enemies. In this feeling of assurance the
intellect is delighted, the memory is recreated, the will is
rejoiced and all the powers of the devout soul enjoy the
sweetness of the most exalted activity. For they are entirely
taken up with this supreme Goodness, Holiness and infinite
Power, which has need of none outside Itself and whose will
governs all created things (II Mach. 14,35, Apoc. 4,11). O
how many thousand-fold blessings do those creatures lose
who, forgetful of their true happiness, employ all the time of
their life and all their powers in attending upon visible
things, pursuing the momentary pleasures and seeking the
apparent and deceitful goods of this world! In the knowledge
and light vouchsafed to thee I would wish, my daughter, that
thou withdraw thyself from this danger, and that thy intellect
and memory occupy themselves continually with the reality
of the existence of thy God. In this endless sea, engulf and
annihilate thyself, repeating without cessation: "Who is like
to God our Lord, that dwells on high and looks upon the
humble in heaven and on earth?" (Ps. 112, 5). Who is like to
Him, that is almighty and depends upon no one? that hum-
bles the proud, and casts down those whom the blind world
calls powerful, that triumphs over the demon and hurls him
to the abyss?

652. In order that thy heart may dilate so much the more upon these truths and attain a greater power over the enemies of the Most High and of thyself, I wish that, as far as is possible, thou imitate me, glorying in the victories and triumphs of his mighty arm and seeking thyself to have a share in those which he gains over this cruel dragon. No created tongue, not that of the seraphim, can describe what my soul felt when I beheld my most holy Son working such wonders against his enemies for the benefit of the souls blinded and terrorized by their errors and for the exaltation and honor of the Most High. In this jubilation I magnified the Lord; and in company with my Son I composed new hymns of praise as his Mother and as Spouse of the Holy Ghost. Thou art a daughter of the holy Church and a spouse of my most blessed Son, favored by his grace: it is therefore just that thou be zealous in acquiring this glory and honor for Him, striving against his enemies and battling for the triumphs of thy Spouse

Chapter XXV

IN ACCORDANCE WITH THE DIVINE WILL JESUS, MARY AND
JOSEPH SETTLE DOWN TO DWELL NEAR THE CITY OF HELI-
OPOLIS AND THEY REGULATE THEIR DAILY LIFE DURING
THEIR BANISHMENT.

653. The traditions, which in many parts of Egypt kept alive
the remembrance of wonders wrought by the incarnate
Word; gave rise to differences of opinion among the sacred
and other writers in regard to the city, in which our Exiles
lived during their stay in Egypt. Some of them assert that
they dwelt in this city, some in another. But all of them may
be right and in accordance with facts, since each one may be
speaking of a different period of the sojourn of our Pilgrims
in Memphis, or Babylon of Egypt, or in Matarieh; for they
visited not only these cities, but many others. I for my part
have been informed that they passed through these and then
reached Heliopolis, where they took up their abode. Their
holy guardian angels instructed the heavenly Queen and saint
Joseph, that They were to settle in this city. For, besides the
ruin of the temples and idols, which, just as in other places,
took place at their arrival here, the Lord had resolved to
perform still other miracles for his glory and for the rescue of
souls; and the inhabitants of this city, (according to the good
fortune already prognosticated in its name as "City of the
Sun"), were to see the Sun of justice and grace arise over

them and shine upon them. Following these orders, saint Joseph sought to purchase for a suitable price some dwelling in the neighborhood; and the Lord ordained that he should find a poor and humble, yet serviceable house, at small distance from the city, just such as the Queen of heaven desired.

654. Having therefore found this dwelling near Heliopolis, they took their abode therein. At the first entrance of the heavenly Lady with her divine Son and saint Joseph, She prostrated Herself to the ground, kissing it in profound humility and lovingly thanking the Most High for having secured them this place of rest after their prolonged and laborious journeyings. She thanked also the earth and the elements for bearing with Her, since in her matchless humility She persisted in esteeming Herself unworthy of all favors. She adored the immutable being of God in this prostration, dedicating all that She was to do in this place to his honor and worship. Interiorly She made a sacrifice of all her powers and faculties, offering to assume readily and with joy all the labors by which the Almighty could be served during her exile; for in her prudence She foresaw and affectionately embraced them all. By means of her divine knowledge She set a great value on sufferings; understanding how highly they are esteemed at the divine tribunal, and how her most holy Son looked upon them as a rich treasure and inheritance. Having performed these exalted acts of devotion, She set about humbly to clean and arrange the poor little house, borrowing the instruments for this purpose. Although our heavenly strangers were thus sufficiently provided with the shelter of bare walls, they were in want of all else pertaining to the sustenance and comfort of daily life. As they now lived in an inhabited country, the miraculous assistance, which they had enjoyed in the desert through the ministry of the angels, failed them; and the Lord left them to the last re-

source of the poor, namely, the begging of alms. Having come to these straits of suffering hunger, saint Joseph went forth to seek this kind of assistance for the love of God; giving thereby an example to the poor not to complain of their affliction and, all other means failing, not to be ashamed to have recourse to this expedient. For so early the Lord of all creation allowed Himself to fall into this extreme of being obliged to beg for his sustenance, in order that He might have an occasion to return the alms a hundredfold.

655. During the first three days of their arrival in Heliopolis, just as in other places of Egypt, the Queen had for Herself and for her Onlybegotten no other sustenance than what was begged by his foster father saint Joseph. When he began to earn some wages by his work, he made an humble couch for the Mother and a cradle for her Son; while he himself had as a resting place only the bare ground; for the house was without any furniture until by his own labor he succeeded in making some of the most indispensable pieces for the convenience of all three. In this connection I must not pass over in silence the fact that in their extreme poverty and need most holy Mary and Joseph regretted not their house in Nazareth, nor thought of the aid of their relations and friends, nor of the gifts of the kings, which they had given away and which, if they had saved them, would now be useful. All of these regrets were far from their minds, nor did they complain of the great privation and destitution, thinking of the past or worrying about their future. But they bore all with incomparable equanimity, joy and tranquillity, resigning themselves to the divine Providence in their extreme need and poverty. o smallness of our unfaithful hearts! In what excruciating anxieties we are apt to be cast at finding ourselves threatened with poverty or privation immediately we begin to rail at occasions lost, at having missed or neglected this or that advantage, or at not having done this or that,

by which we would have evaded our misfortunes. All these complaints are vain and most foolish, since they can bring no relief. Although it would have been good if we had not committed the sins by which we are thus punished, yet very often we are sorry for them only on account of the temporal disadvantages, and not for the guilt connected with sin. Slow and stupid of heart are we to perceive the spiritual things conducive to our justification and growth in grace (Luke 24, 25); while on the other hand we are full of fleshly and earthly rashness in entering upon temporal affairs and anxieties. The example of our Exiles is indeed a severe reprimand for our low-minded earthliness.

656. The most prudent Lady and her spouse, forsaken and destitute of all temporal help, accommodated themselves joyfully to the poverty of their little dwelling. Of the three rooms, which it contained, they assigned one to be the sanctuary or temple of the Infant Jesus under the tender care of the most pure Mother; there they placed the cradle and her bare couch, until, after some days, by the labor of the holy spouse, and through the kindness of some pious women, they could obtain wherewith to cover it. Another room was set aside for the sleeping place and oratory of saint Joseph. The third served as a workshop for plying his trade. In view of their great poverty, and of the great difficulty of sufficient employment as a carpenter, the great Lady resolved to assist him by the work of her hands to earn a livelihood. She immediately executed her resolve by seeking to obtain needlework through the intervention of the pious women, who, attracted by her modesty and sweetness, were beginning to have intercourse with Her. As all that She attended to or busied Herself with was so perfect, the reputation of her skill soon spread about, so that She never was in want of employment whereby to eke out the slender means of livelihood for her Son, the true God and man.

657. In order to obtain the indispensable victuals and clothing, furnish the house ever so moderately, and pay the necessary expenses, it seemed to our Queen that She must employ all day in work and consume the night in attending to her spiritual exercises. This She resolved upon, not for any motives of gain, or because She did not continue in her contemplations during the day; for this was her incessant occupation in the presence of the infant God, as I have so often said and shall repeat hereafter. But some of the hours, which She was wont to spend in special exercises, She wished to transfer to the night-time, in order to be able to extend the hours of manual labor, not being minded to ask or expect God's miraculous assistance for anything which She could attain by greater diligence and additional labor on her own part. In all such cases we ask for miraculous help more for our own convenience than on account of necessity. The most prudent Queen asked the eternal Father to provide sustenance for her divine Son; but at the same time She continued to labor. Like one who does not trust in herself, or in her own efforts, She united prayer with her labors, in order to obtain the necessities of life like other men.

658. The Infant Jesus was much pleased with the prudence of his Mother, and with her resignation in the midst of her dire poverty, and in return for her fidelity He wished to lessen the labors She had undertaken. One day He spoke to Her from the cradle and said: "My Mother, I wish to set up a rule for thy daily life and labors." Immediately the heavenly Mother knelt before Him and answered: "My sweetest Love, and Lord of all my being, I praise and magnify Thee because Thou hast condescended to meet my secret thoughts and desires; may it please Thee to direct my footsteps according to thy holy will, to regulate all my labors according to thy wishes, and to order all my occupations in each hour of the day according to thy divine pleasure. And since thy Deity

became incarnate' and thy Majesty condescended to take heed of my longings, speak, Light of my eyes, for thy servant hears." The Lord replied: "My dearest Mother, from the time of nightfall" (that is, from the hour called by us nine o'clock) "thou shalt take some sleep and rest. And from midnight until the break of day thou mayest occupy thyself in contemplation with Me, and We will praise the eternal Father. Thereupon prepare the necessary food for thyself and Joseph; and afterwards give Me nourishment and hold Me in thy arms until the third hour, when thou shalt place Me in the arms of thy husband, in order to afford him some refreshment in his labors. Then retire until it is time to prepare his meal and return to thy work. Since thou hast not with thee the sacred Scriptures, which were wont to console thee, thou canst, by my holy science, enter into the doctrines of eternal life, in order that thou mayest follow Me in perfect imitation. And continually pray to the eternal Father for the sinners."

659. By this rule of life the most holy Mary governed her doings during her stay in Egypt. Every day three times She nursed the infant God at her breast; for when He pointed out to Her the hour in which She was to nurse Him in the morning, He did not forbid Her to afford Him nourishment at other times, as She had been accustomed to do since his Nativity. Whenever the heavenly Mother was engaged in any work, She always performed it in his presence and upon her knees; and it was very usual, during their colloquies and conferences, that the King from his cradle and the Mother at her work, broke out in mysterious canticles of praise. If they were all written, they would outnumber all the psalms and the hymns used by the Church, and all that are written; for there can be no doubt that God conversed with the source of his humanity, his most blessed Mother, in a more exalted and wonderful manner than with David, Moses, Mary, Anne and all the Prophets. By these hymns the heavenly Mother

was continually filled with new influences of the Divinity, and new longings to be united to his unchangeable being; for She alone was the Phoenix which could be renewed in this conflagration, and the royal Eagle which could penetrate into the ineffable light and soar from height to heights, whither no other created being could venture to wing its flight. She fulfilled the end for which the divine Word had assumed flesh in her virginal womb, namely, to draw on and elevate the rational creatures to the Divinity. As She was the only Creature which did not present the hindrance of sin and its effects, nor from disordered passions and appetites, but was free of the downward tendency of our earthly nature, She flew upward to her Beloved and to his exalted habitation, not resting until She reached her Center, which was the Divinity. Moreover She had always in view the way and the light (John 16, 6), the incarnate Word, and all her desires and affections met in the immutable being of the Most High; and therefore She hastened on in burning fervor, embracing Her goal rather than flying towards it, and living more in her love than in her life.

660. Sometimes, also, the infant God slept under the watchful care of his happy and fortunate Mother; in order that also this saying might become true: "I sleep, but my heart is awake" (Cant. 5,2). And as this most holy body of her Son was for Her a most clear mirror, in which She saw and penetrated the secrets of his deified Soul and its operations (Wis. 7, 16), She beheld Herself therein again and again. Especially consoling to the heavenly Lady was it to see the most holy Soul of her Son revealed to Her in all its heroic operations as a Pilgrim and yet a Comprehensor, while at the same time his bodily faculties were lost in the tranquil and beauteous sleep of childhood, his whole humanity being hypostatically united to the Divinity. Our language is incapable of describing the sweet affections and flights of love,

and the heroic acts of the Queen of heaven on these occasions, and falls far short of the reality; but where words fail,
let faith and love supply the deficiency.

661. Whenever She wished to afford saint Joseph the consolation of holding the Infant Jesus, the Mother of God said:
"My Son and Lord, look upon thy faithful servant Joseph
with the love of a son and father, and delight Thyself in the
purity of his affectionate soul, so acceptable in thy eyes." And
to saint Joseph She said:

"My Spouse, receive in thy arms the Lord, who holds in
his hands all the orbs of heaven and earth, and who has given
them existence out of his mere bounty. Refresh thyself from
thy labors in Him who is the glory of all creation." For these
favors saint Joseph returned most humble thanks; and he was
wont to ask his Spouse whether he could dare to caress the
Child. Encouraged by Her, he would do so; and this privilege
made him forget all the hardships of his labor, and made
them easy and sweet in his eyes. Whenever Mary and Joseph
were at their meals they had with them the Infant; in serving
the meals, the heavenly Queen held Him in her arms, partaking of the food with great modesty and, in holding Him, She
at the same time afforded her most pure soul a sweeter and
more nourishing food than to the body, adoring and loving
Him as the eternal God, and caressing Him with the tenderness of a Mother. It is impossible to conceive the attention
which She paid to this double duty; on the one hand, to
fulfill all obligation that was due to Him as from a creature to
its Creator, looking upon Him in his Divinity, as Son of the
eternal Father, as King of kings, and Lord of lords, as the
Maker and Preserver of all the universe; and on the other
hand, to give to Him all the attention that He deserved as an
Infant, serving Him and nursing Him. Betwixt these two
extremes She was entirely inflamed with love, and her whole
being consumed in heroic acts of admiration, praise and

affection. Of all the rest which the two Spouses did it can only be said that they were the wonder of the angels, and that they attained the summit of holiness and of divine pleasure.

Words of the Queen

THE VIRGIN MARY SPEAKS TO SISTER MARY OF AGREDA

662. My daughter, I came into Egypt, where I knew no relations or friends, in a land of foreign religion, where I could offer no home or protection or assistance to my Son, whom I loved so much. It can easily be understood, then, what tribulations and hardships we suffered, since the Lord permitted them to come over Us. Thou canst not understand with what patience and forbearance We accepted them; and even the angels cannot estimate the reward I merited from the Most High by the love and resignation with which I bore them, and which were greater than if I had been in the greatest prosperity. It is true, I grieved much to see my husband in such necessity and want; but at the same time I blessed the Lord to be able to suffer them. In this most noble patience and joy of spirit I wish that thou imitate me whenever the Lord offers thee an occasion; and that thou learn to act with prudence interiorly and exteriorly, ordering well thy actions and thy thoughts, without hindrance to either of them.

663. When the necessaries of life are wanting to those under thy charge, exert thyself properly to obtain them. If sometimes thou must sacrifice thy own tranquillity in fulfilling this obligation, thou needst not on that account lose thy peace of mind; especially if thou art mindful of what I have so often told thee: not to lose sight of the presence of the Lord; for by his divine light and grace, if thou art careful and preservest thy peace, thou canst do all things. Whatever can duly be procured by human exertion, is not to be ex-

pected by a miracle, nor must one try to exempt himself from labor in the hope of a supernatural interference on the part of God; for the Lord sweetly concurs with the ordinary and natural course of created things. The labor of the body is serviceable to the soul as a sacrifice and as an increase of the merits due to that kind of activity. While at work the rational creature can praise God and adore Him in spirit and in truth (John 4, 23). In order to fulfill this duty, direct thy activity according to his pleasure, consult his will in regard to them, weighing them with the scales of the sanctuary and riveting thy attention upon the divine light which the Almighty infuses in thy soul.

Chapter XXVI

OF THE WONDERS WHICH THE INFANT JESUS, MOST HOLY
MARY AND JOSEPH WROUGHT AT HELIOPOLIS IN EGYPT.

664. Isaias says that the Lord shall enter Egypt upon a light
cloud in order to work miracles for that country. Isaias, in
calling the most holy Mary, or, as others think, the humanity
derived from Her, a cloud, no doubt wishes to indicate that
the Lord was to fertilize and water the barren land of the
hearts of its inhabitants, in order that henceforth they might
produce the fruits of sanctity and of divine knowledge. And
so it really happened after that heavenly cloud had overshadowed this land. For immediately the belief in the true God
began to spread, and idolatry to be destroyed; the paths of
eternal life began to be opened, which until then had been
held closed by the demons. To such an extent was all this
true that there was scarcely any province in that land in
which the true God remained unknown, as soon as the
incarnate Word had arrived therein. Although some of the
people came to this knowledge through intercourse with the
Hebrews, which existed between these two nations at that
time (Kings IV, 17, 24); yet a great many errors, superstitions
and worship of the demons were mixed up with it; just as
was the case with the Babylonians, who at another time came
to live in Samaria. But after the Sun of justice began to

illumine Egypt, and Mary most holy, the taintless cloud, began to overshadow that land, it became so fertile in holiness and grace that it gave forth abundant fruit for many centuries. This is witnessed by the many saints that lived in it afterwards, and by the thousands of hermits that made its mountains gather up and distil such sweet honey of sanctity and Christian perfection.

665. As I said, in order to secure these blessings to the Egyptians, the Lord took his dwelling in the city of Heliopolis. As it was so full of idols, temples and altars of the demons, which at his entrance all fell to the dust with great crashing and noise, the whole city was set in commotion and confusion by the suddenness of this ruin (Is. 19, 1). People rushed about astonished and as if crazed in mind; curiosity brought to the newly arrived strangers numbers of men and women, who sought to speak to the great Queen and saint Joseph. The heavenly Mother, who was aware of the mysterious designs of God, spoke to their inmost hearts with great wisdom, prudence and sweetness. They were filled with wonder at her incomparable gentleness and her exalted teachings, which undeceived them of their errors; and as She immediately cured some of their sick, She quieted and encouraged them so much the sooner. These miracles were so rapidly noised abroad that in a short time an immense concourse of people gathered to see the heavenly Strangers; and the most prudent Lady was forced to consult her most holy Son as to her further conduct toward this great multitude. The infant God told Her to instruct them in the knowledge of God, teach them his true worship, and exhort them to desist from sinful life.

666. In this office of preaching to the Egyptians, and of teaching them, our heavenly Princess served as the instrument of her most holy Son, who lent power to her words. The effect of it was so great that many books would be

required to describe the wonders and the conversions of souls that took place during the seven years of their stay in this province; for in her ministry She was filled with the benedictions of sweetness (Ps. 20, 4). Whenever the heavenly Lady listened to and answered those that came to Her, She held in her arms the Infant Jesus, as the One who was the Author of all the graces to be dispensed to sinners. She spoke to each one in the manner suitable to his capacity and serviceable for teaching him the doctrine of eternal life. She enlightened them concerning the Divinity and made them understand that there cannot be more than one God. She explained to them the several articles of truth pertaining to the Creation and Redemption of the world. She impressed upon their minds the commandments of the decalogue, founded upon the natural law; and She showed them the manner of adoring and worshipping God, and how they were to expect the regeneration of the human race.

667. Concerning the demons, She explained how they were enemies of God and men; how deeply they kept men in error by their idol-worship and the false answers of their oracles; how they induced men to commit the vilest abominations and afterwards secretly tempted them by exciting the disorderly passions. Although the Queen of heaven was so pure and free from all that is imperfect, nevertheless, for the glory of the Most High, She did not deem it beneath Her to speak to them of those vile and impure excesses in which all Egypt was sunk. She also declared to them that the Repairer of so many ills, who was to overcome the demons as it was written of Him, was already come into the world, although She did not say that She held Him in her arms. In order that her teachings might be accepted so much the more readily, and the truth might be more apparent, She confirmed her words by great miracles, curing all sorts of people who were sick or possessed by the devil and who came from all parts of

the country. A few times the Queen went to the infirmaries and conferred admirable blessings upon the sick. Everywhere She consoled the sorrowful and brought relief to the afflicted and the unfortunate, winning all by loving kindness and beneficence and admonishing them with sweet earnestness.

668. In regard to the cure of the sick and wounded the heavenly Lady hesitated between two different sentiments: the one of charity, which drew Her to nurse the wounded with her own hand, and the other of modesty, which forbade Her to touch anyone. In order that all propriety might be observed, her most holy Son empowered Her to cure the men by her mere word and exhortations; while She might cure the women by the touch of her hands and cleansing their wounds. This course of action She maintained thence-forward, taking upon Herself as well the office of a mother as of a sick-nurse. respectively. But, as I will narrate, after they had lived two years in that place, saint Joseph also began to cure the sick, while the matchless charity of the Queen busied itself more particularly with the cure of the women. Though She was Herself endowed with such unsullied purity, free from all infirmities and sufferings, yet She hesi-tated not to tend their festering ulcers and apply with her own hands the coverings and bandages required. All this She did with such tender compassion, as if She herself were afflicted with their misfortunes. Sometimes it happened that, in order to relieve and cure the poor, She asked permission of her divine Son to place Him in the cradle; thus permitting the Lord of the poor to witness in another way the loving charity of this humble Lady. But in all these occupations and cures (O wonderful to relate!) this most modest Mistress never looked upon the face of either man or woman. Even when the wound was in the face, her modesty was so exquis-ite that She would not have been able to recognize any of her

patients by their features if She had not known all men by another interior kind of vision.

669. On account of the excessive heat prevailing in Egypt, and on account of many disorders rampant among the people, the distempers of the Egyptians were widespread and grievous. During the years of the stay of the Infant Jesus and his most holy Mother, pestilence devastated Heliopolis and other places. On this account, and on account of the report of their wonderful deeds, multitudes of people came to them from all parts of the country and returned home cured in body and soul. In order that the grace of the Lord might flow more abundantly, and in order that his kindest Mother might have assistance in her works of mercy, God, at the instance of the heavenly Mistress, ordained saint Joseph as her helper in the teaching and healing of the infirm. For this purpose he was endowed with new light and power of healing. The holy Mary began to make use of his assistance in the third year of their stay in Egypt; so that now he ordinarily taught and cured the men, while the blessed Lady attended to the women. Incredible was the fruit resulting from their labors in the souls of men; for her uninterrupted beneficence and the gracious efficacy of her words drew all toward our Queen, and her modesty and holiness filled them with devoted love. They offered Her many presents and large possessions, anxious to see Her make use of them: but never did She receive anything for Herself, or reserve it for her own use; for they continued to provide for their wants by the labor of her hands and the earnings of saint Joseph. When at times the blessed Lady was offered some gift that seemed serviceable and proper for helping the needy and the poor, She would accept it for that purpose. Only with this understanding would She ever yield to the pious and affectionate importunities of devout persons; and even then She often made them a present in return of things made by her own

hands. From what I have related we can form some idea how great and how numerous were the miracles wrought by the holy Family during their seven years' stay in Egypt and Heliopolis; for it would be impossible to enumerate and describe all of them.

Words of the Queen

THE VIRGIN MARY SPEAKS TO SISTER MARY OF AGREDA

670. My daughter, thou art full of wonder at the works of mercy which I exercised in Egypt, curing the sick of their infirmities and helping the poor in their necessities, in order to relieve them in body and soul. Thou wilt be able to understand how all this comported with my love of modesty and retirement, when thou takest into consideration the immense love that urged my most holy Son to hasten immediately after his birth to the assistance of these people and pour out over them his immense love in his longings for their salvation. This love He communicated to me, and thus made me an instrument of his power, or I should not have dared to enter upon such a great enterprise. For though I always preferred to abstain from speaking or communicating with others, yet the will of my Son and Lord governed me in all things. Of thee, my friend, I desire, that in imitation of me, thou work for the benefit and salvation of thy neighbors, seeking to follow me in the perfection and quality of my works. Thou needst not seek occasions, for the Lord will send them. In some extraordinary circumstances, however, thou mayst find it advisable to offer thy services. But seek to exert thy influence upon all, teach and exhort them according to thy light; not presuming to take upon thyself the office of a teacher, but of one that seeks to console, and one that pities the hardships of her brothers; as one who with much

reserve and humility and with great charity seeks to exhort them to patience.

671. As for those under thy charge, exhort and reprove them, govern and direct them to greater and greater perfection of virtue and to fulfill the divine pleasure. For next to seeking thy own perfection, God wills that thou encourage and teach those under thy charge according to power and graces given to thee. Pray without ceasing for those to whom thou canst not speak; thus extending thy charity towards all men. Since thou canst not go outside to tend the sick, make up for it by taking care of those living with thee, zealously serving them personally in whatever pertains to their comfort and wants. Do not consider thyself above this service because thou art their superioress; for on this very account thou must act as their mother and show thy loving care as such toward all, while in other things thou must interiorly esteem thyself below them. Since the world ordinarily leaves the care of the sick to the most poor and despised, simply because it does not know the high value of this service; therefore I, too, assign to thee as to one who is poor and the least of all, this office of tending the sick, in order that thou mayest follow me in the performance of it.

Chapter XXVII

HEROD RESOLVES TO MURDER THE INNOCENTS; MOST
HOLY MARY IS AWARE OF THIS. SAINT JOHN IS CONCEALED
BY HIS RELATIVES.

672. We will now leave the Infant Jesus, most holy Mary and
Joseph in the work of sanctifying Egypt by their beneficent
presence, and return to Judea, which was unworthy of it.
Thus we will understand the course of the devilish cunning
and hypocrisy of Herod. That wicked king was waiting for
the message of the Magi concerning the newly born King of
the Jews, ready to devote Him to an inhuman death. He
trusted for a while to his own cunning, until his anxiety
caused him to inquire. But when he was informed of their
stay in Bethlehem, their departure, their escape from Palestine on a different route, and of other happenings in the
temple, he awoke to the fact that he had been foiled in his
purpose. He consulted anew some of the experts of the Law;
and as their interpretation of the Scriptures concerning
Bethlehem and the happenings at Bethlehem coincided with
his suspicions, he ordered a strict search to be made for our
Queen, her Child and the glorious saint Joseph. But the
Lord, who had commanded their flight from Jerusalem in the
night, also concealed them on their journey, so that there was
none that knew anything of it, or that could discover a trace
of their flight. Not being able to find Them, and no one

having any knowledge of Them, the henchmen of Herod brought back the answer that no such man, woman or child could be found in the whole country.

673. This inflamed the fury of Herod (Matth. 2, 16) and increased his anxiety; in vain he sought some means to prevent the evil threatening Him from a rival King. But the devil, who knew him to be ready for any wickedness, stirred up in his heart the enormous thought of using his royal power to murder all the children under two years of age around Bethlehem. For in that way the King of the Jews, recently born there, would inevitably be murdered among them. The tyrant was highly satisfied with this scheme, which never yet had been thought of by any even the greatest barbarian; and he set about its execution without any of the aversion of horror that it was apt to excite in other rational beings. Having studied out his wrathful plans to his satisfaction, he ordered some troops to be gathered in that region and privately instructed some of the more intimate of his officers under severe penalties to kill all the children under two years in Bethlehem and its vicinity. The command of Herod was executed and the whole country was filled with confusion and wailing, and with the tears of the parents and of the other relations of the innocent victims, who were thus doomed without any possibility of resistance or prevention.

674. This command of Herod was issued six months after the birth of the Savior. When it began to be executed the great Queen happened to hold her divine Son in her arms, lost in contemplation of his most holy Soul. Looking into it as into a clear mirror, She saw all that passed in Bethlehem more clearly than if She herself had been present to hear the wailing of the children and the parents. She saw also how her Son prayed to his eternal Father for the parents of these innocents; that He offered up the murdered children as the first fruits of his own Death; asking Him also that they

receive the use of reason, in order that they might be a willing sacrifice for their Redeemer and accept their death for his glory. Thus He would be able to reward them with the crowns of martyrdom for what they suffered. All this the eternal Father granted, and as it was made known to the Queen in her Onlybegotten Son, She joined Him in his prayers and sacrifices. She also pitied the parents of the martyred infants in their heartrending tears and sorrows for their sons. She, indeed, was the first and true Rachel weeping for the children in Bethlehem (Jer. 31, 15); and there was no mother who sorrowed for them as She did, since no one could be such a Mother as She was to them.

675. She did not know at the time what saint Elisabeth had done in order to safeguard her son John pursuant to the warning of the angel sent to her by the Queen Herself, as narrated in the twenty-second chapter. Although She had no doubt as to the fulfillment of all the mysteries known to Her concerning the Precursor by divine enlightenment, yet She was uncertain of the troubles and anxieties caused to saint Elisabeth and her son, and of the manner in which they had forestalled the cruelty of Herod. The sweetest Mother did not presume to ask her divine Son concerning this event, on account of the prudence and reverence always observed by Her in regard to such revelations; for in her humility and patience She counted Herself as unworthy and as dust in the sight of the Lord. But the Almighty took notice of her pious and compassionate desires and informed Her that Zachary, the father of saint John, had died four months after her virginal parturition and about three months after She had left Jerusalem. The widowed saint Elisabeth now had no other company than that of her son John, with whom she was passing the days of her widowhood in a retired and secluded place. For on account of the warning of the angel, and knowing of the cruel disposition of Herod, she had resolved to flee

to the desert with her child and live there in the company of wild beasts rather than within the dangerous reach of Herod. This resolve she had taken with the approbation of the Most High and, guided by his impulse, She was now hidden in a cave or cleft of the rock where, with great hardship and difficulty, she obtained sustenance for herself and her son.

676. The heavenly Lady also knew that saint Elisabeth, after three years of this solitary life, died in the Lord; that saint John remained in the desert, commencing to live an angelic life, and that he was not to leave his solitude until he should be commanded by the Almighty to preach penance as his Precursor. These sacraments and mysteries the Infant Jesus manifested to his most holy Mother with many other hidden and profound blessings conferred upon saint Elisabeth and her son in that desert. All this She perceived in the same way as She now perceived the death of the innocent children. It filled Her with joy and compassion; the one because She saw saint John and his mother in safety, the other, on account of the hardships to which they were exposed in the desert. She immediately asked of her most holy Son permission to take care thenceforward of Elisabeth and her son. From that time on She frequently sent her holy angels to visit them with the consent of the Lord; and through them also She sent them provisions, which afforded them better sustenance than they could find in the wild abode. Through these angelic messengers the holy Lady kept up a continual intercourse with her relatives during her stay in Egypt. When the last hour of Elisabeth arrived, Mary sent her a great number of angels to assist her and her child, who was then four years old. These angels also helped saint John to bury his mother in the desert. Thereupon the Queen sent to him every day his sustenance, until he was of sufficient age to provide for his living by his own labors and exertions in gathering herbs, roots and woodland honey (Mark 1,6); of

these thenceforward he lived in admirable abstinence, as I shall relate farther on.

677. Neither the tongue of creatures can describe, nor intellect comprehend, the vast merits and increase of sanctity accumulating in the most holy Mary through these continued and wonderful works; for in all things She acted with a prudence more than angelic. What moved Her to the greatest admiration, love and praise of the Almighty was to see how, at the intercession of Herself and her Son for the holy Innocents, his providence showed itself so liberal toward them. She knew as if She were present the great number of children that were killed and that all of them, though some were only eight days, two or six months old, and none of them over two years, had the use of their reason; that they all received a high knowledge of the being of God, perfect love, faith and hope, in which they performed heroic acts of faith, worship, and love of God, reverence and compassion for their parents. They prayed for their parents and, in reward for their sufferings, obtained for them light and grace for advance in spiritual things. They willingly submitted to martyrdom, in spite of the tenderness of their age, which made their sufferings so much the greater and consequently augmented their merits. A multitude of angels assisted them and bore them to limbo or to the bosom of Abraham. By their arrival they rejoiced the holy ancients and confirmed them in the hope of speedy liberation. All these were effects of the prayers of the divine Child and his Mother. Aware of all these wonders, She was inflamed with ardor and exclaimed; "Praise the Lord, ye children"; and joined with them in the praise of the Author of these magnificent works, so worthy of his Goodness and Omnipotence. Mary alone knew of them and appreciated them properly. And She, so closely allied to God himself, perfectly reached the degree of humility required for such appreciation; for though She was the Mother of innocence,

purity and sanctity, She humiliated Herself more than all creatures with all their faults will ever know how to humiliate themselves. Among all creatures most holy Mary reached a degree of humility peculiar to Herself, which fully equaled the high blessings and gifts received by all other creatures; for She alone comprehended fully how insufficient is the return the creature can make for all the blessings flowing from the boundless love of God. Knowing that without this humility no act of a creature can be worthy of a God, She reached the height of all perfection by making all her acts serve as a grateful return for benefits received.

678. At the end of this chapter I wish to draw attention to the fact that in many things which I am describing, a great diversity of opinion exists among the holy fathers and writers; as, for instance, in regard to the time of the slaughter of the innocent children, or whether also the new-born children or those that were only a few days old were included in the slaughter, or concerning other doubtful points, about which I will not speak, since they are not necessary to my purpose. I write only what is being shown or dictated to me, or about which obedience forces me to ask, in order that this history may be more clear. It will not do to start a dispute concerning what I write; for from the beginning I said, that the Lord wishes this whole work to be free from mere opinion and to contain nothing but what is taught me by the divine light To decide whether that which I write is in harmony with the truth of holy Scriptures, or befits the majesty and grandeur of my subject, or whether the events narrated bear the necessary sequence or connection: all this I leave to the learning of my teachers and superiors and to the judgment of the wise and pious. Variety of opinion is as it were inevitable among the writers on these subjects, since they are guided by different authors, and are each following those of the ancient authors that satisfy them best; yet more than a few of the old authors

(if we except the events related in the canonical writings) relied only on conjecture or on doubtful sources. I, as an ignorant woman, cannot enter upon such discussions.

Words of the Queen

THE VIRGIN MARY SPEAKS TO SISTER MARY OF AGREDA

679. My daughter, in what thou hast written I wish that thou learn a lesson from the very sorrow and apprehension with which thou hast performed this task. Well-founded is thy sorrow to see how such a noble creature as man, made according to the likeness and image of the Lord, endowed with such divine qualities, and gifted with the power of knowing, loving, seeing, and enjoying God eternally, should allow himself to be degraded and defiled by such brutal and abominable passions as to shed the innocent blood of those who can do no harm to anyone. This should induce thee to weep over the ruin of so many souls j especially in the times in which thou livest when that same ambition which incited Herod, has kindled such great hatred and enmity among the children of the Church, occasioning the ruin of countless souls and causing the waste and loss of the blood of my most holy Son, poured out for the salvation of men. Do thou bitterly deplore this loss.

680. But likewise be warned by what thou hast seen in others; ponder the effects of passions admitted into the heart; for if once they have mastered the heart, they will either smother it in lust when it finds success, or consume it with wrath at meeting any opposition. Fear thou, my daughter, this danger, not only on account of the results thou seest of ambition in Herod, but also on account of what thou seest going on every hour in other persons. Be very careful not to allow thyself to be mastered by anything, be it ever so small; for in order to start a great conflagration the smallest spark is

sufficient. I have often repeated to thee this same warning, and I shall continue to do so more often in the future; for the greatest difficulty in practicing virtue consists in dying to all that is pleasurable to the senses. Thou canst not be a fit instrument in the hands of the Lord, such as He desires thee to be, if thou dost not cleanse thy faculties even of the images of all creatures, so that they do not find entrance into thy desires. I wish it to be to thee an inexorable law that all things, except God, his angels and saints, be to thee as if they did not exist. These should be thy sole possession; on this account the Lord has opened to thee his secrets, honors thee with his familiarity and intimacy, and for this purpose also do I honor thee with mine, that thou neither live nor wish to live without the Lord.

Chapter XXVIII

AT THE AGE OF ONE YEAR THE INFANT JESUS SPEAKS TO
SAINT JOSEPH AND REQUESTS HIS MOTHER TO CLOTH HIM
AND ALLOW HIM TO WALK. HE COMMENCES TO CELE-
BRATE THE DAY OF HIS INCARNATION AND OF HIS BIRTH.

681. During one of the conversations of Mary with Joseph
concerning the mysteries of the Lord, the Infant Jesus, having
reached the age of one year, resolved to break the silence and
speak in plain words to Joseph, who so faithfully fulfilled the
duties of a foster-father. As I have already mentioned in
chapter the tenth, He had thus conversed with his heavenly
Mother from the time of his Birth. The two holy Spouses
were speaking of the infinite being of God, of his goodness
and excessive love, which induced Him to send his Onlybegotten Son as the Teacher and Savior of men, clothing Him
in human form in order that He might converse with them
and suffer the punishments of their depraved natures. Saint
Joseph was lost in wonder at the works of the Lord and
inflamed by affectionate gratitude and exaltation of the Lord.
Seizing upon this occasion the infant God, resting upon the
arms of his Mother as upon the seat of wisdom, began to
speak to saint Joseph in an intelligible voice, saying: "My
father, I came from heaven upon this earth in order to be the
light of the world, and in order to rescue it from darkness of
sin; in order to seek and know my sheep as a good Shepherd,

to give them nourishment of eternal life, teach them the way of heaven, open its gates, which had been closed by their sins. I desire that you both be children of the Light, which you have so close at hand."

682. These words of the Infant Jesus, being full of divine life, filled the heart of the patriarch saint Joseph with new love, reverence and joy. He fell on his knees before the infant God with the profoundest humility and thanked Him for having called Him "father" by the very first word spoken to him. He besought the Lord with many tears to enlighten him and enable him to fulfill entirely his most holy will, to teach him to be thankful for the incomparable benefits flowing from his generous hands. Parents who love their children very much are touched with consolation and pride to see their children show great signs of wisdom and virtue; and even when this is not the case, they are naturally inclined to extol and make much of their childish pranks and sayings; for all this is the result of their tender affection for their young offspring. Although saint Joseph was not the natural, but the foster-father of Jesus, his love for Him exceeded by far all the love of parents for their children, since in him grace, or even natural love, was more powerful than in others, yea than in all the parents together. Hence the joy of his soul is to be measured by this love and appreciation of saint Joseph as being the foster-father of the Infant Jesus. For he at the same time heard himself called the father of the Son of the eternal Father, and saw Him so beautiful in grace, while listening to such exalted wisdom and knowledge in the Child.

683. During the whole of this first year his sweetest Mother had wrapped the infant God in clothes and coverings usual with other children; for He did not wish to be distinguished in this from others, and He wished to bear witness to his true humanity and to his love for mortals, enduring this inconvenience otherwise not required of Him. The most

prudent Mother, judging that now the time had come to free Him from swaddling clothes and place Him on his feet, knelt down before the Child in its cradle and said: "My Son and sweetest Love of my soul, my Lord, I desire, as thy slave, to be punctual in fulfilling thy wishes. O, Light of my eyes, Thou hast been for a long time oppressed by the swaddling-clothes and thereby gone to the extreme of thy love for men; it is time Thou change this manner. Tell me, my Master, what shall I do to place Thee on thy feet?"

684. "My Mother," answered the Infant Jesus, "on account of the love which I bear toward man, whom I have created and come to redeem, the swathings of my childhood have not seemed irksome to Me, since when I shall be grown up I shall be bound and delivered over to my enemies unto death (Matth. 20, 18). If this prospect is sweet to Me for the love of my Father (Heb, to, 71) all the rest is certainly easy to Me. I wish to possess only one garment during all my life, for I seek nothing more than what is sufficient to cover Me. Although all created things are mine because I have given them being, I turn them all over to men in order that they may owe Me so much the more and in order that I may teach them, according to my example and for my love, to repudiate and despise all that is superfluous for natural life. Clothe Me, my Mother, in a tunic of a lowly and ordinary color. This alone will I wear, and it shall grow with Me. Over this garment shall they cast lots at my death (Ps. 21, 19) ; for even this shall not be left at my disposal, but at the disposal of others; so that men shall see that I was born and wish to live poor and destitute of visible things, which being earthly, oppress and darken the heart of man. At the very moment of my conception in thy virginal womb I made this renunciation and abdication of all that is contained in the world, though all is mine on account of the union of my human nature with the divine. I shall not have anything to do with

visible things except to offer them up to the eternal Father, renouncing them for his love, and making use of only so much as is sufficient to sustain my natural life, which I will afterwards yield up for man's sake. By this example I wish to impress upon the world the doctrine that it must love poverty and not despise it; for I, who am the Lord of the whole world, entirely repudiated and rejected its possessions. Those who know Me by faith should be filled with confusion at seeing themselves desire what I taught them to despise."

685. The words of the divine Child produced in the heart of the heavenly Mother diverse wonderful effects. The allusion to the seizure and death of her most holy Son transfixed her pure and compassionate heart, and the doctrine and example of such extreme poverty and destitution excited her admiration and urged Her to its imitation. His boundless love for mortals inflamed Her with loving gratitude toward the Lord and produced in Her heroic acts of many virtues. Seeing that the Child Jesus desired no footgear and only one garment, She said to Him: "My Son and my Lord, thy Mother has not the heart to allow Thee to go barefoot upon the ground at thy tender age; permit me, my Love, to provide some kind of covering to protect them. I also fear that the rough garment, which Thou askest of me, will wound thy tender body, if thou permit no linen to be worn beneath." "My Mother, I will permit a slight and ordinary covering for my feet until the time of my public preaching shall come, for this I must do barefooted. But I do not wish to wear linen, because it foments carnal pleasures, and is the cause of many vices in men. I wish to teach many by my example to renounce it for love and imitation of Me."

686. Immediately the great Queen set diligently about fulfilling the will of her most holy Son. Procuring some wool in its natural and uncolored state, She spun it very finely with her own hands and of it She wove a garment of one

piece and without any seam, similar to knitted stuff, or rather like twilled cloth; for it was woven of twisted cords, not like smooth-woven goods. She wove it upon a small 100m, by meshes, crocheting it of one seamless piece in a mysterious manner (John 19, 23). Two things were wonderful about it: that it was entirely even and uniform, without any seams, and that, at her request, the natural color was changed to a more suitable one, which was a mixture of brown and a most exquisite silver-gray, so that it could not be called either, appearing to be neither altogether brown, nor silvery, nor gray, but having a mixture of them all. She also wove a pair of sandals of strong thread, like hempen shoes, with which She covered the feet of the infant God. Besides these She made a half tunic of linen, which was to serve as an undergarment. In the next chapter I shall tell what happened when She clothed the Infant Jesus.

687. At this time occurred the anniversary of the Incarnation and of the Nativity of the divine Word, both of them when they had already settled in Egypt. The celestial Queen celebrated these feasts, so joyous for the Mother of God, commencing a custom observed by Her during all the rest of her life, as will be seen in the third part, which treats about the mysteries happening later on. She began to prepare for the feast of the Incarnation nine days before, in accordance with the nine days of preparation, in which She had been visited with such admirable and magnificent graces. At the anniversary of the Incarnation or Annunciation She invited all the angels of heaven, together with those of her guard, to assist Her in the celebration of those great mysteries and to help Her to acknowledge and give worthy thanks to the Almighty. Prostrate before the Infant in the form of a cross, She besought Him to praise in her stead the eternal Father and thank Him for the favors of his right hand towards Her, and for the gift of his Onlybegotten Son to the human race

(John 3, 16). The same petition She made on the anniversary of her divine parturition. On these days the heavenly Lady was regaled with many graces and joys by the Most High; because He renewed the unbroken remembrance and understanding of these exalted sacraments. As She had received intelligence how much the eternal Father was pleased and obliged by this outward manifestation of sorrow exhibited in her prostration in the form of a cross, and by her mindfulness of the crucifixion of the Lamb of God, She practiced this devotion on all the festivals, seeking to appease the divine justice and soliciting mercy for the sinners. Inflamed with charity, She rose up and ended her celebration with wonderful hymns, singing them alternately with the angels; they formed a choir of celestial harmony, the holy angels intoning their songs, and the blessed Lady answering them on her part in hymns more sweet to the ears of God, and more acceptable than those of the most exalted seraphim and all the heavenly choirs. For these were the echoes of his infinite virtues piercing to the very throne and judgment seat of the eternal God.

Words of the Queen

THE VIRGIN MARY SPEAKS TO SISTER MARY OF AGREDA

688. My daughter, neither thyself nor all creatures together can ever comprehend the spirit of poverty of my most holy Son, and what He has taught me concerning it. But from what I have told thee thou canst understand much of the excellence of this virtue, which its Author and Teacher loved so much, and of the horror in which He holds the vice of covetousness. The Creator cannot hate the beings which He has created; but He knows in his wisdom the boundless damage caused in mortals by avarice and covetousness of visible things; and that this insane love would pervert the

greater part of the human nature. His horror of this vice was in proportion to the number of sinners and foredoomed ones, who are lost by the vice of avarice and cupidity.

689. In order to meet this evil and provide some remedy against it, my most holy Son chose poverty, and taught it by word and by example of his admirable abnegation. Thus would the Physician justify his cause before men if they, for whom He prepared this means of safety and restoration, would neglect to take advantage of it. This same doctrine I taught and practiced during all my life, and upon it the Apostles founded the Church. Such was also the teaching and practice of the Patriarchs and Saints, who rejuvenated and confirmed religion in the Church; for all of them have loved poverty, as the only and most efficacious means of holiness. They have abhorred riches as the incentive to evil and the root of all vices (I Tim. 6, 10). This poverty I wish thee to love and seek after with all diligence; for it is the adornment of the spouses of my most holy Son, without which I assure thee, my dearest, He will disavow and repudiate them as unworthy and far removed from Him. For it is preposterous to see a bride overflowing in riches and bedecked with jewels at the side of a poor and destitute bridegroom; nor can true love exist with such inequality.

690. It is clear that though thou wish to imitate me as a legitimate daughter, I, being myself poor, shall not recognize thee as my daughter if thou art not one in reality, nor shall I ever permit that in thee which I abhorred for myself. I remind thee also not to forget the blessings of the Most High, which thou hast received in such abundance; for if thou art not very attentive and solicitous in this duty, thou wilt be drawn into forgetfulness and gross rudeness by the bluntness and sluggishness inherent in the human nature. Renew many times a day the memory of his blessings, always giving thanks to the Lord with humble and loving affection. Especially

memorable among his benefits are that He has called thee, waited for thee, dissembled and excused thy faults, and added thereto such oft repeated favors. This remembrance will cause in thee sweet and strong movements of love; and thou wilt find new grace and favor before the Lord, since He is so much pleased by a faithful and thankful heart. On the other hand, He is much offended if his kindnesses and blessings are not esteemed and appreciated; for, as He confers them in the fullness of his love, He desires a dutiful, loyal and loving return on the part of his creatures.

Chapter XXIX

THE MOST HOLY MOTHER CLOTHES THE INFANT JESUS IN THE SEAMLESS TUNIC; SHE PUTS SHOES ON HIS FEET. THE DOINGS AND OBSERVANCES OF THE LORD.

691. In order to clothe the divine Infant in the small tunic and put on his feet the sandals made by Her, the most prudent Lady cast Herself on her knees before her sweetest Son and addressed Him in the following words:

"Most high Lord, and Creator of heaven and earth, I would wish to clothe Thee, if possible, in such a way as thy Divinity deserves, and I would gladly have made these garments, which are to cover Thee, from my heart blood; but I know that the poor and insignificant coverings I now offer Thee are according to thy desires. Pardon me, my Lord and Master, my faults and accept the loving affection of her, who is but dust and ashes: allow me to clothe Thee." The Infant Jesus was pleased with the loving service of his purest Mother; and thereupon She clothed and shod Him, setting Him upon his feet. The tunic fitted Him perfectly, covering his feet without hindering them in walking, and the sleeves extended to the middle of his hands, although She had taken no measure beforehand. The collar was cut out round, without being open in front, and was somewhat raised around the neck adjusting itself to the throat. Through this opening the heavenly Mother passed it over the head of the

Infant; for the garment gracefully adjusted itself according to her wishes. He never divested Himself of this tunic, until the executioners themselves tore it off to scourge and afterwards to crucify Him; for this garment continually grew with Him, adjusting itself to his body. The same happened also with the sandals and with the undergarment, which the solicitous Mother made for Him. None of all these articles of clothing wore away or became old in the thirty-two years, nor did the tunic lose its color or its newness but remained just as it had left the hands of the great Lady; nor did any of them become soiled or filthy, but they preserved their first cleanliness. The garment which the Redeemer of the world laid aside in order to wash the feet of his Apostles. was a mantle or cape which He wore over his shoulders; and this also had been made by the Virgin after they had returned to Nazareth. Like the other clothing it grew with the Lord, was of the same color only a little darker and was woven in the same way.

692. Thus the infant Lord of the eternities was placed on his feet, after having since his birth been wrapped in swaddling-clothes and held for most of the time in the arms of his most holy Mother (John 13. 4). He was the most beautiful among the sons of men. The angels were astounded at the humble and poor raiment chosen by Him who clothes the heavens in light and the fields with beauty. He walked freely on his feet in the presence of his parents; but before strangers this wonder remained for a time concealed. since the Queen took Him in her arms when outsiders approached or whenever they went abroad. Indescribable was the joy of the heavenly Lady and of saint Joseph as they saw the Infant walking about and exhibit such rare beauty. He received nourishment at the breast of his purest Mother until He was a year and a half old and no longer. His meals thereupon were most frugal as well in quantity as in quality. At first they consisted in broths mixed with oil, and some fruits or fishes.

While He was still in process of growth She gave Him to eat three times a day, as often as She had formerly given Him her milk; in the morning, afternoon and at night. The divine Child never asked for food; but the loving Mother with thoughtful anxiety provided Him his meals at the proper time until later on, when He was already grown up and would not consent to eat oftener or at other hours than the heavenly Spouses themselves. This was his rule until He reached adult age, of which I will speak later on. Whenever He took his meals with his parents they always waited until He should pronounce the blessing at the beginning and give thanks at the end.

693. From the time the Child Jesus was on his feet He commenced to retire and spent certain hours of the day in the oratory of his Mother. As the most prudent Mother was anxious to know his wishes in regard to her intercourse with Him, the Lord responded to her mute appeal, saying: "My Mother, enter and remain with Me always in order that thou mayest imitate Me in my works; for I wish that in thee be modeled and exhibited the high perfection which I desire to see accomplished in the souls. For if they had not resisted my first intentions (I Tim. 2, 4), they would have been endowed with my most abundant and copious gifts; but since the human race has hindered this, I have chosen thee as the vessel of all perfection and of the treasures of my right hand, which the rest of the creatures have abused and lost. Observe me therefore in all my actions for the purpose of imitating Me."

694. Thus the heavenly Lady was installed anew as the Disciple of her most holy Son. Thenceforward passed such great and hidden mysteries between these Two. that not until the day of eternity will they be known. Many times the divine Child prostrated Himself on the ground, at others He was raised from the ground in the form of a cross, earnestly praying to the eternal Father for the salvation of mortals. In

all this his most loving Mother imitated Him. For to Her
were manifest the interior operations of his most holy soul,
just as well as the exterior movements of his body. Of this
knowledge of most pure Mary I have spoken in other parts of
this history and it is necessary to point it out often, because
this was the source of the light which guided Her in her holy
life. It was such a singular blessing, that all creatures together
will not be able to understand or describe it by their united
powers. The great Lady did not always enjoy visions of the
Divinity; but always the sight of the most holy humanity and
soul of her Son with all their activities. In a special manner
She was witness of the effects of the hypostatic and beatific
union of the humanity with the Divinity. Although She did
not always see this glory and this union substantially; yet She
perceived the interior acts by which his humanity reverenced,
loved and magnified the Divinity to which it was united; and
this privilege was reserved solely to most holy Mary.

695. On these occasions it often happened that the Child
Jesus in the presence of his most holy Mother wept and
perspired blood, for this happened many times before his
agony in the garden. Then the blessed Lady would wipe his
face interiorly perceiving and knowing the cause of this
agony, namely the loss of the foreknown and of those who
would be ungrateful for the benefits of their Creator and
Redeemer and in whom the works of the infinite power and
goodness of the Lord would be wasted. At other times the
blessed Mother would find Him refulgent with heavenly
light and surrounded by angels that sang sweet hymns of
praise; and She was made aware, that the heavenly Father was
pleased in his beloved and Onlybegotten Son (Matth. 17, 5).
All these wonders commenced from the time when at the age
of one year He began to walk, witnessed only by his most
holy Mother, whose heart was to be the treasure-house of his
wonders. The works of love, praise and worshipful gratitude,

his petitions for the human race, all exceed my ability to describe. I must refer the understanding of it to the faith and piety of the Christians.

696. The Child Jesus grew in the admiration and esteem of all that came to know Him. Having reached the age of six years He began now and then to visit the sick in the hospitals, seeking out the stricken ones and mysteriously comforting and consoling them in their afflictions. Many of the inhabitants of Heliopolis began to know Him; the secret attractions of his Divinity and sanctity drew toward Him the hearts of all, and many offered Him gifts. These, according to the promptings of his interior knowledge, He refused or accepted for distribution among the poor. The admiration caused by his wise counsels and his modest and considerate behavior, caused many to extol and congratulate the parents on such a Son. Although all of them were ignorant of the mysteries and of the dignity of the Son and the Mother; yet the Lord of creation, being desirous of honoring his Mother, permitted them to reverence Her as far as was possible under the circumstances, without their learning the special reason for doing so.

697. Many of the children of Heliopolis gathered around the Child Jesus, as it is natural with children of similar age and condition. Since they were free from great malice and were not given to inquire, whether He was more than man, but freely admitted the heavenly light, the Master of truth welcomed them as far as was befitting. He instilled into them the knowledge of God and of the virtues; He taught and catechized them in the way of eternal life, even more abundantly than the adults. As his words were full of life and strength, He won their hearts and impressed his truths so deeply upon them, that all those, who had this good fortune, afterwards became great and saintly men; for in the course of

time they ripened in themselves the fruit of this heavenly seed sown so early into their souls.

698. The blessed Mother was well-informed of all these happenings. Whenever her most holy Son returned from these errands, in which He had fulfilled the will of his eternal Father by looking after his flock, the Queen and the angels prostrated themselves before her divine Son and gave Him thanks for the benefits done to those innocents, who did not yet know Him for their true God, and She kissed his feet as those of the Highpriest of heaven and earth (Heb. 4, 1). This She also did whenever the Child was about to go forth; on such occasions He would raise Her up from the earth in filial reverence and love. The Mother also asked for his blessing upon all her undertakings; and She never lost an occasion for practicing virtue with all the intensity of her love and divine grace. Never was any grace in Her without its fruit, but it operated in all its plenitude and increased in operation. The great Lady sought new means and ways of humiliating Herself, adoring the incarnate Word by her genuflections and prostrations and other most loving and profound ceremonies as outward tokens of her prudence and holiness. This She attended to with such wisdom, that She excited the admiration of the angels themselves, who, interchanging among themselves the praises of the Divinity, said to each other: "Who is that pure Creature, so full of delight to our Creator and her Son? (Cant. 1, 2). Who is this One, that so wisely and attentively honors and reverences the Most High, far exceeding us all in her loving alertness and attention?"

699. In his intercourse and conversation with his parents, this most wonderful and beautiful Child, after He had begun to walk and grow larger, showed more gravity than when He was younger. The tender caresses, which always had been tempered and measured, were now withheld, for in his countenance shone forth such majesty as a reflection of his

hidden Deity, that, if He had not mixed it with a certain sweetness and affability, reverential fear would have prevented all intercourse with Him. The heavenly Mother and saint Joseph felt the effects of a divine power and efficacy, as well as the kindness and devotedness of a loving Father, proceeding from his countenance. Joined with this majesty and magnificence was his filial affection toward his heavenly Mother, while on the other hand He treated saint Joseph as one, who had as well the name as the duties of a father toward Him; and therefore He obeyed them both as a most devoted Son obeys his parents. In his whole behavior the incarnate Word practiced the virtues of obedience, humility and human kindness with such an admirable mixture of majesty and gravity, that his divine wisdom shone forth in all his actions and that none of his grandeur was impaired by triviality or smallness. The heavenly Queen was most attentive to all these mysteries and She alone, as far as a mere creature could, comprehended befittingly the work of her most holy Son and understood the ways of his infinite wisdom. I would attempt the impossible to try to describe in human words the effects of all his doings on her most pure and prudent soul, or how closely She imitated his ineffable sanctity. The souls which were converted and saved in Heliopolis and in all Egypt, the sick that were cured, and the wonders wrought during their seven years' stay in that country, cannot be enumerated: such a blessed crime did the cruelty of Herod turn out to be for Egypt. The goodness and wisdom of God draws from the very wickedness and evils of sin the greatest good. If in one direction men cast away his mercies and shut them out, He calls upon them in other directions to open their hearts and admit his blessings (Job 34, 24). His ardent desires to benefit the human race cannot be quenched by the floods of our sins and ingratitudes.

Words of the Queen

THE VIRGIN MARY SPEAKS TO SISTER MARY OF AGREDA

700. My daughter, from the very beginning of this history of my life thou wast made to understand, that among other purposes, the Lord wished to call the attention of mortals to the debt contracted by their unfeeling forgetfulness of his divine love and of mine toward them. It is true that all his love is included and made manifest in his having died on the Cross for them, for this was the extremity of his immense charity (John 3, 16). But many ungrateful men are loath to remember even this blessing. For such and for all others the knowledge of what He did for them during the thirty-three years should be a new incentive and spur of love; since each of his acts was worth an infinite price and merited our eternal gratitude. The Almighty set me as a witness to all of them: and I assure thee, that from the first instant of his conception in my womb, He ceased not to clamor to the Father for the salvation of men. From that moment He began to embrace the Cross (Heb. 10, 5), not only in desire, but also as far as was possible in effect, placing Himself in the position of one crucified from his infancy and continuing these exercises during his whole life. I also imitated Him in this, joining Him in his prayers and labors for mankind and in the very first acts of his most sacred humanity by which He rendered thanks for the salvation of men.

701. Let therefore mortals beware, lest I, who was a Witness and Co-operatrix of this salvation, be not also a Witness and Co-operatrix in the day of judgment, proclaiming how well justified is the cause of God with men. If on that day I most justly refuse my intercession to those, who have foolishly despised and forgotten so many and so great favors and blessings, the results of the divine love of my Son and my own: what answer, what excuse or evasion shall those then

bring forward, who have been so well informed, so much admonished and enlightened by the truth? How can these ungrateful and pertinacious mortals expect mercy of the most just and righteous God, when He has given them sufficient and opportune time, invited them so often, called them, waited and worked for them, and conferred upon them immense blessings, while they abused and wasted all of them in the pursuit of vanity? Fear, my daughter, this, the greatest of all blindnesses. Refresh ever the memory of the most holy works of my Son and of me, and imitate them with all thy fervor. Continue the exercises of the cross under the guidance of obedience, in order to keep thyself mindful of what thou must imitate and give thanks for. Take notice at the same time, that my Son and Lord could have redeemed the human race without suffering so much and that He wished to increase his sufferings only on account of the immensity of his love for souls. The return for such condescension should be, that the creature content not itself with little, as is ordinarily the case with ignorant men. Add thou virtue to virtue and seek thereby evermore to meet all thy obligations, imitating the Lord and me in our labors for the salvation of the world. All thy merits offer up for souls, uniting them with his merits in the presence of the eternal Father.

Chapter XXX

JESUS. MARY AND JOSEPH RETURN TO NAZARETH AT THE COMMAND OF THE LORD.

702. The Child Jesus reached the end of his seventh year while in Egypt, which was also the term set by the eternal Wisdom for his mysterious sojourn in that land. In order that the prophecies might be fulfilled, it was necessary that He return to Nazareth. This decree the eternal Father intimated to his most holy Son on a certain day in the presence of his holy Mother and while She was with Him in prayer. She saw it mirrored in his deified soul and She saw how He submitted to it in obedience to the Father. Therein the great Lady joined Him, although they had already become better acquainted and habituated to their present abode than to their own native city of Nazareth. Neither the Mother nor the Son made known to saint Joseph this new decree of heaven. But in that very night the angel of the Lord spoke to him in his sleep, as Matthew relates (Matth. 2, 19), and bade him take the Child and its Mother and return to the land of Israel; for Herod and those who with him had sought the life of the Child, were dead. So much value does the Almighty set on the proper order in created things, that, though Jesus was the true God and his Mother so highly exalted above saint Joseph in sanctity, He did not permit the arrangements

of this journey to proceed from his Son nor from his Mother, but from saint Joseph, who was the head of this Family. God intended to teach all mortals, that He wishes all things to be governed by the natural order set up by his Providence; and that the inferiors and subjects of the mystical body of the Church, even though they may excel in virtue and in certain other respects, must obey and submit to their superiors and prelates in the visible order.

703. Saint Joseph immediately notified the Child Jesus and his Mother of the command of the Lord; and both of them answered, that the will of the heavenly Father must be done. Thereupon they resolved upon their journey without delay, immediately distributing among the poor the little furniture contained in their dwelling. This was done by the hands of the divine Child; for the heavenly Mother often consigned into his hands what She had destined as alms to the poor, knowing that the Child, as the God of mercy, loved to exercise it with his own hands (Matth. 25, 40). When She gave Him these alms the most holy Mother falling on her knees, said: "Take, my Son and Lord, whatever Thou desirest, in order to share it with the poor, our friends and brothers." The blessed dwelling, which had been sanctified and consecrated for seven years by the presence of the Highpriest Jesus, was left in the possession of certain of the most devout and pious persons in Heliopolis. Their virtue and holiness had gained them a favor which they could not now fully estimate; although, on account of what they had seen and experienced, they counted themselves indeed fortunate to occupy the same house, in which these Strangers had lived for seven years. This affectionate devotion was rewarded by abundant light and grace for their eternal salvation.

704. They departed for Palestine in the company of angels as on their way thence. The great Queen sat on the ass with the divine Child on her lap and saint Joseph walked

afoot, closely following the Son and Mother. On account of the loss of such great Benefactors their acquaintances and friends were very sorrowful at the news of their departure; with incredible weeping and sighing they saw Them leave, knowing and loudly complaining, that they were now losing all their consolation and refuge in their necessities. If the divine power had not interfered, the holy Family would have found great difficulty in leaving Heliopolis; for its inhabitants began to feel the night of their miseries secretly setting upon their hearts at the parting of the Sun, which had dispersed and brightened its darkness (John 1, 9). In traversing the inhabited country they passed through some towns of Egypt, where They scattered their graces and blessings. The news of their passage spreading about, all the sick, the afflicted and disconsolate gathered to seek Them out, and they found themselves relieved in body and soul. Many of the sick were cured, many demons were expelled without their knowing who it was that thus hurled them back to hell. Yet they felt the divine power, which compelled them and wrought such blessings among men.

705. I will not tarry to relate the particular events of this journey of the Child Jesus and his most blessed Mother out of Egypt; for it is not necessary, nor could it be done without extending this history too much. It will suffice to say that all who came to Them with greater or less devotion, left their presence enlightened with truth, assisted by grace and wounded with the love of God. They felt a secret force, which urged and compelled them to the pursuit of virtue and, while withdrawing them from the paths of death, showed them the way of eternal life. They came to the Son, drawn to Him by the Father, and they turned to the Father, sent there by the divine light of Christ's truth, which enkindled their souls with the knowledge of the true God (John 6, 44). Nevertheless He concealed Himself, since it was not yet

time to reveal Himself openly. But the fire, which He had come to enkindle and spread in this world, secretly and incessantly produced its divine effects among men.

706. Having thus fulfilled the mysteries decreed by the divine will and issuing from the inhabited regions of this country, which They had signalized by their miracles, our heavenly Pilgrims entered the desert through which They had come. In it They again suffered labors and difficulties similar to those of their flight from Palestine; for the Lord continued to permit hardships and tribulation in order to afford Them occasion of merit and provide a proper relief. He administered to these necessities by the hands of the angels as in the first journey, or sometimes the Child Jesus himself commanded them to provide sustenance. Very often saint Joseph, in order that he might become more sensible of the divine favor, was permitted to hear these commands and saw how these spirits obeyed and readily procured what was wanted. This greatly encouraged and consoled the holy Patriarch in his sorrow and anxiety for the King and Queen of heaven. At other times the divine Child made use of his Omnipotence and created all that was necessary to supply their wants out of a crumb of bread. The rest of the journey was similar to the journey described before in chapter the twenty-second; therefore I do not think it necessary to repeat the description. When, however, They arrived at the confines of Palestine the anxious husband was informed, that Archelaus had succeeded Herod his father in the government of Judea (Matth. 2, 22). Fearing that with the sovereignty he had inherited also his cruelty, saint Joseph turned from his route without going to Jerusalem or entering Judea and passed through the land of the tribe of Dan and Issachar below Galilee, following the coast of the Mediterranean sea and passing Jerusalem to his right.

707. They reached Nazareth, their home, for the Child was to be called a Nazarene. They found their former humble house in charge of the devout cousin of saint Joseph, who, as I have mentioned in the twelfth chapter of the third book, had offered to serve him while our Queen was absent in the house of Elisabeth. Before They had left Judea for Egypt, saint Joseph had written to this woman, asking her to take care of the house and what it contained. They found it all in good condition and his cousin received Them with great joy on account of her love for the great Queen, though at the same time she did not know of her dignity. The heavenly Lady entered with her Son and saint Joseph, and immediately She prostrated Herself in adoration of the Lord and in thanksgiving for having led Them, safe from the cruelty of Herod, to this retreat, and preserved Them in the dangers of their banishment and their long and arduous journeys. Above all did She Tender thanks for having returned in company with her Son, now grown both in years and in grace and virtue (Luke 2, 40).

708. Taking counsel with her divine Child She proceeded to set up a rule of life and regulate her pious practices; not that She had failed to observe a rule of life on her journey; for the most prudent Lady, in imitation of her Son, had always observed the most perfect order according to circumstances. But being now peacefully settled in her home She wished to include many exercises, which on the journey were impossible. Her greatest solicitude was always to co-operate with her most holy Son for the salvation of souls which was the work most urgently enjoined upon Her by the eternal Father. Toward this most high end our Queen directed all her practices in union with the Redeemer, and this was their constant occupation, as we shall see in the course of this second part. The holy Joseph also ordered his occupations and his work so as most worthily to earn sustenance for the

divine Child and his Mother as well as for himself. That which in other sons of Adam is considered a punishment and a hardship was to this holy Patriarch a great happiness. For while others were condemned to sustain their natural life by the labor of their hands in the sweat of their brows, saint Joseph was blessed and consoled beyond measure to know, that he had been chosen by his labor and sweat to support God himself and his Mother, to whom belonged heaven and earth and all that they contain (Esther 13, 10).

709. The Queen of the angels herself undertook to pay the debt of gratitude due to saint Joseph for his labors and solicitude. Accordingly She provided his meals and attended to his comforts with incredible care and most loving gratitude. She was obedient to him in all things and humbled Herself before him as if She were his handmaid and not his spouse, or, what is more, not the Mother of the Creator and Lord of all. She accounted Herself unworthy of existence and of being suffered to walk upon the earth; for She thought it just, that She should be in want of all things. In the consciousness of having been created out of nothing and therefore unable to make any return for either this benefit or, according to her estimation, for any of the otters, She established in Herself such a rare humility, that She thought Herself less than the dust and unworthy to mingle with it. For the least favor She gave admirable thanks to the Lord, as to the first cause and origin of them all, and to creatures as to the instruments of his bounty. To some She gave thanks because they conferred favors upon Her, to others because they had denied them; and to others again because they bore with Her in patience. She acknowledged Herself as indebted to all of them, though She filled them with the blessings of sweetness and placed Herself at the feet of all, seeking ingenious means and artifices to let no instant and no occasion pass for practicing the most perfect and exalted virtues to the

admiration of the angels and the pleasure and the delight of the Most High.

Words of the Queen

THE VIRGIN MARY SPEAKS TO SISTER MARY OF AGREDA

710. My daughter, while journeying at the command of the Lord from one country to another and during the works enjoined upon me, my heart was never troubled nor my spirit cast down; for I always held myself prepared to fulfill entirely the will of God. Although the Lord made known to Me his high ends, yet this was not always done at the beginning, thus permitting me to endure so much the greater sufferings; for in obeying the Lord no further reason is necessary than that the Lord Creator so commands and disposes. The souls must accustom themselves to look for this motive alone and to learn solely to please the Lord, without distinguishing between fortunate or unfortunate events and without looking to their own inclinations. In this kind of wisdom I wish that thou advance. In imitation of me and to satisfy thy obligations toward my most holy Son, do thou receive prosperity or adversity in this mortal life with unmoved countenance and with equanimity and peace of mind. Let not the one grieve, nor the other vainly rejoice thee; but attend only to all that which the Almighty ordains according to his pleasure.

711. Human life is interwoven thus variously with both kinds of events; some of them according, others contrary to the likings of mortals; some which they abhor, others which they desire. As the human heart is limited and narrow it immoderately inclines to extremes, boundlessly desiring what it loves and likes, and, on the other hand, grieving and sorrowing at what it abhors and dislikes. These changeful moods and fluctuations create danger for all or many virtues.

The disorderly love for one creature which it cannot attain, moves the soul presently to desire another, expecting a balm for its disappointment in the former. And if it is successful, the soul becomes involved and flurried in the desire of retaining what it possesses, thus casting itself by these velleities into still greater disorders and passions. Attend, therefore, dearest, to this danger and attack it at the root by preserving thy heart independent and riveted only on the divine Providence, without ever allowing it to incline toward what it desires or longs for, or to abhor what is painful to it. Let the will of the Lord be thy only delight and joy. Let neither thy desires draw thee on, nor thy fears dishearten thee. Let not thy exterior occupations, and much less thy regard or attention to creatures, ever impede thee or divert thee from thy holy exercises, attending always to my example. Seek thou lovingly and diligently to follow in my footsteps.

CATHOLIC WAY PUBLISHING

QUALITY PAPERBACKS AND E-BOOKS

THE MYSTICAL CITY OF GOD
BY VENERABLE MARY OF AGREDA

The Conception
Volume I, Part I, Books I & II in one Book:
     Paperback 5" x 8" Edition: ISBN-13: 978-1-78379-280-1
     Kindle E-Book Edition:...................................ISBN-13: 978-1-78379-281-8
     EPUB E-Book Edition: ISBN-13: 978-1-78379-282-5

The Incarnation
Volume II, Part II, Books III & IV in one Book:
     Paperback 5" x 8" Edition: ISBN-13: 978-1-78379-283-2
     Kindle E-Book Edition:...................................ISBN-13: 978-1-78379-284-9
     EPUB E-Book Edition: ISBN-13: 978-1-78379-285-6

The Transfixion
Volume III, Part II, Books V & VI in one Book:
     Paperback 5" x 8" Edition: ISBN-13: 978-1-78379-286-3
     Kindle E-Book Edition:...................................ISBN-13: 978-1-78379-287-0
     EPUB E-Book Edition: ISBN-13: 978-1-78379-288-7

The Coronation
Volume IV, Part III, Books VII & VIII in 1 Book:
     Paperback 5" x 8" Edition: ISBN-13: 978-1-78379-289-4
     Kindle E-Book Edition:...................................ISBN-13: 978-1-78379-290-0
     EPUB E-Book Edition: ISBN-13: 978-1-78379-291-7

Popular Abridgement
     Paperback 5" x 8" Edition: ISBN-13: 978-1-78379-063-0
     Kindle E-Book Edition:...................................ISBN-13: 978-1-78379-064-7
     EPUB E-Book Edition: ISBN-13: 978-1-78379-065-4

True Devotion to Mary: With Preparation for Total Consecration
by Saint Louis de Montfort
     6" x 9" Hardback:...ISBN–13: 978-1-78379-004-3
     6" x 9" Paperback: ISBN–13: 978-1-78379-011-1
     5" x 8" Paperback: ISBN–13: 978-1-78379-000-5
     MOBI E-Book:...ISBN–13: 978-1-78379-001-2
     EPUB E-Book: ISBN–13: 978-1-78379-002-9

www.catholicwaypublishing.com
London, England, UK
2013